Second Edition

Think Right Live Right

A 21-Day Plan to *Overcome Negative Thoughts*

To: Cassie

Read this book, Apply its principles
and learn to renew your mind one
thought a time. You will be glad
you did! :) Rm. 12:2; 2Cor. 10:5

Sincerely yours,

Dr. _____

5-29-21

I would love to hear from you. Please send your comments about this book to the address below. I want to stay in contact with you and send you inspirational emails occasionally, if you would like. I would also like to notify you when/if I will be speaking in your area. If you would like to contact me about the possibility of speaking in person, you can email or call me.

Dr. Paul Chipman
Thinkrightliveright84@gmail.com
804.271.2423
www.thinkrightliveright.com

Published by Think Right Live Right Press
An imprint of Hope for the Home Inc.
6933 Commons Plaza, Suite 242
Chesterfield, VA 23832
Printed in the United States of America
ISBN 978-1-7339535-4-2

Unless otherwise indicated, all scripture notations are from the New American Standard Bible, © 1960, 1962, 1963, 1968, 1971, 1972, 1973, 1975, 1977, 1995 by the Lockman Foundation. Used by permission. (www.lockman.org)

All other Scripture versions cited in this book are identified in appendix D, which hereby becomes a part of this copyright page.

Graphic design illustrators
Eric Collins: www.oobust.com
Chris Reed: www.christopherreed.us

Artistic drawings
Eric Collins, Kayla Eaglin, Myles Lawings,

Cover design
Angie @ pro_ebookcovers.com

Interior formatting
Istvanszaboifj @ fiverr.com

Printed in the United States of America

Contents

Foreword

This thought-provoking book was written to help you understand and examine your thought life on a whole new level. As a Believer in Christ, you are admonished in Scripture, "be transformed by the renewing of your mind" (Romans 12:2). While many Christian authors have written and taught about mind renewal, few have included the neurological evidence to explain the process of how faith in God's Word literally rewires your brain. I believe that Paul Chipman, in this book, *Think Right Live Right,* does a masterful job of combining the theological underpinnings of Biblical mind renewal with evidence-based neuroscience research.

Paul, in his unique and insightful manner, has provided the Body of Christ with a stellar tool designed to equip believers with the knowledge and requisite skills to identify and manage their thoughts and navigate their way through an array of negative and distorted thinking patterns. By reading this book, you will learn an effective way to replace automatic negative thoughts with the truth of God's Word. I am happy to recommend this timely book to you. *The 21-Day Plan* employs practical scriptural principles, thought provoking self-reflective questions, and relevant personal applications throughout each lesson to help you to "take every thought captive to the obedience of Christ" (2 Corinthians 10:5).

Now a word about the author, I have known Paul Chipman for over 30-plus years as my son in the ministry, a former minister on staff under my leadership at Oak Cliff Bible Fellowship Church, and as one of my former students at Dallas Theological Seminary (DTS). Upon graduating from DTS, I commissioned him to his first pastorate in Baltimore, MD. He has faithfully served His God in marriage, ministry, and family life for the past 30-plus years.

Dr. Tony Evans,
Senior Pastor, Oak Cliff Bible Fellowship Church,
President, The Urban Alternative
Author of *The Tony Evans Study Bible*

What People Are Saying About *The 21-Day Plan*

"As a pastor for over 20 years, I have had the privilege of ministering to thousands of individuals who struggled through times of discouragement in their lives. Many times, this discouragement has led to the disintegration of families or worse. One constant I have seen is that many times this discouragement is a direct result of not external circumstances, but what was going on in the hearts and minds of individuals. My friend, Paul Chipman, has developed a wonderful resource to help each of us discover the peace that passes all understanding through trusting God, no matter the circumstances. I encourage you to read this book, and then to share it with others, so we will know the promise of God's presence in our lives every single day."

--**Jonathan Falwell**, Senior Pastor, Thomas Road Baptist Church

"Everyone struggles with negative thoughts from time to time. Dr. Chipman, in *The 21-Day Plan*, helps us to trace the origin of our thoughts and provides the readers with a memorable thought management strategy. Pastors, this book is a must read for any Christian serious about taking control of his or her negative thoughts. It is soundly researched and provides a detailed explanation of how Scripture and science complement each other in the mind-renewal process."

--**Dr. Fred Luter**, Former President of the Southern Baptist Convention, Senior Pastor of Franklin Avenue Baptist Church, New Orleans

"Really, is it possible to have a transformed soul, but an unchanged life? The path to life transformation is mental change. That's the secret that Dr. Paul Chipman reveals in this provocative new work. Mapped out of his own personal challenges, he shows us the way to shake our negativity and retrain our minds in 21 days. Joining scripture with science, he weaves his way between those two worlds to build this insightful work. It is a must read for any persons serious about transforming their own lives and the lives of others."

--**Dr. Lance Watson**, Senior Pastor and Chief Dreamer, Saint Paul's Baptist Church

"The Word of God says for as a man thinks in his heart so is he. Pastor Chipman deals with the mind in his own unique way to expose truths that many have not considered. Everyone has their niche, and the mind happens to be the area where this man of God excels."

-- **Bishop Daniel Robertson, Jr.**, Senior Pastor, Mount Gilead Full Gospel International Ministries

"In the pressure-packed world of professional football, in order to win consistently, we need to have a winning game plan. *The 21-Day Plan* provides its readers with a winning game plan to successfully win the 'mind games' that we encounter on a daily basis."

--**Anthony Pleasant**, NFL veteran of 14 years & two-time
Super Bowl Champion with the New England Patriots

"Pastor Paul Chipman is totally transparent in presenting the painful journey that led to this work. His *21-Day Plan* is solidly Biblical and offers practical reasons for understanding why your thoughts are so important in rebounding from adversity. This book is a must read for anyone going through struggles or working with others who may be struggling. Paul shares God's way of overcoming life's challenges in a very user-friendly format."

--**Dr. Melvin Pride**, Ph.D., LPC, NCC, Director of Clinical Training,
Clinical Mental Health Counseling, Liberty University

"Many men struggle to walk faithfully with Christ and lead with confidence because circumstances, choices, relationships and regrets have filled their hearts and minds with defeat and despair. Satan's grip on their thought life keeps them from loving and leading according to God's plan. Dr. Chipman's book, *Think Right Live Right*, helps us to understand the brain science and the Spirit's influence behind Romans 12:2. Many will be blessed by his Biblical perspective and personal insights."

--**Mike Young**, Founder & President of Noble Warriors

"The book provides a very personal, yet provocative look into the thoughts that kept him in the quagmire of negativity and self-pity. His mind learned to find freedom from negativity by employing Biblically based thought management strategies with key neurological practices. Chip makes it clear in his book that even Christians can have mental and emotional struggles but can overcome them through Christ-centered help."

--**Dr. Jerry Mungadze**, Ph.D., Professional Counselor, author,
Founder and Director Right Brain Therapy Clinic, Dallas, Texas

"*The 21-Day Plan* for mind renewal is well written, biblically sound, thoroughly researched, and effectively used to rewire your brain and renew your mind to function as God intended. This book is a must read for laypeople, seminary professors, seminary students, pastors, pastoral counselors, and professional counselors."

--**Dr. Charlie Davidson**, Director of Doctor of Ministry
Liberty University Baptist Theological Seminary

"*The 21-Day Plan* is an encouraging and stimulating book that will give whip-lash to your old thinking. If you wish to control your thoughts rather than having your thoughts control you, then this book is absolutely a must read for you. In this insightful book, Dr. Chipman will walk with you step by step, helping you identify and replace destructive, negative thought patterns that alter your brain chemistry with Bible-based productive thoughts that improve brain functioning and produce positive change in your life."

--**Dr. Joel Freeman**, Ph.D., Professional Counselor, author, CEO/President of the Freeman Institute, former chaplain of Washington Wizards

"Experts say it takes 21 days to build a habit. I couldn't think of anyone I'd rather walk me through those 21 days than Pastor Paul. His compassion and wisdom jump right from the page, straight into your heart. God has truly gifted him with the unique ability to turn spiritual concepts into practical solutions. With his direction, anyone can learn to take authority over their thoughts and renew their mind."

--**Hannah Keeley**, author of Total Mom Makeover, Founder of Mom Mastery University, and TV host of Hannah Help Me!

"In this must-read book Think Right Live Right, Dr. Chipman addresses the biggest problem facing all people today—mindset. This book will empower the reader to develop a breakthrough mentality. I'm encouraging all of my students of the World famous 21-Day Breakthrough Challenge to get this book ASAP. It's just that good!"

--**Dr. Stan "Breakthrough" Harris**, Ph.D., mentor, author, Hall of Fame motivational speaker & martial artist—10th degree black belt.

"A huge YES! I find all of this immensely interesting! Who doesn't struggle at some time or another with bad thoughts and need to rewire their thinking pattern? You have certainly convinced me of my need for your work and undoubtedly you would do the same for anyone reading your work."

--**Betty Tryon,** Midlothian NOW Magazine, Editor & Writer

"*The 21-Day Plan* is transparent, practical, instructional, and based on biblical principles. The scientific aspect of it is interesting but not overwhelming. The anecdotal stories included at the end of some of the days are a nice inspiration and reinforce the message of the day's lesson. The best thing about it is that it can easily be referred to again and again."

-- **Renee Chambers**, Th.M., Dallas Seminary, Women's Bible teacher

Second Edition

Think Right Live Right

A 21-Day Plan to *Overcome Negative Thoughts*

Dr. Paul R. Chipman

Think Right Live Right Press

Dedication

This book is dedicated to Vonda, my beloved wife of 34 years and partner in parenthood, as we've raised our three wonderful adult sons: Paul (PC2), Mark-Anthony (He-Man) and Allan-Charles (The Professor). I dedicate this book to you because no one sacrificed more than you to bring this book to fruition. Most of the concepts I have written about in this book I learned from what you daily demonstrated. Vonda, you are a rare combination of beauty and brains, tethered to a bodacious love for Jesus and hurting people—making you the perfect ministry partner. The two songs that best describe you are *One in a Million You* (by Larry Graham) and *Through the Years* (by Kenny Rogers). Through the years you have ALWAYS stood by my side, praying for me, encouraging me, supporting me, and confronting me when I needed it. Through the years, you've cried with me and for me. In my darkest hours of failure and disappointment, it was you who kissed my tears away; always directing me back to the TRUE source of my joy and strength—Jesus. I'm convinced heaven must be missing an angel because you're here with me right now.

Acknowledgments

First, I must thank my Lord and Savior Jesus for the storms He brought me through. Out of these tumultuous storms flowed the concepts of *The 21-Day Plan*. Thank you, Jesus, for daily delivering me and choosing me to help set fellow strugglers free from their toxic thoughts and deadly emotions.

Thank you, Pastor Hal Johnson, Dr. Haywood Robinson III, and Mr. Frank Weiss. I don't believe this book would have ever been written if it had not been for you brothers with whom I explained the book's concept. All three of you independently exclaimed, "Chip, you need to put these concepts into a book." However, you didn't stop there; you went the extra mile by reaching into your pockets and sending the seed money to begin writing *The 21-Day Plan* and opened doors to share these concepts. Thank you for being such loyal friends.

A special thank you to my childhood friend, Barry DeSaw who agreed to serve as my first editor, and to his wife, Young, for her willingness to allow Barry to devote so much of his precious time on this project. Other members of my editing/consulting team include Vonda Chipman, Paul Chipman II, Jasmine Chipman, Allan Chipman, Mark-Anthony Chipman, Stanley Rayfield, Becky Schmidt, Debra Shaw, Maureen McCamey, Nickie Babcock, Dr. Elizabeth Cannings, Howard Tryon, Allen and Renee Chambers, Michele Tennesen, Principal Mary Jean Hunt, Diann Merit and my final editor, Nancy "Eagle Eye" Kirsh. As well, I want to thank my graphic artists Christopher Reed who worked tirelessly over 2 years, as a college intern, honing and coordinating the graphics for this project. I'd be remiss if I didn't acknowledge my sketch artist Myles Lawings and other graphic artist who created the images in this book. Your creativity delighted me time and time again. Thank you, Kayla Eaglin and Rayanna Hill. A very special shout out to Mr. C (Eric Collins) for stepping up and illustrating the most challenging of all graphics—The Toxic Ten chart and contributing to the perfecting of many of the other graphics.

Thank you, EK my computer engineer who repaired my damaged flash drive which contained the entire contents of *The 21-Day Plan* even as tech experts said recovery was impossible!

Thanks to all the members of Berean Bible Church (my first pastorate) and the former members of Light of the World church for lovingly supporting me and laying the foundation for this book. A special thank you to all the people who prayed for and or attended *Think Right Live Right* Seminars. You were my sounding board. It was to you that I first introduced the concepts of this book in a public forum.

Thank you, Dr. Tony Evans and Dallas Theological Seminary, for teaching me how to exegete the Word of God and preach it with passion, practicality and persuasive humor. Thank you, Liberty University professors Dr. Melvin Pride for your mentorship and Dr. Charlie Davidson and Dr. David Hirschman, for being the readers of my dissertation and encouraging me to rewrite it and publish it.

I would like to sincerely thank all the Pastors who encouraged me not only about this project specifically, but personally as well. A special thank you to Pastor Andy Rist, Pastor Jon Morton the members and staff of Oak Grove Baptist Church, my man Rocky, and his wife Phyllis, the SBC of Virginia staff and pastors for your ongoing encouragement. Thank you, Pastor Jonny Fleming, Pastor Pete Hypes and Pastor Kevin Bordeaux and the staff and members of Thrive Church. Thank you, Bishop Daniel Robertson Jr and Co-Pastor Elena Robertson, for your extensive teachings on the mind, and encouraging me through your messages to not quit until I brought into manifestation this insightful work. Thank you members of Mt. Gilead FGIM for all your prayers, encouragement, and support on this project. A special thank you to Charles Boyd, Minister Terry Graves, Mary Searcy, Ministers Dominic and Amie Carter, Minister Pranati Battaile, Minister Greg Mitchell and all my students in the Transformation Institute. Thank you Victor Canas, Susan Weiss, Pastor Leonard Davis, Donna Breedlove, Felicia and Noah Hankerson, Santesa Pope, Monica Vaughn, Cynthia Brown, Alfred Brown, Mike Young, Chaplin Curtis Muldrow, Michael Robertson and Dr. Stan "Breakthrough" Harris for your assistance in the marketing of this book. A special thank you to our Texas host families: Dr. Martin, Shirley and Melissa Hawkins and Pastor Gary and Marilyn Randle. Thank you for extending to us your warm southern hospitality each time we traveled to Dallas to host a TRLR Seminar. A special shout out to my barbers, The Blue Brothers: Brian, Otis and Rudy Blue, for your constant encouragement to complete the writing of this book. Thank you Pastor Gerald and Mary Carpenter and the saints of Annapolis Church of God and all the other pastors and their churches for help in the marketing of this book and the use of your facilities for the presentation of *Think Right Live Right* seminars.

Thank you to all who shared your inspiring testimonials. Your transparency and authenticity richly blessed me, and I'm sure those who read them will also draw much needed strength and encouragement.

Next, I want to thank those of you who are not included in the above acknowledgements, but who nevertheless contributed in a myriad of ways to this project. You know who you are. God knows who you are. And of course, I know who you are. Words cannot express my heartfelt appreciation. Without your prayers, financial support, and encouragement *The 21-Day Plan* would have forever remained a dusty doctoral dissertation. You didn't have to do it, but you did. For this reason, as Paul said to fellow supporters in Philippians 1:3, "I thank my God every time I remember you."

Finally, I would like to thank my parents, Raymond and Betty Chipman for bringing me into this world and modeling key life skills. Thank you to all 13 of my siblings for your thoughtful contributions to my life and this writing project. A special thank you to my siblings Sarah, Margaret, Joe, Sekou and Barbara for your ongoing accountability in asking me, "Is the book finished yet?" Additionally, I want to thank my Italian family Mom and Pop Placendo, Pip (aka The Kid), Debbie, Rick and Barb (aka Amazing Grace) and their daughters Jenny and Lauren for your love, encouragement and model of family life.

Preface to the Second Edition

I have been greatly encouraged by the enthusiastic reception I have received from the initial publication of *Think Right Live Right: A 21-Day Plan to Overcome Negative Thoughts* in 2019. I've seen it straddle and reconcile the gap between faith and science as it has successfully woven together theology, neurology and psychology and given the reader confidence that truth-based science and Scripture complement rather than contradict one another. My original purpose has not changed, nor have I altered my basic approach to provide readers with a practical faith-based thought management strategy to rewire their brains to overcome negative thoughts. The 21-Day Plan is rooted and grounded in the scriptures, and backed up by science, holding to the conviction that a*ll truth is God's truth.*

The Second Edition includes additional material designed to make the book even more practical and life-changing. This Second Edition includes: an updated index to make it easier to find subject matter more quickly; the effects of trauma on the brain (Day 2); ten steps to resolve relational conflict and how to ask for a time-out before tempers flare (Day14); how to ask for forgiveness (Day 15); learn to forgive yourself and receive God's forgiveness (Day 11). I incorporated The Filthy Five Memory Verse chart (Day 14), explained the difference between the mind and brain (Day 3), provided examples of additional ways to guard the mind against undesirable thoughts (Day 9), discussed assertiveness and active listening (Day 18), demonstrated how the law of attraction works (Day 4). I have also shown how the conscious and subconscious interface with one another (Day 8). Additional headings were added to help separate longer texts. Memory work was reduced and daily assignments were revised to give the reader clearer instructions (Days 14-21).

I am pleased that many have profited from this book in the past, and I *pray* that God will use the new edition to help you master your thoughts, rather than be mastered by them, and to deepen your walk with Him.

Paul R. Chipman
June 2020

The 21-Day Challenge

Getting the Most from *The 21-Day Plan*

Do something today that your future self will thank you for.
--Unknown--

Are you controlling your thoughts, or are your negative thoughts controlling you? Are you mastering your thoughts, or are your thoughts mastering you? You don't think it's a big deal? Think again.

- Depressive thoughts, serious bouts of anxiety, and panic attacks are the result of systematic distorted thinking patterns.[1]

- Based on a joint study conducted by the Harvard School of Public Health and the World Health Organization, by 2020 depression is expected to be the world's second leading cause of disability, surpassed only by cardio-vascular disease.[2]

- Researchers estimate "more than 90% of us will have a bout with depression at some point in our lives and… almost all of us will have serious anxiety bouts that will restrict us from enjoying life's opportunities."[3]

Once again, I must ask you, are you controlling your negative thoughts or are your negative thoughts controlling you? If you are tired of being a pitiful pawn of your toxic thoughts and emotions and want to learn how to master your negative thoughts rather than your thoughts mastering you, you've picked up the one book perfectly designed to set you free from your mental misery. That's because this book takes a *holistic* approach to the mind renewal process. *The 21-Day Plan* is built upon three abstract disciplines: (1) The Bible; (2) Neuro (brain) science; (3) Cognitive Behavior Therapy (CBT). All three disciplines attest to the fact that changing the way one thinks is possible.

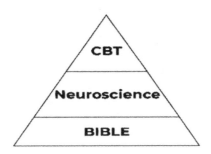

Academic Foundations of The 21-Day Plan

Take The 21-Day Challenge

If you are serious about changing the way you think, I encourage you right NOW to take The 21-Day Challenge. Today, the average life span is 25,550 days.[4] That is how long you will live if you are typical. Do you think it would be a wise use of your time to set aside 21 of those days to learn the thought management skills necessary to control your thoughts for the rest of your life? In so doing, your mind will be renewed to such a degree that you will be better able to both discover and fulfill God's purpose and plan for your life.

The 21-Day Plan is more than a book; it is a spiritual journey that will transform your thought life. This book is divided up into 21 lessons. I encourage you to read only one lesson per day. Should you feel inclined to reread the lesson several times per-day or even divide it into a morning and evening lesson, do so. In fact, do whatever works best for you, because the more you interact with the information and apply the thought management principals the faster your thought life will be transformed. Read it, reread it. Mark up the book. Write down your thoughts in the margin and underline them. Personalize it as your book.

Over the next twenty-one days you will be introduced to new concepts, strategies and practices that your brain will *automatically resist*. But you will learn in these pages how to push back on your brain's pushback. In addition, don't allow yourself to be intimidated by a few 25 cent words or new psychological terms concerning different aspects of your brain. I've heard it said, "your *'I will'* is more important than your *'IQ'."* Tell yourself, "I am more than able to comprehend all pertinent concepts that I may encounter in *The 21-Day Plan*. You will be glad you did.

Seven Features to Help You Succeed

To help you grasp and interact with the material presented in *The 21-Day Plan*, each lesson includes the following items:

- **Brain Fact** A neurological fact about your brain; so you will learn how to work along with your brain and not against it, the goal being to help you discover how God so designed your brain to aide you in the spiritual transformation you desire.
- **Key Thoughts** The main take away of the day's lesson.

- **Scripture** One or more Bible verses that undergirds the truth of the lesson; to illustrate how scripture and science complement each other in the mind renewal process.

- **Questions for Reflection** These questions are designed to help you to interact with the material so you can see how it applies to you personally and spiritually.

- **Confessions** Repeated statements made on a daily basis to aid in the rewiring of your brain to overcome negative thinking.

- **Memory Work** This is daily memory work including scripture memory designed to replace automatic negative thoughts (ANTS) with spiritual automatic thoughts (SATS).

- **Motivational Songs** Daily songs designed to uplift your spirit and soul and swing your negative mood in a more positive direction. "Music changes virtually all areas of the brain responsible for regulating emotion." [5]

A Better Way to Think

Like me, you may have grown accustomed to thinking the first negative thoughts that pops into your head. While it may be common, it is definitely not healthy. *The 21-Day Plan* exposes you to a better way to think; it's called thought management. My life has been dramatically changed and transformed by learning these thought management strategies. I want to challenge you to make the commitment to daily read *The 21-Day Plan*—not missing a single day. If you do miss a day, don't be discouraged. Just pick up where you left off and continue your 21-Day spiritual journey.

The plan is called *The 21-Day Plan* because that is how long it takes the brain to rewire itself and create a new mental habit.[6] Neuroscience researcher, Caroline Leaf, expounded upon this habit-forming process by pointing out, **"Intentional daily focus over a minimum of sixty-three days, in twenty-one day cycles, allows a habit to form."** [7] To affect the type of desired change in your thought life, you will need to practice the thought management principles and daily confessions multiple times per day. The more you practice, the faster you will change the way you think. If you commit to the plan and the process and the procedures it includes, the result will be a profound effect on retraining your brain, renewing your mind, and transforming your thought life from negative to positive.

If you are willing to accept this challenge, as a means of mutual accountability, *let's sign a covenant together.* Your life is worth taking 20 minutes daily to read a lesson to help you gain mastery over your negative thoughts so that you can use your mind to think as your heavenly Father intended. In so doing, you will accomplish the works He created you to do (Jeremiah 1:5; 29:11; Ephesians 2:10). Take heart, knowing my staff and I, at Think Right Live Right Ministries, are praying for your successful completion of the plan, daily.

My Covenant

With God's help, I purpose over the next 21 days or
longer, to read and apply the principles of *The
21-Day Plan* daily. In so doing, I will
learn to overcome my negative
thoughts by replacing them
with positive, faith-filled,
God-honoring thoughts.

_____

Your Name

_____

Accountability Partner's Name

Dr. Paul Chipman
_____

Dr. Paul Chipman

*"Two are better off than one, because together they can work
more effectively. If one of them falls down, the other can
help him up...Two people can resist an attack that
would defeat one person alone. A rope made of
three cords is hard to break."*
Ecclesiastes 4:9 (TEV)

Author's Note

The only true disability in life is a bad attitude.

--Unknown

Welcome. If you picked up this book it is probably because you are struggling to manage your negative thoughts to some degree. You are not alone. I invite you to come along with me on a personal journey that will help you learn how to overcome those negative thoughts and toxic emotions that have robbed you of the clarity of thought and peace of mind you so desperately desire. It's a 21-day journey especially designed to help you learn to overcome your negative mental cognitions. Does it work? *The 21-Day Plan* in its doctoral research studies was shown to have a 92.8% [1]success rate for those participants who read every page, completed all assignments and diligently practiced the scriptural and scientifically based thought management principles. Satan, "the father of lies", will do anything he can to stunt your spiritual growth and keep your mind in a vortex of negativity. But don't let him. This book contains information that you will need to break free from Satan's stronghold over your mind and henceforth learn to manage your thoughts skillfully for the rest of your life.

As you prepare to read this book, there are a few things you need to know to make this reading/spiritual journey a truly mind transforming experience:

- **Quick Start** If you are asking yourself, where should I begin reading to get the most immediate impact? I suggest you begin by reading **Days 1, 9, 10, and 11 in that order.** Once completed, go back to Day 2 and begin reading concurrently.

- If you are seeking relief from or insights into **relational conflicts,** I suggest you begin reading **Days 1, 13, 14, p. 241,** *Conflict Resolution: Rules of Engagement, and pp. 313-314, Assertiveness and Active Listening.* Once completed, go back to Day 2 and begin reading concurrently.

- *DO NOT* **stress yourself to complete reading this book or trying to memorize all the mantras,** affirmations, acrostics and scripture memory verses in twenty-one days. *The 21-Day Plan* is the condensed product of a compilation of four years of thought management research and detailed analysis. Your primary goal should be to *complete the plan*—be it in 21, or 41 days or longer. **You may choose to read just 2 to 3 pages per day. Find a pace that works for you and stick with it.** *Don't Quit!*

- *The 21-Day Plan* should be viewed as a **reference tool that you will read and reread as you seek deeper insights into the thought management strategies** that will assist in the rewiring of your brain to overcome negative thoughts. Re-reading provides an ideal time to devote the necessary time to the plethora of Scripture memory work.

- **To foster spiritual growth and greater chemical, structural/functional changes in the brain,** it is imperative that you read all your daily lessons. Each lesson will take **25-35** minutes to complete. Therefore, you might consider dividing your reading into AM and PM reading. Consistently read each day, as consistency greatly enhances the power and effectiveness of the program.

- ***DO NOT* skip listening to the daily musical selections.** Do it daily. Music changes virtually all areas of the brain responsible for regulating emotion.[2]

> *In consistency lies the power.*

Inspiring music stimulates the release of the brain's feel good chemical, dopamine.[3] In addition to altering our mood, music has been used to treat a wide array of emotional disorders including anxiety, depression and other stress-related afflictions like post-traumatic stress disorder (PTSD).[4] For these reasons music is included in *The 21-Day Plan*. (If you find it very difficult to motivate yourself to read *The 21-Day Plan* at the start of the day, try listening to the recommended song(s) of the day before you begin your daily reading.)

- *The 21-Day Plan's* memory work at times is challenging, but don't let it intimidate you. It is challenging for a reason. Brain researcher, Dr. Laura Boyd, of the University of British Columbia, has discovered "increased difficulty, increased struggle in practice actually leads to both more learning and results in greater structural change in the brain... **The best driver of neuroplastic change in your brain is your behavior."**[5] No one can rewire your brain for you – therefore, challenge yourself. Say to yourself, "If it's going to be, it's up to me!" Stop looking for the easy way out. Short cuts lead only to places not worth going. Fredrick Douglas, former slave, author, and national abolitionist leader, said, **"If there is no struggle, there is no progress."**

I once heard it said there are two types of pain: the pain of discipline and the pain of regret. Which pain will you choose to endure? The choice is up to you. *You have what it takes, but it will take everything you have to change the way you think.* If you want to change, make a change. There is no better time than *NOW*!

"Their own emotions are their god..."
(Philippians 3:19 GW)

****

"The Spirit of the Lord is on me,
because He anointed me
to preach good news to the poor.
He has sent me to proclaim
freedom to the captives and
recovery of sight to the blind,'
to set free those who are
oppressed..."
(Luke 4:18 EHV)

****

"[The Lord] will give to [you]
beauty for ashes,
the oil of joy for mourning,
the garment of praise
for the spirit of heaviness..."
(Isaiah 61:3 MEV

Week 1
The Science of Thought (Days 1-7)

*"We cannot
solve our problems
with the same
level of thinking that
created them."*

—Albert Einstein

Day 1

Do You Wish to Get Well?

You are today where your thoughts have brought you;
you will be tomorrow where your thoughts take you.
--James Allen

Daily Food for Thought

- **Brain Fact** "Research indicates as much as 75% of everything we think is negative, counterproductive, and works against us."[1]

- **Key Thought** "Push back on the pushback": Because the brain was not designed to change suddenly, it will push back on most new changes that are introduced to it.[2] Consequently, to introduce new mental habits, participants must learn to "push back on the brain's pushback" if they are to experience permanent change.

- **Scripture** "Think the same way Jesus Christ thought" (Philippians 2:5 WE).

Disclaimer: *The 21-Day Plan* **is for informational purposes only. It is not designed to serve as a mental health treatment plan, or substitute as counseling and therapy you may be receiving or to replace prescribed medications your medical professional may have prescribed for you.**

Reminder: If you have not read *The 21-Day Challenge, and* signed the *covenant,* or read the *Author's Note*, please consider doing so now. They are found on pages 14-21.

Daily Reading

Perhaps life's pressures have caused the peace and joy you once enjoyed to take flight. Such was the case with me. A series of negative circumstances involving the loss of two jobs, false accusations levied against me by fellow clergy and ex-members, three lawsuits, and IRS liens leveled against the church I pastored, back-to-back ministry failures, fears of economic calamity, marital distress, and a plethora of regrets of the past had robbed me of my joy. I felt as if an ominous cloud of negativity had engulfed me, causing me to undergo intense feelings of low self-esteem, self-hatred, and helplessness. Seemingly powerless to quell the accuser's harassing voice within my head, it felt as if I could hear him torment-ing me hourly with such a feverish fluidity, declaring: "Things will never get any better for you. It's over! What's the use of even trying again? You are a worth-less, faithless, fearful, failure. God could never use someone like you. You were a fool to have placed your trust in God. Look where it got you. Even He has for-saken and abandoned you, just like so many others." **But God!**

Reaching for a thread of hope, I fell to my knees and cried out to God—one last time before succumbing to the irrepressible toxic undertow of self-pity, an-ger, despair and hopelessness. At my lowest ebb, the Spirit of God, after listening to my lament, compelled me to dry my eyes, rise up from my knees, and visit my local bookstore. There, the Lord directed me to a work entitled, *A Better Way to Think*, by Dr. H. Norman Wright. That book revealed to me that it was not only my depressing circumstances that had me feeling lower than the fattest pig at a barbeque, it was primarily my stinking thinking over a period of years that had systematically turned me into a full-fledged **"negaholic"**— with a persistent negative outlook—badly in need of detoxification. Over the next sev-eral days and months I devoured that book and many more like it. Gradually, the clouds of depression gave way to the loving light of God's Son. Hope, love and joy slowly returned to my life. Over time, my sorrows were replaced with a tri-umphant confidence in God's love for me and His plans for my life, bringing about a renewed excitement. Through the process, I made the vital discovery that *I could master my thoughts, instead of my negative thoughts mastering me.*

Having now learned, through my studies, how to significantly silence the tormenting chatter of Satan, *"the Accuser"* (Rev. 12:9), my mind was then clear enough to hear the loving voice of my *"Advocate"* –Jesus (1 John 2:1). Loving-ly, He reminded me that He had neither forsaken nor abandoned me even in my failures, but had used my years of trials, failures, and heartache to prepare me for a new phase of ministry. God's perceived rejection was merely His *redirection*. God had been preparing me to be a vessel through whom *He* can deliver an untold multitude of people still held in bondage to their twisted and distorted thinking patterns and self-destructive behaviors. I was to take what I had experienced and use it to help others whose toxic thinking patterns stole their dreams, robbed their joy, destroyed their hope, and undermined their confidence in God's promises.

God has been, and is, daily delivering me, each day, so that I can "comfort others with the comfort that I had received from God" (2 Corinthians 1:3-5). Concerning Simon Peter's test of faith, Jesus said to him, "Simon, Simon! Indeed, Satan has asked for you, that he may sift you as wheat. But I have prayed for you, that your faith should not fail; and when you have returned to Me, strengthen your brethren" (Luke 22:31-32). *The 21-Day Plan* that you now hold in your hands is the road map that God used to help deliver me and renew my mind—one thought at a time. He used this plan to restore the joy of my salvation, my purpose and meaning in life. The plan is built upon the Bible, neuroplasticity research, and Cognitive Behavior Therapy (CBT) analyses and practices. Does the plan work? While conducting my doctoral research trials, *The 21-Day Plan* had a 92.8% success rate for those who read every page and consistently completed all corresponding activities.

As I began conferring with my ministry colleagues about what I had been going through mentally, as well as my subsequent research, several confided in me that they too struggled with negative discouraging feelings. As I continued my research, I happened upon the following grave statistics compiled by such institutions and organizations as The Barna Group, Focus on the Family, and Fuller Theological Seminary. They analyzed the thought lives of many members of the clergy across denominational lines. They discovered the following:[3]

- A total of 1,500 pastors leave the ministry permanently each month in the United States of America.

- Over 50 percent of pastors feel so discouraged that they would leave the ministry if they could, but they have no other way of making a living.

- A total of 71 percent of pastors stated they were burnt out, and they battled with depression beyond fatigue on a weekly and even a daily basis.

- A total of 80 percent of pastors and 85 percent of pastor's wives feel discouraged in their roles.

- A total of 50 percent of pastors' wives feel that their husbands' entering ministry was the most destructive thing to ever happen to their families.

- A total of 70 percent of pastors do not have a close friend, confidant, or mentor.

These statistics reflected my mindset. I was an ex-pastor who had left the ministry due to unmet expectations and setbacks, all of which fed into my already-fear-based, pessimistic attitude. However, it was not until much later that I learned it wasn't the external factors that caused me to leave the ministry feeling despondent and hopeless; rather, it was my internal processing of those experiences. It was stinking thinking that caused so many of my fellow colleagues and I to become wounded warriors—ministry casualties.

As my mental fog lifted, it gradually dawned on me that if we, the pastors who are considered the "most spiritual," are struggling with depression and dropping out of the ministry at a rate of 50 per day,[4] due in large part to distorted thinking, then surely those in the pews and in the larger public are struggling equally if not more so. My suspicions were confirmed:

- "According to the National Institute of Mental Health… about one in four adults – a little more than 25 percent of Americans ages eighteen and older – suffer from a diagnosable mental disorder in a given year."[5] And that's accounting for only one year. That equates to around fifty million people in the United States.[6]

- "If your church is typical of the US population, on any given Sunday, one in four adults and one in five children sitting around you are suffering from a mental illness. Many of them are under the influence of powerful antipsychotic drugs and their side effects." [7]

The National Alliance on Mental Illness (NAMI) defines mental illness as "medical conditions that disrupt a person's thinking, feelings, mood, ability to relate to others and daily functioning" and "often results in a diminished capacity for coping with the ordinary demands of life." [8] By this definition, long- and or short-term depression is considered a mental illness.

> ***Your thoughts are killing you!***

- "As much as **75%** percent of everything we think is negative, counterproductive and works against us."[9]

- "Around **87%** of illnesses can be attributed to our thought life, and approximately 13% to diet, genetics, and environment."[10]

When I considered that three out of every four thoughts are negative, I realized that I could no longer just accept the first thought that popped into my head. I had to become more selective. I had to learn a better way of thinking. After reading the second statistic, I came to grips with the fact that my thoughts were killing me both spiritually and physically. I needed to change.

27

Why You Can't Afford Another Negative Thought

That is right. Your negative thoughts are killing you! Renowned neuroscience researcher, Dr. Caroline Leaf discovered, in her groundbreaking research, a correlation between negative thoughts and their impact on our health:

- "Studies conclusively link more chronic disease (also known as lifestyle diseases) to an epidemic of toxic emotions in our culture. These toxic emotions can cause migraines, hypertension, strokes, cancer, skin problems, diabetes, infections and allergies, just to name a few." [11]

- "Negative thoughts secrete 'downer' chemicals (i.e. cortisol and adrenaline) in the brain which cause people to feel depressed, anxious, worried, stressed, or fearful, etc. While on the other hand, positive thoughts release 'upper' or 'feel good' chemicals (i.e. serotonin and dopamine) in the brain, which in turn causes people to feel happy, excited, joyful, and positive."[12]

> *Negative thoughts secrete "downer" chemicals in the brain.*

Dr. Norman Wright, author of *A Better Way To Think,* points out additional effects of both positive and negative thinking on both mind and body.

Positive attitudes cause the secretion of the correct amount of chemicals, and negative attitudes distort the chemical secretions in a way that disrupts their natural flow. The chemicals are like little cellular signals that translate the information of your thought into a physical reality in your body and mind, creating an emotion. The combination of thoughts, emotions and resulting attitudes, impact your body in a positive or negative way. This means your mind and body really are inherently linked, and this link starts with your thoughts.[13]

Perhaps by now you are more cognizant of why you cannot afford the luxury of another toxic thought. The longer you fail to address your negative (toxic) thoughts, the more time the thoughts have to become neurologically entrenched

> *Positive thoughts release "feel good" chemicals in the brain.*

in both your mind and body. King Solomon, the wisest man who ever lived, made the following observation: "Being cheerful keeps you healthy. It is slow death to be gloomy all the time" (Proverbs 17:22 GNT).

Don't waste another day allowing your toxic stinking thinking to predictably poison your mind and body. "Antipsychotics are now the top-selling class of drugs in the United States. This is because of their growing use not only to treat serious psychotic disorders but also to address a broader array of problems. These drugs [often] have powerful side effects, which "...can impair a person's functioning as powerfully as an illness can."[14] *Medication is no cure all. Even with it, you must learn to better manage your negative thoughts and toxic emotions if you hope to improve the quality of your mental, emotional and physical health.* (Be sure to read today's closing testimony.)

The 21-Day Plan equips its readers with the requisite thought management skills to...

- retrain your brain to overcome negative thoughts;
- identify and take captive The Filthy Five negative thoughts that seek to master your mind;
- break self-destructive behavior patterns, and replace them with productive behaviors;
- identify and reject The Toxic Ten thought patterns that lead to sadness and depression;
- break the negative habit loop of excessive worrying;
- overcome painful regrets of the past;
- interrupt and replace negative self-talk;
- build a healthy God-centered self-esteem and self-identity;
- break addictions and other spiritual, mental, and emotional strongholds.

The 21-Day Plan illustrates practically what it means to take negative thoughts captive to the obedience of Christ (2 Corinthians 10:5). Only as we learn to better manage our thoughts will our minds be transformed to fully embrace the mind of Christ (Romans 12:2; 1 Corinthians 2:16).

I'd Like to Change the Way I Think, But...

Psychologist, Dr. Archibald D. Hart, author of the book *Habits of the Mind,* observes three significant factors contributing to the reasons people think negatively. First, he observes that most people do not enjoy being negative; they are that way because of stress, the pressures of life, fear, and busyness.[15]. Secondly, most people will modify their negative thinking patterns once they acquire the knowledge and confidence to do so. Finally, many people fail to change or they relapse back into negative thinking patterns because of a taunting inner voice telling them something like, "You will never change" and reminding them of previous failed attempts to change. Their inner voice derides them, saying perhaps, "Things will never get any better for you, so why bother to try."[16] Take it from an ex- "negaholic". Don't believe that lie! With God's help you can change the way you think. In the final analysis, it's your thoughts that are keeping you from changing. That is why it is imperative that you learn to control your negative thoughts—rather than your negative thoughts controlling you.

Push Back on Your Brain's Pushback

As with any new habit you seek to establish, I encourage you to anticipate a few false starts because of the nature of *how* the brain works. As the brain was not designed to change suddenly, it will push back reflexively on most new changes that are introduced to it.[17] That includes something as simple as trying to think positively for a change. Hence, you should expect to experience some resistance from your brain. In order to renew your mind, you must learn to push back on the brain's pushback.

Do you remember the Bible story of the woman with the issue of blood hemorrhaging? She suffered twelve years of false starts in her efforts to be healed. I can only image the countless number of times she had to push back against the thought, "You will never be healed; there is no cure for your condition." However, when she heard Jesus was coming to town, she pushed back on her brain's pushback, shook off all discouragement and tried one more time. The Bible says, "She pressed her way into the crowd and touched the hem of Jesus' garment and instantaneously she was healed. Her hemorrhaging stopped immediately (Mark 5:25-34). What an amazing God we worship! In like manner, if you are to be healed of your negative way of thinking, you too are going to have to press through and push back on your old way of thinking. You will need to get into the habit of pushing back on your brain's pushback until your brain recognizes you are serious about introducing a new mental habit—a better way to think. You will hear a voice saying to you, "What's the use in trying again? You tried to change your negative thinking before and failed, and you will probably fail again." At that time, you will have to push back on the pushback and say to yourself, "I never tried *The 21-Day Plan* before. I believe this plan will lead to my breakthrough! I'm going for it!"

Let me tell you what you can expect, according to Dr. Leaf: "The first four days will be the most difficult. The fifth through the twenty-first days will become easier as you progress. By the time you get to the twenty-first day, you will feel a marked change."[18] Over the next twenty-one days, you will be introduced to new concepts, strategies and practices that your brain will automatically resist. Hence, grow accustomed to the phrase: *Push back on the pushback!* Take heart. You are not alone. Jesus walks beside you. He knows you are suffering; He suffers with you. The Holy Spirit lives within you, therefore you have the strength you need to press past all your negative thoughts to triumph.

Do You Wish to Get Well?

The Rev. Dr. James Allen, author of *As a Man Thinketh,* asserts, "You are today where your thoughts have brought you; you will be tomorrow where your thoughts take you."[19]

God used this statement to jerk the slack out of my chain and motivate me to ask Him for the grace and strength to change the way I was thinking. I did not want my life to continue on its current trajectory. Not knowing any better, I had grown accustomed to not challenging the first negative thought that popped into my head. In ignorance, I thought, if a thought popped into my head, then I ought to at least consider it before dismissing it outright.

Wrong! I knew I had to make a dramatic change in my thought life. The Bible declares, "A cheerful disposition is good for your health; gloom and doom leave you bone-tired" (Proverbs 17:22 MSG). I was sick and tired of being sick and tired and was ready for a change.

Are you sick and tired of your mind being filled with negative, anxiety-ridden, and toxic thoughts? Have life's stresses and pressures turned you into a "negaholic"? Are you tired of being a pawn of your mood swings? Change is possible, but…only if you want it badly enough! And remember the things we want badly are the things we pray about. In other words, pray, with all the earnestness you can muster when the voice of negativity interposes.

In the fifth chapter of the Gospel according to Saint John, Jesus posed this same question to a disabled man at the pool of Bethesda. The man with disabilities had remained at the proximity of the pool for thirty-eight years, hoping to be healed. That's a long time to be dealing with a spiritual, physical, or emotional problem. Although physically impaired, the man's real problem was rooted in his thought life. The man *thought* he couldn't be the first in the pool. He *thought* no one was willing to help him. He *thought,* even after thirty-eight years of failing to be the first in the pool, that the pool was his only option for healing. Finally, perhaps on a subconscious level, he concluded that being "a cripple" was all that someone like him could expect from life.

Jesus, sensing the man's desperation and discouragement, asked him, "Do you wish to get well?" Amazingly, the man did not respond to Jesus' question with an emphatic, "Yes, Jesus please, pretty please, heal me! I've been waiting for thirty-eight years now! Where have you been?" The text does not say why the man did not answer Jesus with an emphatic "Yes"! Allow me to suggest one possible reason. On the surface, it seems like a simple yes or no question, but we know Jesus' questions are always multifaceted. In essence, Jesus was asking the man if he was willing to dream again—to have hope again after thirty-eight years of disappointment and failure. Perhaps, it was this deeper question that the man was avoiding. Sure, the man began offering a litany of excuses, (v.7) but was he really trying to camouflage his lack of faith and hope?

Speaking from personal experience, repeated failure, if internalized, (i.e. I failed, therefore I am a failure) can leave you in a perplexed and dismal state of mind. On the one hand, you've come to expect failure—reasoning that you don't deserve any better because of your past or maybe God is mad at you and wants to punish you. On the other hand, a part of you wants to believe and have hope yet fears being disappointed again. This leaves you in a perplexed state of mind in which you are afraid to verbalize what you really want. Your defeated mentality causes you to conclude, if I don't *ever* expect anything good to happen, then I won't be disappointed—*ever* again. Hence, you resolve within yourself to play it safe and take whatever life brings your way. Perhaps that's one plausible explanation of why the man with disabilities did not answer Jesus' question. He was playing it safe; protecting himself from yet another disappointment.

Coming from a man who has experienced multiple "failures", I've learned this. Without an edifying theology of failure, without an insightful definition of success and without being tethered to an undaunted faith in the infinite goodness and sovereignty of God, failure will eat you alive. It will spit you out, and leave you feeling like roadkill on the highway of life, while happier people drive by and stare. (The issue of failure is discussed in greater detail in Day 20 of *The 21-Day Plan*.) The disabled man in our story had his reasons for being pessimistic and hopeless, just as you may have. However, Jesus wants you to know that while you may have your reasons, you don't have a right to remain negative, hopeless, and pessimistic when He is available to help you. Jesus offered the man with disabilities hope, healing, and a new lease on life. Are you also in need of healing from a self-defeated, negative mindset?

Joyce Meyer, a popular TV Bible teacher, was a victim of incest. In her book, *Battlefield of the Mind,* she said this about negative thinking; "The hardest part of being set free from negativism is facing the truth and saying, 'I'm a negative person, and I want to change. I can't change myself, but I believe God will change me as I trust Him. I know it will take time, and I'm not going to get discouraged with myself. God has begun a good work in me, and He is well able to bring it to full completion."[20] She concludes that the admission of a problem is the first step toward healing.

Ultimately, I had difficulty admitting to my wife and sons my chronic propensity toward a negative thought life. My wife tried to point it out to me, but I just did not want to accept it. She would often ask me, "What happened to the guy I married? I want the old Chip back, the guy I fell in love with because he made me laugh."

I was speechless. The truth be told, I had begun to wonder what had happened to him myself. Who has God brought into your life to lovingly confront you about your negative and pessimistic attitude? Are you ready to admit it? Jesus is asking you today, "Do you wish to get well?" God wants to help you change the way you think and introduce you to a better way to think.

> *The hardest part of being set free from negativism is facing the truth and saying, "I'm a negative person, and I want to change."*

How Bad Do You Want It?

Perhaps the following information will help motivate you to change the way you think. Dr. Caroline Leaf, author of the book, *Think, Learn, Succeed*, observed the following:

> A growing body of evidence shows how our thought lives have incredible power over our intellectual, emotional, cognitive, and physical well-being. Our thoughts can either limit us to what we believe we can do or free us to develop abilities well beyond our expectations or the expectations of others. When we choose a mindset that extends our abilities rather than limits them, we will experience greater intellectual satisfaction, emotional control, and mental and physical health.[21]

If you were not interested in changing the way you think, you probably would not be reading this book. How badly do you want to change? Take a moment to identify where you are along what is known as The Stages of Change Continuum.[22]

The following personal assessment has been designed to help you assess how committed you are to changing not just your thoughts, but also any troublesome area in your life.

Stage 1. Pre-contemplation—no intention of changing behavior
Stage 2. Contemplation—aware a problem exists, but no commitment to action
Stage 3. Preparation—intent upon taking action
Stage 4. Action—active modification of behavior
Stage 5. Maintenance—sustained change: new behaviors replacing old
Stage 6. Relapse—falling back into old patterns of behaving
Stage 7. Victory—getting back up after each relapse and trying again until the goal is achieved

Where do you estimate you are now on the stages of the change spectrum? (Circle one.)

Stage 1   Stage 2   Stage 3   Stage 4   Stage 5   Stage 6   Stage 7

You will notice that Stage 6 is named "Relapse." If you experience a relapse in your 21-day journey, just pick up where you left off and begin again. But do so prayerfully, knowing that God is your strongest advocate. God fervently wants you to succeed. Appeal to God in prayer in the wake of every apparent "failure." The reason we fail is because in ourselves we are flawed and weak and we just don't know the infinite transformative power of God's love. But earnest prayer is the readiest access to God's power.

The book of Proverbs states, "The godly may trip seven times, but they will get up again" (Proverbs 24:16 NLT). Know that your negative thought processes will resist any new change. We Christians call the enemy of the fulfillment of God's plans for our lives by the name "Satan." Satan will partner with your brain's resistance by causing you to quit any positive, wholesome undertaking regarding your thought life. But *stand your ground*! "Set your mind and keep it set" (Colossians 3:2 AMP) on your goal. After every false start, get back up and try again. Persevere; knowing that with God you already have the victory. Christ secured it for you 2000 years ago (1 Corinthians 15:57; 2 Corinthians 2:14). Remember, "Greater is He who is in you than he who is in the world" (1 John 4:4). Dependence upon God and perseverance are key to success. If you continue to get up and try again *whenever* you find your mind in the clutches of negativity, you will ultimately make it to Stage 7, VICTORY!

Referring back to the Stages of Change Continuum introduced previously, it would be helpful for you to be in stage 3 or below to derive the maximum benefits from this 21-Day Plan. To successfully complete *The 21-Day Plan*, a total commitment is required. Regarding commitment, perhaps you've heard the story about the pig and the chicken that both walked out of the farmyard and stopped in front of a church. The marquee outside the church read, "Give to the Lord's Work." The chicken read the words and fell under a strong chicken conviction and said to the pig, "I think we ought to give something to the Lord's work, TODAY!" The pig paused momentarily from his search for food, read the marquee for himself, looked at the chicken and asked, "What exactly do you have in mind?" The chicken replied, "Well, I plan to give at least a couple of eggs, and I figure you could give a slab of bacon." In astonishment, the pig snorted, shook his head and said, "Easy for you to give a few eggs; for you that would be a contribution, but for me to give a slab of bacon, well, that requires a TOTAL COMMITMENT. To restate this in the words of the illustrious motivational speaker Les Brown, "You gotta be *hungry*!"

This program requires a total commitment, (all 21 days and longer) not a half-hearted effort. Your commitment is essential because each lesson will require your full participation. Push back on the temptation to skip your daily reading, practice exercises, Bible studies, mantras, or reflective questions. Skipping questions or readings may compromise the effectiveness of the plan. Allow God, through this study, to do amazing things in your thought life as you grant Him full access to your mind, will, and emotions.

Finding the Motivation to Change

At times, we struggle to make a difficult decision that we know in the deep recesses of our minds we need to make; it helps at such times to ask ourselves the following seven questions:

1. What will it cost me if I don't change?
2. Ultimately, what will I miss out on in my life if I don't make the change?
3. What is it already costing me mentally, emotionally, physically, spiritually and financially?
4. If I do change how will that make me feel about myself?
5. What kind of momentum could I create if I change this in my life now?
6. What other things could I accomplish if I really made this change today?
7. How will my family and friends feel? [23]

God Has Supplied the Power You Need

Now back to our story of the disabled man in the gospel of John. Despite the lame man probably making excuses, Jesus healed him anyway. Hallelujah! What a gracious Savior we serve. Even after all you have read today, like the man miraculously healed, you may not be entirely resolute in your decision to change how you manage your thoughts. However, know that He who began a good work in you is faithful to complete what He began (Philippians 1:6). As you participate in this 21-Day Plan, I encourage you to not rely upon your will power, but rather upon the indwelling power of the Holy Spirit. In so doing, it will take pressure off you and enable you to relax and trust the process. Like the faithless healed man, Jesus has sought you out for divine healing. Your part in your healing is to be faithful and pray to show up at the right place every day, for as long as it takes. The healed man showed up at the same pool for thirty-eight years, so keep on keeping on! As you proceed through this plan, and even when you miss a day or suffer some setback, know that Jesus will supply you with His grace. Rest on His promise: "Yes, it is God who is working in you. He helps you want to do what pleases Him, and He gives you the power to do it" (Philippians. 2:13 ERV). Do you want sympathy or victory?

How God Wants You to Use Your Mind

We are called to be proactive in our thought life, by remaining cognizant of the nature of our thoughts on a constant basis. Instead of accepting the first negative thought that pops into your mind, determine that with the Lord's help you will not be mentally passive, but will challenge any harmful, destructive, or unholy inner voice. This mindfulness is referred to as metacognition.[24] Metacognition means to deliberate upon our thought process. So, attend critically to all detractions that may come into your mind reflexively. In other words, *think about what you are thinking about.*

The 21-Day Plan is designed to equip you with the requisite tools to learn to monitor every thought and to challenge its worthiness. If the thought is in direct opposition to the Word of God, you must cast it down and discard it (2 Corinthians 10:5). Why? Because whoever and whatever controls your thoughts will control your feelings and behaviors and ultimately control your life. Unlike any other created being, God designed you and me in such a way that our thoughts control every aspect of our lives. Because of our uniquely designed cogitation (thinking), God, in His Word, informs us how He wants us to think. "Think the same way Jesus Christ thought" (Philippians 2:5 WE).

How to Think Like Christ

You think like Jesus when you...

1. **Use your mind to dwell on positive thoughts.**

   Finally, believers, whatever is true, whatever is honorable and worthy of respect, whatever is right and confirmed by God's word, whatever is pure and wholesome, whatever is lovely and brings peace, whatever is admirable and of good repute; if there is any excellence, if there is anything worthy of praise, think continually on these things, center your mind on them, and implant them in your heart (Philippians 4:8 AMP).

2. **Use your mind to obey (the will of) God.**

   "You shall love the Lord your God with all your heart, and with all your soul, and with all your *mind,* and with all your strength" (Mark 12:30).

3. **Use your mind to understand the Word of God.**

   "Then He opened their minds to understand the Scriptures" (Luke 24:45).

4. **Use your mind to dwell on spiritual things.**

   "The mind set on the Spirit is life and peace" (Romans 8:6).

5. **Use your mind to experience the peace of God.**

   "Thou wilt keep him in perfect peace whose mind is stayed on thee [God]" (Isaiah 26:3 KJV).

6. **Use your mind to be transformed into the image of Christ.**

   "Don't copy the behavior and customs of this world, but let God transform you into a new person by changing the way you think. Then you will learn to know God's will for you, which is good and pleasing and perfect" (Romans 12:2 NLT).

7. **Use your mind to remain on the lookout for Satan's next sneak attack.**

"Keep your mind clear and be alert. Your opponent the devil is prowling around like a roaring lion as he looks for someone to devour" (1 Peter 5:8 GW).

Questions for Reflection

1. Are you accustomed to accommodating the first thought that comes to your mind?

Yes or No

2. If yes, why do you believe God may want you to think in a positive and praiseworthy way versus accepting the first negative idea that pops into your head?

_____

_____

3. "You are today where your thoughts have brought you; you will be tomorrow where your thoughts take you." Explain what this means to you.

_____

_____

4. Are you aware that God designed you in such a way that your thoughts control every aspect of your life? Your thoughts control your emotions, your attitude, and ultimately your behavior. Explain:

_____

_____

5. Would you say you are shaping your thoughts, or your negative thoughts are shaping you? To what extent?

_____

_____

Congratulations. You have completed your first lesson. You are well on your way to winning the "thought wars" that are taking place in your mind. Each day you will learn a little more and more and become stronger mentally and spiritually. This is the plan. The old devil is scared because he knows that as long as you remain engaged in this kind of mindful thought management, he does not stand a chance of keeping you in bondage any longer. You are on your way to victory! God be praised!

Real Life Testimonies to Help Build Your Faith

We close today's lesson with a sharing of a personal story of a man I call Roosevelt. He is an example of a man who daily faces mental challenges due to his diagnosis. He is a man who knows what it means to be kept by God's grace.

Roosevelt's Story: Kept By God's Grace

At the age of 18, I was told I had bipolar disorder and schizophrenia, diagnoses that I flatly rejected. Confused and afraid, I became angry and especially suspicious of psychiatrists and all other mental health care specialists. Years after this gut-wrenching diagnosis, in my confusion, self-pity, and anger, I began self-medicating my pain with street drugs from the age of 20 to 41. During those years, I was involuntarily admitted into mental health facilities a minimum of 5 to 6 times. In my full-blown manic states, triggered by other illegal drugs, I was uncontrollable, leaving authorities no other choice than to place me in a strait jacket and admit me into the nearest psychiatric hospital. Even after these types of episodes, I still believed there was nothing seriously wrong with me.

After decades of escaping into drugging and partying, in 2010, (then 43), I was sick and tired and desperately wanted to change my life. Having been reared in church and baptized as a teen-ager, I knew it was time to return to the God of my youth. I sensed God through my circumstances speaking to me. Humbled and broken, I invited Jesus into my heart. Immediately, the scales that hung like curtains from my eyes were lifted, and I could clearly see that something had happened down on the inside of me. My mind was clear. I felt as though my confused mind was being replaced with the mind of Christ. I began reading the Bible and praying every day. Having lived in emotional torment and confusion for most of my life, it felt good to know that I was now headed in the right direction.

As to my diagnosis of bipolar disorder and schizophrenia, I can now accept the fact that I do have a chemical imbalance in my brain and therefore need to take my medication as prescribed every day. But my medication has its side effects. For example, it makes me talk and walk slower than I normally do. At other times, my medication seems to intensify my negative thoughts and fuel my paranoia.

Over the years, I've prayed for healing. Through trial and error, I have found that I must take my medication to get the results I seek. I still hear a voice telling me that I don't need to take my medication, but fortunately I've learned to ignore that voice. I still have negative thoughts, but I rebuke them. I take those thoughts captive. I refuse to allow a harmful thought to so dominate me that it drags me into negativity and depression.

Satan does at times come around trying to bring thoughts of condemnation, telling me that God doesn't love me and has failed me. He tries to convince me that I should feel ashamed that I am on medication. I quickly rebuke him saying, "There is therefore no condemnation for those who are in Christ Jesus" (Romans 8:1). I remind the devil that when God wants me off the medication, I'll know it because I'll no longer need it. I thank God that despite my diagnosis, I'm able to work each day, minister in church, care for my aging mother, and maintain a vigorous exercise regimen.

God is good!

* * *

Roosevelt's story attests to the fact that medication is not a cure-all. While on medication, you still must learn to manage your thoughts, emotions and work to maintain a positive attitude. Roosevelt is one of several people in his family who have received a similar diagnosis. His growth has enabled him to acknowledge this chemical imbalance while praying for healing and total deliverance. He is learning to be content with his situation until complete healing manifests. He refuses to allow this one burden to overshadow all the other blessings in life. Roosevelt is learning what it means to be kept by grace—God's grace.

* * *

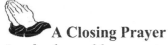**A Closing Prayer**

Lord, please bless me to experience tremendous transformation in my thought life over the next 21 days or for as long as it takes me to complete this journey. Give me the desire to daily pray, to read your Word, and strengthen me to complete my daily lessons. I recognize I need to learn how to master my thoughts so that my negative thoughts do not master me. I will cooperate with your Holy Spirit, as I learn to renew my mind —one thought at a time. In Jesus' Name. Amen.

♪ For an inspirational pick me up, I recommend these songs (found on YouTube music):

- *Better* by Hezekiah Walker
- *The Comeback* by Danny Gokey
- *Nothing Is Impossible With God* by The Brooklyn Tabernacle Choir

*If the musical recommendations above are not to your liking, here or elsewhere, find music that makes you feel happy and inspired.

Until tomorrow, do this:

1. Throughout the day, reflect upon the 7 positive ways God wants you to use your mind.

2. Listen to the above song (s) at least 2-4 times to stimulate your brain and uplift your spirit.

You're not Crazy—You're Human:
10 Sources of Your Thoughts

Every troubled person has a troubled mind. When thoughts are crazy, life is crazy.

--Archibald D. Hart

- **Brain Fact** "The National Science Foundation estimated that the human brain produces as many as 12,000 to 50,000 thoughts per day".[1]

- **Key Thought** Thoughts affect emotions and emotions affect attitudes, and attitudes produce behavior.[2] **TEA=B**

- **Scripture** "It will come about on that day, that thoughts will come into your mind..." (Ezekiel 38:10).

Daily Reading

Welcome to Day 2 of *The 21-Day Plan*! Let me ask you a question. Do you at times feel as though your head is swimming in thoughts? Do you at times find yourself asking, *"Whoa? Did I think that?"* or *"Where did those thoughts come from?"* It's as though the thought just popped into your head out of thin air. It did! Our thoughts can be downright scary at times. Do you sometimes find yourself with thoughts that you would not share with anyone else on the face of the earth for fear they would question your Christianity, or worse yet your sanity? If so, you are not alone, nor are you crazy. You're human. If some of your thoughts have you questioning your sanity, check out the tormenting thoughts of a man Jesus encountered in the Gospel of Mark. After reading it, I think you'll conclude that your thoughts are not as destructive as his were.

> When they arrived at the other side of the lake, a demon-possessed man ran out from a graveyard, just as Jesus was climbing from the boat. This man lived among the gravestones and had such strength that whenever he was put into handcuffs and shackles—as he often was—he snapped the handcuffs from his wrists and smashed the shackles and walked away. No one was strong enough to control him. All day long and through the night he would wander among the tombs and in the wild hills, screaming and cutting himself with sharp pieces of stone (Mark 5:1-5 TLB).

The main reason the man was screaming and cutting himself with stones was because he was tormented by the demonic chatter going on inside of his head. These destructive thoughts were prompting him to mutilate his body. In today's teen culture, I often hear stories of teens cutting and mutilating themselves. Observe the fact the man's desire to harm himself emanated from his thought life. However, after Jesus cast out the tormenting spirits which negatively affected his thoughts, emotions, attitudes and behaviors, the onlookers observed the man "sitting down, clothed and in his right mind" (Mark 5:15 TLB).

The text underscores the devastation Satan can wreak in an individual's thought life, once he (Satan) gains control of the victim's mind.

For far too many seasons of my life, my negative thoughts mastered my mind. I identified strongly with the lyrics of a country song that went, "I'm in bad company when I'm all alone." When I was out and about laughing, joking and ministering to people, I was fine; it was when I was alone with my private thoughts that I was most vulnerable to a cacophony of negative thoughts and voices. They did not come from God.

Today's lesson is designed to probe into the primary sources of our thoughts. By the end of today's lesson, I hope that you will be encouraged to learn that you are not demon possessed and that many of your craziest and most bazaar thoughts do just pop into your head out of thin air, and most of this you are not responsible for. No, you're not crazy—you're human; but being human means, you will at times think you are crazy.

What Are Thoughts?

Dr. H. Norman Wright describes a thought in the following manner:

> [Thoughts] are the ways in which we're conscious of things. They are made up of memories, our perceptions, and our beliefs. They are glimpses, even snippets, of ideas. Sometimes they pass fleetingly, barely noticed. Sometimes

they come sharply into focus. Our thoughts determine the orientation of everything we do. They evoke the feelings that frame our world and motivate our actions. And they have the power to change the way we feel.[3]

Based on Wright's definition, I have developed a formula **TEA=B**. Thoughts affect Emotions and Emotions affect Attitudes, and Attitudes result in Behavior. **TEA=B**.[4] Remember it! Commit it to memory. Pronounce it **TB**. It is analogous to the tuberculosis shots of old. Try to imagine each thought as a hypodermic syringe being injected into the brain, influencing everything you think, feel, and do. Why was the demon-possessed man cutting himself? Because his Thoughts stimulated his Emotions which in turn affected his Attitude. That resulted in his bizarre Behavior—**TEA=B**. *Are you aware of the fact that you are happy, sad, or mad, because of the thoughts you are entertaining?* So, if you do not like the way you are feeling at this moment, you just have to change what you are thinking about; what you are accepting as an emotional guide. It

> *Our Creator designed us in such a way that our thoughts influence every aspect of life.*

is literally that simple. Our Creator designed us in such a way that our thoughts influence *every* aspect of life. Thoughts form our spirituality, change our emotions, affect our attitudes, forge our character, influence our immune system, and determine our behavior.[5] The primary goal of *The 21-Day Plan* is to teach you how to better identify and manage your thoughts.

Questions for Reflection

1. As you are reading today's lesson, do you feel happy, sad, mad, worried or angry?

_____

_____

2. In order to change the way you are feeling, what do you need to do?

_____

_____

The Science

The following information serves to provide more of a technical or scientific definition of a thought from some experts in the field.

Dr. Caroline Leaf, a leading researcher in the field of neuroscience, asserts, *"Thoughts are basically electrical impulses, chemicals, and neurons."[6]* Dr. Norman Wright remarks, "Whenever you have a thought and that electrical transmission goes across your brain in a fraction of a second, you become aware of what you're thinking."[7] We become conscious of our thoughts when the dendrites (hair-like follicles'), which are attached to each neuron (brain cells), receive messages from the axon (a long tail-like stem extending from each neuron). When the sending and receiving brain cells connect, we experience a conscious thought.[8] See Figure 2.1. The human brain is made up of approximately one hundred billion (100,000,000,000) neurons.[9]

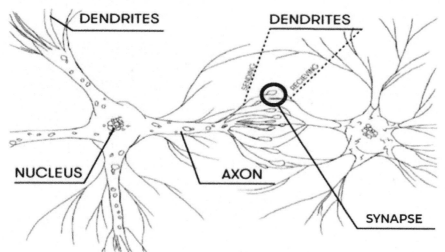

Figure 2.1 Two Brain Cells Participating in Conscious Thought

That there is such a direct correlation between thoughts and health should raise concerns about the things we ponder, because our ultimate well-being surely hangs in the balance.

Dr. Don Colbert, author of *Deadly Emotions*, states, "Thoughts are measurable and occupy mental 'real estate.' Thoughts are active; they grow and change. Thoughts influence every decision, word, action and physical reaction we make."[10] *"Every time you have a thought it is actively changing your brain and your body for better or worse."[11]*Our thoughts are far more powerful than we realize. Hence, it behooves us to examine the factors that influence, direct and produce our thoughts, both positive and negative.

The 10 Sources of Our Thoughts

Have you ever had a thought pop into your head that left you saying to yourself, Where did that thought come from? You are about to be equipped with the tools to trace the origin of your thoughts. Once we discover the origin of our thoughts, we are in a better position to manage them, because we will know what triggers to avoid. I have discovered through my research that the vast majority of thoughts emanate from 10 primary sources—7 natural and 3 spiritual.

Seven Natural Sources

Source #1: Science

The brain is the most complex organ in the universe. "It is estimated that the brain has one hundred billion (100,000,000,000) neurons (nerve cells) and perhaps more connections in it than there are stars in the universe."[12] "Your thinking is phenomenally fast—every thought impacts every single one of the 75 to 100 trillion cells of your body in an instant."[13] The National Science Foundation says "the human brain produces as many as 12,000 to 50,000 thoughts per day,"[14] depending upon how active your brain is. However, not all thoughts are processed. Researchers estimate that 95% of our thoughts are subconscious; hence, we aren't aware of them and don't remember them.[15] Our subconscious *thinking often manifests in our dreams.* But of the 5% we do remember, the vast majority of those tend to be negative. "It is estimated that information in the brain travels at the speed of 268 miles per hour."[16] Is it any wonder that the human brain at times feels overwhelmed by a cascade of negative thoughts? It is within this maze of neurological complexity that our thoughts originate.

The human brain produces a myriad of thoughts – some sensible, others cryptic, and some pure nonsense. "[Thoughts] jump into our consciousness without any planning or conscious prompting."[17] In recognizing the sheer volume of thoughts the brain produces, I discovered that I was not personally responsible for every zany, insane, or sinful thought that came into my head. And neither are you. *You are not responsible for every bizarre thought that pops into your head!*

Before gaining this awareness, on one occasion, I sought out professional counseling because of a troublesome notion that remained lodged in my mind. The counselor asked me a number of exploratory questions, and after thirty minutes or so, we were able to trace the origin of the vexation. Because there was no evidence to substantiate the worthiness of the thought, the counselor told me to ignore it. I followed this advice, and, within two weeks the thought dissipated. I've learned that there are some thoughts that we have to let pass through our minds without paying much attention; without giving them status. Some thoughts are to be seen as clouds just passing through our heads. You are no more responsible for all the thoughts that run through your mind than you are for the clouds that pass over your head. Like everything else in the world, our brain has been impacted by the intrusion of sin. Allow this perspective – that thoughts are like clouds –to free you from feelings of fear, shame, guilt etc. In time you will stop asking yourself, "How could I have thought such a hideously unworthy, truth-trampling thing?" As you read *The 21-Day Plan*, you will learn to ignore such thoughts and say to yourself, *"That's not my thought."* Jesus said, "You will know the truth, and the truth will make you free" (John 8:32).

Questions for Reflection

1. What do you think of the idea of allowing certain thoughts to pass through your head without paying special attention to them and viewing them as mere clouds passing overhead?

_____

_____

2. Did you realize that by dwelling upon a thought you actually give it life?[18]

Yes/No

Source #2: Sensory Mechanisms (5 Senses)

Our five physical senses – seeing, hearing, touching, tasting, and smelling – form our sensory mechanism. A vast majority of our thoughts, feelings, and emotions derive from our sensory mechanism. Based on the five senses, Dr. Wright asserts that thoughts "jump into our consciousness without any planning or conscious prompting."[19] Due to the fickle nature of our senses, at times, we may feel that we are weak, pitiful pawns of our thoughts and emotions, while at other times we feel strong, confident and courageous. A lot depends on what we are sensing or perceiving from our environment. A lot depends on our mood. For example, some people refer to Monday as "Blue" Monday. Why? Because after two days of being away from the job, their senses communicate to their brain an avalanche of negative thoughts: they say to themselves something like, "Boy, I can't believe it's Monday already. Where did the weekend go?" Your brain processes all these thoughts in a nanosecond. It's no wonder you don't want to get out of bed; your senses have told your brain it's another melancholy Monday. Your tiredness can influence your thoughts too. I've heard it said, "The devil likes to jump into your head before you get out of bed."

> _Thoughts jump into our consciousness without planning or conscious prompting._

Our five senses often play a large role in undermining our faith in God's promises and in becoming all that God intended us to be. God has promised to "supply all of our needs" (Phillippians.4:13), but because we don't see how, the enemy may whisper in our other ear something like, "God is not going to come through for you. You're unworthy." Unchecked, we allow our five senses to cause us to become fearful, worried, and anxious. Perhaps this is why God says we are to "walk by faith and not by sight" (2 Corinthians 5:7).

Source #3: Self-Talk

Our self-talk is a major player in thought reproduction. Self-talk has to do with the running internal dialogue or ongoing conversation we have with ourselves.[20] _Our self-talk plays a defining role in the thoughts we experience daily, and this_ *contributes to our self-esteem and self-concept.* For example, if as a child you grew up hearing repeatedly that you were unwanted, unloved, and worthless, subconsciously, and over time consciously, you would probably begin to believe it. Consequently, you might develop an internal dialog that says something like, "I am worthless" or "I am unworthy of love." Wright refers to these thoughts as automatic thoughts. "Automatic thoughts are learned. We listen to others and what they say about us, and we believe the statements. And what is more, we tend to become what we believe."[21] This is why the Bible affirms, "For as he [a man] thinks within himself, so he is" (Proverbs 23:7). If your self-talk is negative, it will generate negative thoughts and feelings; conversely, if your self- talk is positive, it will generate positive thoughts and feelings. To aid you in your efforts to replace your negative self-talk, on Day 3 I will introduce you to a positive *I Am Significant* mantra.

Source #4: Specific Events
Our thoughts are sometimes generated by specific events, replete with imagery, memories of specific events, sometimes very recent, positive, negative, or neutral. These may include: failing or passing a test, grief over things done or insufficiently done;[22] distressing medical news; prolonged periods of stress and anxiety; perceived failures; episodes of extreme embarrassment; a break up; or stress from financial difficulties.[23] Positive events tend to generate positive thoughts and feelings, and might include a marriage engagement, a wedding, a job promotion, the birth of a child, the safe return of a loved one from a military tour, the purchase of a new home, or other blissful experiences.

A word about trauma and its effects on our thoughts and brain chemistry: traumatic events such as physical or sexual abuse, death, an accident, bullying, neglect or abandonment, etc. have a way of instantly rewiring our brain.[24] Imagine that your brain is like a vegetable garden, each row meticulously cultivated, arrayed with an assortment of different vegetables growing side by side. Now imagine a torrential rain so powerful that it totally destroys the vegetable garden, washing away all the aligned rows and uprooting all the vegetables, leaving in its wake a tangled web of demolished vegetation. Dr. David Ziegler, author of, *Traumatic Experience and the Brain*, asserts that childhood trauma is equivalent to the 100-year flood.[25] "New pathways are formed. The experience of trauma makes new imprints on the brain. And that can change thinking forever, unless steps are taken, usually *through therapy*, to reverse the damage."[26] (*Repeated trips to the church altar for prayer, being smeared with oil, or having an "anointed" person lay hands, although beneficial, are not the fullest solutions.*)

Trauma specialist Dr. Norman Wright stresses, "When a child is traumatized, his brain literally forms itself around the experience it encounters. The experience is coded into neural templates. Any experience similar to the original event will then create that same traumatic response."[27] You see more clearly now how specific experiences shape our later moods, temperament and ultimately help form our less-than-confident personality; through self-talk, the experience becomes a part of our core beliefs, defining who we believe ourselves to be.

Source #5: Social Interactions

As you interact with people who are loving, supporting, affirming, and overall positive, they will inspire positive thoughts and feelings in you. For example, the Bible tells of the early Christians socially interacting supportively with one another. "All the believers were together and had everything in common. They sold property and possessions to give to anyone who had need. Every day they continued to meet in the temple courts. They broke bread in their homes and ate together with glad and sincere hearts..." (Acts 2:44-46 NIV). They encouraged and built each other up spiritually. And, very importantly, your kindly, supportive attitude toward others brings generally better thoughts about yourself.

If on the other hand, you intercommunicate with negative, critical, racist, small minded or judgmental people they will likely generate negative thoughts in you. People who habitually associate with negative people will profit from the wisdom of Mr. George Herbert, who said, "He that lies with the dogs, riseth with fleas."[28] The Bible says, "Bad company corrupts good morals" (1 Corinthians 5:51). While it is not always possible to choose whom you interact with, you can sharpen your awareness and regulate your thoughts to nullify the debasing effects of negative social interactions.

Source #6: Specific Drugs and Alcohol

Drugs prescribed by a physician, such as anti-depressants, can adversely affect one's thoughts just like illegal street drugs. Addiction counselors Kenneth McIntosh and Phyllis Livingston, in their book, *Youth with Alcohol & Drug Addiction*, chronicle the effects alcohol and drugs have on the brain. They contend that while drugs and alcohol do produce a high or preferred mental state, they are also known to cause confused and extreme feelings leading to suicidal and homicidal thoughts.

Narcotic drugs often release the feel-good chemicals dopamine and serotonin, which cause a high, also use up (deplete) these hormones, leaving the drug user on a never-ending pursuit of a re-experience of that "first high." The more dopamine released, the more pleasure we feel. Most abused chemical substances affect the limbic system, affording only short-term pleasure.[29]

This short-term "high" exacts a heavy toll on the brain's chemical balance and on the mind psychologically. Alcohol, a depressant, is known to produce a vast array of depressive thoughts once the drug is metabolized and wears off. It is called a depressant for a reason; it makes the user depressed.

Source #7: Specific Foods

The kinds of foods we eat can dramatically affect our mind, mood, and attitudes. Foods high in sugar provide a short-term boost of energy, but not long afterwards you find yourself crashing. This is sometimes referred as a "carb crash." Sugar is a highly caloric carbohydrate. During the crash, you may experience lightheadedness, lethargy, irritability, headache, confusion, difficulty concentrating, anxiety or increased negative thoughts.[30] Some compare the crash to feeling like a hangover. "A sugar crash usually happens within four hours of eating a large amount of carbohydrates" – especially sugar.[31] Why the crash? It is because the blood flow to your brain and other muscles is diverted to your stomach to aid in the digestive process. That is why you may find it harder to think clearly after a big meal. The crash is the result of your blood sugar level declining or "crashing." Additionally, "A carb-rich meal [like pastas and other comfort foods] raises your levels of tryptophan…[which] stirs up your body's favorite sleepy time hormone, melatonin."[32] When this occurs, you may find yourself looking for a place to lie down and go to sleep.

Question for Reflection

When I, "Dr. Chip," eat fatty or high-carbs foods, I often become irritable, lethargic, and lightheaded, and I find it hard to focus. What happens to you when you eat these kinds of foods?

Spiritual Sources

Rounding out my top ten list of sources affecting our thoughts are three spiritual ones: God, Satan (The Great Liar), and Secularism.

Source #8: Spoken Words of God

God has influenced and continues to influence our thoughts. From the beginning of creation, God spoke to Adam (verbally or through his thoughts). According to Genesis 3:9, God would meet with him in the cool of the day in the Garden of Eden. It was perhaps during these evening meetings that God communicated to Adam his role and responsibilities as the chief curator of the Garden of Eden. Just as God spoke to Adam, He also speaks to his children today. Jesus said, "My sheep hear my voice" (John 10:27). The closer Christians walk in fellowship with God, the more inclined they are to hear His "still small voice." God can, and does, speak through the thoughts of Christians in order to renew their minds.

All true believers were first drawn to faith in Christ because of the spiritual thoughts the Father used to influence their minds. The following verses underscore God's adroitness in influencing the thoughts of believers through the third person of the Godhead, the Holy Spirit. God primarily speaks to His children, not so much through audible instruction, but by impressions and most importantly through His written instructions in His Word, the Bible. Consider the following verses:

- Then He opened their minds to understand the Scriptures (Luke 24:25).

- All Scripture is given by inspiration of God, and is profitable for doctrine, for reproof, for correction, for instruction in righteousness, that the man of God may be complete, thoroughly equipped for every good work (2 Timothy 3:16-17 KJV).

God is speaking to us when He instructs us with His Word, on how we ought to live.

- Therefore, I urge you, brethren, by the mercies of God, to present your bodies a living and holy sacrifice, acceptable to God, which is your spiritual service of worship. And do not be conformed to this world, but be transformed by the renewing of your mind, so that you may prove what the will of God is, that which is good and acceptable and perfect" (Romans 12:2).

Source #9: Satanic (Demonic) Influences

The genesis of negative thoughts finds its origin in the Book of Genesis. Satan initiated the fall of mankind by speaking to Eve and manipulating her thoughts, causing her to disobey the command of God (Genesis 3). Satan impelled Eve to question the goodness of God by causing her to think that God was selfishly withholding something good from her by forbidding her and Adam from eating from the tree of the knowledge of good and evil. The serpent beguiled Eve when he said to her, "You surely will not die! For God knows that in the day you eat from it your eyes will be opened and you will be like God, knowing good and evil." When the woman saw that the tree was good for food, and that it was a delight to the eyes, and that the tree was desirable to make one wise, she took from its fruit and ate; and she gave also to her husband with her, and he ate" (Genesis 3:4-6). It is noteworthy to observe that Satan did not coerce Eve into disobeying God. He simply influenced her thinking,

Based on the experiences of the demon-possessed man in Mark 5, as well as my own personal experiences, the primary spiritual factor that contributes to the proliferation of negative thoughts is Satan and the numerous demons that work on his behalf. Consequently, all believers are told to, "Put on the full armor of God, so that you will be able to stand firm against the schemes of the devil. For our struggle is not against flesh and blood, but against the rulers, against the powers, against the world forces of this darkness, against the spiritual forces of wickedness in the heavenly places" (Ephesians 6:11-12).

The following verses illustrate diverse ways in which Satan manipulates the thoughts and minds of believers and non-believers alike.

- During supper, the devil having already put into the heart of Judas Iscariot, the son of Simon, to betray Him (John 13:2; Luke 22:3-4).

- Peter said, Ananias, why has Satan filled your heart to lie to the Holy Spirit and to keep back some of the price of the land? (Acts 5:3).

Satan works 24/7 to influence and gain mastery of our minds. However, *The 21-Day Plan* will teach us how with God's help, we can learn to master our negative, destructive thoughts rather than our negative thoughts mastering us.

Source #10: Secularism

Webster's dictionary defines secularism as "a system of doctrines and practices that disregards and rejects any form of religious faith and worship."[33] The Scriptures refer to secularism as a worldview that excludes God. This secular world view is lamentable because, "…the whole world lies in the power of the

> *The secular person is encouraged to live for himself, get all he can, and can all he gets.*

evil one" (1 John 5:19). Satan, through the media, bombards the minds of people with pictures, products, and the alluring opportunity to indulge lustful desires with little, if any, regard for the consequences. When subscribing to a secular worldview, what God decrees is rendered insignificant, as infinitely flawed human judgment replaces the judgment of God. Therefore, people feel free to do as they please, without the guidance of wisdom and without seeking permission or instruction from God. The essence of human secularism: *God is not my Sovereign*. Hence, Christians are admonished in scripture to shun the secular perspective along with its evil practices:

- Do not love the world, nor the things in the world. If anyone loves the world, the love of the Father is not in him. For all that is in the world, the lust of the flesh and the lust of the eyes and the boastful pride of life, is not from the Father, but is from the world. The world is passing away, and also its lusts; but the one who does the will of God lives forever (1John 2:15-17).

Accordingly then, "…be transformed by the renewing of your mind, so that you may prove what the will of God is…" (Romans 12:2).

This secular worldview seeks to bombard and dominate our mind so that we think like the world thinks, desire the evil things of the world, and mimic the behaviors of worldly people. The secular person is encouraged to live for himself, get all he can, and can all he gets (Luke 12:16-21). That is the essence of the secular life. However, the Christian worldview is expressed in the words of Jesus: "If anyone wishes to come after Me, he must deny himself, and take up his cross daily and follow Me. For whoever wishes to save his life will lose it, but whoever loses his life for My sake, he is the one who will save it" (Luke 9:23-24). True life is found in knowing, serving, and following Christ, not in excluding Him.

Question for Reflection

What areas of your thought life are substantially influenced by the secular worldview?

_____

_____

Congratulations! You have completed your second lesson. There are many more empowering Christian principles to be learned through this program. Stay with it. And if you find yourself doubting, pray, knowing the Lord hears you. Continue to push back on any negative thinking, in the confident awareness that it is not from God and push ahead to Day 3.

A Closing Prayer

Dear Father in Heaven help me to become more aware of the sources that are influencing my thoughts, both positive and negative. Help me, whenever possible, to avoid people, places, and things that may trigger negative ideation. Father, help me to continually push back on the belief that I am responsible for every discouraging, unclean or compromised thought that comes into my mind, and help me to not let those kinds of initial impressions go unchallenged. Let such unhelpful notions not evoke any embrace, and thus an emotional response on my part. Please help me to identify such thoughts outright. Having been previously deceived by the enemy in my thought life, I am now going to mount a serious comeback. In Jesus' name. Amen.

For an inspirational pick me up, I recommend:

- *The Breakup Song* by Francesca Battistelli
- *Wanna Be Happy?* by Kirk Franklin
- *Thankful* by Johnny Lang (featuring Michael McDonald)

Until tomorrow, do this:

Memory Work— Continue to memorize the following:

1. Begin to memorize **TEA=B** – Thoughts affect emotions and emotions affect attitudes, and attitudes produce behavior.

2. If you find the songs inspiring, listen to them several times to uplift your spirit.

A Case of Mistaken Identity:
Discovering the Real You

Man is obviously made for thinking. Therein lies all his dignity and his merit; and his whole duty is to think as he ought.

--Blaise Pascal

Daily Food for Thought

- **Brain Fact** Of the brain's five lobes - the frontal lobe, the prefrontal lobe, the occipital lobe, the temporal lobe and the parietal lobe [1] - it is within the parietal lobe that our spiritual DNA is hardwired.[2]

- **Key Thoughts** You are a spirit. You have a soul. You live in a body.

- **Scripture Verse** "Now may the God of peace Himself sanctify you entirely; and may your **spirit** and **soul** and **body** be preserved complete, without blame at the coming of our Lord Jesus Christ" (1 Thessalonians 5:23).

Daily Reading

Identity theft has become a major criminal enterprise. According to the U.S. Department of Justice, "An estimated 17.6 million persons, or 7% of all U.S. residents age 16 or older, were victims of one or more incidents of identity theft in 2014[3]…costing the American economy a staggering $15.4 billion...."[4]

    I myself recently fell prey to identity theft at the hands of a cyber hacker. Hacking into my email account, and pretending to be me, the criminal sent hundreds of my contacts a distress letter stating that I needed help out of a financial bind because I was robbed while traveling internationally. A thief supposely stole all my money, my passport and airline tickets, "I" was calling upon all those who knew me to send money to the American embassy in Bangkok, Thailand, so I could purchase new tickets to fly back to the United States. Sounding a little fishy, the e-mail immediately generated calls from family members, friends, and colleagues questioning the validity of it. Within minutes I sent out an alert to my contacts about the scam. In retaliation for my quick response the hacker wiped out fifteen years of precious email contacts. That hurt! Has this sort of thing ever happened to you?

Today, I want to alert believers to another kind of identity theft. Satan, the enemy of our souls, has hacked into believers' minds and while he may not have actually *stolen* their identity, he has at least confused them as to their Christ-directed identity. Many believers view themselves as victims, rather than victors, as failures rather than overcomers, as cowards rather than the courageous saints. Call it a case of confused, obscured identity if you will.

Biblical Mind Renewal

Today's lesson is designed to help you restore your true identity by renewing your mind regarding who you really are as a Christian believer, what you are, and *whose* you are. Biblical mind renewal is the lifelong process of replacing our perspective (thoughts, opinions, and beliefs) with God's perspective as revealed in His Word.[5]

> *It is the brain's plasticity that enables the believer to be transformed into Christ-likeness.*

According to C. Samuel Verghese, MD., Ph.D., it is the "brain's plasticity that enables the believer to continually modify personality and behavior into Christ-likeness."[6] As believers in Christ, we have the responsibility to take on the mind of Christ. By the dynamic of brain plasticity, God has made it possible for us to renew our minds one thought at a time. When we fail to renew our mind in the realm of our higher and truer spiritual identity, we, by default, become victims of Satan's "identity theft."

> *Satan wants to keep you confused as to what your true identity is, so he can tell you who you are.*

The primary reason Satan wants to keep you confused about your true identity is so that *he* can tell you who you are. Satan wants that divorce to define you, that abortion to define you, your family of origin to define you, that experience of rejection, that insult to define you, etc., etc., and today you are going to rediscover the *real* you. Allow the Holy Spirit to renew your mind, one thought at a time, so you can see yourself as God sees you—no more and no less (Romans 12:3). Pray earnestly for this deliverance!

Who Are You, Really?

When you look in the mirror, what do you see? Do you like what you see? You are more than the image you see staring back at you. You are such a complex and multidimensional individual that the looking glass cannot capture your total essence. And this is true of you whether you consider yourself a Christian or a non-Christian.

The triune God of the Bible, your Creator, said, "Let Us make man in Our image, according to Our likeness" (Genesis 1:26). God is a tripartite being: He is one in essence, but three in *"person,"* conceptually: Father, Son, and Holy Spirit—referred to as the Trinity. *We, therefore, having been made in God's image and likeness, are also trichotomous in our nature: comprised of a spirit, soul, and body.* This is referenced in the following Scripture: "Now may the God of peace Himself sanctify you entirely; and may your spirit and soul and *body* be preserved complete, without blame at the coming of our Lord Jesus Christ" (1Thessalonians 5:23).

Who are you, really?

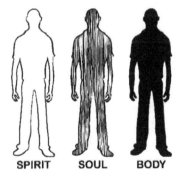

SPIRIT   SOUL   BODY

Figure 3.1 Man's Three-fold Nature (Part 1)

As a spiritual being, you can relate to God. *From a neurological standpoint, the human brain is hardwired to experience a deep and intimate relationship with God.* Of the brain's five lobes, the parietal lobe is where our spiritual essence is housed.[7]

> *From a neurological standpoint, the human brain is hardwired to experience a deep and intimate relationship with God.*

Before going into greater detail, I am going to segue momentarily to answer a question perhaps looming in your mind: What is the difference between the mind and the brain? Are they one and the same, or two distinct entities – one physical and the other conceptual? Through my research, I have discovered that *the mind is the brain at work.* I believe this is the simplest, most pragmatic way to describe these inner-workings.

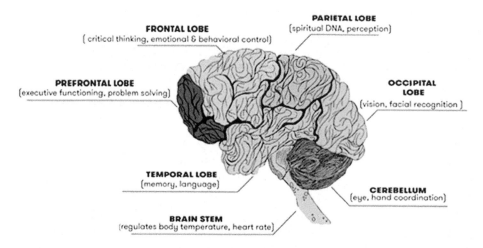

Figure 3.2 Map of the Human Brain

Within your brain you have a God-spot. Dr. Tim Clinton, president of the Association of Christian Counselors and author of the book, *God Attachment,* maintains that all humanity are born with a "God attachment."[8] For this reason God is worshiped in the most advanced cultures to the most primitive cultures the whole world over.

Who are you, really? *You are a spiritual being made in the image of God and hardwired to know Him personally.*

Although possessing a spirit, the Bible affirms that man's spirit is dead until spiritually awakened: "And you were dead in your trespasses and sins" (Ephesians 2:1). That begs the question, *When did man die spiritually?* In all probability, you are familiar with the story of Adam and Eve told in the Book of Genesis. The happy couple had it made. While living in luxury and privilege, and without want in the Garden of Eden, this happy couple was given one prohibition: God said, "From the tree of the knowledge of good and evil you shall not eat, for in the day that you eat from it you will surely die" (Genesis 2:17). Not surprisingly, they ate the forbidden fruit of that tree. Still Adam and Eve continued to live, in every physical sense. In fact, it is told that Adam did not physically die until the age of 930 (Genesis 5:5). *However, when Adam sinned, he died spiritually* and became separated from God. This is commonly referred to as "the Fall" (Genesis 3). Another consequence of their sin was that God expelled the couple from the Garden of Eden.

God, motivated by his love for mankind, promised Adam that He would send a deliverer; One who would die for the sins of mankind, thereby extending forgiveness to all who come to Him in faith and repentance. Some two thousand years ago, God fulfilled his promise when He sent His Son Jesus into the world. Upon seeing Jesus, John the Baptist declared, "Behold, the Lamb of God who takes away the sin of the world!" ... "For God so loved the world, that He gave His only begotten Son, that whoever believes in Him shall not perish, but have eternal life" (John 1:29; 3:16). Whenever an individual makes the decision to ask

God to forgive him of his sins, and prayerfully asks Jesus to become his personal Lord and Savior, instantaneously his or her once-dead spirit becomes alive to God. In that instant, the person becomes spiritually alive. And so profoundly altered is he or she that we use the term "Born-Again" (John 3:3-8). Denominational traditions may express this spiritual experience in different terms but in any case, this new spiritual person is now the real you. The Bible declares, "For if a man belongs to Christ, he is a new person. The old life is gone. New life has begun" (2 Corinthians 5:17 NLV). Let there be no mistaking your true born-again identity.

Questions for Reflection

1. Based on the above text, do you think you are spiritually alive?

_____

_____

2. If you are spiritually alive, did the new birth occur when you were a child, a teen, young adult, or later in life?

_____

_____

3. Why did this religious conversion happen when it did?

_____

_____

If you answered spiritually not alive, or not sure, your dead spirit can be spiritually born-again at this very moment. God's enormous love for us makes this possible. All you need to do is to intently pray the following prayer:

Lord, Jesus, forgive me of my sins, come into my heart. Change me. I'm tired of living for myself. I want to now live for You. I make you Lord and Savior of my life. Thank You for never giving up on me and patiently loving me in my ignorance and sinfulness. I am Yours, Lord, yielded to You, to use me as You please. Amen.

If you have sincerely prayed that prayer, the Bible declares you have been born again spiritually (Acts 2:21; Romans 10:13; 2 Corinthians 5:17). You are now spiritually alive. Welcome to the family of God. Tell a friend, begin reading the Gospel of Saint John and consider joining a good Bible teaching church that will help you to grow spiritually.

Your Born-Again Spirit

As a born-again child of God, your born-again spirit is attuned to:

- spending time in God's presence (Psalm 105:4; Isaiah 55:6)
- praying to God and listening to His promptings (Matthew 7:7-8,11;1 Thessalonians 5:17)
- praising and worshiping God in song (Psalm 7:17; 9:11; Philippians 4:4)
- reading and memorizing the Bible (Joshua 1:8; Psalms 1:1-3; 119:11, 97)
- worshiping as part of a community of believers, etc. (Hebrews 10:24)

From now on, born-again child of God, this is the real you. The Holy Spirit living on the inside of you is the driving force that motivates your born-again spirit to live like Christ, love like Christ, and share Christ. This is the real you!

As a new spiritual being, you have the "mind of Christ" (1 Corinthians 2:16; Philippians 2:5). This means that you now have the ability to think like Christ, to "cast down" negative thoughts and to choose positive God-honoring thoughts. However, your new spiritual mind now exists in seed form only (Matt. 13:4; 2 Peter 1:3). It must be watered by the word of God, prayer, and the other spiritual habits mentioned earlier if it is to grow and be empowered. You must renew your thinking from that of your worldly mind (Romans 12:2). *Your spiritual mind must be cultivated spiritually lest it fall prey to figurative spiritual malnutrition and its growth be stunted.* As a result, your spirit will be too weak to exercise controlling influence over both your soul and body. Zechariah 4:6 informs, 'Not by might nor by power, but by My Spirit,' says the Lord of Hosts." You are a spirit and you have a soul.

Figure 3.3 Man's Three-fold Nature (Part 2)

Your Soul

Your soul is comprised of your mind (thinking, reasoning), your will (choices), your emotions (feelings), in addition to your conscience and personality. *Unlike*

58

your born-again spirit that is sensitive to God, your soul is radically independent, thinking primarily about self and doing its own thing. Your soul is not the real you. When the Bible uses the term "natural man" or "natural mind" it is referring to your soul (1 Corinthians 2:14; James 1:23). Your soul is in the process of being delivered, submitted, and conformed to the image of Jesus (sanctification). Sanctification is a lifelong progression. The major problem with your soul is that it suffers from an "I" problem. Examine the following verses:

- And I will say to my soul, 'Soul, you have many goods laid up for many years to come; take your ease, eat, drink and be merry' (Luke 12:19).

- Because the mind [soul] set on the flesh is hostile toward God; for it does not subject itself to the law of God, for it is not even able to do so (Romans 8:7).

- And He [Jesus] was saying to them all, 'If anyone wishes to come after Me, he must deny himself [soul], and take up his cross daily and follow Me' (Luke 9:23).

If you want to know whether your soul-based thoughts are dominating your thought life, observe how frequently your thoughts begin with the personal pronouns I, me, my, and consider whether you make other self-centered statements like these:

- "I don't need to pray."
- "I'm strong enough. I can handle this; it won't bother me to_____...."
- "In my opinion..."
- "I don't need to learn about that stuff. I'm good the way I am."
- "I don't need anybody telling me what to do."

What do we do with such thoughts? My wife told me about a mother who walked into her child's messy room and told the child, "I think it's time you clean up your room." The child, looking up from the toys she was playing with, replied to her mother, "That's not my thought!"

Here are some egoistic soul-based non-Biblical ideas that often pop up in our minds and come out of our mouths …

- "I've waited on God long enough; it's time for me to take matters into my own hands."
- "I feel my heart is leading me to..."
- "I'm fine the way I am."

When thoughts such as these come into your mind, say to yourself, "That's not my spirit talking; that's my soul talking."

Remember, your soul is not necessarily the real you, the highest you. You are a born-again spirit. One of the goals of *The 21-Day Plan* is to strengthen your born-again spirit to such a degree that it controls both your soul and body and brings them into conformity to its will. Your soul desires to control and dominate your spirit. But you must push back on your soul's pushback. God wills that your spirit, which is born-again, should control both your soul and body.

Questions for Reflection

1. Name one characteristic about your spirit and soul that you did not know prior to today's lesson.

_____

_____

2. How often each day do you feel you are experiencing troublesome soul-based self-talk?

_____

_____

Reviewing: You are a spirit, you have a soul, and you live in a body.

Figure 3.4 Man's Three-fold Nature (Part 3)

Your Body

The body is often referred to in the Scriptures as "the flesh." It is your external physical layer—the part visible to the eye. *Like your soul, your body is hostile to the things of God, unless brought under submission to your born-again spirit.* As a consequence of "The Fall," your flesh and natural mind are inherently sinful. I remind you: your fleshly body is not the real you! Your sin-riddled flesh loves nothing more than to dominate both your soul and your spirit. See above the diagram showing the flesh (body) on the outer circle. Examine how the Word of God describes the nature of the flesh:

- But I say, walk by the Spirit, and you will not carry out the desire of the flesh. For the flesh sets its desire against the Spirit, and the Spirit against the flesh; for these are in opposition to one another, so that you may not do the things that you please (Galatians 5:16-17).

- Now the deeds of the flesh are evident, which are: immorality, impurity, sensuality, idolatry, sorcery, enmities, strife, jealousy, outbursts of anger, disputes, dissensions, factions, envying, drunkenness, carousing, and things like these…(Galatians 5:19-21).

- The mind of the flesh [with its carnal thoughts and purposes] is hostile to God, for it does not submit itself to God's Law, indeed it cannot. So, then those who are living the life of the flesh [catering to the appetites and impulses of their carnal nature] cannot please or satisfy God or be acceptable to Him (Romans 8:7-8 AMP).

You may ask, how can I know when the real me, my spirit, is being controlled and dominated by my flesh? For starters, the flesh always seeks ease and comfort; it is lazy and loves to indulge its carnal appetites as is illustrated in the aforementioned verses.

You know when your flesh is dominating and controlling your soul and spirit when…

- You chafe at anything spiritual, like reading your Bible, going to church, praying, fasting, journaling, memorizing scripture, singing spiritual songs, etc.
- You find yourself indulging in any sinful activity like watching pornography, drinking, smoking, or any form of sexual immorality, or perversion.
- You eat the entire pizza and a dozen donuts instead of just one. You have obviously overeaten.
- Your self-talk is of this ilk:
  --"I don't feel like it."
  --"I'm too tired to go to church; it's been a rough week on the job."
  --"I don't feel like praying on my knees. I'd rather pray in the bed – it's more comfortable."
  --"Everybody is doing it!"
  --"Just doing this once can't hurt!"
  --"It can't be wrong when it feels so right."
  --"I'll just ask for forgiveness later."
  --"I've already blown my diet, so I might as well go all out now. I can restart my diet again tomorrow."
  --"I'll just enjoy tonight. Everybody has the right to a little enjoyment."

Spiritual Alignment

When such thoughts pop into your mind, say to yourself, "It's my flesh talking." Your born-again spirit will tell you to deny the sinful desires of your flesh. Because of the inherent sinful nature of the flesh, we are told in scripture to "Put on the Lord Jesus Christ and make no provision for the flesh in regard to its lusts" (Romans 13:14). Because your flesh was not completely sanctified at salvation, it will perpetually war against your born-again spirit. Therefore, Paul said, "…present your bodies a living and holy sacrifice, acceptable to God, which is your spiritual service of worship" (Romans 12:1). God wills that you push back on your fleshly appetites and rely upon the power of the Holy Spirit to strengthen your spirit so that you can walk in victory. Figure 3 illustrates how spiritual victory is won by bringing your soul and body into alignment with your spirit.

Figure 3.5 Spiritual Victory Is Won Through Alignment

Questions for Reflection

1. Name some characteristics of your "fleshly desires" that you did not deeply consider prior to today's lesson.

_____

_____

2. Why is it essential that you "push back on your soulish and fleshly thoughts?

_____

_____

Separating Your "Who" From Your "Do"

Importantly: *The 21-Day Plan* is not a self-help, pop psychology book. This is a book designed to be used in partnership with the Holy Spirit who resides within every born-again believer. As the Holy Spirit works to renew our minds—one thought at a time, we must cooperate with Him. The Holy Spirit's job is to both remind us of God's will (John 14:26) and empower us to do God's will (Acts 1:8). Our job, as spirit-filled believers, is to obey the Holy Spirit when He brings to our remembrance things we ought not to be thinking or doing. When the soul and flesh rise up in opposition to our godly spirit, it is our job, to push back on their pushback. Our pushback may be to simply say, "Get thee behind me, Satan" (Matthew 4:10).

The above familiar quote from Matthew reminds me of a story about a woman who had promised her husband that she would not buy any more new dresses. To help her resist the temptation she asked her husband to hold her accountable. Well, one day while window shopping, her eyes fell upon a stunning dress—on sale, 40% off. She remembered what she had told her husband, but the dress was too pretty to pass up. So, she went in and tried the dress on. It fit her perfectly and accented all her attractive features. So, she bought it, knowing she was going to have to tell her husband. Her husband met her at the door and noticing the shopping bag asked, "What's in the bag, certainly not a dress?" With great timidity the wife confessed her transgression. Her husband exploded and angrily said, "You just couldn't resist the temptation. Why didn't you tell Satan to 'get thee behind me'?" She replied, "I did tell him that, and he said, it looked especially good from behind!"

Hey, let's face it; we are going to fail at times. But always remember that the Holy Spirit is always available to help us get back up, even after we've repeatedly failed.

When our soul and flesh get the best of us and we royally blow it, Satan often goes on the offensive, exploiting an excellent opportunity to bombard our minds with all kinds of self-condemning thoughts. He may say things like, "You are a poor excuse for a Christian." "God could never use a mess up like you." "Your sins are too plentiful; God has his limitations; He's not going to forgive you." In addition to tempting us to sin, Satan seeks to define us by our mistakes, our failures and our mess-ups. But push back on Satan's pushback and say to him, "I recognize your voice. Yes, you are a liar!" Then, if you haven't done so already, confess your transgression to God and ask his forgiveness. Have faith in his promise (1 John 1:9). The Bible tells me, "there is no condemnation for those who are in Christ Jesus" (Romans 8:1). God's mercy is greater than your mistakes. Let the devil know that you refuse to allow him to try to define you based on your errant or perhaps sinful actions. Every person is more, much more than his or her worst mistake. Furthermore, because of your faith in Christ Jesus and the infinite grace of God, you are who God says you are, even and in spite of mistakes

63

you make, and actions you may do. Practice separating your 'who' from your 'do'.

Each day, remind yourself that your soul and flesh will war against your spirit and lure you into any number of sins. However, you need to practice separating your spirit—the real you, from the actions and proclivities of your often sin-sick soul and body. Consciously separating your 'who', "your Christian essence" from your 'do', a specific, sinful action, is essential in order to avoid a tiresome plethora of discouraging, self-condemning thoughts.

The Apostle Paul wrote about his personal struggle with sin as his soul and flesh warred against his born-again spirit. Paul lamented, "For the good that I want, I do not do, but I practice the very evil that I do not want. But if I am doing the very thing I do not want, I am no longer the one doing it, but sin which dwells in me" (Romans 7:19-20). Paul learned to separate his 'who' from his 'do' and we can learn to do the very same thing. With your spirit, you love God and desire to serve Him faithfully. That is your truest self. But when we fail to separate our 'who' from our' 'do', we by default allow Satan to insidiously thwart the truth regarding our spiritual identity. You are a spirit. You have a soul. You live in a body.

Building on a Firm Foundation

"Know who you be!" These are words of admonition that Omoro, the father of Kunte Kinte, spoke to his son in the movie, *Roots*. That advice is quite appropriate and necessary for building a firm foundation of our identity in Christ. If, for example, you build your identity upon externals such as your looks, then who are you when your looks begin to fade? If you build your identity upon a specific human relationship, who will you be or become if that relationship dissolves? If you build your relationship upon your monetary successes, who will you be when finances fail? Jesus warns against building our lives and identities upon the arbitrary constantly shifting sands of our secular culture when he says,

> All who listen to my instructions and follow them are wise, like a man who builds his house on solid rock. Though the rain comes in torrents, and the floods rise, and the storm winds beat against his house, it won't collapse, for it is built on rock. But those who hear my instructions and ignore them are foolish, like a man who builds his house on sand. For when the rains and floods come, and storm winds beat against his house, it will fall with a mighty crash (Matthew 7:24-27 TLB).

Truth be told, despite being a preacher of the Gospel, I had built my self-concept upon the shifting sands of superficial success. Like so many others, I had built my identity upon my 'do' and not my 'who'. Life was good for several decades, but just around the bend, life was waiting to take me on an unsettling journey that would shake me to the very core of my being. Failure, setbacks, disappointments, economic calamity, marital distress, bouts of depression, and anxiety attacks, the likes of which I had never previously known. When the superficial identity props were washed away, my self-respect and identity came crashing down. It was then that I was forced to ask myself, Paul Chipman, who are you? Sadly, it took years before I found myself able to answer that question. As I searched for an answer, I recalled an elder Christians who said, "You never know that Jesus is all you need until Jesus is all you have." At my lowest point Jesus was all I had. Over the course of several years, stone by stone and brick by brick, the Lord helped me to build my identity upon Christ as my solid rock. As I read His word, studied His word, and preached His word, I discovered that God did not see me as I saw myself. In my heavenly Father's eyes, I was special. I was absolutely redeemable. God's unfathomable love avails this. I discovered that I am forever the recipient of His divine love, and He loves me just as much as he loves his Son Jesus (John 17:23).

I Know Who I Am!

In my search for my true spiritual identity, God gave me the following Bible mantra/confession/affirmation which I have over the years repeated to myself countless times.

Affirmation: I Am Significant. Why? *(Because)* God loves me and sent his Son to die upon the cross for my sins. He has adopted me into His family and has given me a new name. I am a born-again* Christian, fearfully and wonderfully made in the image of God (John 3:16; Ephesians 1:5; 2 Corinthians 5:17; Psalm 139:14).

If your church or Christian affiliation uses a term other than "born-again," such as: "child of God", "Christ follower", "spirit-filled believer", "believer", "saint", "saved", or "Christian", feel free to insert it into the mantra. The important thing is to remain mindful that God's tremendous love and advocacy is what empowers us.

This time say it in the second person in front of a mirror. Do not hesitate to point your finger at your reflection in the mirror and say it repeatedly. You may or may not feel it emotionally but repeat it anyway.

You are significant. Why? *(Because)*God loves you and sent his Son to die upon the cross for your sins. He has adopted you into His family and has given you a new name. You are a born-again Christian, fearfully and wonderfully made in the image of God.

This mantra/confession replaces your negative self-talk. Each time you are tempted to label yourself in a negative way, repeat the whole *I am significant* mantra. As you consistently do this, you are retraining your brain to see yourself as God sees you and to speak about yourself as God speaks about you. The topics of negative self-talk, self-esteem, and your spiritual identity will be discussed in greater detail later in *The 21-Day Plan*.

FYI: Concerning Bible affirmations: We make Bible confessions not because we are trying to make them true. We make Bible confessions because they are true whether we believe them or not. However, when we confess them, we become conscious of our spiritual identity. We sense it. Our new spiritual persona becomes powerful and real in our lives at this time. As you consistently repeat this confession with faith and conviction, you will begin to renew your mind—one thought at a time. "It takes a thought to replace a thought. It takes a right belief to replace a wrong belief."[9]

> *We make Bible confessions because they are true whether we believe them or not.*

Exercise believing faith and refuse to base your identity on your fickle feelings. You are who God says you are.

Everything we receive from God we receive by faith. We are saved by faith, healed by faith, and made righteous by faith.

After assuring me that I was significant in Christ, the Lord gave me the N-O-W-M-O-V-E-F-O-R-W-A-R-D acrostic. He challenged me to N-O-W-M-O-V-E-F-O-R-W-A-R-D in embracing my true spiritual identity based on His infallible Word. He commanded me to stop procrastinating and stop allowing Satan to perpetrate his insidious identity theft. I had to build my self-image upon my 'Who' (who I am in Christ) rather than my 'Do' (what I do). I am a spirit. I have a soul. I live in a body. Normally, we consider *doing* very important, but our *being* - becoming who God has called us to be - is of primary importance. Our faith and spiritual rebirth mean that now, any *doing* is to be based on our *being* one with Christ. (Eph. 2:10). Although you will not always behave or act perfectly (your DO), your born-again relationship with Christ, your spiritual identity, (your WHO) never changes.

> *Biblical mind renewal is the lifelong process of replacing our perspective with God's perspective.*

The *I Am Significant* mantra and the N-O-W-M-O-V-E-F-O-R-W-A-R-D spiritual identity acrostic will become the basis of rewiring your brain neurologically and spiritually for you to see yourself as God sees you—no more and no less (Romans 12:3). You will learn it incrementally over the next 21 days and beyond. Initially, your soul (mind) and flesh will resist this new description of yourself. Hence, the real spiritual you, empowered by the Holy Spirit, will need to step up and tell your soul and flesh to submit; they are no longer in charge. There is a new spiritual sheriff in town. You know who you are! You are a spirit empowered by the Holy Spirit to control your soul and body in order to fulfill God's glorious plan for your life.

This is how you employ the N-O-W-M-O-V-E-F-O-R-W-A-R-D spiritual identity acrostic. When the Enemy says to you that you haven't changed much since being born again spiritually and you are the same old worthless person you have always been, instead of agreeing with that negative thought, the spiritual you will say, "No Satan!" based on the Word of God, spiritually,

I am (a)...
   New creation in Christ Jesus (2 Corinthians 5:17).
   Ordained and chosen by God to fulfill His purpose for my life (Jeremiah 1:5; 29:11).
(And I...)
   Walk in the power of the Holy Spirit (Ephesians 5:18; Acts 1:8)

(Because I walk in the power of the Holy Spirit...)

I Am (an) (a)...
   More than a conqueror (Romans 8:37)
   Overcomer (1 John 5:4)
   Victor, not a victim (1 Corinthians 15:57)
   Eternally loved (Romans 8:35, 38-39)

I Am...
   Favored of God (Psalm 5:12)
   Oh, so bold, confident and courageous (Proverbs 28:1; 2 Timothy 1:7)
   Reconciled to be a reconciler (2 Corinthians 5:18-20)
   Well protected (Isaiah 54:17; Psalm 23:4-6)
   Assured of success (Psalm 1:3; Nehemiah 2:20; Joshua 1:8)
(the) **R**ighteousness of God in Christ Jesus (2 Corinthians 5:21; 1 Peter 2:9)
   Destined to win if I do not quit (2 Corinthians 2:14; Romans 8:31; Isaiah 41: 9-10; 43:1-4)

IMPORTANT: While standing in front of a mirror, repeat this acrostic in the 2nd person ("You are...").

Use the Scriptures above and others to see yourself through your Father's eyes. The reason Satan desires to keep you confused about your true identity is so that he can tell you who you are. He wants to define you. Push back on his pushback. Cast down all negative thoughts and mental images and believe what the Word of God says about you. Commit it to memory. You will be glad you did!

As you conclude today's lesson, you have your first homework assignment. Locate a 3x5 card and write on it the I Am Significant statement exactly as it appears here:

I Am Significant

I Am Significant. Why? *(Because)* God loves me and sent his Son to die upon the cross for my sins. He has adopted me into His family and has given me a new name. I am a born-again Christian, fearfully and wonderfully made in the image of God (John 3:16; Ephesians 1:5; 2 Corinthians 5:17; Psalm 139:14).

Figure 3.6 I Am Significant Mantra

Topic: I Am Significant

I Am Significant. Why? *(Because)* God loves me and sent his Son to die upon the cross for my sins. He has adopted me into His family and has given me a new name. I am a born-again Christian, fearfully and wonderfully made in the image of God.

To hardwire it into your brain, you will need to repeat it to yourself a minimum of 10-12 times per day. If you find yourself not accomplishing this, pray earnestly. The more often you practice, the quicker you will wire it into your brain, and experience less negative self-talk. The rewiring process will be explained in greater detail on Days 5-7.

As Seen Through Our Father's Eyes

It's often hard to fathom how God views us and the depths of our heavenly Father's magnanimous love. "This is love: not that we love God, but that He loved us…" (1 John 4:10a EHV). "God's love is uncaused and spontaneous. His love is born from within him, not from what he finds in us. Our goodness doesn't enhance his love. Our weakness doesn't dilute it." [10] Selah! From His infinite love, God asserts, "I'll call nobodies and make them somebodies; I'll call the unloved and make them beloved" (Romans 9:25 MSG). Christ was stripped bare so we would be adorned with his righteousness. Before you performed any righteous deeds, God called you *righteous*. Before you broke any bad habit, God pronounced you an *overcomer*. Before you won a single victory, your designer decreed you a *champion*. Before you ever behaved righteously, God declared you a *saint*. That is how we are viewed through our Father's eyes.

Using Downtime to Memorize

Someone might say, "I'd like to memorize this mantra, but I can't seem to find the time" You do have the time, but it's just not a priority. Some people say, for example, "I need to exercise, but I just don't have the time." Everybody has the time to exercise. Those who don't exercise but are physically able to, have just not prioritized it. Satan tricks us in this and a million other ways.

Let me help you find some time. In the Gospel of Luke, Chapter 17, Jesus healed 10 lepers. However, they were not healed instantaneously. Instead they were healed as they were going to the temple to show themselves to the priest. If you want to be healed from a negative self-image brought about by negative self-talk, practice memorizing this mantra as you are going through your daily activities. Take time to memorize it whenever you find yourself in the following situations:

- When your mind is idle
- Stuck in traffic or at a red light
- Your morning and evening commute
- Standing in line at the bank, DMV, mall, amusement park, etc....
- As you are waiting for church service to start or class to begin
- While you're vacuuming, mowing the lawn, or washing your car
- Doing dishes, washing laundry, preparing meals
- Halftime at sporting events
- Preoccupied with worrisome thoughts
- During break times on the job or in the rest room
- On break while playing video games or while exercising
- When you wake up first thing in the morning
- During radio, TV, or internet commercials
- Before, during, and after your prayer or quiet time
- When you wake up during the night and cannot fall back to sleep
- Putting on your make up, shaving, or bathing, etc....

You don't need to carve out extra time. Memorize it as you are going through your day. You will be glad you did!

Keys to Memorizing the Mantra

1. Write it on a 3x5 card.
2. Start with the Topic: I Am Significant.
3. Repeat the 1st phrase, I Am Significant...multiple times.
4. After you've memorized that, move to the next word or phrase. "Why? (Because...) God loves me", etc.
5. Do not seek to memorize the 3rd phrase until you have the 1st and 2nd totally memorized.
6. Always repeat the memorized phases as a group starting from the beginning and continuing to add on.
7. PRACTICE! PRACTICE! PRACTICE!
8. Employ your imagination. See it first, and then say it.

Do not stress yourself over this memory work. Proceed at your own pace.

> *Because of how deeply entrenched our old, toxic thoughts are, we may need to say the new ones hundreds of times before we truly change our thinking for the better.*

Congratulations! You have completed your third lesson. You are well on your way to winning the "thought wars" that are taking place in your mind. Each day you will learn a little more that will make you mentally and spiritually stronger. The devil does not stand a chance of keeping you in bondage. We've got the victory. *Trusting in God, we've got the victory!*

Real Life Testimonies to Help Build Your Faith

We close today's lesson by sharing Charles's personal story of how he came to experience his spiritual rebirth.

Charles's Story: At My Worst You Found Me

My name is Charles. I was born and raised in Brooklyn, New York. Through a series of bad choices and bad associations, I became addicted to alcohol and heroin at the age of 21. With my twisted mind obsessed with nothing but getting high at any cost, my criminal actions lead to my being incarcerated in the North Carolina penal system. It was there in the dark pit of prison that a loving God reached out to me. At my very worst, He found me and lovingly drew me to himself. How? It just so happened I started attending Bible studies with my cell mate and there I discovered the good news of the Gospel. God demonstrated His love for me by sending Jesus to die upon the cross for my sin (John 3:16). Humbled and broken by my addiction, right there in that prison cell, I opened both my mind and heart to receive God's love by inviting Christ Jesus into my heart to become my personal Lord and savior. He replaced my cravings for drugs with a craving to know Him and His Word. As I daily read my Bible and attended Bible studies, Jesus began replacing old practices with new practices. He replaced my self-hatred, shame, and guilt with a healthy self-love and self-acceptance and love for others. I am truly amazed at the transformation in my life. Now I know that God can change the worst of sinners. Why? Because He did it for me.

A Closing Prayer

Dear God, help me to see myself as You see me, no more and no less. Lord help me to yield to your Holy Spirit as He reminds me to repeat my mantra. Help me to obey his promptings. Thank you for loving me and reminding me of my true identity. In Jesus' name. Amen.

For an inspirational pick me up, I recommend:

- *You Say* by Lauren Daigle
- *I Know Who I Am* by Sinach
- *Hello, My Name Is* by Matthew West
- *I Am* by Jason Nelson

Until tomorrow, do this:

Memory Work— Continue to memorize the following:

1. Remember **TEA=B** – Thoughts affect emotions and emotions affect attitudes, and attitudes produce behavior.

2. Practice reciting the *I Am Significant* mantra (Repeat 10-12 times per day – for example say the *I Am* mantra – 2 times a day per meal and snack and 2 times in the morning and evening while in bed).

I Am Significant. Why? (Because) God loves me and sent his Son to **d**ie upon the cross for my sins. He has **a**dopted me into His family and has given me a **n**ew name. I am a born-again Christian, fearfully and wonderfully made in the image of God.

*To aid in the memory of this mantra, I have highlighted the "d" in die, the "a" in adopted, and the "n" in new. It spells the name Dan. Hopefully this small memory device will serve you well.

3. Listen to the above song (s) at least 1-3x's to stimulate your brain and uplift your spirit.

71

The Power of Your Imagination:
What You See is What You Get!

Imagination is everything. It is the preview of life's coming attractions.
--Albert Einstein

- **Brain Fact** "The imagination is far stronger than any other power which we possess, and the psychologist tells us that on occasions, when the will and the imagination are in conflict, the imagination always wins."[1]

- **Key Thought** What you see is what you get. What you consistently imagine, you will consistently get.

- **Scripture** "Glory to God, who is able to do far beyond all that we could ask or imagine by his power at work within us" (Ephesians 3:20 CEB).

Daily Reading

Welcome to Day 4.

During my formative years, I remember hearing a Motown Song by the soul stepping Temptations entitled, *Just My Imagination*. Are you familiar with the song? The lead vocalist sang about his love of a particular woman that he watched pass by his window each day. He is in love with the woman and imagines in his mind that she loves him too. He imagines confessing his love to her, marrying her, raising a family together and living happily ever after. However, when brought back to reality, he laments, *"It was just my imagination running away with me."* Reader, may I ask you a question? Can you imagine yourself controlling your thoughts rather than your negative thoughts controlling you? Can you imagine you shaping your thoughts rather than your thoughts shaping you? Can you imagine 75% of your thoughts being positive and only 25% negative? Or, do you, like the love smitten singer above, conclude, *"It's just my imagination running away with me."*

In today's lesson, you are going to discover the power of your imagination and how you can use it to work for you rather than against you. You are in for some exciting discoveries.

The Power of Your Imagination

A.W. Tozer, author of *The Value of a Sanctified Imagination*, describes the unique power of your imagination:

Like every other power belonging to us, the imagination may be either a blessing or a curse, depending altogether upon how it is used and how well it is disciplined. We all have to some degree the power to imagine. Every advance made by mankind in any field began as an idea to which nothing for the time corresponded. The mind of the inventor took bits of familiar ideas and made of them something altogether nonexistent. Thus we "create" things and by so doing prove ourselves to have been made in the image of the Creator. [2]

Just as God first conceived Adam and Eve in His mind before He created them, you and I are made in the image of God and possess the same ability to first cognitively see a thing before it comes into being. For example, as I was writing *The 21-Day Plan*, I held in my mind this image of placing my completed manuscript in an attachment and pressing the send button on my computer as I sent it electronically to the publisher. I maintained that image on the canvas of my mind years before it actually happened.

Rev. Dr. Alexander Whyte, the famed 19th century Scottish preacher, professor of New Testament studies at New College in Edinburgh, author and astute student of the mind, makes an even more profound statement about the power of our imagination: "The imagination is far stronger than any other power which we possess, and the psychologist tells us that on occasions, when the *will and the imagination are in conflict, the imagination always wins.*" [3]

> **Your Imagination creates your reality.**

When I first read the statement "When the will and the imagination are in conflict, the imagination always wins," I had an Oprah "aha" moment! In that moment, I discovered why I had failed in some endeavors and succeeded in many others. In large part it was due to the mental images that I had painted on the canvas of my imagination.

Allow me to explain. In previous undertakings that had ended in failure, I recognized that while I spoke words of faith concerning the endeavor and had so wished and wanted to succeed, truth be told, I had entertained countless images of the endeavor failing. In fact, I had engaged in many internal conversations rehearsing my concession speech! In the end, the negative mental images won. I failed in several ministry endeavors just as I had imaged I would. The more I anticipated failing, the darker my moods became, and one by one my support staff at the church plant began to leave. Figuratively speaking, sensing the imminent demise of this endeavor, I felt like the few remaining faithful followers forsook me and ran for the hills

For quite a while, I erroneously remained angry and harbored resentment toward the people whom I falsely believed had abandoned me. However, once the mental fog lifted, I realized that these people truly admired and respected me. They were subconsciously fleeing from the pessimistic person I had become, in large part because of the negative images looming in my mind and the negative "vibes" that were emanating from me. They had not abandoned me. I had abandoned *them* by failing to safeguard against the negative mental images that I had allowed to play on the movie screen of my mind. I thought because I rarely verbalized my negative mental conceptions, except to my wife, that no one else was aware of the fear-riddled thoughts and images in my head. But I was wrong. As was the case with the Bible character Job, "The thing I feared has overtaken me, and what I dreaded has happened to me" (Job 3:25 CSB). How was that possible?

The Law of Attraction

Dr. Bruce L. Moyle, III, an electrical engineer, explains how my negative thoughts although unspoken were nevertheless communicated to my would-be followers.

Each thought exists as a minute wave of energy called a thought form. A thought form is real—it exists. It happens to not be noticed by you because its energy vibration (frequency) is outside the range of human senses. It operates faster than the speed of light and is therefore, not visible to you. It might be helpful for you to understand this concept by relating it to something you already know… If you're like most of us, you have a favorite radio station. Perhaps an FM station…Let's say it's 102.7 on the dial. What the number means is that the frequency of transmission for the station is 102.7 megahertz (megacycles). Mega is the metric designation for one million. The energy transmitted by the station vibrates continuously in the space around you. But unless your radio is tuned to the frequency of 102.7 million cycles per second, you are unaware of it. My point is this: There is a lot of information vibrating in the space around us that we are not aware of because our senses are limited to a specific range of frequencies. And some of the information vibrating in the space is in the form of tiny, subtle thought forms. In effect, you are like a radio station, WYOU, broadcasting your desires, intentions, and ideas out into the universe—completely uncensored.[4]

While the term "thought form" may seem strange, the idea that people transmit their thoughts, intentions, and desires into the universe around them is not. A term often used to refer to this phenomenon is "vibes". People have sometimes commented, "That person is sending off certain vibes." The vibes could be perceived as either good, bad, or indifferent; nevertheless, the individual feels them. Christians with the spiritual gift of discernment are more acutely aware of people's "thought forms." Jesus, on several occasions, mentioned he knew the thoughts of his disciples and the Pharisees even before they uttered a word (Matthew 9:4; Luke 5: 22; 9:47). Our thoughts are powerfully omnipresent.

Our negative thoughts which translate into toxic mental images, subtly work themselves into our unconscious mind and into the world around us via thought forms and ultimately make their way into our vocabulary. If you really want to know what you truly believe, observe the images in your mind and listen to the words coming from your mouth.

What's Playing on the Movie Screen of Your Mind?

It's safe to say that most of us would not spend our hard-earned money to see a movie that we knew was dreadful. On the one hand, while we would not pay to see a horrible movie, how often have we found ourselves mentally watching depressing images of ourselves on the movie screen of our minds? We may have repeatedly viewed depressing images of ourselves as weak, performing poorly, fleeing instead of fighting, and compromising our morals just to be accepted. Sadly, many of us do it every day, sometimes every hour of the day. Admission to our own bad movie is free of charge, yet it costs us much heartache, misery, and depression.

Concerning these negative mental images, Dr. Whyte, points out that believers, "should vow by the Savior's help never to throw the wrong kind of pictures on the screen in our mind, for the imagination literally has the power of making the things we picture real and effective."[5] It's my desire here in *The 21-Day Plan* to help us to replace those negative mental images. This does not mean that, because of our ongoing battle with our old nature, we will not slip and watch a few negative reruns from time to time. But it does mean that these times should increasingly be the exception, rather than the rule.

A Truth About the Imagination

Because of the Fall of Adam (Genesis 3), man's imagination has been compromised, contaminated, and corrupted. The word imagination first appears in Genesis 6:5, *"And God saw that the wickedness of man was great in the earth, and that every imagination of the thoughts of his heart was only evil continually"* (KJV). We see here why a person's imagination can either be a blessing or a curse. Take note: the vast majority of the negative mental images in your head did not just pop into your head overnight. Quite the contrary, many of them were planted in our minds early on in life from childhood and adolescent experiences, our family of origin, as well as other negative and traumatic events that we experienced later in life. As a result, we are admonished in Scripture to manage both our thoughts and imaginations. The Apostle Paul writes, *"Casting down imaginations and every high thing that exalteth itself against the knowledge of God and bringing into captivity every thought to the obedience of Christ"* (2 Corinthians 10:5 KJV). Keep in mind the imagination can be used either positively or negatively. Imagination is neutral; it's a blank canvas.

The root of the word imagination is image. It has to do with images like still photos or still images on an 8-millimeter reel. The phrase casting down means to "take down, put down, or pull down." [6] Similarly, as you drive on the freeway, you are probably accustomed to seeing giant commercial billboards advertisements along the highways marketing different types of businesses, medical facilities, churches, etc. Have you had an opportunity to witness the workers who take down those billboards and replace them with new images? I have. I remember watching them pull down and tear off the old image and glue the new one right on top of the old one. That is what Biblical mind renewal is all about. It replaces old thoughts and images of self and replaces them with new Christ centered images. In Christ we have been made brand new (2 Corinthians 5:17). Therefore, as a new spiritual person, it's necessary to replace old mental images with new Bible-based images.

On the subject of our old image, the Apostle Paul emphatically states, *"You were taught, with regard to your former way of life, to put off your old self, which is being corrupted by its deceitful desires; and to put on the new self, created to be like God in true righteousness and holiness"* (Ephesians 4:22,24 NIV). The process of taking off our old self (our mindsets) in order to put on our new self is done in our minds: *"...Be renewed in the spirit of your mind"* (Ephesians 4:23). Biblical mind renewal is the lifelong process of replacing our perspective (thoughts, opinions and beliefs) with God's perspective as revealed in His Word.

Dr. David Eckman, author of the book *Becoming Who God Intended*, makes the case that Christians are weekly presented with truthful information, but observe very little change in their thought lives, emotions, attitudes, and behaviors. Why? Because believers fail to distinguish between information and integration. "With information, the conscious mind has simply placed data into the memory.

With integration, the conscious mind has taken a picture formed in the imagination and placed it in the subconscious, where it will affect emotions."[7] Eckman goes on to say, as you begin to create new Bible-centered mental images of yourself, God, and others, in place of the negative images derived from childhood, adolescence, and negative experiences as adults, your emotions will begin to change and you will begin to feel the positive emotions as you meditate upon new mental pictures.[8]

I encourage you to use your sanctified imagination, to see yourself for who you really are spiritually—in the eyes of your loving heavenly Father. We don't just say, "I am significant." We visualize it. As you N-O-W-M-O-V-E-F-O-R-W-A-R-D in the process of renewing

> *Use your sanctified imagination, to see yourself for who you really are spiritually.*

your mind, take the time to visualize yourself being all that God says you are.

Engage your imagination as you say out loud to yourself...

I Am (a)...
New creation in Christ Jesus (2 Corinthians 5:17).
Ordained and chosen by God to fulfill His purpose for my life (Jeremiah 1:5; 29:11).
(And I...)
Walk in the power of the Holy Spirit (Ephesians 5:18; Acts 1:8).

(Because I walk in the power of the Holy Spirit...)

I Am (an) (a)...
More than a conqueror (Romans 8:37).
Overcomer (1 John 5:4).
Victor, not a victim (2 Corinthians 15:57).

The mental image I use to integrate the acrostics "I am an overcomer" and "a victor, not a victim," originated with an experience I had while a senior in high school. I ran the quarter mile on the school's track and field team. Early in the season I was undefeated. However, on one specific April day, I was scheduled to race against an especially tough opponent. He too was undefeated. His reputation as a freakishly gifted football and track star had preceded him. As the race time neared, I did my routine stretching before removing the warmup gear. Turning to my right, I saw this challenger remove his gear and begin to stretch. I noticed the guy's muscular legs and thought to myself that his calf muscles were as large my thighs. As my eyes moved upward, I saw the massive forearms and chest of what seemed to me the paragon of athletes. All of a sudden, my confidence melted away like super-heated wax. We lined up at the starting line, the official shot the gun, and that was as close as I ever got to beating him. The man ran like a gazelle! I finished a distant second. My brief glorious status in being "undefeated" was over. As I went home and considered my loss, I concluded that the young man had defeated me not because of any peculiar excellence in athleticism, but because I had allowed his aura to get into my head. In a very real sense, I was defeated before the race began. Knowing why I had lost, I purposed in my heart that I would defeat him in the conference championships six weeks later. As I looked for a weakness in my nemesis, I learned (through a couple of rumors) that the young man was famously undisciplined. He didn't enjoy training and relied upon his youthful physical nature to achieve all he had. I strongly believed my only hope of defeating him was to out train him. Over the ensuing weeks I pushed myself in my practice sessions and as a result outperformed my competitors, picturing each of them as the hot shot who had ruined my record and my image of myself as a superb runner.

As I had *imagined*, 6 weeks later we met at the conference championships. At the starting line, I totally ignored him. My mind was set not on his prowess, but rather on the finish line. My strategy was to get out in front and stay in front. He and the other competitors were going to have to run me down from behind if they were going to catch me. That was my attitude. The starting gun fired, and I sprinted into the lead. I ran so fast; it was as if wings were attached to my track shoes. I didn't come into contact with another runner until the last few yards of the race when Hot Shot arrived beside me, brushing my arm. Then something happened that had never happened before in my 3-year track history. Fatigued, I broke my stride and fell forward toward the finish line. My body hit the ground with a thump. But pinned beneath my chest was the finish line tape. Bouncing up, covered in dirt from head to toe, I raised both my hands in victory. I was the Tri-County 440-yard Champion! I had overcome! I was more than a conqueror. I was a victor not a victim. God had given me the victory. Reflecting upon this achievement years later, I felt it must have been an angel that pushed me over the finish line before I was overtaken.

When I repeat the phrase, I am more than a conqueror, I now hold this mental image in my mind. This is one example of what Dr. Eckman means when he says believers are to use their imagination to integrate Biblical information into emotion-based mental pictures that result in real mind renewal and life transformation. So, as you rehearse the I am significant mantra and the N-O-W-M-O-V-E-F-O-R-W-A-R-D spiritual identity acrostic, use your sanctified imagination to make the mantra come alive emotionally. Neurologically, your brain feeds on these images to aid in the transformation process.

Practice it with the next one; *"I am Eternally loved"* (Romans 8:35, 38-39). For example, you might picture Jesus standing a short distance from you. Love is shining out from him like sunlight from the sky as he walks toward you smiling. Your heart melts as you smile in return. You are engulfed in His magnanimous love which draws you towards Him like a magnet. As you approach Him, He opens wide His arms to warmly embrace you and says, "(insert your name), you are my beloved child in whom I am well pleased." Can you see it? Use your sanctified imagination to experience the power of His special love and admiration for you. You are everything to the Father that Jesus is. John 17:23 says that God loves you as much as He loves Jesus. Imagine that! If you dare to believe, it will radically alter your life.

The Power of a Sanctified Imagination

See it. Say it.

I Am…

    Eternally loved (Romans 8:35, 38-39)

I Am…

    Favored of God (Psalm 5:12)

    Oh, so bold, confident and courageous (Proverbs 28:1; 2 Timothy 1:7)

    Reconciled to be a reconciler (2 Corinthians 5:18-20)

    Well protected (Isaiah 54:17; Psalm 23:4-6)

    Assured of success (Psalm 1:3; Nehemiah 2:20; Joshua 1:8)

(the) **R**ighteousness of God in Christ Jesus (2 Corinthians 5:21; 1 Peter 2:9)

    Destined to win if I do not quit (2 Corinthians 2:14; Romans 8:31)

Speaking of the importance of imagining, Dr. Norman Wright comments,

> Imagining is the forming of mental pictures or images. And interestingly, the way we imagine ourselves we are likely to become. If we imagine ourselves as failing, we're more likely to fail. If we see ourselves as succeeding in some task, there's a greater likelihood that we'll succeed…and images we believe and reinforce eventually seep into the unconscious part of our minds, becoming part of who we are.[9]

Wright's observation parallels the sentiments of the writer of Proverbs 23:7, "For as he [a man] thinks in his heart, so is he." I have paraphrased it to read, "As a man thinks, so he will become." Our imagination is far more powerful than many of us may realize. Pull down those negative imaginations and…

    -see yourself healed.

    -see yourself living stress free.

    -see yourself succeeding where you had previously failed.

    -see yourself accepting your challenges gracefully.

    -see yourself prospering where you previously found yourself fretting over financial matter.

    -see yourself loosing that extra 40 pounds and working out in the gym.

    -see yourself rejoicing in the success of others.

-see yourself victorious in that struggle you've had for years or decades.

-see yourself achieving your dreams and living the life God designed for you.

Envisioning Your Life's Story

Take a moment to think about a few of your favorite movies. Who plays the starring role? Every movie has a character that plays the leading role, and in the movie of your life you have the leading role. You are mortal; and as you were born you will surely die. When you die, the engraver will engrave on your tombstone the day and year you were born and the day and year you die. In between those two dates, the engraver will place a dash (—). The dash represents the life you lived. As you star in the lead role of your life story, know that people are watching your movie frame-by-frame, reel-by-reel. The Sacred Scriptures inform us that our lives are being watched by others. "We are surrounded by a great cloud of people whose lives tell us what faith means. So, let us run the race that is before us and *never give up*. We should remove from our lives anything that would get in the way and the sin that so easily holds us back" (Hebrews 12:1 NCV). As we look to lay aside any thing that may hinder our Christian race to the finish, for certain, we need to lay aside the negative mental images, the "evil imaginations," that daily flash upon the mental screens in our minds. If for example you are struggling financially, push back, recall the solid fact that God is our most trusted Shepherd and He leads us through every difficulty. We don't have to worry when we walk stride and stride with our Eternal provider.

As my family and I were going through financial uncertainty, the Enemy would flash on the movie screen of my mind: a foreclosure sign staked on my front lawn, with several white 8x10 pieces of paper plastered on our front door with the word FORECLOSURE in bold red lettering. If I were to maintain my peace and stay in an attitude of faith and victory, I had to push back on the thoughts and pull down that negative mental image. How? By replacing it with the following promise of God found in Bible, words that echo through the ages:

When you pass through the waters, I will be with you;
And through the rivers, they will not overflow you.
When you walk through the fire, you will not be scorched,
Nor will the flame burn you.
For I am the Lord your God,
The Holy One of Israel, your Savior
You are precious in my sight…honored…and I love you. (Isaiah 43:2-4a)

If you choose to, write this verse carefully on a 3x5 card. Take it out and read it every time you begin feeling anxious, any time you see negative images flash on the canvas of your mind.

If at the reading of this lesson, you are suffering a relationship difficulty, it would be to your advantage to remove from your imagination the picture of separation and discord and see yourself in peace with others. If you are under intense mental stress and pressure these days, push back on your initial negativity and pessimism and pray to God for wisdom, strength, and sustaining grace to hold fast to His exceeding great promises. Shift your focus away from the problem you are facing toward praising God and thanking Him for all the other blessings in your life. Recall the blessing of health, opportunity, close friends, education, skills, edifying experiences, happy memories, and reasons to be hopeful. Talk to a trustworthy friend, or seek professional or pastoral counseling, begin a journal or diary, listen to sermons or read books to strengthen your faith. Recalling Whyte's words: "Believers, should vow by the Savior's help never to throw the wrong kind of pictures on the screen in our mind, for the imagination literally has the power of making the things we picture real and effective."[10] Such is the power of the imagination. Run your race to the end, in unbridled faith, free of the mental clutter that might have distracted you from your divine destiny.

As you star in the movie of your life, remember, God wants to participate in the creation of your life's story. He created you and cast you in the leading role. Jesus is the executive producer; He funded your life's story with his own blood. The Holy Spirit is both the director and your supporting actor. He is there with you in every scene, to make you look your best and support you in every possible way. My question to you is, "How do you envision your story ending? It is up to you. Do you imagine the situation you are presently facing ending in the thrill of victory or in the agony of defeat? The ending is largely predicated upon how you see yourself and your Savior. As the star of your life's movie, do you see yourself as a hero or a zero, a victor or a victim? Despite whatever setbacks, failures, or hardships, do you have the faith to believe that God can still bring you out on top? You still have a tomorrow. A better tomorrow begins by putting the proper mental images in your mind today. Albert Einstein said, *"Your imagination is your preview of life's coming attractions."*

"I have a Dream!"

In August 1963, Dr. Martin Luther King, Jr. spoke to his nation on national television about human dignity and social justice. His immortal words, "I have a Dream", were spoken that hopeful summer day by a man who was simply imagining. Decades later, his dream became a reality! If Dr. King's imagination for a desegregated United States of America with equal opportunity for all Americans superseded the seemingly insurmountable atrocities of legalized institutional hatred and racism, certainly you my friend, can unleash your powerful imagination to change your own life with the assistance of *The 21-Day Plan.*

Despite what you may have been through or are presently going through, I challenge you to begin thinking positively about your future. Resolve that your story will end well. You will not limp to the finish line. You will finish strong. Despite our human propensity toward negativity, God wired into the human brain a "bias toward optimism...if not, we would be prone to increased anxiety and depression,"[11] Despite your pessimism, your brain is ready and willing to believe again and can envision a positive future despite past disappointments and unmet expectations. I challenge you to dream again. One's ability to dream again is visually illustrated in the life of fatherless Abraham, who became the progenitor of the Judeo-Christian faith.

Abraham's original name was Abram. Throughout much of Abraham's adult life he wanted an heir, but his dream had not come to pass. God, the consummate dream giver, acutely aware of the desires of Abraham's heart, spoke to Abraham when he was 75 years of age. God asked him to exercise his faith and believe that God wanted to grant him the desire of his heart—a son. Hence, God invited Abraham on a walk so they could discuss the matter in more detail. "And He [God] took him [Abraham] outside and said, "Now look toward the heavens, and count the stars, if you are able to count them." And He [God] said to him [Abraham], "So shall your descendants be" (Genesis 15:5,16). During Abraham's encounter with God, it is probable that Abraham used his imagination to see a *child's smiling face* upon every star in the sky. Abraham's faith in the promise of God shed light on how Abraham wanted his story to end. Despite many years of disappointment, failure and frustration, Abraham kept the dream alive. He had to trust God *today* for a brighter tomorrow. Using his sanctified imagination, he saw himself as a father and his wife Sarah as a mother. Nearly 25 years later, God fulfilled his promise. Nearing his 100th birthday, her 90th, Abraham and Sarah gave birth to their son Isaac (Genesis 21:1-5).

The Bible affirms, "God has given to each a measure of faith" (Romans 12:3). Use your measure of faith to dream about a glorious future. It may be surprising for many to learn, but neurologically speaking, there is a direct correlation between your faith and your brain's health.

Faith: The Number One Brain Exercise

In *How God Changes the Brain*, Dr. Andrew Newberg contends that the number one brain exercise is faith. He defines faith as "intrepid trust in your beliefs." "...Faith is equivalent with hope, optimism, and the belief that a positive future awaits the believer...even when there is no proof that such beliefs are accurate or true." Dr. Newberg underscores the importance of faith by referencing a medical curiosity: "Faith in an optimistic future may be a placebo, but it's important to remember that placebos can cure, on average, 30 percent of most physical and emotional diseases."[12] Such evidence underscores the power of the imagination.

This begs the question, does positive thinking work? The answer is an emphatic, YES! Furthermore, what we are specifically interested in here is the power of faith-filled thinking and prayer.

A study conducted by the famed Mayo Clinic on the importance of optimistic thinking as an assist to maintaining optimal health discovered that positive thinking had the following effects on the body:

"(1) It decreases stress; (2) It helps you resist catching the common cold; (3) It reduces the risk of coronary artery disease; (4) It eases breathing if you have certain respiratory diseases; (5) It improves your coping skills during hardships; (6) It reduces the stress-eliciting cortisol levels in your body."[13]

Feel free to visit the site to view the list of all the benefits of positive thinking yourself. There you have it. If you happen to be uncomfortable with the term "positive thinking," replace it with the term "healthy thinking" or "positive— Bible-based" thinking. However, for the sake of your brain's health, I caution you not to throw the baby out with the bath water.

By contrast however, pessimistic people tend to experience or to be more at risk of the following:

"(1) more at risk for depression; (2) more anxiety; (3) more sleeping problems; (4) more obsessive–compulsive behaviors; (5) impaired social functioning; (6) shorter life span; (7) poorer mental functioning."[14]

According to Newberg, doubt and fear of the future put the human brain in an unstable, insecure, and unsafe state of mind. These are the exact same sentiments expressed by the Apostle James, who said, "A man of two minds (hesitating, dubious, irresolute), [he is] unstable and unreliable and uncertain about everything [he thinks, feels, decides]. Consequently, that man will not receive anything from God" (from James 1:6-9 AMPC).

Surely, God wants His children to be optimistic about their future. That is why He said to a depressed and demoralized group of Hebrew exiles, "I know the plans that I have for you, declares the Lord, plans to prosper you and not to harm you, plans to give you hope and a future" (Jeremiah 29:11). It bears repeating; for the brain to function healthily, it needs to be secured in a promising future and an intrepid faith in a promise-keeping God. King David, a man who faced many dark days and challenging nights, routinely used his faith to remain optimistic about his future. He said on one occasion, "I would have despaired unless I had believed that I would see the goodness of the Lord in the land of the living" (Psalm 27:13). *Believe God! Exercise your faith to believe the rest of your days shall be the best of your days! The best is yet to come!* Learn to make your imagination work for you and not against you.

No matter how faith filled and optimistic you might be, inevitably a tinge of doubt is bound to creep back in to undermine your resolve. What should you do with the doubt? Newberg addresses it in the following manner:

Truth can only be approximated by the brain. Instead what the brain does best is calculate the odds of success. Here is where faith kicks in because it is essential to remain optimistic about your chance of reaching your goal. So, what do you do when all of the subtle, and not so subtle, self-doubt kicks in? You can do several things, suppress them, evaluate them, or ruminate on them. Neurologically, it's actually easier to suppress them, because the more you keep your mind focused on your optimistic belief of success, the more you will inhibit the functioning of the limbic system, [Day 8] which generates doubt and fear. Ruminating, unfortunately, strengthens the neural circuits that generate anxiety and embed the information into long term memory banks.[15]

Newberg reminds us that what we think about we bring about—both positive and negative. Manifestation begins in the mind.[16] God wants us to use our minds to imagine a great future. When times are at their worst, God has equipped you with an imagination empowered by the Holy Spirit, so that in the darkest of times when you feel all hope is lost, you can turn your mind's eye inward to the great I AM, who resides on the inside of you to encourage you. He'll open your eyes to see yourself,

-going back to school and graduating with honors.
-getting married.
-prospering financially.
-emotionally whole and healthy—free of anxiety, worry, bitterness and resentment.
-getting that promotion, making that team, and getting accepted into that program, organization or school.
-in control of your mindset, moods, and attitudes.
-living your best life now—no longer tormented by regrets of the past.
-starting a new career or ministry.
-fully vested in your marriage.
-reconciled with your children and all attending church together.

Neurologically speaking, what you see consistently is what you'll get consistently. What you think about, you bring about. If someone sees you staring off into space, sitting in

> *What you see is what you'll be.*

deep peaceful contemplation with a big smile upon your face, and then they ask you what you are thinking about, reply, "It's just my imagination running away with me. I'm reflecting upon the glorious future that awaits me."

A Closing Prayer

Dear God, I resolve by your strength to no longer dwell on negative mental images without pushing back. I now know that by ruminating on such negative images, I cause my fears and doubts to grow. I understand that what I think about I will bring about. I pray that you would make these truths more real and compelling. In Jesus' name. Amen.

For an inspirational pick me up, I recommend:

- *Overcomer* by Mandisa
- *I Gotta Believe* by Yolanda Adams
- *I Can Only Imagine* by Mercy Me

Until tomorrow, do this:

Memory Work

1. Remember **TEA=B** – Thoughts affect emotions and emotions affect attitudes, and attitudes produce behavior

2. **Biblical mind renewal** is the lifelong process of replacing our perspective (thoughts, opinions, and beliefs) with God's perspective as revealed in His Word.

3. Practice reciting the *I Am Significant* mantra (Repeat 10-12 times per day – or 2 or 3 times in the morning and evening while in bed and at each meal daily.)

I Am Significant. Why? *(Because)* God loves me and sent his Son to die upon the cross for my sins. He has adopted me into His family and has given me a new name. I am a born-again Christian, fearfully and wonderfully made in the image of God.

4. My spiritual identity

N-O-W-M-O-V-E-F-O-R-W-A-R-D acrostic. Review it but do not seek to memorize now.

Day 5

What You Think About You Bring About

We are what we think. All that we are arises with our thoughts. With our thoughts, we make our world.

--The Buddha

Daily Food for Thought

- **Brain Fact** "The wiring in the brain contains our beliefs and assumptions. With enough deliberate practice, we can rewire ourselves."[1]

- **Key Thought** Neuroplasticity (brain flexibility) describes the "plastic (changeable) nature of the brain...."[2] The brain is not static, but is forever changing.

- **Scripture** "For as he [a man] thinks in his heart, so is he" (Proverbs 23:7AMPC).

Daily Reading

Well done! You've made it to Day 5. The next three lessons hold the primary keys to understanding the process of mind renewal. While the lessons may get a little technical at times, don't let that intimidate you. Push back on any intimidating thoughts and commit to expanding your mind. After all, you have the mind of Christ, and with His mind you can grasp the most difficult of concepts (1 Corinthians 2:16). I am confident that you will find today's lesson both practical and inspirational. We begin today's lesson with a quote by that optimist of optimists, Dr. Norman Vincent Peale:

86

Most people appear quite self-sufficient, composed, self-controlled. That is the way we are expected to look in public. But, as someone once observed, in every human being there is a frightened child. There is one in you and in me, too. Appearances notwithstanding, most human beings are plagued with self-doubt, shyness, a sense of inferiority, and low self-esteem. We are afraid of ourselves, of the future, and of the world. It is something we have to struggle against all the time. Very few people have wholly transcended this feeling of self-putdown and achieved complete, serene self-confidence. I do not think anyone has done so *without definite change in his basic thinking*[3].

Peale's final two sentences are most instructive. Read them again if necessary, to make sure you grasp what Peale means. *The 21-Day Plan* is all about changing the way you think—changing the way you deal with yourself, your thoughts, feelings, God, and people. This list also includes the countless ideas, organizations, occupations, and activities you encounter daily. It takes the grace and power of God to make substantive changes in your thinking across so many areas. I discovered that it was impossible for me to change the way I was thinking by my own strength. The good news is, God doesn't expect us to! "The things that are impossible with people are possible with God" (Luke 18:27). God has made it organically possible for all of us to change the way we think through the process of neuroplasticity. The prefix *neuro* refers to the brain. The root word *plasticity* connotes, "The idea of the plastic (changeable) brain, the recognition that our brains change and grow physically in response to life experience. New brain cells are constantly being formed; new networks between cells keep growing as we learn new things."[4] It is through the process of neuroplasticity that the Holy Spirit works in conjunction with any believer who dares to yield, to give up his prideful individuality, to transform his spirit, soul (mind), and body.

For a more scientific explanation of the brain's ever-changing nature, Dr. Laurence Tancredi describes neuroplasticity as, "the ability of neurons at the synapses to forge new connections, thereby essentially bringing about a rewiring of the brain. Neuroplasticity results not only in the setting down of new pathways through the cortex, but also the remodeling of neural networks."[5] In laymen's terms, every time you consistently think a new thought, have a new idea, increase your education, expand your vocabulary, memorize the lyrics of a song, or receive any instruction in moral conduct, a new neurological pathway is forged in your brain.

Have you ever wondered why you are able to multitask? It is because of the innumerable neuropathways in your brain. Thus, you can drive your car barreling around a curve at 65 miles per hour while talking on your car's communication system, all the while looking out for "the boys in blue," and as you munch on a juicy chicken sandwich (I don't recommend this). Furthermore, as all this is occurring, your stomach acids are working to digest your sandwich, as you hum along to your favorite worship song playing in the background. The reason you can multitask is because your thoughts and actions run on their own separate neurological grid.

"One part of the brain responds to one's words, another part to what one sees, another to what one feels, and another to what one tastes."[6]

Amazing! The more you repeat a given behavior, the more it becomes deeply rooted in your brain's wiring and becomes easier to do, say, and repeat the next time.

Tancredi goes on to inform us that individuals who consistently engage in any sort of dangerous or addictive behavior, such as drugs, sex, gambling, or pornography, do so because it is a matter of neuroplasticity. Neuroscientists point out that what often starts as an innocent experiment—drinking alcohol, or smoking pot—can develop over time into compulsive, addictive behavior. Patterns that are repeated over time become wired in the central nervous system (the brain and spinal cord).[7] Substantiating this fact, the human brain is forever changing, growing, and adapting to new stimuli and information. The brain changes and adapts via the development of new circuitry which induces more and more of either good or bad behavior.[8] Remember that the wiring of our nervous system is neutral; it has no preference for ideas or thinking patterns that are either positive or negative, optimistic or pessimistic, kind or cruel, trustworthy or cynical. It has been said, "We are not slaves to our minds, but we are slaves to the habits that control our minds"[9] This book, *The 21-Day Plan*, is all about the deliberate, rewiring of the brain to overcome negative thinking.

Questions for Reflection

1. By what process do habits get wired into our brains?

_____

_____

2. Why are we able to multitask? Explain.

_____

_____

To demonstrate the power of neuroplasticity, Dr. Edward Taub, at the University of Alabama, has developed a novel technique that utilizes the brain's capacity for neuroplasticity. When a particular limb is affected by a stroke, he immobilized the functioning limb, thus forcing the patient to use the injured limb, resulting in brain rewiring and ultimately a speedier restoration of the damaged limb to a functioning level.[10] The brain has an awesome ability to adapt, change, and rewire itself to adapt to new information and the novel realities it experiences.

Thinking for a Change

Are you thinking for a change or are you still thinking you can't change? Renowned psychotherapist Dr. Richard O'Conner informs us that, "The wiring in the brain contains our beliefs and assumptions. With enough deliberate practice, we can rewire ourselves."[11] For this reason, the 21-Day program involves memorizing and quoting multiple times daily the I Am Significant mantra and the N-O-W-M-O-V-E-F-O-R-W-A-R-D spiritual identity acrostic. Each time you repeat it with focus and with a resolute attitude, you are rewiring your brain. You probably didn't know it was that simple to rewire your brain. It may be simple, but that doesn't mean it's easy. Go ahead and repeat the mantra and the acrostic now. It functions as more than information if you use your sanctified imagination

> *With enough deliberate practice, we can rewire ourselves.*

to tap into your emotions. Repeat it enough times and it will become real to you and empower you. You will be glad you did!

**I Am Significant.**
Why? *(Because)* God loves me and sent his Son to die upon the cross for my sins. He has adopted me into His family and has given me a new name. I am a born-again Christian, fearfully and wonderfully made in the image of God.

I can N-O-W-M-O-V-E-F-O-R-W-A-R-D knowing my true spiritual identity.

I Am (a)...
New creation in Christ Jesus (2 Corinthians 5:17)
Ordained and chosen by God to fulfill His purpose for my life (Jeremiah 1:5; 29:11)
(And I...)
Walk in the power of the Holy Spirit (Ephesians 5:18; Acts 1:8).

(Because I walk in the power of the Holy Spirit...)

I Am (an) (a)...
More than a conqueror (Romans 8:37)
Overcomer (1 John 5:4)
Victor, not a victim (1 Corinthians 15:57)
Eternally loved (Romans 8:35, 38-39)

I Am...

Favored of God (Psalm 5:12)

Oh, so bold, confident and courageous (Proverbs 28:1; 2 Timothy 1:7)

Reconciled to be a reconciler (2 Corinthians 5:18-20)

Well protected (Isaiah 54:17; Psalm 23:4-6)

Assured of success (Psalm 1:3; Nehemiah 2:20; Joshua 1:8)

(the) Righteousness of God in Christ Jesus (2 Corinthians 5:21; 1 Peter 2:9)

Destined to win if I do not quit (2 Corinthians 2:14; Romans 8:31; Isaiah 41: 9-10; 43:1-4)

Replacement Therapy

In repeating the mantra and spiritual identity acrostic daily, you are rewiring your brain by replacing automatic negative thoughts (ANTS)[12] with spiritual automatic thoughts (SATS). This replacement therapy will be discussed in greater detail in a future lesson but allow me to lay the groundwork now. In replacing ANTS with SATS you are rewiring your brain to begin the habit of thinking and speaking positively about yourself, thus, reducing the amount of negative self-talk. Because of our old nature, bad habits are much easier to pick up than good ones.[13] Unfortunately, mental "habits cannot be eradicated—they must be replaced."[14]

> *Mental habits cannot be eradicated—they must be replaced.*

Allow me to illustrate this in a more practical way. Imagine that you have decided to clean your house. You are tired of all the clutter and broken furniture, especially the worn-out recliner and three-legged sofa that you've placed books under to replace the missing leg. You have procrastinated long enough—today is the day. You call your best friend and he agrees to help you move your old furniture into your garage to make room for new furniture. After arduous hours of work, your house is clean. You walk around your house admiring its beauty. You notice the ornate detail in the crown molding as the dazzling sunlight reflects off your hardwood floors. You walk over to the refrigerator and pour yourself a cold glass of lemonade and head for your favorite recliner. However, it's no longer in the corner beside the lamp stand. You begin to reflect upon how comfortable that chair was and how it was a birthday present from your parents. A smile captures your face. You reason, it wouldn't hurt to bring one piece of furniture back inside; after all, you do need to sit on something. Hence, you remove it from the garage and bring it back inside your house. But what good is a recliner without a stand on which to rest your glass of lemonade? So, you retrieve the stand from the garage. Next, while in the garage you notice that cracked plant vase and three-legged stool that you had impulsively thrown out...after all, it was a gift from your ex fiancé. You guessed it. Over the course of one week, all of your old broken furnishings and little

90

knickknacks are back inside your house because of their familiarity and senti-mental value. Now, there is no room or desire for the new furniture.

Holding that image in mind, think about this parable Jesus told in Matthew 12:43-46, "Now when the unclean spirit goes out of a man, it passes through wa-terless places seeking rest, and does not find it. Then it says, I will return to my house from which I came…then it goes and takes along with it seven other spir-its more wicked than itself, and they go in and live there…" By way of analogy, our toxic thoughts can be likened unto unclean spirits. We may seek to suppress them or even cast them out, but unless a new, positive, healthy thought "a clean spirit" is introduced to compete with the negative one, the old negative thought will return with a vengeance to re-entrench its hold neurologically.[15] Unless new, positive and healthy thoughts fill the mind, the vacuums in the mind are ulti-mately filled with what our brain is more familiar with, the old thoughts, just as the individual in the above story returned to his old furniture. It is hard to intro-duce new change to the brain because the brain was not designed to change rapidly. Consequently, it takes a minimum of twenty-one days, and for some twice that long, to introduce permanent change into the neurological connectivity of the brain.[16] The brain is a creature of habit, and habits are hard to break.[17]

> *It is hard to introduce new change to the brain because the brain was not designed to change rapidly.*

Our need is to introduce a new mindset and way of living to effectively and continually re-place an old mindset. Regarding this, the Apostle Paul reminds believers what he taught them, "Instead, renew the thinking in your mind by the Spirit and clothe yourself with the new person created according to God's image in justice and true holiness" (Ephesians 4:23-24 CEB). In summary, Paul says, believers are to replace their old method of thinking with a new Christ centered method. Readers, you have been taught that Biblical mind renewal is the lifelong process of replacing our perspective with God's perspective. If we are to renew our minds, we must take off our old way of thinking and replace it with a new way of thinking; that is the essence of replacement therapy. That is what the *I Am Significant* mantra and the N-O-W-M-O-V-E-F-O-R-W-A-R-D acrostic are designed to do—replace the old negative self-talk with new positive self-talk. Throughout several years, I have repeated this mantra thousands of times. I can't help it. It has become my brain's default setting. I just keep adding new Scripture references. When I first began the N-O-W-M-O-V-E-F-O-R-W-A-R-D acrostic, I had one Scripture memorized for each letter. Now, I have three to five Scriptures per letter. *Relax.* If the Holy Spirit empowered me to do it, as messed up and confused as my mind was, He can do the same for you.

This is important to remember: Your success with *The 21-Day Plan* will not set any precedent; your success is fully predictable.

Feed Your Positive Thoughts and Starve Your Negative Thoughts

Neuroscience researcher, Dr. Caroline Leaf, concurs that thoughts (via brain cell/ neuron activity) have the power to change our brains through the process of neuroplasticity. She illustrates the brain's changeable nature by observing similarities between our thoughts and trees.

Thoughts look like trees with branches. As thoughts grow and become permanent, more branches grow, and the connections become stronger. As we change our thinking, some branches go away, new one's form, the strength of the connections change, and the memories network with other thoughts. (See Figure 5.1)

Figure 5.1 A Thought Tree

Picture 1 of Figure 5.1 illustrates two brain cells. Picture 2 illustrates how the two brain cells multiplied to six brain cells as the same thoughts were mulled/ considered/meditated upon. Picture 3 illustrates the voluminous growth of a brain cell connectivity consequent to meditative or thought processes. As a consequence, the series of thoughts, through habit, achieved a physical presence in the brain. "Neurons that fire together, wire together."[18] Picture 4 above illustrates a thought that was at one time a mature growing thought but has been starved by the introduction of a competing thought.

> *You literally have the power to starve a negative thought to death.*

Leaf concludes, "What an incredible capacity of the brain to change, rewire, and grow! Spiritually, this is renewing the mind."[19] Did you realize that you can empower your positive thoughts by dwelling and meditating upon them and starve your negative thoughts to death, by not dwelling and meditating on them? The dendrites begin to deteriorate and die. As a result of deliberate positive thinking, you literally have the power to starve a negative thought to death.[20]

> *"Those who ruminate about their problems are four times more likely to develop major depression than those who don't."*
> *Dr. Norman Wright*

Dr. Charles Swindoll describes the power of our thoughts this way:

92

Thoughts, positive or negative, grow stronger together when fertilized with constant repetition. That may explain why so many who are gloomy and gray stay in that mood, and why others who are cheery and enthusiastic continue to be so, even in the midst of difficult circumstances. Please do not misunderstand me. Happiness (like winning) is a matter of right thinking, not intelligence, age or position. Our performance is directly related to the thoughts we deposit in our memory bank. We can only draw on what we deposit. What kind of performance would your car deliver if every morning before you left for work you scooped up a handful of dirt and put it in your crankcase? The fine-tuned engine would soon be coughing and sputtering. Ultimately, it would refuse to start. The same is true of your life. Thoughts about yourself and attitudes toward others that are narrow, destructive, and abrasive produce wear and tear on your mental motor. They send you off the road while others drive past.[21]

Are you off on the side of the road, stuck in a mental ditch? You don't have to remain mired in a quagmire of negativity. God has designed a way to get you out of the ditch of pessimism and self-criticism by choosing to starve your negative thoughts to death and feed your positive thoughts. You've got the POWER!

Questions for Reflection

List some negative thoughts that you need to starve to death?

_____

_____

You Thought I Forgot, Didn't You?

When you think a thought (negative or positive) consistently, you are laying down a mental (rail) road track in your mind.[22] For our purposes here, let's say the thought is negative. However, after reading *The 21-Day Plan*, you resolve to change the direction of your thinking; you decide that you are going to exit that negative railroad and begin to think positively. You decide to lay down a new positive mental track. FYI: Beware that the old negative railroad tracks are still in place! They remain lodged within your amygdala [uh-mig-duh-lee] —your emotional memory bank. Because old negative mental tracks have not removed, an alcoholic, remains sober for 10 months and then takes just one drink (falls "off the wagon"), and becomes as hopelessly addicted to alcohol as he was before. Likewise, old mental tracks remain lodged in the brain. They just succumb to disrepair, but they remain.[23]

This truth of my old negative mental tracks remaining within my mind was dramatically brought to my attention several years ago. I have a major sweet tooth, but for a period of 10 years or more I had given up eating sweets like cookies, cakes, pies, and junk food like pizza. By God's grace and strength, I did not really miss eating the junk. I was glad to give it up because whenever I previously overindulged, I would develop an ugly rash on my neck, and the sweets caused a major expansion of my girth—if you know what I mean. After ten years, I knew I had kicked the habit. I was free, or at least I thought so. Then one day at work, I allowed myself to get hungry by skipping breakfast. I walked into the teacher's lounge during the Christmas Holiday time, and I saw something that looked like a dumpling covered in white powdery sugar. Right away, my flesh brought the thought into my mind, "What is that? It looks really good. I'll bet it tastes good too." My opportunist soul said, "You haven't eaten anything all day." My flesh agreed, saying, "I am hungry." and, "One little bite won't hurt you. After all, you have the self-control to eat just one." The battle was on! Like Adam and Eve, I moved in for a closer look. It did look very appetizing! My flesh hollered out, "Grab it and eat it quickly before someone sees you!" My spirit said to resist the temptation and leave the room immediately. My soul, pushed back on my spirit and said, "No, I think I will try just one." The flesh in full agreement shouted, "EAT IT! NOW! I ate. My spirit said, "Why did you do that? You know you had the power to resist." I asked the Lord's forgiveness. To soothe my guilty conscience, I vowed, "I'll not eat any more." It was about 9:30 in the morning. One hour later, I was back for more. I came back every hour on the hour. By the end of the day I had wrapped 15-20 of these small delicacies into a napkin and ate them on my commute home. I discovered that day that the old tracks had not been removed or taken up; they had just fallen upon ill repair due to lack of use. One tasty Munchkin led me to a dissolute 20 more. I was once again struggling with eating sweets and other junk food; just as I had been 10 years earlier. For the next several weeks and months, I struggled to resist temptation. Eventually, I had to call upon the Lord for His grace to supply me with the strength to resist the lure of constant temptation. He once again set me free.

Praise the Lord! Do I have a witness?

This is an important neurological principle to remember, especially as it relates to being delivered from some self-destructive habit. Having had friends who struggled with alcohol and drug addictions, I, on occasion, would accompany them to their Alcoholics Anonymous (AA) or Narcotics Anonymous (NA) accountability meetings. When it was my friend's turn to introduce himself, he would stand and say, "My name is_____. I am an alcoholic. But I have been sober for 10 years." Initially, I didn't understand the reasoning behind such an introduction, but I do now. The tracks remain. Whether having been delivered, or in the process of being delivered, we have the onus to work along with the Holy Spirit as He renews our minds and transforms our lives. Why? Because as he did with Christ, the Devil will come back at a more opportune time to tempt us (Matthew 4:1-11; James 4:7). Satan knows the old tracks are still there. That is why he "goes about as a roaring lion, seeking those he may devour" (1 Peter 5:8).

Questions for Reflection

Name an experience where you were reminded of your old mental tracks still remaining. For example, you may have gained the victory over _____ _____, until you _____ and it seemed to start all over again.

A Trace of Grace

Perhaps at the time you are reading this you have hit a wall or "fallen off the wagon" in some area of your life in your struggle against a self-destructive habit, or you feel yourself reverting to your old habit of thinking negatively. Don't quit trying. Pray for the motivation through the power of the Holy Spirit to continue to press on to victory. Concerning the motivation to continue, Hart makes the following astute observation: "Motivation also survives better if you are flexible and build in some room for failure. Rigid programs of change fizzle precisely because they are inflexible. A healthy mind is a mind that can tolerate setbacks, then bounce back."[24]

Push back on the thought that you will never change and that you are a failure. It's not true, you know! Take it from a guy who has failed many times: just because you failed does not mean you are a failure. I remind you, failure is a circumstance, —not a person. Separate your *who* from your *do*. Push back on the thought that God has given up on you; *it is a lie from the enemy*. I've heard it said, "A setback is a setup for a comeback." God has not given up on you, so don't give up on Him or yourself. Accept the fact that you will falter and fail at times. We all do. Accept the fact that you are a mess in your flesh. However, you are not your flesh. You are a powerful supernatural spirit empowered by God's Holy Spirit. That is why Jesus said, "With God all things are possible" (Luke 1:37). Despite a few setbacks, know that your efforts to improve yourself and work through *The 21-Day Plan* are never lost. With a dedication, you will find someday that God has hardwired a bounce back and a victorious attitude into your brain. What do I mean by that? Dr. O'Conner makes this concluding observation,

Learning is never lost. When we're trying to break a bad habit by practicing more constructive behavior (eating right, exercising, being assertive), we can easily be discouraged by a bad day. We can give up and feel that we've wasted a lot of effort, but that's not the case. Every day you practiced left its traces in the brain; you can get back on the horse after a fall and expect it soon to be as easy and rewarding as ever.[25]

Hallelujah! Hallelujah! Praises be to God! That's great news!

You can begin again. God has left traces of grace upon your neuro-circuitry. You can begin again. Dream again. Use your sanctified imagination to see your-self walking in victory over distorted thought patterns that lead you into discouragement and depression. God has left traces of grace upon your mind; be not discouraged. See yourself walking in victory over that addiction, anger, bit-terness, unforgiveness, perceived failure, rejection, disillusionment, grief, insult or diminished confidence. The choice is up to you. Choose to bounce back by shaking off the disappointment, discouragement, and failure.

God told the prophet Joel to tell His people to follow His Commandments. Joel's hearers had failed in their efforts to follow God faithfully. As a conse-quence, the Nation of Israel was in bondage. Despite having caused their own misery, God declared, "I will give you back what you lost in the years when swarms of locusts ate your crops" (Joel 2:25 GNT). Negativity, like plagues of locusts, may have overtaken your mind, leaving you somewhat hopeless, dis-couraged, and depressed. However, believers, we can focus and shake off that discouragement. We can start again. Our efforts have not been in vain. God de-clares, "I will give you back what you lost..." (GNT). Verbalize your pushback, if necessary.

To illustrate the concept of dealing with negative situations, let me share a story told about a farmer who discovered one morning that his donkey had fallen in a well. The farmer worked all morning trying to figure out how to get the don-key out of the well. By noontime, he had exhausted all his options and decided that since he could not get the donkey out of the well, he would just have to bury the donkey in the bottom of the well. He called a friend who hauled dirt and asked him to drop a load of dirt right beside his well. The farmer immediately began shoveling dirt down into the well, praying as he shoveled: "Lord, Betsy has been a good donkey. I am so sorry to see her go this way." However, Betsy, in the bottom of the well wasn't ready to go out like this. So, with each shovel of dirt that fell on Betsy's back, she shook it off, trampled it under foot and stepped up a little higher. The more dirt the farmer threw down on her the more she shook it off, trampled it under her feet and stepped up a little higher. After hours of shoveling dirt down the well, much to the farmer's surprise, he began to realize that the animal could get out of the well that way. The farmer found himself de-lighted with what Betsy had been doing with the dirt. In a frantic rush the farmer began to shovel more dirt into the well. Shortly, he could see Betsy begin to emerge. Eventually Betsy stepped over the end of the well and trotted down to-ward the pasture.

What's my point? Believer, you need to shake off that discouragement and flattened confidence, and all that negative thinking, trample it under foot and step on up to a higher level of thinking through a deliberate reinvigoration of what our gracious Lord has made available to us through the process of neuro-plasticity. Whatever it is, shake it off, and remind yourself, "I know who I am!" Remember, "With enough deliberate practice, we can rewire ourselves."[26] Practice reading the Word. Practice the proactive measure articulated in *The 21-Day Plan*. Do not ever be afraid to cry out to God for help. He is the most steadfast friend you will ever have. Practice getting back up every time you fall, knowing that each attempt at improving yourself has impacted your brain. The result of this impact is evidence of God's grace assuring you that deliverance is sure to come. You have the grace to…

--begin again,
--know that victory is yours,
--know that God is with you,
--know that God loves you,
--maintain faith that God knows what He is doing, and…
--know that the best is yet to come!

On a different occasion, God made another promise to his dispirited children: "To all who mourn in Israel he will give: beauty for ashes; joy instead of mourning; praise instead of heaviness. For God has planted them like strong and graceful oaks for his own glory" (Isaiah 61:3 TLB).

The best is yet to come because:

--God is not through with you yet.
--God wants to bestow glory upon your life.
--God will, in his perfect timing, bring you out bigger and better and stronger. You will be like a strong and graceful oak tree.
--as you daily work your way through *The 21-Day Plan*, your mind is being renewed—one thought at a time.

The great missionary Hudson Taylor once said, "All our difficulties are only platforms for the manifestation of God's grace, power, and love."[27] With God, there is always something that can be done to improve our prospects and make ourselves happier. Think of your life as God's worthy platform.

Question for Reflection

How might the statement by Hudson Taylor help you to alter your perspective about some of your previous failed attempts at change?

_____

_____

_____

**A Closing Prayer**

Dear God, I thank you for bringing the truths of neuroplasticity to my eyes. Thank you, Father, for designing me in such a way that I can change with your magnanimous help. With your loving grace, Lord, I don't have to stay the same. Allow me to tap into your ever-flowing supply of grace, so that I can begin to starve my negative thoughts and fulfill your promise of salvation and restoration. I choose to meditate on who I am in the light of your love instead of who I used to be, treading in constant negativity and doubt. In Jesus' name. Amen.

For an inspirational pick me up, I recommend:

- *Unfinished* by Mandisa
- *Right On Time* by Aaron Cole
- *I Believe I Can Fly* by R. Kelly

Until tomorrow, do this:

Memory Work

1. Remember **TEA=B** – Thoughts affect emotions and emotions affect attitudes, and attitudes produce behavior.

2. **Biblical mind renewal** is the lifelong process of replacing our perspective with God's perspective as revealed in His Word.

3. Practice reciting the I Am Significant mantra (Repeat 10-12 times per day – at minimum – or every hour of the day).

I Am Significant. Why? God loves me and sent his Son to die upon the cross for my sins. He has adopted me into His family and has given me a new name. I am a born-again Christian, fearfully and wonderfully made in the image of God.

4. **My spiritual identity**:

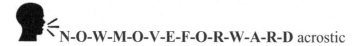**N-O-W-M-O-V-E-F-O-R-W-A-R-D** acrostic

Day 6

What You Talk About You Bring About

Your brain is like a supercomputer and your self-talk is the program it will run.
--Jim Kwik

Daily Food for Thought

- **Brain Fact** Due to the ever-changing nature of the brain (neuroplasticity) it is constantly re-inventing itself in response to our self-talk—both positive and negative. As new neuropathways are forged through repetition and focus, un-used pathways fall away.[1]

- **Key Thoughts** Neuroplasticity describes "the plastic (changeable) brain, the recognition that our brains change and grow physically in response to life experience."[2]

- **Scripture** "Death and life are in the power of the tongue, and those who love it and indulge it will eat its fruit and bear the consequences of their words" (Proverb 18:21 AMP).

Daily Reading

Words are very powerful! How many of us have been the recipient of injurious words, or, worse yet, have hurt others with our words? Harsh, critical words sting! As a child, if you complained to your parents that someone called you a bad name, they may have repeated the old cliché, "Sticks and stones can break my bones, but words will never hurt me." Now that you are grown, you know better. Words *do* hurt, and you have the emotional scars to prove it. What a curious power words have. This truth is affirmed by the writer of the Book of Proverbs who said, "Death and life are in the power of the tongue, and those who love it and indulge it will eat its fruit and bear the consequences of their words" (Proverbs 18:21 AMP). Pause for a moment and grasp the gravity of that statement: "Death and life are in the power of the tongue...." Do you routinely speak words of death or words of life? The Message Bible translates Proverbs 18:21 this way: "Words kill, words give life; they're either poison or fruit—you choose." From Proverbs 18:21, we discover that our words impact our lives for better or for worse. Positive words give life, healing and refreshment. Negative words bring forth discouragement, depression, and self-doubt. To safeguard himself, the psalmist David asked God to, "Set a guard over my mouth, O Lord; keep watch over the door of my lips" (Psalm 141:3 KJV). I have personalized it and paraphrased it to read, "God, put a muzzle over my big mouth so I won't have to eat my own words later or experience regret because of the lamentable or foolish things that I have said." The wisdom of Proverbs warns us against speaking impulsively: "You are trapped by the words of your mouth. You are ensnared with the words of your mouth" (Proverbs 6:2 WEB). Other verses concerning the impact of spoken words, both negatively and positively, are mentioned in the following verses: Proverbs 8:8, 10:19, 15:1, 26, 16:24, and 17:27.

Many of us are cognizant of the pitfalls of speaking negative words, few of us, however, realize how much more destructive are the words we speak to ourselves in the form of negative self-talk. What is self-talk? Self-talk has to do with the running internal narrative or ongoing conversation we have with ourselves every second of every day.[3] While much of our negative self-talk never proceeds out of our mouth, it nevertheless, remains lodged in our minds (in specific thoughts) and hearts. Although generally not verbalized, our negative self-talk is still impacting us emotionally, physically, and neurologically. According to doctors at the renowned Mayo Clinic in Minneapolis, Minnesota, "Negative self-talk can induce physical as well as emotional stress, harming your cardiovascular health, gut health, and immune system."[4] Whether you are aware of it or not, we all talk to ourselves all day long. The million-dollar question is, when you talk

> *Self-talk has to do with the running internal narrative we have with ourselves every second of every day.*

to yourself, are you speaking words that contribute to success or failure? Hope or despair? Death or life? Here are some things you need to know about your self-talk:

- The majority of mind chatter is negative rather than positive in most people.
- Self-talk also includes thoughts in the form of pictures that flash through our mind, virtually unnoticed. These often correlate to actual memories.

- Self-talk can happen so quickly that just one thought leads to an almost instantaneous stream of related thoughts.
- The subconscious mind accepts all of our self-talk as the truth. It *is* truth neurologically whether it is true in fact or not. But know this: the mind will then go about attempting to create circumstances to match or validate the thoughts.[5]

Before proceeding further, I want you to focus on the gravity, the fullest import, of that last bullet point: "The subconscious mind accepts all of our self-talk as the truth, even if it is not...."

> *The subconscious mind accepts all of our self-talk as the truth, even if it is not.*

Through my research, I've discovered that much of our self-talk is mere mental chatter and bogus lies that we have come to believe over the course of time. Today we will learn one approach to quelling a lot of our negative self-talk. After all, this book is about the imperative of challenging and changing a negative narrative that is inconsistent with our intended goals.

The Origin of Self-Talk

Margie Meacham, Dr. Norman Wright and other researchers and psychologists point out that our self-talk is rooted in our core beliefs. Core beliefs are beliefs that govern our lives; they are the beliefs that we hold deep down in our hearts. Jesus said, "...the things that come out of a person's mouth come from the heart..." (Matthew 15:18NIV). When the Bible writers use the word "heart," it almost always refers to "The comprehensive term for a person as a whole; his feelings, desires, passions, thoughts, understanding, and will".[6] Our self-talk is comprised of the things we believe in our hearts to be true—whether they are true or not.

The deep-seated beliefs that you have right now, right or wrong, however you came to them, are guiding your life, nonetheless. In fact, many psychologists believe that "by age 7, or as early as 4 to 5 years of age, a child's personality is substantially formed, but continues to develop throughout the rest of his or her life."[7] One's personality and core values were shaped and influenced by his or her family of origin (FOO), caregivers, peers and role models. Our personality is also influenced by the town or place where we grew up, our religious and moral instructions, traumas and other life experiences. All of this influences how we process information. This processing brings what we call beliefs. These beliefs are reflected in our self-talk.

Meacham makes the following observation about our self-talk:

The self-talk that goes through our heads also creates emotions. It is always the thought that comes first, and then the feelings will follow. So, the type of inner talk that you have going on will decide how you feel throughout the day. As hard as it can be to accept, no one or nothing can "make us" feel anything. It is the thoughts we think in response to certain situations and events that determines how we feel, not the external situation itself. Words and thoughts have their own energy, including self-talk. Everything you think and say affects your personal vibration, and the way you feel.... This is true whether we are reacting to spoken words delivered by someone else, or to the inner self-talk that we hear ourselves "saying" inside our heads.[8]

Because of the ongoing inner dialog that we engage in all day long, it is easy to comprehend how our words rewire our brain. The brain is rewired through repetition.[9] That is how you learned your ABCs and multiplication facts—rote memorization. Due to the ever-changing nature of the brain (neuroplasticity), it is constantly re-inventing itself in response to our self-talk—both positive and negative. As new neuropathways are forged through repetition and focus, unused pathways fall away.[10] The goal of *The 21-Day Plan* is to teach you how to rewire your brain by creating new positive neuropathways. We do this by using positive thoughts and words, thus renewing our minds—one thought and one word at a time.

Dr. Caroline Leaf points out, "Since your core beliefs are rooted deeply in your brain, it will take a concerted effort, over a period of time to dislodge certain forms of distorted thinking, but change is possible".[11] As believers, we know that we cannot change ourselves, but the Holy Spirit working through the word of God can. The words we speak verbally or internally will either serve to hasten or stymie the mind renewal process. "The brain's plasticity (flexibility) enables the believer to continually modify personality and behavior into Christ-likeness."[12] How to discover your core beliefs will be discussed in greater detail on Day 15 and Day 18.

Your Self-Talk Reflects How You See and Feel About Yourself

"Your self-talk plays a defining role in the thoughts you experience daily and contributes to your self-esteem and self-concept. For example, if, as a child, you grew up hearing repeatedly that you were unwanted, unloved, and worthless, subconsciously, and over time consciously you would very likely begin to believe it to be true. Consequently, you would develop an internal dialog which says, for example, "I am worthless," and perhaps also "I am unworthy of being loved." Wright refers to these thoughts as automatic thoughts. "Automatic thoughts are learned. We listen to others and what they say about us, and we believe the statements. And what is more, we tend to become what we believe."[13] This is why the Bible affirms, "For as he [a man] thinks in his heart, so is he." (Proverbs 23:7 NKJ). The text does not say, as a man thinks in his head, but "in his heart." In Scripture, we are told to "...Guard thy heart; for out of it flows the issues of life" (Proverbs 4:23 JUB). The reason you are to guard your heart with all diligence is because from your heart flow the issues, the forces of life. Flowing from your heart can be a force of optimism or a force of pessimism. There can be a force of success and joy, or failure and hopelessness. The choice is up to you.

Hooked on a Feeling

Singer BJ Thomas sang a song entitled, "Hooked on a Feeling." He was singing about a loving feeling. But what do you do when your self-concept is hooked on a negative feeling? Personally, and through my research, I have discovered feelings that constantly recur come from the deepest beliefs in our hearts. At various stages of writing this book, my inner critic/negative self-talk harassed me with two toxic assertions: You can't write, and You are stupid. Before addressing the second assertion "You are stupid," allow me this one aside. As believers, we are quick to hold Satan culpable for every negative thought we have. Satan is the bogeyman and we blame him for every sinful thought. However, such a bogeyman theology can leave you in bondage and prevent you from digging down deep enough to locate the true cause for some of your more challenging thoughts, feelings, and behaviors. You can rebuke Satan, and cast him out, but if and when the feelings return, pause to consider perhaps there may be a deeper natural cause for the persistent thoughts and feelings. It is probably some core belief or misbelief that Satan is using to keep you in bondage. It's not enough to simply rebuke Satan; you must learn to DISARM him by proactive behaviors. I ask myself, how was Satan able to convince me for almost my entire adult life that I was stupid—lacking intelligence? After all I earned three degrees: the bachelors, a master's, and doctorate. In the doctoral program, I achieved summa cum laude—highest honors, with a 4.0 GPA! Pretty impressive! To God be the glory!

Do you see, reader? I had every objective reason to believe I was smart, but sadly, the hard-wired lie trumped the truth. Through asking the hard questions, I discovered the genesis of the "I am stupid" core belief that took root in my heart soil in kindergarten. I was one of thirteen children raised in a southern New Jersey family. We lived in a rural area. I was one of the middle children but occupied a "youngest child role" for a brief period. I was emotionally close to my mother; I never left her side. One day, at the age of 5 or 6, my mother told me I was old enough to go to school. The next day when the yellow bus with flashing lights stopped in front of my house, my mother said to me, "Paulie, you are now old enough to go to school." I immediately buried my face in her dress and with the herculean grip of a 6-year-old, I bear hugged my mom around her legs. I held on for dear life, pleading with her to not make me climb aboard the yellow bus. Momma pried my arms off her, dried my tears with her dress, and said, "Paulie, it's time for you to go to school." I remember crying all the way to school, all throughout the school day, and all the way home from school. I never stopped crying for one and a half years. I'm not kidding! I remember being the only student in kindergarten who couldn't say the alphabet from A to Z or count to 100. I got hung up on 19, 29, 39, etc., and I didn't have a clue which number came next. But who fails kindergarten? So, I was socially promoted to the first grade. However, my first-grade teacher did not believe in social promotions, so I failed first grade. I was still crying. There, I was dubbed with the nickname "Paulie Blue." It was there that the "I am stupid" core belief took root. I muddled my way through grade school showing few flashes of intelligence. Middle school fed my negative core belief once again. Due to my poor academic performance, I was once again socially promoted into the eighth grade and warned that if I did not perform well, I would be immediately demoted to the seventh grade. The thoughts and feelings of stupidity and laziness never left me because they were part of my core beliefs. I could have continued to rebuke Satan every time those thoughts arose. I did try to do this for almost my entire life. However, God, through my research, revealed to me a way to disarm Satan. How did I replace that "I am stupid" core belief? I had to present my brain with some evidence to counter my negative self-talk. Hence, I picked up my pen, opened my quiet time journal, and wrote down the following evidence:

- My 4th grade teacher, Mrs. Rondilski, told me I could do my work if I tried hard. In her classes I earned A's and B's. I later that year earned an award for making the most academic improvement.

- At 16, I became a born-again Christian, and I began to embrace my new identity. I was a new creation in Christ with a new core belief, "I can do all things through Christ who gives me strength" (2 Corinthians 2:17; Philippians. 4:13). After a change of friends, I began making the honor roll.

- After I received a high B on a very difficult physics test, my 12th grade physics teacher, Dr. Herman, complemented me in front of the entire class, stating that I was both an athlete and a scholar.

- In college, I took Dr. Warton's Sociology class. I was told by upper classmen who had previously taken the course that the best I could hope to receive was a C. After a semester of arduous work, I received a higher grade than I was told was possible.

- I earned both graduate and post graduate degrees.

- *I discovered that my inability to focus at times, my lack of motivation and comprehension, procrastination and difficulty spelling words were associated with an untreated condition: Attention Deficit Disorder (ADD). This is unrelated to intelligence, and sometimes even geniuses have ADD.*

Buttressed with this evidence, I told my inner critic that a stupid, lazy person would not be able to accomplish all of that. I combined all that evidence with the new thought management principles and the *I Am* mantras I learned in *The 21-Day Plan*, and take such thoughts captive. By God's grace, I was able to pull up the taproot of my misbelief. Satan, the father of lies, still sometimes tries to deceive and discourage me, but by now, I can recognize his villainous voice.

Questions for Reflection

1. Are there any negative feelings that you can't seem to shake? Yes/No

2. Are you willing to pray to God and ask Him to help you get to the root cause of the troubling thoughts or feelings?

_____

_____

3. If you find yourself hesitant in prayerfully asking God for help, what might be the causes of your hesitancies, the impediments?

_____

_____

Putting a Stop to Your Negative Self-Talk

In cases where your negative self-talk begins its chatter, here are seven things you can do:

1. Present your inner critic with evidence to the contrary as I showed you above. Present all evidence large or small. Write these points of evidence on a piece of paper or a 3x5 card, and when your inner critic begins to criticize you, take out the paper or card and read it over and over again until the chatter stops. You're countering the lies with the truth.

2. Vigorously clap your hands and shout "Stop it!" or "Shut up!" Don't laugh. Try it; it works. You have startled that negative inner critic and interrupted the negative habit. In situations where you're in public and cannot verbalize, simply clinch your fist and say, "Stop it!" in your mind.

3. When you recognize that some negative chatter has begun in your mind, you might immediately challenge that voice with a forceful admonition such as, "I know your voice, Satan. I've heard it before!" Take the thought captive by breaking out in a song of praise that affirms the goodness of God and His unconditional love for you.

4. Verbally repeat the negative self-talk in the second person. For example, "You are stupid, are you?" "You are worthless, are you?" "So, you are unlovable"? By stepping outside of yourself, you can hear how stupid and irrational your self-talk sounds.[14]

5. Pray and ask God to purge your mind of negative, sad, frustrating, depressing, embarrassing, and demoralizing memories.

6. Renew your mind by meditating upon, memorizing, and repeating Bible-based words of life, remembering that "Life and death are in the power of the tongue" (Proverbs 18:21).

7. Replace negative self-talk by daily, and especially in the instrumental moment, repeating your *I Am Significant* mantra and the N-O-W-M-O-V-E-F-O-R-W-A-R-D acrostic at least 10-12 times daily. Dr. Wright reminds us, "Repeated self-talk, over time, turns into attitudes, values and beliefs." [15]

Questions for Reflection

> *Repeated self-talk, over time, turns into attitudes, values and beliefs.*

1. Write down some things your inner critic is constantly saying to you?

_____

_____

2. List some evidence that contradicts those assertions and write these counter assertions in complete sentences.

_____

_____

3. Which of the seven strategies explained above will you most likely try the very next time negative self-talk begins?

_____

_____

What to Say When You Talk to Yourself

I firmly believe *you will not be defeated by what others say about you. You will be defeated by what you say about you.* In the final analysis, all of us have certain beliefs that control us. It is through the process of renewing our minds that our deep-seated heart values will be changed. Biblical mind renewal is the life-long process of replacing our perspective (thoughts, feelings, and beliefs) with God's perspective. Just as a caterpillar is transformed into a beautiful butterfly, at salvation, we too were transformed into a new creation (2 Corinthians 5:17). As a new creation in Christ, your new mind must be retrained to see yourself as God sees you—no more and no less. For your faith-filled words to change and rewire your brain, they cannot be words that you speak only occasionally but repeatedly. Remember, the brain is rewired through repetition.

Mind renewal starts from the inside out. It requires meditating upon and saturating our minds with the word of God (Joshua 1:8; Romans 12:2; Ephesians 4:23-24). We have a lot of misbeliefs. The Holy Spirit's purpose is to bring to our minds, the truth of God's word (John 16:13). The light of God's word will shine into the darkened areas of our minds and hearts to replace those misbeliefs. Once you realize who you are, you will be able to more truthfully and freely declare who you are based on the authority of God's word.

As we begin to think about what it will take to renew our minds and change the way we're thinking, we may hear a little voice saying, "Managing my thoughts, changing my self-talk is hard work. I don't feel like it." I remind you of the words spoken by actor Tom Hanks in the movie, *A League of Their Own.* Hanks' character, speaking to his lackadaisical and undisciplined baseball team complained about how hard baseball practice is and says, "It's supposed to be hard. If it weren't hard, everyone would do it. The hard is what makes it great." True, mind renewal is hard work! All positive change is hard! Push back to your negative self-talk and tell it, "I'm committed to doing the hard work. I'm committed to changing the way I have been thinking. There is a better way to think and I'm committed to discovering it." Now shake off any negativity and lethargy and repeat this mantra with enthusiasm. Say it in faith. Receive it in faith. Act on it in faith.

What do you say when you talk to yourself? Say *only* what God says about you.

107

I Am Significant. Why? *(Because)* God loves me and sent his Son to die upon the cross for my sins. He has adopted me into His family and has given me a new name. I am a born-again Christian, fearfully and wonderfully made in the image of God.

I can N-O-W- M-O-V-E-F-O-R-W-A-R-D in life, knowing…

I Am (a)
New creation in Christ Jesus.

- Therefore, if anyone is in Christ, he is a *new creation*; the old has passed away, and see, the new has come (2 Corinthians 5:17 CSB)!

Ordained and chosen by God to fulfill His purpose for my life.

- Before I formed you in the womb I knew you, and before you were born I *consecrated* you; I have appointed you…. (Jeremiah 1:5).

(And I…)

Walk in the power of the Holy Spirit.

- You will receive *power* when the Holy Spirit has come upon you and you shall be my witnesses…. (Acts 1:8).

(Because I walk in the power of the Holy Spirit…)

I Am (a) (an)…
More than a conqueror

- No, in all these things we are *more than conquerors* through him who loved us (Romans 8:37 NIV).

Overcomer

- For whatever is born of God *overcomes* the world; and this is the victory that has overcome the world—our faith (1 John 5:4).

Victor, not a victim

- But thanks be to God, who gives us the *victory* through our Lord Jesus Christ (1 Corinthians. 15:57).

Eternally loved

- Nothing in all creation can separate us from *God's love* for us in Christ Jesus our Lord (Romans 8:35, 38-39 CEV)!

I Am…

Favored of God.

- For it is You who blesses the righteous man, O Lord, You surround him with *favor* as with a shield (Psalm 5:12).

Oh, so bold, confident and courageous.

- The wicked flee when no one is pursuing, but the righteous are *bold* as a lion (Proverbs 28:1).

Reconciled to be a reconciler.

- Now all these things are from God, who reconciled us to Himself through Christ and gave us the *ministry of reconciliation* (2 Corinthians 5:18).

Well protected.

- No *weapon* that is formed against you will prosper (Isaiah 54:17).

Assured of success.

- And in whatever he does, he *prospers* (Psalm 1:3).

I Am …

(the) **R**ighteousness of God in Christ Jesus.

- [God] made Him [Christ] who knew no sin to be sin on our behalf, so that we might become the *righteousness of God* in Him [Christ] (2 Corinthians 5:21).

Destined to win if I do not quit.

- But thanks be to God, who always leads us in *triumph* in Christ… (2 Corinthians 2:14).

Meditate upon the *I Am Significant* mantra and repeat it to yourself all throughout the day. When experiences trigger your negative self-talk, replace the negative with your new God-centered self-talk. Remember that repeated self-talk, over time, turns into attitudes, values, and beliefs.[16] For this very reason memorizing this mantra is part of this program. You are literally rewiring and retraining your brain. If you, in faith, consistently repeat this mantra, it has the potential, over time, to begin to change your mental image of yourself.

Your negative self-talk will not change overnight, but little by little, day by day, your mind will be renewed, and you will be transformed by the very faith affirmations you are declaring. Feel yourself moving forward with each action even if the action is verbalization. Greater focus on the short-term gain enables us to think in terms of the glass half full, in terms of accomplishment. Understand that every faith-based action, however small, enables our progression toward the goal. Give yourself more wholly to the momentary task, process, practice, or routine. You will be glad you did! It will be to your benefit to get this mantra down into your heart because your mouth will speak what is put in your heart (Matthew 12:34-35). If doubt and unbelief are put into your heart, words of doubt and unbelief will come out. If faith-filled words are put into your heart, faith-filled words will come out. We must first see it on the inside, and this allows God to bring it to pass on the outside.

However, you not only have to state the affirmations, but you have to align them with your emotions. Beliefs lodged in our subconscious minds are changed not solely through intellect and mental fashioning, but by our emotions as we utilize the power of our imagination. Information (ideational conception) plus emotion leads to transformation. We are emotional beings, and the more intensely emotional we feel about something, the faster we are able to reprogram our subconscious mind. "If you just read your affirmation you can expect a 10% success rate. If you read and visualize the end result you can expect about a 55% success rate. If you read your affirmation, picture the end result and *feel the emotion* behind what you are picturing, you can expect a *100% success rate*."[17] This three-step process is referred to as imprinting or tattooing.[18] The more emotionally compelling the statement, the more you will want to repeat it. Strangely, the more you repeat something the more compelling it becomes. An unenthused affirmative statement is like a boring TV commercial that you ignore. With the positive affirmation, you are trying to sell yourself emotionally on the concept or idea. You have to sincerely want what you are affirming, and if you want it (whatever your "it" is) bad enough, your hunger for it will draw you like a magnet to the outcome sought.[19]

Why You May Feel Your Affirmations May Not Be Working

Perhaps by now you have begun to encounter a bit of noticeable mental resistance in your efforts to establish a new spiritual identity. Such resistance may come in the form of questioning whether such affirmations are true and whether you are trying to convince yourself of a lie. Here are several techniques to help resolve some of the incongruence you may experience.

First, most importantly, recognize that the affirmations are true of your *new* spiritual identity and not your old self, your soul (mind, will, and emotions) and body (2 Corinthians 5:17; Ephesians 4:23-24). However, know that if you continue believing and believe with conviction that the affirmations are not true, that skepticism will form an obstacle to your progress. For as the Bible affirms, "For as he thinks in his heart, so is he." (Proverbs 23:7 NKJV).

Secondly, if you feel that you are lying to yourself when you repeat the affirmations, for example, "I am more than a conqueror" or "I am an overcomer," here is a technique I recommend to address this mental incongruence. Try stating it this way: "I *choose* to believe that I am more than a conqueror," "I *choose* to believe I am an overcomer," "I *choose* to believe that I am a victor and not a victim." By employing the phrasing "I choose to believe," we meet with lesser resistance, because we are stating what we elect to believe instead of declaring who we are. This subtle alteration in phraseology has the effect of diminishing your experience of psychic resistance ("pushback"). When you begin repeating these "I am" affirmations, you must maintain awareness that you are not saying something based on your current level of belief in it; you speak based on another's belief, not yours. And that "other" is, of course, God Himself. The whole idea is not to practice saying what you already believe, but what God has always believed. And it is a proven causal relationship of behavior research that a person grows in the conviction that something is true by continually repeating the statement or mantra (Proverbs 18:21). Do not expect to believe immediately. Believe rather that God believes it.

> **Believe God's word more than what you feel.**

Another reason affirmations may not be working for you is because you may, on a subconscious or preconscious level, be "double-minded": you may hold two mutually contradictory thoughts simultaneously. As a common indicator, one moment you feel you want to change your life in a certain way, and the next moment you don't. In the Book of James, the biblical author maintains that a double-minded man will not receive anything from God (James 1:6-8). The reason he will not receive an answer to his prayers is because to be double-minded is to have two minds, one of fear and one of faith. For example, a woman may have been praying to God to help her lose weight. But she has trouble verbally affirming, "I am getting slimmer and trimmer with each passing day." Her inability in some forms of verbalization suggest that she may be double-minded. In the back of her mind, she may be thinking to herself, "If I lose weight, people will be expecting me to keep the weight off," or some other contrarian concern. It's not that positive affirmations do not work; they are not working for this particular woman because her heart is divided, and she is experiencing mixed signals in her brain. All this has the effect of impeding neurological rewiring.

A final reason your affirmations may not be working for you is the possibility that you are not spending enough time and focus repeating them. This is only Day 6, and you need at least twenty-one days to ensure a new mental habit.

See it! Say it! Seize it!

We are going to end today's lesson with a story of a woman who saw herself healed and used her words to talk herself out of sickness and into wholeness. What is the woman's name? The Bible doesn't tell us. The Gospel writer Mark just says, "And a certain woman, which had an issue of blood twelve years" (Mark 5:25 KJV). The King James Bible relates that, the woman had an issue of blood. Take heart, reader, the people in Biblical days also had issues. How many troubles and vexations are you dealing with today? Perhaps your major concern is a personal relationship, a financial difficulty, or being continually haunted by a bad memory. The text declares the woman had "an issue." However, I'd like to suggest to you that she had at least four issues. First, as indicated in the text she had a medical issue. She had been diagnosed with an incurable and unstoppable menstrual flow. One day her monthly cycle started as usual, but after 5 to7 days when it should have stopped it continued day after day, month after month, and she suffered for the next 12 long years. What an ordeal! Secondly, she had a religious issue. Because of her unabated menstrual flow, she was considered ceremonially unclean and not permitted to participate in any of the religious temple services. Thirdly, she had a social issue. Because of her unusual medical situation, she was treated like a leper, and therefore considered unclean; she was forced to live as a social outcast, even separated from her closest kin. *Lastly,* but very importantly she had a financial issue. "[She] had suffered many things of many physicians, and had spent all that she had, and was nothing bettered, but rather grew worse." (v.26). Despite her terrible problems, the woman maintained a healthy mindset. How do I know that? It is said that "A healthy mind is a mind that can tolerate setbacks, then bounce back."[20] Her healthy attitude allowed her to steadily bounce back again and again for twelve long years. A nod to her for struggling through! While her money may have been gone, her hope likely was not. Her undying desire to be healed probably drove her to consider an option she had not considered before, the one-of-a-kind miracle worker, Jesus. His name is one that echoes through the ages with a luminous hope. She must have reasoned Jesus can help me—Jesus alone!

See it!

The woman saw herself healed, whole and restored with the help of Jesus. Painted on the canvas of this woman's heart was a mental image of herself totally healed. Mentally, she didn't picture herself remaining sick and a social and religious outcast. She pushed back on such images. Sometimes desperation can bring a person to do what this plan teaches one to do. "For the imagination literally has the power of making the things we picture real and effective."[21] She refused to allow mental images of herself--perpetually bleeding for the rest of her life--to remain lodged in her mind. Instead, she replaced those negative images with mental images of her reaching out, touching the hem of Jesus' garment and seeing herself instantaneously healed. This is what it means to see it. After seeing it, she went on to say it.

Say It!

With the image of her body healed firmly etched in her mind, her mouth spoke what she believed in her heart. "For she kept saying, 'if I only touch His garments, I shall be restored to health'" (Mark 5:28 AMPC). Persistently she kept up her positive self-talk. The woman's mindset equivalent was, "I believed; therefore I spoke..." (2 Corinthians 4:13). Your words have power! God declares, "Let the weak say, I am strong" (Joel 3:10 KJV). Don't use your words to describe the situation. Use your words to change the situation. Believing only what you see requires no faith. Do what the woman did and speak what you want to see happen. Speak words of faith and life over your body, over your finances, over the dissatisfactions of your personal relationships, over nagging doubts and discouragements, over challenges and tribulations and watch things change. Exercise your God-given faith.

The Psalmist declares, "Let the redeemed of the Lord **say** so..." (Psalm 107:2). What are you saying about your circumstances? Still saying you can't learn to control your thoughts. You can't lose any more weight? You can't take life's pressures anymore without exploding? Your words have power. Speak life, not death. Instead say, "I can do all things through Christ who gives me strength" (Philippians 4:13). Say. "I am more than a conqueror. I am an overcomer. I am a victor, not a victim." Remember, the brain is rewired through repetition. That is why the Bible commands believers to never stop speaking the promises of God (Joshua 1:8).

Concerning the importance of words, Dr. Samuel C. Verghese points out that "a rewiring of the brain occurs with verbal treatment as well as with medications. Moral training...as well as lectures and reading...offers the opportunity to bring about beneficial neuroplastic changes."[22] Indeed, words can change and rewire your brain, providing they are repetitively heard and spoken in faith—negative or positive. Remember, what you talk about you bring about.

Seize it!

The woman from scripture, mentally seeing herself healed by faith and then having spoken words of faith knew it was time for her to seize the opportunity to meet Jesus, the healer. Observe the progression: See it! Say it! Seize it!

Aware that Jesus was coming to her area, she was going to have to seize the opportunity and proactively seek him out. However, she had two obstacles standing in her way: one internally and the other externally. Internally she probably had to battle her negative self-talk that was constantly discouraging her. It may have gone something like this:

Who are you kidding? Do you think Jesus would heal someone like you? You are a social outcast—a bloody mess! You haven't been to Temple in how many years? Jesus' miracles are reserved for His faithful Temple worshipers. You don't qualify! Why even waste his time? All the doctors couldn't help you... why this Jesus? Why get your hopes up? You will only be disappointed once again. It's been twelve years. Don't you think if God were going to heal you, He would have done it by now?

Pushing back on every negative internal voice, she pressed her way into the crowd, determined to touch, in faith, the miracle worker.

Externally, just as she had imagined, the teaming masses of desperate people pushed her, bumped her, and jostled her from side to side. But the woman was undeterred. After twelve years of hearing a discouraging "No!" she was determined to get her yes, yes, you can be healed. As she had envisioned in her mind, she got close enough to Jesus and reached out and touched his garment. Immediately the flow of blood ceased, and she felt in her body that she was healed of her affliction (Mark 5:29-33). Her healing became manifest because she recognized that the compass of Jesus' divine powers was extraordinary. She believed that things would get better in the future. Hence, her strong faith enabled her to push back on her negative self-talk and persevere until victory was achieved.

Questions for Reflection

1. Are there any personal goals that you've allowed your inner critic to talk you out of pursuing?

Yes/ No

2. Are you willing to renew your faith and dream again and once again venture toward your goal? See it, say it, and seize it? Explain, if you wish to.

_____

_____

Real Life Testimonies to Help Build Your Faith

I've heard it said that most adults' mental and emotional problems have their origin in their childhood. We close today's lesson with the personal testimony of a woman whose adult life was marked by a painful childhood experience. So traumatic was the experience that it marred her self-image giving way to a negative internal dialogue which led her into addiction and bondage for decades until her heart and mind were unshackled.

CJ's Testimony: I Thought I Was Over It, But...

I was born in Annapolis, MD, into a loving Christian home. I was the 6th child of 7; the youngest girl; I was doted upon and protected. Blessed with intelligence, I consistently made the Honor Roll throughout elementary school. Because of my academic standing, I was one of 7 African American students chosen to integrate the all-white Annapolis Junior High School in 1959. Boy, were my parents proud of me. As a 12-year-old child, I wanted nothing more than to make my parents proud, but at the same time, I felt pressure and uneasiness. However, the internal pressure I felt, paled in comparison to the vitriol that I was about to encounter from the all-white student body at Annapolis Junior High School.

For the first time in my life, I came face to face with unadulterated racism. The white students spit on us, pushed, shoved, and threatened to beat us up in the bathroom. I felt totally alone and abandoned with no one to protect me. Where was Mom? Where was Dad? Why would they send their baby girl into such a horrible habitat? Why would they leave me to face this all alone? Each day walking into that school was like entering a war zone. The experience literally traumatized my 12-year-old brain. Strangely enough, I never told my parents about the racial hostility and abuse that I encountered daily. Why? Because they were so proud of me. I didn't want to disappoint them. So, I kept it all inside. Daily, I felt trapped in a schoolhouse of horror with no one there to protect or look out for me. Feeling alone and abandoned with no one to talk to or support me, I made the decision that I would find a way out of this living hell. After completing the 7th -9th grades and maintaining excellent grades, I put my exit plan into action. With the help of a sympathetic white teacher, I forged my parent's signature and I transferred myself back to the all-black high school in my district. I was now free from the verbal and physical harassment, but by now the *damage was done*. Little did I know that the painful trauma I was forced to endure would create a painful wound in me that would serve as the genesis of a long-lasting drug addiction.

One thing we all have in common is pain. Once under the influence, (of drugs and alcohol) the painful memories seemed to dissipate. I could forget my pain and just have fun. Having ceased attending church, I had no spiritual coping skill or for that matter no natural coping skills to help deal with my pain, so alcohol and pills become my way of coping with past and present pain. The alcohol and tobacco were just a bandage that I kept putting on an open wound. The only problem was that the bandage kept falling off my wound. As my body built up a tolerance to alcohol, I began to turn to illegal street drugs like marijuana and ultimately cocaine. Cocaine was my drug of choice, but little did I know that it would hold me in its addictive claws for close to 40 years.

Now life really became complicated. I was a functional addict. I worked hard to support my habit and my daughter. I had several good jobs where I connected with other colleagues who were also struggling with the disease of addiction.

Knowing I needed to stop self- medicating, I began attending Narcotics (NA) and Alcoholic Anonymous (AA) meetings. I went to hundreds of sessions, but never really changed because I wasn't seriously committed to changing my lifestyle. However, the information proved to be extremely helpful because they brought me to the realization, that I couldn't beat my addiction without a higher power. My higher power was the God of my childhood. Although I had wandered from Him, He was there all the time—waiting patiently for my return. Throughout my addiction, my mother, brother, and many family members never ceased praying for me. Their prayers, I believe in part caused me to call out to God for help. Incrementally, my life began to change. I was hoping that God would deliver me instantaneously as He had delivered my brother. However, for me, my deliverance came through a much longer process. I initially stopped using cocaine, but I still smoked and drank beer socially. As I began praying and reading the Bible more, I was reminded of how much my heavenly Father loved me and I knew that He would eventually deliver me from alcohol and drug addictions. I became increasingly hopeful knowing that I was not going to die an addict. In response to my prayers, the prayers of my parents, family and friends, God moved in a surprising way.

One day as I was driving in my car, I was overcome with God's presence to such a degree that I felt like I was in a vacuum. I could not even hear the radio playing. I don't even know how I was able to keep driving the car. God spoke to me and told me that He had heard my prayers and today He was answering my prayers. I just began grinning and grinning. It's hard to describe the feeling and put it in words; it's almost as though I was engulfed in a liquid love that resulted in joy, unspeakable joy. All I could say was *thank you Jesus!* I knew that I was finally delivered. From that day forward, I stopped drinking and smoking. I no longer see myself as being in recovery. I am in delivery. God has delivered me and is daily revealing to me His purpose for my life. He has greatly used the Body of Christ and especially my Bishop to help disciple, coach, and mentor me. I now keep myself busy working in the church, writing a monthly newsletter, working with new members, and keeping myself surrounded with *only quality people* (OQP). When thoughts of my past life pop up in my mind, I pray to God for help or I talk back to Satan and tell him my mind and life no longer belong to him. I am a new creature in Christ Jesus. I am now God's property (1 Peter 2:9) so you'd better back off!

* * *

Like the woman that Jesus healed after 12 years, Jesus also over time healed and delivered CJ. But first, CJ decided she wanted to be delivered. Secondly, she had to see herself drug free in her mind's eye. And once she made the decision and could *see it* on the inside, God could bring it to pass on the outside. Next, she had to *say it*: "I shall not die an addict." Finally, she had to *seize it*. As an addict, she attended hundreds of NA and AA meetings. In these small group gatherings, she learned many thought management strategies, and was able to make the connection between her painful childhood trauma and her later use of drugs and alcohol to escape her pain. As she continued to cry out to God for help, He totally delivered her from her dependence upon drugs and alcohol.

Proverbs 18:10 reminds us, "The name of the Lord is a strong tower; The righteous run into it and are safe." We all know pain, suffering, and disappointment. The question is where do you run? To what or to whom do you turn? CJ has learned to stop turning to cocaine and instead turn to the Source of her strength—His name is Jesus. Jesus has the power to heal your brokenness, to deliver, and set you free from all things that enslave you and to empower you to walk in newness of life—His life.

* * *

 **A Closing Prayer**

Father help me to draw upon your strength and to do the hard work of renewing my mind. Father, "May the words of my mouth and the meditations of my heart be acceptable in your sight" (Psalm 19:14 KJV). May I use my tongue to speak life and not death. In Jesus' name. Amen.

For an inspirational pick me up, I recommend:

- *Speak Life* by Toby Mac
- *Speak* by Tina Campbell
- *Blessings on Blessing* by Anthony Brown

Until tomorrow, do this:

 Memory Work

1. Remember **TEA=B** – Thoughts affect emotions and emotions affect attitudes, and attitudes produce behavior

2. **Biblical mind renewal** is the lifelong process of replacing our perspective (thoughts, opinions, and beliefs) with God's perspective as revealed in His Word.

3. Practice reciting the *I Am Significant* mantra (Repeat 10-12 times per day – every hour on the hour).

I Am Significant

I Am Significant. Why? *(Because)* God loves me and sent his Son to die upon the cross for my sins. He has adopted me into His family and has given me a new name. I am a born-again Christian, fearfully and wonderfully made in the image of God (John 3:16; Ephesians 1:5; 2 Corinthians 5:17; Psalm 139:14).

Figure 3.6 I Am Significant Mantra

4.  **My Spiritual Identity**

The N-O-W-M-O-V-E-F-O-R-W-A-R-D acrostic is your new spiritual identity. Write the first part of the acrostic on a 3x5 card and carry it with you wherever you go. You can also write it on multiple cards; place a card in your Bible; tape another to your car dashboard for example, bathroom mirror, refrigerator, or workstation. Do not concern yourself with memorizing the scriptures at this point. Just begin to memorize the transitional phases and what each letter stands for and repeat it as often as the Holy Spirit prompts you to do so. You will be glad you did!

My Spiritual Identity

I Am (a)...

New creation in Christ Jesus (2 Cor. 5:17),
Ordained and chosen by God to fulfill his
   purpose for my life (Jeremiah 1:5; 29:11) *(And I...)*
Walk in the power of the Holy Spirit (Eph. 5:18; Acts 1:8)

Figure 6.1 My Spiritual Identity (Part 1)

118

Why You Do What You Do?

There is nothing as powerful as a changed mind. You can change your hair, your clothing, your address, your spouse, your residence, but if you don't change your mind, the same experience will perpetuate itself over and over again, because everything outwardly changed, but nothing inwardly changed.

--T.D. Jakes

Daily Food for Thought

- **Brain Fact** The basal ganglia is the portion of your brain where habits are formed.[1]

- **Key Thought** "Left to its own devices, the brain will try to make almost any routine into a habit, because habits allow your mind to ramp down more often."[2]

- **Scripture** "And [Jesus] came out and went, as was His *habit*, to the Mount of Olives…" (Luke 22:39 AMPC).

Daily Reading

How many times have you asked yourself, "Why did I do that?" Plenty of times, I'm sure. Now, we all have a lot of different reasons for doing what we do. Some people do things because they have a "disease to please." Some of us do things out of fear, guilt or insecurity. Still others do things to get even or to maintain their reputations. Today, you're going to discover, neurologically speaking, why you do what you do and how you can change. You are going to discover why you often think the same thoughts, engage in the same activities, and hold on to the same destructive mental habits, when you know at some level of consciousness that they are hurting you. Neurologically, we do what we do out of *habit*. What exactly is a habit? Habits are the routinized actions, large and small, that have been partially removed from the process of decision making which you perform typically every day. According to researchers at Duke University, habits account for about 40 percent of our behaviors on any given day."[3] Behavioral strategist James Clear asserts,

> Your life is essentially the sum total of your habits, how in shape or out of shape you are is a result of your habits. How happy or unhappy you are – a result of your habits. How successful or unsuccessful you are - a result of your habits. What you repeatedly do (i.e. what you spend time thinking about and doing each day) ultimately forms the person you are, the things you believe, and the personality that you portray.[4]

Clear makes it very clear (no pun intended) that we are a composite of our habits, both good and bad. Christian psychologist Dr. Archibald Hart affirms, *"We are not slaves to our minds, but we are slaves to the habits that control our minds.* We weave patterns of thoughts out of ignorance and neglect. We let bad habits become dominant. The result is pain and unhappiness, self-defeat, and self-destruction."[5] Stephen R. Covey, author of *The 7 Habits of Highly Effective People,* asserts *"Sow a thought, reap an action; sow an action, reap a habit; sow a habit, reap a character; sow a character, reap a destiny."*

> *Your life is essentially the sum total of your habits.*

If we are honest, we must confess that we've all tried to change some of our bad habits and inculcate more positive ones. No doubt all of us can testify to the fact that bad habits are hard to break. Try to stop smoking or biting your fingernails down to the quick, cursing, overeating, gossiping, gambling, viewing pornography, checking your cell phone every minute, or checking to make sure all the doors and windows are locked for the fifteenth time. The primary reason it is hard to break any habit is because our brains are essentially creatures of habit. "Habits, scientists say, emerge because the brain is constantly looking for ways to save effort. *Left to its own devices, the brain will try to make any routine into a habit, because habits allow your mind to ramp down more often."*[6] Consequently, the brain will attempt to make any repeated action, whether

> *Habits emerge because the brain is constantly looking for ways to save effort.*

good or bad, into a habit. It will be referred to later in today's reading, but the basal ganglia is the portion of your brain where habits are formed.[7] (See Figure 7.1).

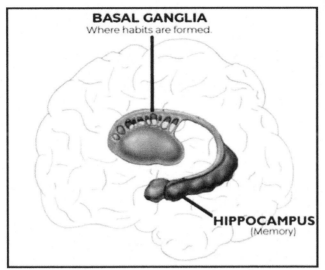

Figure 7:1 The Basal Ganglia

The Habit Loop

According to Charles Duhigg, author of *The Power of Habit: Why You Do What You Do In Life And Business*, the habit forming " process within our brains is a three-step [process] beginning with a cue, routine, reward; cue, routine, reward-[when it] becomes more and more automatic... a habit is born."[8] (See Figure 7.2 below:)

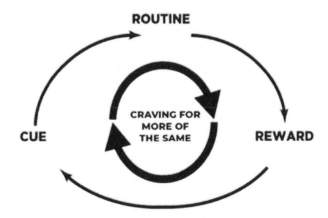

Figure 7:2 The Habit Loop

1. Cue—a **trigger** from the environment that initiates the behavior and begins the habit loop.

2. Routine–the behavior you engage in as a result of the cue.

3. Reward—the benefit you derive from performing the behavior.

Here is how this habit loop is evident each time you answer your phone.

Cue: The phone rings.

Routine: You answer it.

Reward: If it was someone you wished to talk to it is a reward; if not it is dismissed, or it is felt as punishment.[9] Are you beginning to see it more clearly?

Now let us apply this cue, routine, reward habit loop to a negative mental habit many people struggle with—getting up in the morning with a positive attitude. I've heard it said, "The devil likes to get into your head, before you get out of bed." Why? Satan knows that the attitude you get up with in the morning tends to set your emotional tone for the first half of, if not the entire day. With this in mind, let's take proactive measures to stay one step ahead of the enemy with a discussion of the old, then new, habit loop.

The Old Habit Loop

This is the morning **routine** for many who struggle to get out of bed. The **cue** is the morning alarm signaling it is time for you to wake. The **routine** is the negative thoughts you think which lead to the negative self-talk you engage in—before getting out of bed. Your automatic negative thoughts (ANTS)[10] may prompt you to say such things as, "I hate getting up in the morning" or "I am so doggone tired" or "I am so tired that I feel I could sleep all day; it feels like I just went to sleep a half hour ago."

After convincing yourself how terrible you feel and why you would like to stay in the bed, you hit the snooze button and **reward** yourself with fifteen more minutes of sleep. The alarm sounds once again. You are now behind schedule, so you jump out of bed in a panic. Your brain chemicals begin secreting large doses of cortisol (the stress hormone) and adrenaline as you rally yourself to complete all the morning chores in preparation for your day. This is your **cue, routine,** and **reward.** This example of the morning routine shows the way our brain chemistry automatically tips the balance and helps us move and do the things we need to do. Your reward is the 15 minutes extra sleep. Though you don't think about it, that 15 minutes has functioned as a sort of reinforcement. Was this the first time you hit your snooze alarm? No! Was it the second time? No! You've hit that snooze alarm probably a hundred times before arising. It's automatic, because it has become a brain habit.

The New Habit Loop

The first step in rewiring your brain starts with a strong desire or craving to do so. It is pictured in the center of Duhigg's brain habit loop (Figure 7.2). If your craving is strong enough to make you want to change the way you wake up (dreading the start of a new day) and you prefer to set a more positive emotional tone when you arise to face the day, then you need a replacement, or a new **cue, routine,** and **reward**. Duhigg insists that "habits [of thinking] cannot be eradicated—they must be replaced."[11] Imagine waking up in the morning to a new **cue, routine,** and **reward**. Here is the **HELP** you need.

> *Habits cannot be eradicated—they must be replaced.*

Cue: The alarm clock is the cue signaling you it's time to wake up. **Routine:** After shutting off the alarm, you immediately begin to yawn. Yawning has a useful physiological function. It is a reflexive drawing of oxygen into the lungs. This is the oxygen that ends up in the brain. Empirical research has revealed that a person needs to yawn ten to twelve times to realize the full benefits to waking. Yawning helps to wake up your brain. Yawning is one way of exercising the brain, similar to smiling, and has several neurological benefits. Yawning "lowers stress, improves cognitive (brain) functioning, stimulates alertness and concentration, optimizes brain activity and metabolism, relaxes every part of your body, and increases memory recall [and] enhances consciousness and introspection."[12] These are just a few of the benefits of yawning.

When the ANTS line up and begin to uniformly march lockstep into your mind, with complaints about your daily concerns, and hassles, interrupt and replace them by asking yourself five questions. They are thought-provoking questions designed to help you tap into the positive emotions that you need to start your day off with a positive attitude. As you lie in bed and after you have finished (12 times) yawning, ask yourself:

1. What am I **happy** about in my life now?
2. What am I **excited** about in my life now?
3. Who **loves** me and whom do I **love** right now?
4. What am I most **proud** of in my life now?[13]
5. What can I **praise** God for right now?

Resist the thought to answer "Nothing." Some of us will just have to search for a moment to answer each question. Possible answers: I am **happy** about the fact that I have a job that allows me to provide for my family and me. I am **excited** that I'm healthy, spiritually wealthy and wise. Who **loves** me? God loves me! "My children love me, and I love them." (Doubts about whether others love you must not stop you from answering #3. People do love you, whether they routinely express that love or not.) #4: I am **proud** of the fact that I am not a quitter. #5:

123

I **praise** God for blessing me with so many abilities (to learn, to cope, to increase my spirituality, to encourage others, and more). The psalmist, David, declared,

> It is wonderful to be grateful
> and to sing your praises,
> LORD Most High!
> It is wonderful *each morning*
> to tell about your love
> and at night to announce
> how faithful you are.
> I enjoy praising your name…
> (Psalm 92:1-3 CEV)

For the questions to be effective in tapping into your positive emotions, you need to engage your imagination to visualize the people, places, and things that make you feel positive. The potential of this exercise (visualizing) is extraordinary. It can transform your life.

To aid in recall, the word **HELPP**, (*H*appy, *E*xcited, *L*ove, *P*roud, *and Praise*) will serve as a useful acrostic for these five questions. The questions serve a twofold purpose: First, they wake up your brain to tap into the positive emotions needed to help you have a positive attitude. Second, as you consistently practice the **HELPP** questions each morning, you are rewiring your brain to replace the old negative thoughts and emotions. In time your brain will do it automatically. When this happens, it will have become a habit. However, for the routine to become a brain habit, you must have a strong desire to change. One can feel the positive efforts of this exercise almost immediately, and sometimes in as little as two or three days. Your brain's craving serves as a prompt to your reward.

Reward: Your days will begin in a more positive manner and your reward is that you will become a more positive person making your life more pleasant in the morning (or whenever your day begins). In addition, you will feel less stressed and more relaxed because the yawning and **HELPP** questions are serving to buttress and balance your brain chemistry, lowering stress, and bringing about a calming homeostasis in your brain. By getting up a little earlier, and not hitting the snooze button for more sleep, you will have extra time to do additional things like reading your Bible, praying, reciting the *I Am Significant* mantras, or reading several pages of *The 21-Day Plan*. By establishing these new habits, your mind is being renewed; your brain is rewired one thought at a time.

Sometime ago, I watched an interview of Jack Canfield, coauthor of the popular *Chicken Soup for the Soul* book series. During that interview, he told the story of how his friend, before getting out of bed in the morning, would ask himself a series of gratitude questions, much like the ones I listed above. Jack recounted how his friend would not get out of his bed, to start his day, until he had brought himself to cry tears of joy and gratitude for the many blessings in his life. By so doing, he assured himself to have a positive mental perspective regardless of whatever unexpected circumstances or problems that he would perhaps encounter that day.

I am mindful of the Bible character David whose day took an unsuspecting turn when he encountered a giant named Goliath. After receiving permission, from King Saul, to fight Goliath, young David stopped by a brook and picked up 5 smooth stones (1 Samuel 17:40). He placed one stone in his sling shot and whirled the sling shot over his head as he ran toward the behemoth. As he drew closer, he released the stone in the direction of the giant Philistine's head. Upon impact, the stone brought the Philistine giant to the ground—out cold. He was defeated with one smooth stone. Upon reflection, should you decide to inculcate the 5 **HELPP** questions into your morning routine, which is equivalent to 5 smooth stones to help you slay the giants of fear, discouragement, defeat, despair, and regret that seek to dominate your mindset at the start of each day? Since you have been equipped with HELPP, you can now *use the rock you got* to defeat the mental giants that seek to enslave you. Try it. You'll be glad you did!

Examine the pictures below to see how an old negative habit loop can be replaced with a new positive habit loop; thus, enabling you to wake up in a better mood. (See Figure 7.3).

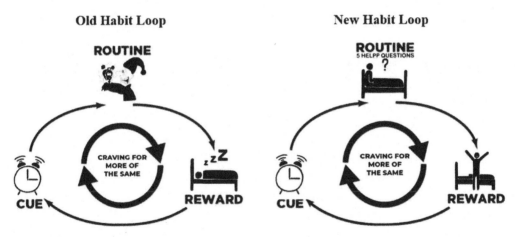

Figure 7.3 Wakeup Habit Loop

Questions for Reflection

> *If you change nothing, nothing will change.*

1. Which habit loop best describes your morning routine?

_____

_____

2. Are you willing to try a new approach?

_____

_____

Initiating a New Habit Loop

When battling discouraging thoughts, here's a way to start a new habit loop.

Old Habit Loop: The **cue**: When a barrage of negative thoughts would come to Sam's mind, he would dwell upon them and begin to feel depressed. To relieve the depression, Sam's old routine was to take an alcoholic drink. His **reward** was that the alcohol lifted his spirits momentarily, before the depressive component of the alcohol kicked in. (See Figure 7.4).

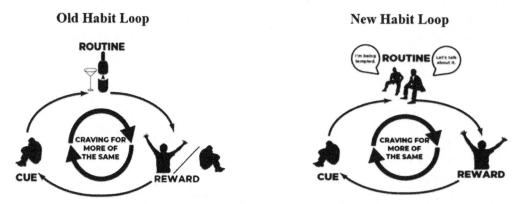

Figure 7.4 The Alcoholic Habit Loop

New Habit Loop: The **Cue**: A negative thought entered Sam's mind; he meditated upon it and began to feel depressed. However, this time Sam pushed back on the thought and his old **routine**. Instead of drinking, Sam made the quality decision to start a new habit. Hence, Sam called his friend Bob to talk about what was really bothering him. His **reward** was that his spirit was lifted, his friendship was deepened, and he avoided a hangover. And most importantly, he felt empowered by resisting temptation.

Questions for Reflection

Explain your habit loop when you're stressed, discouraged, depressed, angry or frustrated. For example, I overeat, I lash out, I watch TV, etc.

Describe the habit loop you engage in at such challenging times. Begin with the Cue. Keep in mind that these antecedent causes or triggers are sometimes subtle and invisible. You need to think about why your mood is changing.

1. Cue:

_____

_____

2. Routine: I tend to

_____

_____

3. Reward: I feel

_____

_____

Describe how you could create a new habit loop. What would be your reward?

_____

_____

_____

Positive and Negative Mental Strongholds

In Christian circles, the term *stronghold* is frequently bandied. What is a stronghold? It can be defined as a fortress, which is established and hard to penetrate. In the context of this discussion, it is understood as a negative thought or series of negative thoughts that a person failed to notice and control. Neurologically speaking, a stronghold is any pattern of thinking (positive, negative, neutral or mixed) that the brain has turned into a habit. Concerning negative mental strongholds, the Bible informs Christians that we are to be actively engaged in "pulling down strongholds" (2 Corinthians 10:4 NKJV). Anxiety, worry, fear, doubt, and all forms of immoral thoughts can become mental strongholds if we consistently and habitually dwell on them. However, as there are negative strongholds to pull down, there are also positive strongholds that we need to establish. Concerning the development of positive strongholds, the Apostle Paul said, "…you'll do best by filling your minds and meditating on things true, noble, reputable, authentic, compelling, gracious—the best, not the worst; the beautiful, not the ugly; things to praise, not things to curse" (Philippians 4:8 MSG). As we consistently focus upon these positive things, the brain will attempt to make the actions into a habit.[14]

> *A stronghold is any pattern of thinking that the brain has turned into a habit.*

Thinking for a Change

Duhigg reminds us that "habits cannot be eradicated—they must be replaced."[15] One of the objectives of today's lesson is to teach you how to break your old habit loops and replace them with new, positive habit loops as illustrated above in figures 7.3 and 7.4. The entrance of an automatic negative thought (ANTS) [16]is the cue.

Cue: The cue is always itself. We must understand that it is typically unalterable. It is external, not something you do. In psychology it may sometimes be called a stressor.

Routine: Instead of pondering and mulling over the ANTS until they evoke an avalanche of negative emotions, attitudes and behaviors, immediately push back on the negative thought and replace it with a spiritual automatic thought (SATS). It is said that, *"nature abhors a vacuum."* This simply means that we cannot operate on a "don't" principle; *we must have something substantial to take the place of* the thought or action (the "don't") we are trying to eliminate.

Reward: Your mind will be calmer and more peaceful as a result of your pushback. The toxic chemicals that were released into your brain will be reduced. They will be less likely to cause stress headaches, high blood pressure, and panic attacks. God said, "I will keep him in perfect peace whose mind is stayed on me" (Isaiah 26:3).

Note how using the information about ANTS and SATS, the New Habit Loop takes an entirely different approach. (See Figure 7.5).

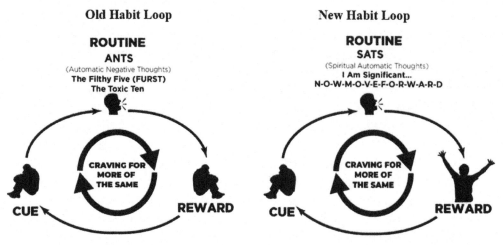

Figure 7.5 The ANTS Habit Loop vs. The SATS Habit Loop

You are learning to replace *worry* with the *Word*. In the new habit loop, you will replace the ANTS with SATS by taking out your 3x5 cards and repeating your *I Am Significant* mantra. You may also repeat it aloud. When you speak aloud your mind has to stop and listen to what your mouth is saying. Therefore, your mind is not available to receive the next negative thought. Continue by reciting the N-O-W-M-O-V-E-F-O-R-W-A-R-D acrostic in order to drown out the voice of your enemy, the father of lies. The Bible says, "Resist the devil and he will flee from you" (James 4:7).

Stomping Out the ANTS

Satan flees for a moment, but comes back at a more opportune time, perhaps for example, the next time you slip up or make a mistake. Satan, speaking through the voice of your conscious (self) will attempt to convince you that you are such an idiot and a real screw-up. You are the one person that grace can never change. Whenever that happens, employ the **"but" or "but God"** strategy. Satan says, "You are_____!" You finish the sentence with **"but" or "but God."** For example:

- "I'm overweight and out of shape, *but God* will help me to get my body back in shape."
- "My thoughts are crazy, *but The 21-Day Plan* is teaching me how to control my thoughts."
- "I failed again, *but God* reminds me that everyone fails from time to time. I will persevere."

Satan, the father of lies, will continually try to deceive us. It is his fulltime job and he never sleeps, but you must resist him and push back on his pushback. Satan will flee but he will return. Therefore, it is to our advantage to learn as many strategies as possible to shut his vile, reprobate mouth.

In addition to the **"but"** strategy, you may also find the **"at least"** strategy equally effective. The devil tries to cloud your mind with doom and gloom thoughts, to blind you to all the positive things in your life. You think to yourself (maybe)

- "I only made an 85 on the test. I was hoping to earn a 95. *At least* I passed it.
- "I failed my driver's test again. *At least* I did better than last time."
- "My marriage is not all that I hoped it would be. *At least* we have the opportunity to go to marriage counseling."
- "I am only making the minimum wage. *At least* God is allowing me to pay many of my bills. And God is allowing me to seek other employment."

Use all these ("but," "but God," "at least") strategies until they become a habit.

A final strategy to stomp out the ANTS is to discover the power of **"yet."** For example, when the Liar attempts to convince you that you are academically slow and will never measure up or catch up to others around you, never achieve your goals, or experience the financial prosperity you desire etc., rebuff him by declaring:

- "I can't do this...*yet*."
- "I'm not good at this...*yet*."
- "I don't know the answer...*yet*."
- "I've not reached my career or financial goals...yet."

Reward: You will become a *spin-doctor* by putting a *positive* spin on every negative thought. You will "take every thought captive" (2 Corinthians 10:5). As you apply these techniques, you will begin to feel more empowered because Satan will no longer dupe you into thinking his accusations are from God. You will recognize his insidious voice. Your mind will become more positive than negative because you will know how to renew your mind one thought at a time.

Craving to Change

Here is perhaps the most encouraging and intriguing thing about the habit loop. In the very center of Duhigg's Habit Loop are the words *"Craving for more of the same."* Not only do you have the desire for change, your brain is so wired that it helps you make the changes. God has built an organic change mechanism into your brain.

> *Patterns that are repeated over time become wired in the brain and body.*

Concerning the brain's neurological cravings: Dr. Tancredi, author of *Hardwired Behavior*, maintains, "Patterns that are repeated over time become wired in the brain and body... The brain changes adapt because of the development of new circuitry and *induces* more and more of the...behavior."[17] The brain's wiring does not discriminate between good and bad behavior. It just craves more. It will take whatever data you give it consistently and make it into a habit and create its very own neurological craving to perpetuate the habit.[18] God so designed the brain to reaffirm whatever behaviors we perform consistently. The basal ganglia converts the information or action into a habit and initiates a perpetual drip-drip-drip, a craving for more and more of the same activity.[19] That is the main reason breaking a bad habit is so difficult.

How Did You Become So Spiritual?

Have you ever wondered why David, the psalmist, loved the Lord so much? He tells us how he became "a man after God's own heart" (Acts 13:22). "His delight is in the law of the Lord, and in His [God's] law he meditates day and night" (Psalm 1:2). David goes on to say, "O how I love your law! It is my meditation all the day" (Psalm 119:97). Again, he states, "Your word I have treasured in my heart, that I may not sin against You" (Psalm 119:11). Practicing spiritual habits caused David to fall helplessly in love with the Lord—his Shepherd. Do you want to know how Joshua cultivated a heart for God? He tells us, "This book of the law shall not depart from your mouth, but you shall meditate on it day and night, so that you may be careful to do according to all that is written in it: for then you will make your way prosperous, and then you will have success" (Joshua 1:8). He had a hunger down on the inside to know God.

These men were not born spiritual giants as we might presume. They were people of flesh and bone like you and me. What differentiated them from you and me were their mental habits. Neurologically, they inundated their minds with the Word of God by meditating on it, at first in small portions. Their brains responded to their actions by ingraining it into a mental habit. The more they spent time in the word, their brains created a neurological craving, which caused their brains to crave Bible meditation more and more.[20]

Dr. Andrew Newberg, author of *How God Changes the Brain*, states "The longer you focus on your goal, the more real it begins to feel and if you stay focused long enough you'll alter the neural circuitry in your brain. The same is true for any principle in life. Focus on God long enough and God becomes neurologically real. Focus on peace and your body becomes relaxed and serene."[21]

Why are some people more spiritually inclined than others? In the final analysis, we are as close to God as we choose to be. The first step in getting closer to God begins by determining to cultivate a daily quiet time (QT). The brain cannot create a neurological craving for something that is not done repeatedly. A daily QT would serve to prime your spiritual pump.

Speaking of priming the pump, in 2016, while on a missionary trip in Ghana, West Africa, I saw the village children coming down to the community water station. They carried huge water pails, basins, and pots upon their heads. However, before they could access all the water underground, they first had to prime the pump. To do this, they first had to take the jug of water that was stationed beside the community pump and pour it down into the pump opening. Now, I am not sure of all the dynamics of physics and why it works, but I know if you pour water into the pump opening (head) and pump the handle 5 to 10 times, water comes gushing out. Spiritually speaking, if you are a believer, there are reservoirs of spiritual water residing on the inside of you. However, before gaining access to this spiritual supply of water, you must first prime your spiritual pump. You prime your spiritual pump by daily cultivating the spiritual habits of spending time with God in prayer, Bible reading, journaling, etc. If done consistently, over time your brain will create its very own desire for more. Goodness and satisfaction are timeless motivators; what we do that works well is almost certain to be done again.

How to Have a Daily Quiet Time

Here are some quiet time arranging ideas:

A. **Cue:** Set your alarm clock or put a daily reminder in your smartphone or other device to notify you it's time for your QT. The alarm is your trigger (cue). You can't start a new habit if you don't remember and schedule it. I strongly recommend having your QT the very first thing in the morning. I know some of you may be thinking, "I don't do mornings!" But we are talking about prayerful meditation here, and do you know you are talking to someone--God--who already knows precisely how tired you are? Do you understand, reader, that prayer is different than other ideational functions, that it can inspire us to feel more purposeful in literally any situational context. Morning (or waking) QT can set the spiritual/ attitudinal tenor of your entire day.

B. **Routine**:

1. *Get up 10 to 15 minutes earlier.*

   When the alarm sounds, shut it off, push back on the negative thoughts as you immediately begin your 10 to 12 yawning exercises. If you are one of those individuals who struggle to get up in the morning with a positive attitude, as you are yawning ask yourself the five **HELPP** questions. Whisper a prayer to God, thanking Him for giving you purpose and direction in your life and asking Him for strength and guidance throughout the day. Also, ask Him to forgive you for sins you knowingly and unknowingly may have committed.

2. *Find a quiet place to read.*

   The night before, be sure to place your Bible, devotional or 3x5 memory cards in the place you have chosen to have your quiet time (QT). You might do it right there in your bed. The goal is to make it as convenient as possible.

132

3. *Read your daily devotional, Bible or Bible app on your cellphone.*

Start small. Caution: If you are just establishing the habit of a QT, avoid the Bible reading plans. They are too laborious and time consuming. Instead, find a daily devotional such as the *Daily Bread,* or *Faith Talk*: A *90 Day Devotional* by Vonda Chipman. Start small, just minutes a day. Feel free to increase the length of your QT as the weeks go by. You want immediate success to help build momentum. A good place to also begin reading is in the Book of Proverbs, or the Gospels, in an easily understood modern translation. Limit yourself to one chapter or less per day. After reading, pray, asking God to help you to meditate on one important concept or verse throughout the day. In time, you may consider journaling your thoughts and Bible observations. As your spiritual hunger increases evidenced by a growing desire to gain deeper insights into God's word, consider asking yourself 4 questions each time you read a select passage of scripture. Ask what does this passage:

- reveal about God's character?
- reveal to me about myself?
- instruct me to do or stop doing?
- teach me about how to best relate to others?

4. *Seek out an accountability partner.*

Share your goal of having a daily QT over the next 21 days with a family member or friend and ask if he or she will help to hold you accountable. Preferably, this will be someone who already has a consistent QT or who is also seeking to establish a QT.

5. *Anticipate setbacks.*

Allow for the possibility of failure and setback. You may miss one day but try not to miss two days in a row. That's important! This is the crucial turning point, the precise point where success turns into failure; a day's setback becomes two. To miss two consecutive days impedes the habit formation process. Don't expect to fail but do plan for the possibility of transient failure. The brain tends to reject rigidity. If you miss your morning QT, you should schedule time to do it later in the day. Use that minor setback as something positive: use it as a reminder that you need to schedule it later in the day. Should you miss the entire day, push back on all self-condemning thoughts and immediately resume where you ended.

6. *Couple your QT with another existing habit.*

In order to help your brain remember to cue you to have your daily QT (especially if you miss the morning or waking time) it is best that you combine your QT with something you are already doing on a daily basis. For example, if you shower every morning, tell yourself, "Immediately after (or before) I shower I will have my QT." Or you might say, "During my morning coffee, I will have my QT." You may prefer to say, "after brushing my teeth, I will have my QT." In so doing, the shower, the coffee, and the teeth brushing function as your neurological cue to begin your new QT routine. Integrating the QT with a daily routine element helps to eliminate the problem of forgetting it. Similar to taking a lunch break on your job, or after arriving home each evening and sitting on the couch for some down time, your old habit becomes the cue for your new habit—your QT. You could have your QT before or after your daily reading of *The 21-Day Plan* to assimilate it with your goal to read 21 consecutive days. When you reach that goal, the brain will create a craving for more continued Bible reading and spending time with God. You will know it has become a neurological habit when you miss your QT and your brain seems a bit out of sorts. You will ask yourself, what is the anomaly. You brain will remind you that it misses its soothing QT.

C. **Reward:** Your reward will be an increased feeling of peace and closeness to God. In addition, your spirit may begin to come alive and may begin to crave more of God and His presence. Daily cultivation of a closer friendship with God will heighten your awareness of your true spiritual identity in God, and His purpose and plan for your life. Furthermore, you will be able to handle the pressures of life better, because you will no longer be relying upon your own power, but the power of the Holy Spirit that resides within you. As you invest your time in seeking God's presence and meditating on His Word, you will discover that your mind is being transformed and renewed–one thought at a time.

Questions for Reflection

1. Will you begin today to commit to having a daily QT over the next 21 days?

Yes____ No_____

Signature _____ Date _____

2. To what daily routine elements do you think you will be able to attach a quality QT time (before getting out of bed, after showering, or while drinking my coffee)?

_____

_____

_____

Real Life Testimonies to Help Build Your Faith

We close today's lesson with the personal testimony of a young man caught up in a negative habit loop who found deliverance after he was able to develop new habits.

Dominic's Testimony: Bound No More!

My own sinful nature led me into a pornography addiction at age 12. I had a strong sex drive, a strong need for intimacy, and a lack of positive social outlet for those feelings. This problem was further exacerbated when certain situations presented themselves to me. For example, I remember meeting a gentleman in middle school who lived in my neighborhood. He kept a stash of porn magazines in his house. One day I went with him to his house and viewed these magazines, and I asked to borrow a couple of them. I also had an instance where my next-door neighbor went out of town for two weeks and needed someone to watch his cats. The neighbor was gracious and open with his home and told me that I could watch his cable TV. I soon discovered that he had two porn channels on his TV. Over the next several weeks, I feasted on those pornographic images.

The desire to stop began early. I had given my life to Christ at age 7 and grew up in the church, so I knew that watching porn was wrong. Nevertheless, I continued to view pornography while away at college and into early adulthood. I would watch it either on my computer or cellphone, and I would often involve active sex with women with the watching. But all this was about to change.

The turning point for me arrived in 2011. I was 28 years old, and I used my computer to watch two cross-dressed men engage in vile and abominable sexual acts. I felt totally disgusted with myself, afraid of what I was becoming. I decided I desperately needed to change. Now resolute in my decision to change, I could sense God's presence affirming His desire to deliver me from this affliction. God reminded me that what I desired was intimacy with him and that only Jesus Christ could fill the void that I had tried to fill with porn for all those years. Committed to the process of deliverance, I recommitted my life to Jesus as an adult. There was no question in my mind that I was powerless alone to break this pattern of behavior. God's help was essential!

Since that 2011 turning point, I learned to replace the time I spent viewing pornography with far more constructive, wholesome behavior. My daily focus now consists of seeking God and spending time with Him and His Word, and this includes waking up and getting alone with God, kneeling in His presence, reading the scriptures, meditating on the Word and memorization. In the moment of fellowship with the Lord, I pray to God for strength to resist temptation; I praise Him for the victory and even dance in His presence. I replaced channel surfing and spending countless hours staring at the TV with attending church services three times a week along with my wife and son. Additionally, I listen to my pastor's sermons online at least 3 to 4 times a week. In so doing, I continue to strengthen my spirit, making it easier to resist temptation.

The Bible says, "Walk by the Spirit, and you will not fulfill the lust of the flesh" (Galatians 5:16-17). As my spirit man is empowered by the Holy Spirit, I can get in agreement with Job, who said, "I have made a covenant (agreement) with my eyes. How then could I gaze lustfully at a virgin" (Job 31:1 AMP)? Job had promised himself and his God that he would not stare at any woman apart from his wife with the intent of arousing himself sexually, and I have made the same solemn promise to God.

In terms of my deliverance from watching porn, it appears now to have been a process. The desires still come back from time to time, and sometimes almost as strong as they did before, but my reaction to the temptation is different. I recognize that my faith is being tested, and I realize that I now must fight the good fight of faith daily, knowing that I will always have to trust God for my healing and deliverance in this area of susceptibility regarding pornography. But my God is awesomely powerful, and I am up to the task!

* * *

Dominic's deliverance was not instantaneous. The desire to view porn still tempts him occasionally, but he resists. He has replaced his old habit loop of viewing pornography with a new habit loop that includes reading, praying, attending church and other spiritually fortifying and faith building activities. Through this process his life has been marvelously transformed; he has found deliverance. He is renewing his mind one thought at a time. He is no longer bound.

* * *

A Closing Prayer

Father, I have made the quality decision to cultivate the habit of meeting you daily and to complete The 21-Day Plan. I recognize that I may miss my mark, but when I do, please strengthen me to start again. I pray for discernment to recognize my negative habit loops and in that moment draw upon your strength to replace them with new positive habit loops. In Jesus' Name. Amen.

For an inspirational pick me up, I recommend:

- *When I Rose This Morning* by The Mississippi Mass Choir
- *Good Morning* by Mandisa
- *Cycles* by Jonathan Mcreynolds
- *I Miss My Time With You* by Larnell Harris
- *The Center of My Joy* by Richard Smallwood

Until tomorrow, do this:

Memory Work

1. **TEA=B** – Thoughts affect emotions and emotions affect attitudes, and attitudes produce behavior.

2. **Biblical mind renewal** is the lifelong process of replacing our perspective (thoughts, opinions, and beliefs) with God's perspective as revealed in His Word.

3. Practice reciting the *I Am Significant* mantra (Repeat 10-12 times per day – for example say the *I Am* mantra – 2 times a day per meal and snack and 2 times in the morning and evening while in bed).

   I Am Significant. Why? *(Because)* God loves me and sent his Son to die upon the cross for my sins. He has adopted me into His family and has given me a new name. I am a born-again Christian, fearfully and wonderfully made in the image of God.

4. Practice reciting the My Spiritual Identity acrostic.

   My Spiritual Identity –N-O-W-M-O-V-E-F-O-R-W-A-R-D acrostic. Continue writing the acrostic on a 3x5 card and carry it with you wherever you go. You can also write it on multiple cards, place a card in your Bible, and tape another to your car dash, or bathroom mirror, or workstation. Do not concern yourself with memorizing the scriptures at this point unless you are exceptionally motivated. Just work on memorizing the acrostic a little better each day. In the future, memorize the Scriptures associated with the above acrostic found on pages 108-109.

I Am Significant

I Am Significant. Why? *(Because)* God
loves me and sent his Son to die upon the cross
for my sins. He has adopted me into His family and
has given me a new name. I am a born-again
Christian, fearfully and wonderfully made in the
image of God (John 3:16; Ephesians 1:5; 2 Corinthians
5:17; Psalm 139:14).

Figure 3.6 I Am Significant Mantra

My Spiritual Identity

I Am (a)...

New creation in Christ Jesus (2 Cor. 5:17),
Ordained and chosen by God to fulfill his
    purpose for my life (Jeremiah 1:5; 29:11) *(And I...)*
Walk in the power of the Holy Spirit (Eph. 5:18; Acts 1:8)

Figure 6.1 My Spiritual Identity (Part 1)

My Spiritual Identity

(Because I walk in the power of the Holy Spirit,)
I Am (a,an)...

More than a conqueror (Romans 8:37)
Overcomer (1 John 5:4)
Victor, not a victim (1 Cor. 15:57)
Eternally loved (Romans 8:35, 38-39)

Figure 7.7 My Spiritual Identity (Part 2)

My Spiritual Identity

I Am...

Favored of God (Psalm 5:12)

Oh so bold, confident and courageous (Pr.28:1; 2Tim.1:7)

Reconciled to be a reconciler (2Cor. 5:18-20)

Well protected (Isaiah 54:17; Psalm 23:4-6)

Assured of success (Psalm 1:3; Nehemiah 2:20; Joshua 1:8)

Righteousness of God in Christ (2Cor. 5:21; 1Pet 2:9)

Destined to win if I do not quit (2Cor. 2:14; Romans 8:31)

Figure 7.8 My Spiritual Identity (Part 3)

138

Week 2
Thought Management (Days 8-14)

*"Self-discipline
begins with the
mastery of your thoughts.
If you don't control
what you think,
you can't
control what you do."*

--Napoleon Hill

Day 8

How Your Brain Manages
Your Thoughts and Emotions

"The undisciplined [minds] are slaves to moods, appetites and passions."
--Stephen R. Covey

Daily Food for Thought

• **Brain Fact** The human brain is divided into several semi-distinct parts. The part of the brain that deals with logic or reason is called the frontal lobe. Another part of the brain controls feelings and emotions; this is the limbic system. "The anterior cingulate acts as a kind of fulcrum that controls and balances the activity between the frontal lobe and limbic system."[1]

• **Key Thought** We can maintain a balanced brain chemistry by deliberately focusing on positive, optimistic thoughts and ideas, and we can do this by developing the habit of challenging the negative (destructive, hateful, judgmental, angry, resentful) ideas when they arise in our thinking.

• **Scripture** "Be anxious for nothing, but in everything by prayer and supplication with thanksgiving let your requests be made known to God. And the peace of God, which surpasses all comprehension, will guard your hearts and your minds in Christ Jesus" (Philippians 4:6-7).

140

Daily Reading

While Week 1 focused on the science of thought, Week 2's general focus is thought management. Failing to manage your thoughts and emotions can mean the difference between sickness and health or life and death. I have chosen to begin today's lesson with a thought-provoking story that underscores the importance of this concept.

Nick's Story

Nick, age 45, was an overly pessimistic railroad yard worker, who chronically feared something bad was going to happen to him. Nick's worst fears were confirmed; one summer day, Nick and his fellow yard workers were told that they could go home an hour early in order to celebrate the birthday of one of the foremen. All the workers left, but somehow Nick accidentally locked himself in a refrigerated boxcar that had been brought into the yard for maintenance. The boxcar was empty and not connected to any of the trains. When Nick realized that he was locked in the refrigerated boxcar, he panicked. He began beating on the doors so hard that his arms and fists became bloody. He screamed, but his coworkers had already gone home to get ready for the party and nobody could hear Nick's desperate calls for help.

Again, and again he called out until finally his voice became a raspy whisper. Aware he was in a potentially lethal situation, Nick found himself guessing that the temperature in the unit was well below freezing. He feared the worst. He thought," What am I going to do? If I don't get out of here, I'm going to freeze to death. There's no way I can survive in here all night." The more he thought about his circumstances the more grimly he felt the frigid air about him. With the door hopelessly locked and having no apparent means of escape, he sat down to await his inevitable death by freezing or suffocation. To pass the time, he decided to chronicle his demise. He found a pen in his shirt pocket and noticed an old piece of cardboard in the corner of the car. Shivering uncontrollably, he scribbled a message to his family. In the message, Nick detailed his tragic circumstance as best he could. "Getting so cold. Body numb. If I don't get out soon, these will probably be my last words."[2]

The next day, Nick's coworkers returned to work and found Nick crumpled in the corner of the refrigerated car dead. Nick's subsequent autopsy revealed that he had frozen to death. Astonishingly; Nick died of hypothermia in a sixty-one-degree Fahrenheit refrigerated boxcar. The refrigerated unit of the car had been broken for some time and had been pulled into the yard for repair. This is a true story, and it illustrates the incredible power of the mind and the devastating effects it can wreak in our lives if we neglect to manage our negative thoughts.

Could it be that your negative thoughts are figuratively killing you, narrowing the scope of your outlook, shortening your life span by infecting your body with all sorts of maladies? [3]

Failing to manage our negative thoughts may not kill us overnight, as with Nick, but cumulatively they have the potential to do so. We must learn to effectively manage them. Thought management is not automatic. We must diligently employ our maturity, spirituality, and intelligence to guide our thoughts favorably and wholesomely.

> *The anterior cingulate controls and balances the activity between the frontal lobe and limbic system.*

The Brain's Thought Manager

What happened to Nick? How is it possible to freeze to death in sixty-degree weather? Let us glean some keen insight from Drs. Newberg and Waldman, authors of the book, *How God Changes Your Brain.* In their book, they explain how our thoughts are regulated within our brains. They suggest imagining the brain divided into two halves. They invite us to conceive of the brain this way: one-half of the brain—the frontal lobe—controls logic and reason, and the other half of the brain—the limbic system—controls feelings and emotions. Our focus now is the purpose of the anterior cingulate (AC). "The anterior cingulate acts as a kind of fulcrum that controls and balances the activity between the frontal lobe and limbic system."[4] (See Figure 8.1 below).

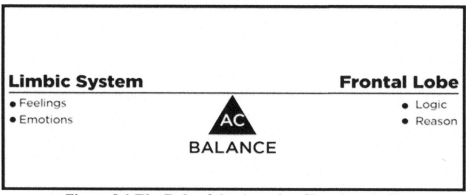

Figure 8.1 The Role of the Anterior Cingulate (AC)

If we were to analyze Nick's demise, we might quickly surmise that the most probable cause of Nick's death, from a neuroscience perspective, was the result of a weakness in the anterior cingulate, very much related to linear thinking. The results were from an overly stimulated amygdala. The amygdala [uh-mig-duh-lee] is that portion of the brain "responsible for processing emotional memories as well as storing them in the long-term memory."[5] When Nick became panic

142

stricken, fear tipped the balance in favor of the limbic system, shutting down Nick's frontal lobe, where logic and reason reside.

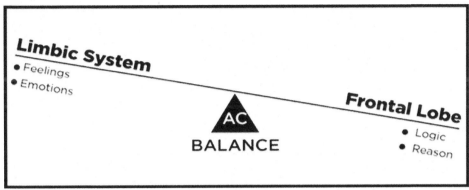

Figure 8.2 Limbic System Shutting Down the Frontal Lobe

Evidence supporting a limbic imbalance is confirmed by Nick's frantic behavior of banging on the boxcar door until his hands bled and ear-piercing screaming until his voice became a raspy whisper. His limbic system overload prevented his weakened anterior cingulate (AC) from balancing his inter-lobe electro-chemistry. This kind of correction likely would have allowed Nick to logically reason a way out of his predicament. It is worthwhile to reflect that in such a frenzied state, Nick believed that he was freezing to death as he was trapped within a sixty-one-degree freight car.

When the emotion-laden limbic system is frenetically charged, it has the potential to severely impede the logic and reasoning capacities in the frontal lobe, rendering the individual a pitiful pawn of his or her unbridled emotions.[6] For this reason, I contend, failing to properly regulate your thoughts and emotions can sometimes even mean the difference between life and death.

To further enhance your understanding of the role of the anterior cingulate (AC), I will compare it to a childhood object that is familiar to many of us, the seesaw. Imagine the anterior cingulate as a seesaw inside of your brain. *(To identify the location of the anterior cingulate in the brain, see Figure 10.2)* Visualize the seesaw. As one side of the seesaw goes up, the other side goes down. Whenever fear or anxiety or other aversive experiences upset our brain chemistry, the limbic side of the seesaw goes up, and the frontal lobe functions go down, suppressing logic and reasoning capacities. However, when the frontal lobe side of the seesaw goes up, the limbic system side goes down, thus suppressing the (emotional) limbic system.

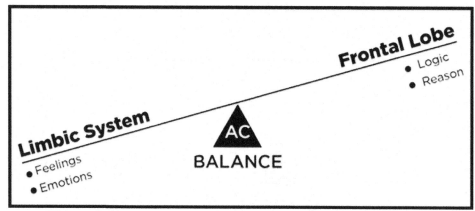

Figure 8.3 Frontal Lobe Shutting Down the Limbic System

The AC is the fulcrum upon which the seesaw rests. If the AC is weak, it will not be able to properly balance the brain chemicals, causing the brain to get stuck in one position or the other for a protracted period of time. If chemically tilted to favor the limbic system, you can end up an emotional wreck (like Nick). On the other hand, if you are stuck in a chemical tilt favoring the frontal lobe, you can end up feeling emotionless, devoid of affect much like Mr. Spock from the iconic 1960s television series *Star Trek*. Remember him? Let me caution you, both extremes are equally hazardous to emotional, mental, and relational health. The AC is the thought manager for the brain, designed to keep your brain in perfect chemical balance.

Ways to Strengthen Your Anterior Cingulate (AC)

According to Newberg and Waldman, to regulate your thoughts "it is essential that you nurture that inner negotiator (anterior cingulate), which is what meditation and spiritual practices do."[7] The information that you will be exposed to in *The 21-Day Plan* is designed to strengthen your anterior cingulate so it can perform at its optimum level. Your anterior cingulate is strengthened as you consistently engage in the following spiritual practices:

1. Think God-honoring thoughts (Day 1).
2. Refuse to define yourself by the satanically influenced negative thoughts that pop into your head (Day 2).
3. Allow your born-again spirit to influence your thoughts, and bring your soul (mind, will and emotions) and body in alignment with your spirit so that you can walk in victory (Day 3).
4. Use your imagination to visualize a positive you with a more promising future (Day 4).
5. Rewire your brain to think positive thoughts to replace negative ones (Day5).

6. Speak words of life and hope versus destruction and pessimism (Day 6).
7. Establish spiritual practices such as prayer and a daily quiet time, which includes such things as reading the Bible, memorizing scripture, joined with times of spontaneous praise, worship, and thanksgiving to God for his many blessings (Day 7).
8. Consistently check, challenge and change your negative thoughts and replace them with positive, faith filled, God honoring thoughts (Days 8-21).
9. Listen to inspirational music (Days 1-21).

Additionally, meditating upon Biblical truths strengthens the anterior cingulate. The concept of meditation has suffered a bad rap in most conservative Christian circles, primarily due to Eastern mysticism and New Age practices, but let me enlighten you. Satan did not invent meditation. He is a thief; Satan stole the concept of meditation from the Bible. In the KJV translation, the term meditation or meditate is used as many as 20 times, as exemplified in the following select passages:

- "My *meditation* of him shall be sweet: I will be glad in the Lord" (Psalm 104:34).
- "O how I love thy law! It is my *meditation* all the day" (Psalm 119:97).
- "But his delight is in the law of the Lord; and in his law doth he *meditate* day and night" (Psalm 1:2).

Biblical meditation means to ponder, think about, or to mull over in the mind. Meditation was invented by God. For example, you might choose to meditate upon God's love for you. I recall a situation where a Bible teacher explained how one might meditate in this way:

You would begin by asking the Holy Spirit to reveal that truth [God's love] to you. You might sit quietly in your prayer time, thinking about God's love. During that time, you might reflect on times when you've experienced God's love. You then might study scriptures that speak of His love, maybe even slowly and thoughtfully studying them, one at a time. Or you may choose to study the word 'love' in Greek, Hebrew and Aramaic. This contemplative process may last for a day, a week, a month or longer.[8]

Such meditation serves to strengthen the anterior cingulate by helping it to regulate and balance the chemicals in your brain. David the psalmist declared, "I will meditate on Your precepts, and contemplate Your ways" (Psalm 119:15 NKJV). God invented meditation; Satan perverted it. I herein contend that the issue is not meditation per se, but the *focus* of your meditation. Newberg and Walden point out that meditation "is one of the best ways to enhance the neural functioning of your brain."[9] *The 21-Day Plan* will encourage you to meditate on the Triune God, His love, His Word, and His proclamations concerning your true identity in Christ.

David's Story

Prayer and meditating on God's Word serves to strengthen the anterior cingulate.

Having examined the role and function of the anterior cingulate, let's now turn our attention to the Holy Scriptures to examine an incident in the life of David. Allow me to set the historical context. After killing Goliath, young David spent the next several years fleeing from insanely jealous Saul (king of Israel), who saw David as a threat to his rule as king. David, while on the run, in order to support himself and a growing number of loyal comrades, picked up a few odd jobs. The story is recorded in 1 Samuel 25:4-35. David and his men took it upon themselves to guard the sheep of Nabal during the sheep-shearing season. As was the custom, they expected compensation for their security detail work. Afterward, David sent ten of his servants to Nabal's house to request food and supplies from him. Nabal, who owned the sheep, responded in full limbic mode:

Nabal tore into them, "Who is this David? Who is this son of Jesse? The country is full of runaway servants these days. Do you think I'm going to take good bread and wine and meat freshly butchered for my sheepshearers and give it to men I've never laid eyes on? Who knows where they've come from?" (1 Samuel 25:9-11 MSG).

David's emissaries communicated this to David, who responded likewise in a fully hyperactive limbic state.

David said [to his army of men], "Strap on your swords!" They all strapped on their swords, David and his men, and set out, four hundred of them... [David saying to himself] "That sure was a waste, guarding everything this man had out in the wild so that nothing he had was lost—and now he rewards me with insults. A real slap in the face! May God do his worst to me if Nabal and every cur in his misbegotten brood aren't dead meat by morning!" (1 Samuel 25:12-13, 20-22 MSG).

Remember how the seesaw works, when one side goes up, the other side goes down. Therefore, when the frontal lobe side is up, the limbic side is down and when the limbic side is up, the frontal lobe side is down. David's limbic portion of his brain was in full tilt, thus suppressing his rational thinking, resulting in an inclination to commit homicide. But God had provided a way for David to escape such a horrific fate. His escape came from a very unexpected source.

Meanwhile, one of the young shepherds told Abigail, Nabal's wife, what had happened: "David sent messengers from the backcountry to salute our master, but he tore into them with insults. Yet these men treated us very well. They took nothing from us and didn't take advantage of us all the time we were in the fields. They formed a wall around us, protecting us day and night all the time we were out tending the sheep. Do something quickly because big trouble is ahead for our master and all of us. Nobody can talk to him. He's impossible—a real brute!" (1 Samuel 25:14-17 MSG).

Abigail, the faithful wife, sprang into action to intercept David. Unlike the men, she operated in concert with her frontal lobe.

How many times has a close friend or caring confidant, or significant other saved you from disaster?

As soon as Abigail saw David, she got off her donkey and fell on her knees at his feet, her face to the ground in homage, saying, "My master, let me take the blame! Let me speak to you. Listen to what I have to say. Don't dwell on what that brute Nabal did. He acts out the meaning of his name: Nabal, Fool. Foolishness oozes from him. "I wasn't there when the young men my master sent arrived. I didn't see them. And now, my master, as God lives and as you live, God has kept you from this avenging murder—and may your enemies, all who seek my master's harm, end up like Nabal! Now take this gift [the provision he originally asked for] that I, your servant girl, have brought to my master, and give it to the young men who follow in the steps of my master. She got up, and then bowed down, face to the ground, saying, "I'm your servant, ready to do anything you want. I'll even wash the feet of my master's servants!" (1 Samuel 25:23-27,41 MSG).

After hearing Abigail's heartfelt plea for mercy, moved with compassion, David replies:

Blessed be God, the God of Israel. He sent you to meet me! And blessed be your good sense! Bless you for keeping me from murder and taking charge of looking out for me. A close call! As God lives, the God of Israel who kept me from hurting you, if you had not come as quickly as you did, stopping me in my tracks, by morning there would have been nothing left of Nabal but dead meat" (1 Samuel 25:32-34 MSG).

Juxtapose to Nick's case study, let's analyze neurologically what probably took place in David's brain that calmed him. David was initially operating from a limbic system at full tilt, but Abigail disrupted his automatic negative thoughts (ANTS) processes by pleading with David to not respond in anger to Nabal's insult. In so doing, she managed to engage David's rational mind (his frontal lobe) and talk him down, to bring him to his finer sensibilities (1 Samuel 25:26-28).

Confronted by Abigail, David was now faced with a choice. Would he respond emotionally or rationally? By the grace of God, David decided to allow the rational side of his brain, his frontal lobe, to rule the day.

By pausing to ponder Abigail's plea to spare the life of her husband and the lives of the entire household, David gave his anterior cingulate (AC) time to balance the chemicals in his brain to create a perfect chemistry for him to make a rational and neurologically sound decision rather than an irrational, foolish, and emotional decision. Instead of responding in anger, David chose to respond rationally and compassionately. Not a single life was lost.

How many of you remember a time when you were a child when a parent or some other adult said to you, or advised you, when you were getting very angry, to pause and count to 10? Did you ever wonder why? By pausing to count to 10 you were giving your anterior cingulate (AC) time to stabilize the chemicals in your brain—tilting the seesaw away from the limbic and in the direction of the frontal lobe, where reason and logic dominate. The adults giving this advice probably had no scientific understanding of it, but modern research in the field of neurology has revealed that this is definitely what is happening.

According to Newberg and Waldman, a strong frontal lobe-AC circuit always inhibits anxiety, depression, and rage.[10] David had a strong AC because he spent a lot of time in the presence of God praying, meditating, journaling, singing, praising, and writing the Psalms. All of these spiritual practices proved to strengthen David's anterior cingulate. As these spiritual practices worked for David, they will also work for us, if we diligently practice them.

Questions for Reflection

1. Is this your first introduction to the role of your brain's anterior cingulate?

Yes or No

2. Take a moment and reflect upon an experience of your own that propelled your limbic system into an extreme overload, getting you hot and bothered, angry or stressed, suppressing your frontal lobe's rational functions. Recall exactly how the episode occurred. Did it continue to an extreme, producing something regrettable or terrible, or was there a moment of calming, where you regained your composer? On reflection, what are your thoughts?

A Check Up From The Neck Up

How healthy is your anterior cingulate? According to Newberg and Waldman, a healthy AC system encompasses these five functions:

1. Ability to shift attention
2. Cognitive flexibility (adaptability)
3. Movement from idea to idea
4. Ability to see options
5. Ability to "go along with the flow"[11]

However, an unhealthy cingulate system will frequently result in the following problems:

1. Cognitive inflexibility ("It's my way or the highway!")
2. Getting stuck on thoughts (obsessions) or behaviors (i.e. compulsive disorders)
3. Worrying
4. Argumentativeness
5. Road rage
6. Holding on to hurts from the past
7. Oppositional behavior/uncooperativeness/recalcitrance
8. Addictive behaviors (alcohol or drug abuse, eating disorders, etc.) [12]
9. A tendency to say "No" automatically[13] (the problem that almost cost Nabal his life)

When your anterior cingulate is unhealthy, it makes you more susceptible to automatic negative thoughts (ANTS), other kinds of unhealthy thinking, and mood swings. When you find yourself in such lamentable states, the devil will often attempt to attribute it to your moral character, perhaps a dearth of spirituality, and bury you under a load of guilt and self-condemnation. However, I contend it's probably an anterior cingulate problem. Work on strengthening your AC by doing something constructive. Idleness is often a very significant factor in chronic debilitating negativity. This observation is entirely consistent with the familiar maxim, "Idle minds are the devil's workshop."

Hooked on A Feeling? How to Get Out of a Rut

If you are like most people, then you have at one time or another experienced being hooked on a negative thought or feeling that you just could not seem to shake. The thought continued to reverberate in your mind. Neuroscientists refer to this familiar phenomenon as "brain looping".[14] Based on what you have learned here in Day 8 about the anterior cingulate seesaw, it is plain to see how the brain can become stuck on an obsessive negative thought. A "stuck" person might say, for example, "I hate being divorced (eight years later)" or "I have to have it my way!" or "You hurt me years ago, and I'll never forgive that" or "Things will never change" or "That was too humiliating." [15] Does any of this sound familiar?

If you find yourself stuck on a negative thought, Dr. Daniel Amen, author of *Magnificent Mind at Any Age*, suggests that you engage in one or more of the following tactics and activities to distract your mind.

1. Distract yourself and come back to the problem or issue later.

Make a list of all the things you could do to distract yourself. Do not concern yourself with whether or not these things seem especially productive. The purpose is only to re-orient the mind, not to necessarily achieve anything else. These proactive diversions may include: "singing a favorite song, listening to music that makes you feel positive, taking a walk, doing a chore, playing with a pet, or practicing structured meditation"[16] Concurring with Amen, one sure-fire way to disrupt a brain loop, and especially a negative brain loop, is to listen to a motivational spiritual song many times, until it shifts your outlook and bolsters your mood. In this way we turn worry into worship. Don't be afraid to dance, sing, hum along or cry. Feel free to let the music overwhelm your soul and allow you a deeper sense of connection (with God and/or with other human beings).

2. Write out options and solutions.[17]

Writing what you are worried about on paper helps your mind to deal with the issue in a rational way. For example, "My finances are dwindling. How can I make more money?" Make a list of all the many things you could do to help remedy the problem, at least in part. By doing this, you will be suppressing the limbic (worried, anxious, etc.) portion of your brain.

3. Seek the counsel of others.[18]

Whenever you find yourself unable to get relief from a negative thought or concern, it may be to your advantage to call a trusted friend with whom you could share your problem; by doing this, you are, of course, seeking counsel. Oftentimes, just discussing our mental perturbations with someone provides an emotional release. The person you confide in may suggest options and perspectives you may not have previously considered. Even if the person offers no strategies or solutions, just receiving their empathy can feel appreciably reassuring. Wise King Solomon said, "If you don't ask for advice, your plans will fail. With many advisors, they will succeed" (Proverbs 15:22, ERV).

4. Recite and memorize the serenity prayer.[19]

Dr. Amen recommends that you recite the serenity prayer every time you are troubled by a chronic negative. For those who are not familiar with it, the prayer states, *"God, grant me the serenity to accept the things I cannot change, the courage to change the things I can, and the wisdom to know the difference."* Dr. Amen's advice echoes the teaching of the Apostle Paul, who said, "Be anxious for nothing, but in everything by prayer and supplication with thanksgiving let your requests be made known to God. And the peace of God, which surpasses all comprehension, will guard your hearts and your minds in Christ Jesus" (Philippians 4:6-7). Prayer is one of those spiritual practices that strengthens the anterior cingulate, thus allowing you to release pent up emotions through the limbic system, allowing your brain chemicals time to stabilize. When worrisome ideas or memories act to dominate your mind, repeat your "I Am Significant" mantra and your "My Spiritual Identity – N-O-W-M-O-V-E-F-O-R-W-A-R-D" acrostic until you experience a satisfactory diminishment.

5. Don't try to convince someone else who is stuck: take a break and come back later.[20]

"When another person is 'stuck' on a thought or behavior, logical reasoning usually will not work."[21] People are not able to listen when they are experiencing deeply emotional (AC intensive) problems. When we are stuck on the same spiraling ruminations, we tend to revisit the same troubling image, memory, and thought pattern again and again without hearing or understanding the point of view of others. To disengage stuck people, move on to another subject to distract them. This strategy can save your marriage or relationship and spare you the pain of hours spent in stressful, fruitless contention. The Bible says, "A fool is right in his own eyes…" (Proverbs 12:15). Save your breath. That is exactly what Abigail, Nabal's wife did.

Abigail must have learned this principle through many years of interaction with her husband, Nabal. Interestingly, Abigail didn't consult with her husband about her plans to compensate David and his men. The Bible specifically says, "…But she did not tell her husband Nabal" (1 Samuel 25:19). Why? The man was stuck in limbic mode. He would not have been able to receive a single word she said in that mode. Remember, the man's name is Nabal, which translates as *fool*. It is foolish to think we can argue a drunk into reasonableness, and likewise it is foolishness to believe we can argue a person in full limbic mode into reason.

Like a good and clever wife, she told him the following morning, and boy was he shocked.

When Abigail got home she found Nabal presiding over a huge banquet. He was in high spirits—and very, very drunk. So she didn't tell him anything of what she'd done until morning. But in the morning, after Nabal had sobered up, she told him the whole story. Right then and there he had a heart attack and fell into a coma…and he died. (1 Samuel 25:36-38 MSG).

We see here that an overactive limbic function can cause a person great harm and even bring about his or her death, just as it was with modern day Nick.

Question for Reflection

Which of Dr. Amen's "unstuck" strategies will you use the next time your brain is troublingly looping? Why?

_____

_____

The Conscience and Subconscious Mind

A final word about Nick. In addition to his limbic system hijacking his brain, there was another law at work in Nick's head. I described Nick as "an overly pessimistic railroad yard worker who chronically feared something bad was going to happen to him." Nick's worst fears were confirmed. I mention this again to illustrate how the conscious and subconscious mind work in tandem to bring certain experiences to pass in our lives based on the beliefs we hold. The Reverend Dr. Joseph Murphy, author of *The Power of Your Subconscious Mind*, makes the following observation:

> There are two levels of your mind—the conscious or rational level, and the subconscious, or irrational level. You think with your conscious mind, and whatever you habitually think sinks down into your subconscious mind, which creates according to the nature of your thoughts.... Whatever you claim mentally, [positive or negative] and feel as true, your subconscious mind will accept and bring forth into your experience.... It works by association of ideas, and uses every bit of knowledge that you have gathered in your lifetime to bring about its purpose. As soon as your subconscious mind accepts any idea, it proceeds to put it into effect immediately.... The law of your mind is this: You will get a reaction or response from your subconscious mind according to the nature of the thought or idea you hold in your conscious mind.

Nick feared (consciously) that some tragedy would befall him. Hence, his subconscious mind arranged things in his physical environment to set the stage for the fulfillment of his long-held pessimistic belief.

FYI: The limbic system is responsible for both pleasure and pain. On the pleasurable side, the limbic system releases a neurotransmitter called 'dopamine,' which creates pleasurable feelings[22] like happiness, excitement, joy, love and laughter. This is its positive side. However, today's lesson focused on the harmful side of the limbic system and the array of negative emotions that come consequent to an insufficiently regulated limbic system.

**A Closing Prayer**

Dear God, help me to use my brain to work for me and not against me. When my emotions sweep me up in anxiety and fear, may I always remember to trust my spiritual training and push back on my fears and receive your peace in the place of my unease, your strength in the place of my weakness. In Jesus' name. Amen.

For an inspirational pick me up, I recommend:

- *I Never Lost My Praise* by The Brooklyn Tabernacle Choir
- *How Can It Be* by Lauren Daigle
- *He Brought Me This Far* by Andrae Crouch
- *My Soul is Anchored* by Douglas Miller

Until tomorrow, do this:

Memory Work

1. Practice reciting the *I Am Significant* mantra (Repeat 10-12 times per day – for example say the *I Am* mantra – 2 times a day per meal and snack and 2 times in the morning and evening while in bed).

2. **I Am Significant**. Why? *(Because)* God loves me and sent his Son to die upon the cross for my sins. He has adopted me into His family and has given me a new name. I am a born-again Christian, fearfully and wonderfully made in the image of God.

3. Practice reciting the *My Spiritual Identity.*

    My Spiritual Identity – N-O-W-M-O-V-E-F-O-R-W-A-R-D acrostic. **Do not concern yourself with memorizing scriptures at this point** unless you feel especially inspired to do so. Just memorize *the transitional statements* and what each letter stands for. You will be glad you did! *The four mantras you are encouraged to memorize are displayed in a form usable as 3x5 cards on page 138.*

The Filthy Five:
The 5 Negative Thoughts That You MUST Take Captive to Remain Positive

It is hard to fight an enemy who has outposts in your head.
--Sally Kempton

• **Brain Fact** "Thoughts are basically electrical impulses, chemicals, and neurons."[1]

• **Key Thought** All of our negative thought habits fall into five categories—the "Filthy Five."

• **Scripture** "Keep your mind clear and be alert. Your opponent the devil is prowling around like a roaring lion as he looks for someone to devour. Be firm in the faith and resist him…" (1 Peter 5:8-9a NOG).

Daily Reading

Have you ever had one of the moments when the light bulb went off and everything made sense? Oprah would call it an "A-ha" moment. After many years of stumbling around in the darkness as far as how to gain control of my undesirable thoughts, the light bulb metaphorically came on for me personally when I discovered the ability to organize my own psyche torment into five distinct categories. They proved to be pivotal and revelatory in enabling me to divide my negative thoughts into categories. Given the ability to categorize and understand the thoughts, I was empowered to move forward in mastering my mind. I had suffered much mental duress for years, but the Lord eventually revealed to me a better way to think. I had to learn to control my thoughts rather than let my thoughts control me. I had to do this because the thoughts were emotionally ruinous. As neurological science informs us that the typical brain encounters between twelve thousand and fifty-five thousand thoughts per day,[2] and as much as three quarters of these are negative, I began to wonder how I could get control of my thought life. Through my research, I discovered that all my negative thoughts fell into five categories. Hence, I was personally responsible for guarding my mind against five categories of thoughts. For my convenience, I labeled them "The Filthy Five". Almost certainly, you have been troubled by some of these thoughts. If you today find yourself drowning in a sea of negative thoughts, consider this lesson a lifeline. Take hold and don't let go.

The key to mastering your negative thoughts begins with first identifying them, and secondly learning to take them captive. These are the five categories of thoughts that you and I must learn to push back on if we hope to remain positive and hopeful.

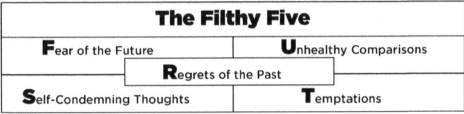

Figure 9.1 The Filthy Five

#1 - Fear of the Future

The first of the "Filthy Five" thoughts that believers must avoid at all costs is the fear of the future. For purposes of our discussion here, fear of the future is defined as anxiety about what unpleasant things tomorrow may bring. A common indication that you are fearing the future is when you find yourself mentally verbalizing, *"What if...."* Today, for example, you may be fretting over speculations about future financial, relationship, or medical concerns. If your thinking begins, "What if..." or *"How am I...,"* it is likely that the gist of the thought is expressive of a fear. If you are mentally stuck on fears about the future, you will find yourself in a negative spin cycle that will likely deplete your experience of joy and fulfillment.

God wants His children to learn to live in the present. He wants us to learn to live in the *now,* not fearing the future, because your heavenly Father has promised to take care of all your tomorrows. Jesus said, "Don't get worked up about what may or may not happen tomorrow. God will help you deal with whatever hard things come up when the time comes" (Matthew 6:34 MSG). This verse is translated elsewhere, "Refuse to worry about tomorrow, but deal with each challenge that comes your way, one day at a time. Tomorrow will take care of itself" (Matthew 6:34 TPT). When fears of the future attack your mind, repeat this verse until the peace of God, working though the anterior cingulate (AC), begins to stabilize your brain chemicals (Day 8). If you are mentally feeding upon fears about the future, you will find yourself in a negative spiral that will prove very harmful. Dwelling upon fear of the future will release negative toxins into the bloodstream.[3] This has been well established by medical and neurological research.

God's prophet Elijah fell prey to a series of fear-of-the-future thoughts when the wicked Queen Jezebel sent word by a messenger, "I swear that by this time *tomorrow,* you will be just as dead as those prophets (1 Kings 19:2ERV).

When we find ourselves *dreading* undesirable activities before they happen, that too is fear of the future. For example, "I dread going into work tomorrow."

We need to learn to develop mindfulness. Mindfulness is a term used in cognitive behavioral therapy (CBT). Mindfulness is the mental practice or habit of maintaining a positive mental focus without emotionally reacting to external stimuli. In other words, mindfulness is the practice of not being emotionally moved or shaken by adverse or intrusive thoughts or events.[4] God wants us to respond to the experience of negative fears without being emotionally devastated or consumed by them, to not be moved by them (Psalm 62). He wants us to adopt the attitude of godly self-direction and positivity. Knowing by relying upon God's power, we possess the inner strength to face every future challenge with poise, determination and confidence.

Questions for Reflection

1. How would you phrase your own "What if" questions regarding the future?

_____

_____

_____

2. What are the feelings those thoughts seem to generate?

_____

_____

_____

#2 - Unhealthy Comparisons

A recent TV airline commercial advertisement showed customers sitting in first class and other customers sitting in coach. A man seated in coach stands up and peers through a curtain into first class. He apparently wants to see how delightfully luxurious the accommodations are there. A female flight attendant observing his approach, pulls the curtain closed with a disapproving look. Then, on the screen appear the words, "FIRST CLASS IS THERE TO REMIND YOU THAT YOU ARE NOT IN FIRST CLASS."

Unhealthy comparisons comprise the second of our "Filthy Five" categories. We must purge our thoughts of these sorts of notions if we are to keep our minds free from toxic, discouraging attitudes and emotions. Those who constantly compare themselves unfavorably will find themselves on a perineal emotional seesaw.

Here's the trap: When you compare yourself to someone whom you feel superior to, then your self-esteem rises. However, when you compare yourself to someone else whom you feel lesser than, your self-esteem plummets.

You'll know that you are engaging in unhealthy comparisons when you find yourself thinking or saying, "I wish I were more like _____ " or "I wish I had _____." Satan desires believers to stay mired in negativity, insecurity and self-doubt. Satan would like us to keep measuring ourselves against others, because Satan knows that feelings of inadequacy and low self-esteem will result. The end result of our unwise and unwarranted comparisons is an impoverished self-concept.

The Apostle Paul, who himself resisted engaging in unhealthy comparisons, said this about those who do, "We won't dare compare ourselves with those who think so much of themselves. But they are foolish to compare themselves with themselves" (2 Corinthians 10:12 CEV).

A classical biblical illustration of unhealthy comparison is found in the unstable relationship between King Saul and his army commander, David. King Saul's unhealthy comparison between himself and David is evident in the following story:

> It happened as they were coming, when David returned from killing the Philistine, that the women came out of all the cities of Israel, singing and dancing, to meet King Saul, with tambourines, with joy and with musical instruments. The women sang as they played and said, "Saul has slain his thousands, and David his ten thousands." Then Saul became very angry, for this saying displeased him; and he said, "They have ascribed to David ten thousands, but to me they have ascribed thousands. Now what more can he have but the kingdom?" Saul looked at David with suspicion from that day on (1 Samuel 18:6-8).

Hence, Saul became green with envy and looked upon David with extreme suspicion. Saul's internal reaction to the women's songs fed into his unhealthy

157

comparison of himself to David. David may have killed ten thousand, but Saul was still the King of Israel. However, Saul's unhealthy construction made him feel inferior and inadequate. He resolved in his heart to kill David, viewing him as a threat to his royal authority.

Advertising executives on Madison Avenue, in order to keep their consumer buying-driven economy going at full speed, keep us spending by causing us, in subtle and overt ways, to engage in unhealthy comparisons. For example, picture a situation where you are standing in a checkout line at a grocery store and there your eyes fall upon the covers of several popular magazines, among them, *Better Homes and Gardens.* On the cover you see, an immaculately manicured lawn with a long, winding aggregate driveway lined with variegated flora in the distance. The publishers who select such photos are aware that we are likely to feel envious of such an idyllic surrounding. They encourage us to admire, aspire and compare. A resultant comparison makes you feel that your humble abode falls woefully short. Now you know why the magazine is entitled, *Better Homes and Gardens* i.e. *better than* your home and gardens. Hence, you place the magazine back in the rack. The next magazine reads on the cover, "The 100 Most Beautiful People." You begin thumbing through the magazine and in less than thirty seconds you feel uglier than you've felt in decades. There's Forbes. Surely, in those pages are some of the richest people in America. Want to feel poor? Open that magazine.

Do you see how we are manipulated by a superficial, materialist, commercial, status-crazed culture? See how you are being manipulated?

But such unhealthy comparisons are not limited to slick advertising campaigns. We frequently compare our IQ, grades, credit rating, neighborhood, school, salary, our children, our occupation, and educational attainments etc. with others. Pastors of smaller churches often unwisely compare their own respective church to the mega churches or to the televangelists' churches on TV. Sometimes we might compare ourselves to another person in church who may appear more sincere or emotional in prayer or worship, but such unhealthy comparisons are subtle traps of the enemy designed to diminish our self-worth.

Questions for Reflection

1. In what other areas does Madison Aveune-style advertizing techniques encourage unhealthy comparisons?

_____

_____

_____

2. What activities or indulgences (TV programs, magizines, internet surfing, social networking etc.) would you be willing to give up in order to free yourself from this error of comparing?

_____

_____

3. In what ways and areas of your life might you be engaging in unhealthy comparisons?

_____

_____

#3 - Regrets of the Past

In scripture (Isaiah 43:18; Philippians 3:13), we are cautioned against dwelling on regrets of the past because Satan uses our past regrets to keep us from ful-filling our God-ordained destiny. You are to learn from your past, not live in your past. Satan wants to keep you bound to your history, so you don't fulfill your destiny. As we dwell negatively on the past, we don't solve anything or come nearer to God's perspective; we just spiral within the negativity and come no closer to understanding our relationship to God and our value in His eyes. These negative images place us at our worst and doing things such as being ashamed or humiliated. The spiraling is like many flaming arrows which ignite other feelings such as disappointment, disillusionment, grief, sorrow, anger, resentment, and bit-terness. You know that you are engaging in regrets of the past when you find yourself thinking or saying such things as, "If only..." or "If only I could redo it," or "I wish (the situation had not happened)," etc. Sometimes the negative corresponds to an image from the past with an associated feeling. In these cases, it may not be worded, but still felt, keeping us tied up in the past.

> *Satan wants to keep you bound to your history, so you don't fulfill your destiny.*

In the Bible, King Saul, nearing the end of his life, reflecting upon his life and past regrets, laments, "I have sinned, return, my son David, for I will no more do thee harm, because my life hath been pre-cious in thy eyes this day: for it appeareth that I have done foolishly, and have been ignorant in *very many things*." (1 Samuel 26:21 DRA). To state it more emphatically, Saul is saying, "I have played the fool!" If we are honest with our-selves, we've all played the fool and have many regrets of the past. However, let me caution you! *We must learn from our past, not live in it.* Don't let your histo-ry rob you of your destiny. Sometimes an embarrassment or regret from the past

159

can afford us some improved understanding of things, but most often there is nothing to be learned except this: *I am no different than anyone else, we all make mistakes and suffer embarrassments, and we all fail.*

In Days 10 and 11, we will detail how to process regrets of the past so that you can be set free from the shackles that have held you in bondage for so long. The prophet Isaiah had this to say, reflective of God's perspective on common regrets of the past:

Do not call to mind the former things,
Or ponder things of the past.
Behold, I will do something new (Isaiah 43:18).

God is doing new things in your life. Your past does not determine your destiny; however, your present-day choices do. Focus on the present. That's key. The open door to your God-ordained destiny is in front of you, not behind you. Constructive present moment decision making is not generally aided by looking back.

Questions for Reflection

1. Do you frequently struggle with negativity about the past?

_____

_____

2. Have you come to the place where you are ready to accept God's forgiveness for your past actions, so you can forgive yourself and others, and move forward in your life?

Yes/No

3. Can you identify any forgiveness you may need to seek so you can move on? If so, do it today. As appropriate, pray for the relevant forgiveness and move on with your life. Refuse to remain in bondage.

#4 - Self-Condemning Thoughts

Self-condemning thoughts are a natural consequence of engaging in unhealthy comparisons. They could be rooted in regrets of the past or a sense of inadequacy in the face of life's vicissitudes. Self-condemning thoughts may originate (perhaps long ago) in the criticisms of a parent or authority figure, acrimony within an intimate relationship, memories of sexual or emotional abuse, a sense of abandonment, a loss or failure of some kind, or regrets, errors, and failures related to adolescence or immaturity.

Similar events were the basis of the self-condemning thoughts expressed by the "prodigal" or "lost" son described in Luke 15:11-24. He left the safety and security of his home to go "sow his wild oats." However, once his money ran out, his so-called friends thinned

> *Self-condemning thoughts are apt to lead down a slippery slope into debasing self-talk, self-hatred, and or negative labeling.*

out and he was left all alone–broke, busted and disgusted. After hitting rock bottom, he bemoaned, "I am no longer worthy..." (Luke 15:18-19). Self-condemning thoughts, if left unchecked, are apt to lead down a slippery slope into debasing self-talk, self-hatred, and or negative labeling. Negative labeling is rooted in the limbic system.

Questions for Reflection

1. The prodigal son labeled himself *unworthy*. What kind of labels have you habitually attached to yourself?

_____

_____

2. Do you recall from Day 3 who first labeled you?

_____

_____

3. How has the I Am Significant mantra and N-O-W-M-O-V-E-F-O-R-W-A-R-D acrostic been working in helping you gain control over self-condemning thoughts and negative labels?

_____

_____

_____

#5 - Temptations

The last of the "Filthy Five" is temptation. When overcome with negative emotions, a person is more susceptible to succumbing to temptation. The temptation may be to throw in the towel and quit, flee instead of fight, become resentful and pout instead of actively engaging and praising; perhaps you overeat or retaliate rather than wait on God to address your feeling of being transgressed. Have you been tempted recently to give someone a piece of your mind because he or she (figuratively) tapped danced on your last nerve? In Gethsemane, just before his capture, Jesus warned his melancholy disciples to, "Keep watching and praying that you may not come into temptation; the spirit is willing, but the flesh is weak" (Mark 14:38; Matthew 26:41).

A classic Biblical example of someone giving in to temptation is found in the story of Samson and Delilah. Samson continued his liaison with Delilah up until the time she seduced him by cropping his hair (Judges 16:19-21). But let's not be too hard on "ole' Samson. We are all a mess in the flesh, so to speak. The story of Samson illustrates what happens when we allow our flesh to master our spirit (Galatians 5:17-21).

A final advisement about tempting thoughts: The crazy and bizarre thoughts and mental images that pop into your mind from time to time—I categorize them as temptations, because we are being tempted to hold onto these thoughts and images. Many of these thoughts are the by-product of your brain's extensive and ongoing cogitative processes (Day 2). However, the devil tempts you to personalize these unpleasant, curious thoughts and images and convince you that you are to blame for your plight. But you know better now. When such notions or impressions pop up in your mind, say emphatically to the Enemy, "Get thee behind me Satan!" Or say to yourself, "That's not *my* thought!" Or, relax and remind yourself, "It's *just* a thought," and dismiss it straight away. Don't mull it over in your head as if it were somehow viable. Cast it down immediately. This is the perfect time to show that you are the boss! You will master your thoughts instead of your thoughts mastering you.

Consistently yielding to the temptation to give in to fear, anger, jealousy, or other harmful cogitative habits can cause chemical imbalances in the brain which bring about a shutdown, impeding the anterior cingulate (AC) – the brain's thought manager – from properly balancing its chemistry.[5] The negative emotions generated by the Filthy Five are all based in the limbic system.

Name That Thought: A Learning Activity

This exercise is designed to help you learn to quickly identity any of the haunting, distracting intrusions among the Filthy Five. Here I use the acrostic (FURST) to help you to memorize them.

Directions: 1. Use the number corresponding to each sentence to identify the type of unwanted thought it is and write the number under the appropriate category. The first two have been done for you. Some may fit into more than one category, as with #9 below.

Fear of the future	Unhealthy comparisons	Regrets of the past	Self-condemning thoughts	Temptations
	1,9		2,9	

1. "I wish I were smart, like him/her." (Unhealthy comparison)
2. "I can never do anything right!" (Self-condemning thought)
3. "If I had tried harder (were smarter, more talented, more industrious, etc.) I would not have failed. I will never be able to forgive myself."
4. "I would love to visit Hawaii one day, but I am too afraid to fly."
5. "People like us are not as important as some other folks."
6. "I wish I hadn't made so many dumb mistakes when I was young."
7. "I am *afraid* that I won't have enough money to pay my bills next month."
8. "I know I need to lose the 15 pounds I've gained, but it's so hard to stop eating my favorites, fried chicken, macaroni and cheese, ice cream, and chocolate chip cookies."
9. "My future doesn't look that bright. I am never going to get a college degree. I am not as smart as the others."
10. "It is hard not to lie, because I don't want to hurt people's feelings." *[1]
11. Make up your own sentence for each of The Filthy Five.

- F_____
- U_____
- R_____
- S_____
- T_____

Beginning today, and for the rest of this week, I want you to become more cognizant of your thoughts. Begin monitoring your thoughts, just as an air traffic controller would monitor the flight of the planes flying into and out of an airport. Each time a regret of the past, or fear of the future appears in your mind (your frontal lobe), identify and categorize it. For example, "That thought was an unhealthy comparison." This is a crucial step in taking control of your thought life. You'll not be able to control your thoughts until you learn to both identify and classify them. By the time you complete *The 21-Day Plan*, you will have mastered this thought identification practice.

---

[1] *(Answers: 1. U 2. S 3. R/U 4. F 5. U 6. R 7. F 8. T 9. F/S/U 10. T)

Perhaps someone may object, "My thoughts come at me so fast. How can I slow them down to such a degree that I can categorize them?" It's not as hard as you think.

Each time you stop to ask yourself what category of thought it is, you cause your mind to pause and think about your question. Now that your brain is engaged in the classification process, your brain's flow is interrupted and cannot immediately proceed onto an additional speculation, rumination, consideration, deduction, or deliberation. You have intruded upon the next thought that might have come. Because your next thought cannot find an open landing pad (in your frontal lobe) it must (figuratively) circle overhead in hopes of eventually landing. Your goal is to keep that next thought or next thoughts circling in your head as long as possible. This is how you slow down your thoughts. Your conscious mind cannot think two simultaneous, independent thoughts at the same time. Don't expect perfection the very first time you try this. Practice it. Eventually, your skills in consciously interrupting will improve. You are beginning the process of thought management (Days 10-14).

Over these past nine days, I have intentionally repeatedly asked you two questions: 1) Are you controlling your thoughts, or, are your thoughts controlling you? We cannot hope to control our mental processes without this "thinking about thinking" (metacognition). This week you will be shown how to regiment your thoughts to a degree that may surprise you. You don't have to try to get a handle on the twelve thousand to fifty-five thousand "thoughts" your brain produces in a day. You just have to identify and control The Filthy Five. You will do this by developing the ability to control one thought at a time. As you practice doing this, you will discover how to renew your mind, one thought at a time.

**A Closing Prayer:**

Dear God, I draw upon your strength and patience to daily monitor my thoughts by asking myself, "What kind of thought is this? Allow your word to fortify my mind against the stresses and pressures of life that come as a result of dwelling upon The Filthy Five, the patterns that have caused me to continue in a state of fear, anxiety and worry. Thank you, Father, for the wisdom that I am gaining from participating in The 21-Day Plan. I pray earnestly for your power, mercy and grace, that I may apply these principles. In Jesus' name. Amen.

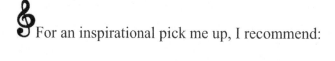For an inspirational pick me up, I recommend:

- *What Mercy Did For Me* by People and Songs
- *Way Maker* by Sinach or The Pentecostals of Alexandria
- *So Long Bye, Bye* by Jonathan Nelson

Until tomorrow, do this:

Memory Work

1. Begin memorizing The Filthy Five **FURST** acrostic.

2. Turn to The Filthy Five Memory Verses (Figure 14.2 on page 242). Begin to familiarize yourself with these Scriptures, as you will be encouraged to memorize them as an indispensable step in the rewiring of your brain to overcome negative thoughts.

3. Practice reciting the *I Am Significant* mantra (Repeat 10-12 times per day – at minimum – or every hour of the day).

4. **I Am Significant**. Why? (Because) God loves me and sent his Son to die upon the cross for my sins. He has adopted me into His family and has given me a new name. I am a born-again Christian, fearfully and wonderfully made in the image of God.

5. **My Spiritual Identity** – N-O-W-M-O-V-E-F-O-R-W-A-R-D acrostic. Write this acrostic on a 3x5 card and carry it with you wherever you go.

Thought Management 101:
Check, Challenge, Change, Reframe

Yesterday I was clever, so I wanted to change the world. Today I am wise, so I am changing myself.

--RUMI, 13ᵗʰ-century Persian poet

Daily Food for Thought

• **Brain Fact** "The amygdala is that portion of the brain responsible for processing emotional memories as well as storing them in the long-term memory."[1]

• **Key Thought** You can learn to manage your thoughts just as Jesus managed his thoughts when he was attacked by Satan.

• **Scripture** "We are taking every thought captive to the obedience of Christ..." (2 Corinthians 10:5b-6a).

Daily Reading

Welcome to Day 10. Thought management is a lot like classroom management. As I was matriculating my way through various educational institutions, most of the time I worked also as a substitute teacher. In over a decade of subbing, I lost control of my class only twice. One of those classes was in a suburban middle school. Due to overcrowding, my class was in a remote trailer. It was a

166

hot Friday afternoon in June. Last period of the day, there were over 25 middle schoolers crammed into the trailer. After the bell signaled the start of class, I attempted to settle the students down and inform them of their class work. However, the students had other ideas. After speaking to them in a firm voice for the fourth or fifth time, they still failed to cooperate. All else failing, I called the office for backup. The phone was dead. The kids must have known the phone was dead, because after I hung up the phone, they began to laugh and got even louder and more defiant. Scratching my head for a backup plan, I began to send the major ring leaders to the office for discipline. One by one, they exited the trailer. I quickly locked the door behind them; only to watch them return within minutes because the trailer door lock was broken. When the insubordinates returned, other students began cheering and clapping as if the defiant brigade had returned victorious from battle. The noise level in the portable trailer reached a feverish, incredible pitch. The class became a mob; they were laughing, joking, flying paper airplanes and launching balls of crumbled paper across the room like hand grenades. I put up a valiant fight, but the best thing that I could do was to try to manage the chaos. In the end, I sat powerless and frustrated at the teacher's desk. No resources or tactics left within reach, all I could do was to pray for the bell to ring—soon and very soon. What a sad sight. I left that experience thinking, God bless the public-school teachers!

As I reflected upon that fiasco, I was mentally confronted with a wild realization: Those rioting students were the living embodiments of the uncontrolled, repetitive thoughts in my head. My negative thoughts frequently overrode all my attempts at resistance and left me feeling stressed, confounded and powerless to control them. Perhaps, like me, you too struggle to control your negative thoughts and emotions. They are easily brought on by the stresses and pressures of life. Here in Day 10, I am going to reveal to you how you can gain the skills necessary to manage those stressful, fearful, anxious, and hopelessly unhelpful cogitative habits that are robbing you of the peace and tranquility you desire and deserve. How, you ask? By following strategies that enable you to check, challenge, change, and reframe negative, debilitating mental habits.

> *God has provided a thought management strategy in scripture utilized by the master teacher himself, Jesus.*

God has provided us a thought management paradigm in Scripture, one that was utilized by the master teacher himself, Jesus. I discovered this paradigm after examining Christ's interaction with Satan in the wilderness (Matthew 4:1-10). Jesus demonstrated for us that whenever a negative thought comes to us, we can manage it. We must learn, through faith and cogent design, to check the thought, challenge the thought, and change the thought. And, in some cases, we must reframe the thought. The thought management strategy is illustrated below in Figure 10.1

167

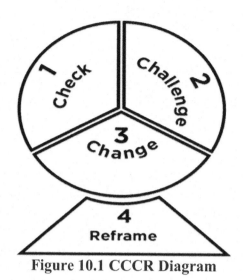

Figure 10.1 CCCR Diagram

Step One: Check It

Immediately following Jesus' baptism by John the Baptist in the Jordan River, "Jesus was led up by the Spirit into the wilderness to be tempted by the devil. And after He had fasted forty days and forty nights, He then became hungry. And the tempter came and said to Him, "If You are the Son of God, command that these stones become bread." (Matthew 4:1-3).

Whenever a negative (i.e. self-critical, self-condemning, distressing, worrisome) thought comes to your mind, you must immediately check it. To "check it" means to recognize which one or more of The Filthy Five it corresponds to. If you are mentally entertaining any one of The Filthy Five, know that the thought is not of God, but the enemy of your soul—Satan. It is the voice of the accuser, not the voice of your untiring advocate—Jesus. God and the devil are at starkly opposing and irreconcilable positions on the moral spectrum, and we must never allow ourselves the self-deception of conjecturing that maybe the devil is partially right.

Observe how Jesus immediately recognized the tempter's voice. Satan started in with Jesus, "If you are the Son of God..." (Matthew 4:4). Satan began by attacking Christ's divine identity, just as he attacks our spiritual identity today. However, Jesus thereupon recognized the tempter's beguiling voice. This is what it means to check a thought. When a (sometimes apparently random) negative thought perchance pops into your head, at once ask yourself what category or categories of The Filthy Five (FURST) it falls within. The thought the Deceiver introduced into the mind of Jesus was a temptation. This is one example of what it means "to take every thought captive to the obedience of Christ" (2 Corinthians 10:5). After checking the thought, progress confidently to step two.

Step Two: Challenge It

After checking the negative thought, Jesus next challenged the thought. Challenging the negative thought is a two-step process. The first is to resist the thought. The second: reject the thought. Jesus challenged (resisted and rejected) Satan's evil treachery. Satan, knowing that Jesus had fasted forty days and was hungry, whispered three temptations in Jesus' ear. (Observe that Satan attempts to entrap Jesus with one of "The Filthy Five," temptations). Satan said to Jesus, "Command that these stones become bread" (Matthew 4:3). Jesus challenged and resisted the thought. His resistance is evident in the fact that he refused to turn the stones into bread and refused to cast himself down from the pinnacle of the temple (Matthew. 4:6) or to bow down and worship Satan (Matthew 4:9). After Jesus resisted, he ultimately rejected all of Satan's subterfuge because he knew the thoughts did not agree with God's Word or desire for his life. Consequently, Jesus rejects Satan's inducement to sin by rebuffing him, saying, "Away from me, Satan!" (Matthew 4:10 NIV). Jesus resisted Satan three times, and Satan ultimately fled. The Scriptures inform believers to, "Resist the Devil and he will flee from you" (James 4:7). If the thought disagrees or seems to disagree with the Word of God, challenge it, resist, and reject it as necessary.

Step Three: Change It

After you check and challenge your dubitable thought, the next step is to change it. We must replace it! Change the negative thought and replace it with Scripture. For example, when Satan suggested to Jesus that He turn the stones into bread, Jesus checked it, challenged it, and *changed it*. He replaced it with Scripture. "It is written: 'Man shall not live on bread alone, but on every word that comes from the mouth of God'" (Matthew 4:4 NIV). To Satan's suggestion that he (Jesus) throw himself from the top of the temple to draw attention to himself and force God to have to save him, Jesus changed it and replaced the thought, retorting unambiguously, "It is also written: 'Do not put the Lord your God to the test'" (Matthew 4:7 NIV). To Satan's entreaty that Jesus fall and worship him, Jesus replaced it with the following Scriptural injunction, "Away from me, Satan! For it is written: 'Worship the Lord your God and serve him only'" (Matthew 4:10 NIV). Jesus shows us how to master our negative thoughts so that

> *Change the negative thought and replace it with Scripture.*

our negative thoughts do not master us: Check, Challenge, Change. For each of us individually to be victorious in our respective thought life, we are charged with following the example of Jesus and developing the skills to FOCUS (Fight Opposition Constantly Using Scripture).

169

When Satan Utters the Lie, You Counter with the Truth

In order to succeed in our thought life struggles, the ability to focus (FOCUS) is the key to victory. Early in the *21-Day Plan*, you were introduced to the *I Am Significant* mantra and *My Spiritual Identity* – N-O-W-M-O-V-E-F-O-R-W-A-R-D acrostic, and on Day 6, I introduced you to corresponding scriptures. By example, I will now demonstrate to you how to utilize that mantra to replace every stinging accusation Satan levels against you, just as Jesus did.

When the enemy speaks to you, and says, "You'll never beat your addiction," or "You'll never overcome your anxiety attacks," or "You can't do this," you CCC (check, challenge, and change) your thoughts, and...

You say, **I Am...**

More than a conqueror. "But in all these things we overwhelmingly conquer through Him [Christ] who loved us" (Romans 8:37).

When Satan says, "You will never overcome... (emotional pain, sadness, fear, doubt, guilt, etc.)." If your experience is of divorce, betrayal, or sexual abuse, your strategy is precisely the same; you CCC that thought and...

You say, **I Am an...**

Overcomer. "For whatever is born of God overcomes the world; and this is the victory that has overcome the world—our faith" (1 John 5:4).

When the thought comes to mind, "There's nothing you can do. You are a victim of circumstances," you CCC that thought and...

You say, **I Am a...**

Victor, not a victim. "But thanks be to God, who gives us the victory through our Lord Jesus Christ" (1 Corinthians 15:57).

When you hear the voice of criticism saying, "You can't...," "You haven't...," "You are not...," or it otherwise derides you or suggests, for example, that you somehow aren't worthy of respect or worthy of being loved, you CCC that untruth and...

170

You say, **I Am...**

Eternally loved. "Who will separate us from the love of Christ? ... [Nothing] will be able to separate us from the love of God, which is in Christ Jesus our Lord" (Romans 8:35,39c).

Talking back to Satan, just as Jesus did, is the key to victory in our proactive thought wars. Immediately confronting your negative inner narrative is essential if you are to overcome stress, anxiety, worry and an array of self-condemning thoughts. Satan is trying to talk your soul (mind, will, and emotions) out of what your spirit man knows—you have the mind of Christ and your victory has already been secured by Christ on the cross over two thousand years ago.

This is not a physical battle, but a spiritual battle. Like it or not, believe it or not, you are in a war—but God has equipped us to win, providing we daily clothe ourselves in His spiritual armor.

Finally, be strong in the Lord and in the strength of His might. Put on the full armor of God, so that you will be able to stand firm against the schemes of the devil. For our struggle is not against flesh and blood, but against the rulers, against the powers, against the world forces of this darkness, against the spiritual forces of wickedness in the heavenly places (Ephesians 6:10-13).

Our task is to stay in an attitude of faith and victory as we learn to replace Satan's lies with the truth of God's word. Faith in God's word will extinguish Satan's outrageous lies and protect our minds from the Great Liar's ability to establish some sort of stronghold.

Step Four: Reframe It

Satan likes nothing better than to keep our minds bogged down in a quagmire of negativity, hopelessness and despair. He loves to see God's people neck deep and drowning in the quicksand of painful memories of the past and dispiriting feelings. If we allow him to, he'll keep our minds fixated on that second DUI that costs you your career, the breast cancer surgery that left you feeling disfigured, the loss of a child, harmful words that were spoken, or the blatant sexual, racial or other discrimination that you experienced. In order to be set free from these painful memories and despairing thoughts, we will need to employ step four of this thought management strategy (CCCR). It is essential that we learn to reframe those painful memories.

Neurologically speaking, all too often, a negative event remains lodged in the amygdala's emotional memory bank, thus becoming a tiring drain on the brain. *The amygdala* [uh-mig-duh-lee] *is the part of the brain that houses our emotional*

171

memories.[2] The thalamus is a large group of nerve cells in the center of the brain that relays information to other parts of the brain.[3] When we become aware of a conscious thought, it is received by the thalamus. It "signals the hypothalamus [and amygdala] to chemically prepare a response."[4] The amygdala attaches an emotion to that thought that requires a response—happiness, sadness, anger, joy, etc. (See Figure 10.2 below.)

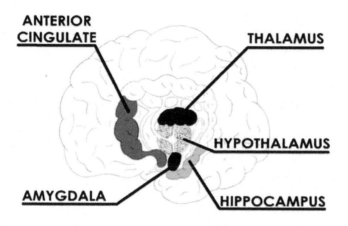

Figure 10.2 Thalamus and Amygdala

Let's illustrate how the thalamus and amygdala interface. One of my favorite Christmas songs is Nat King Cole's version of *The Christmas Song,* the one that begins with the lyric "Chestnuts roasting on an open fire... Jack Frost nipping at your nose." Whenever I hear that song, a smile comes to my face. It surely has the same effect on many people. Why? Because when the thalamus sends that song to the amygdala—the emotional memory bank—it is attached to a pleasing emotional memory. Every one of our experiences has an emotional label coupled with it. Well, you've lived long enough to know that all your memories are not positive. That divorce was painful, as was the miscarriage or abortion, as was the failure in that job interview, as was that time when you were a teenager and you fell down or dropped your things and others nearby laughed at you, as was that time you were attacked or robbed or bullied. Due to the emotional unpleasantness of the experience, the memory is fastened with a feeling tag and stored in your amygdala, and it will remain negative forever, until you learn to reframe it.

The goal in reframing is to neutralize those toxic emotional memories hidden away in your amygdala, secreting toxic chemicals into your mind and body whenever the thought is reactivated by some trigger. By learning to reframe the event, extracting (if possible) from that negative experience whatever positive aspects you can derive from it, you alter the tag that attaches to it. In other words, you find an "at least" or a "purpose"

> *The goal in reframing is to neutralize those toxic emotional memories hidden away in your amygdala.*

or a lesson learned from the pain. Should you choose to not do so, the negative experience will likely forever evoke the same detrimental emotions.

For a biblical example of reframing, the writer of Hebrews shows us how Jesus reframed the gory events of Calvary. "Because his heart was focused on the joy of knowing that you would be his, he endured the agony of the cross and conquered its humiliation, and now sits exalted at the right hand of the throne of God!" (Hebrews 12:2 TPT). From Jesus' vantage point, the joy of securing our salvation coupled with the joy of pleasing his Father, attached purpose to the pain he endured on the cross. Jesus reframed being lied about, spat upon, brutally beaten, and flogged nearly to death. Ultimately, he was nailed to a cross with nine-inch spikes, and there he bled in ghastly misery for many hours. Before expiring, Jesus prayed to his Father, on our behalf, saying, "Father, forgive them, for they do not know what they are doing" (Luke 23:34). Knowing that he had completed the work he had been sent on earth to do, Jesus final words were, "Father, into Your hands I commit My spirit" (Luke 23:46). Jesus then hung his head and died. The joy of knowing that he would be reunited with the Father, and man's sins would be forgiven, mankind would be reconciled to, and have everlasting access to their Loving Creator, made all His inexpressible suffering worthwhile.

If you and I are going to be set free from the painful emotional memories stored in our brain's amygdala, it is not enough to spiritually rebuke the thought and feeling; we must be willing to do what Jesus did: reframe the painful experiences that are clouding our minds with toxic emotions and fear-laden thoughts. The concept of "reframing" is a principle rooted in the often quoted Bible verse, "And we know that God causes all things to *work together for good* to those who love God, to those who are called according to His purpose" (Romans 8:28). Ferreting out some positive in every negative experience is critical to overcoming the related emotional pain. Reframing serves to rid the mind of a great deal of weight, and in so doing helps to strengthen the anterior cingulate (AC) so it can maintain a healthy balance between the frontal lobe and the limbic system.[5]

The Reframe Game

In the den in my home is a framed picture of me in my youth, arms raised in victory as I anchored the mile relay for my high school track team. We set a record around that time that lasted for over 23 years. I know this is a bit of a boast, but when visitors look at the photograph, they often assume that I am reliving a past glory. However, I use the picture as a powerful reframing device. When I receive some disappointing news, or I am processing regrets of the past, I sometimes ponder the picture as I stand before it and I think to myself how I might reframe this situation so that I might come out as victorious as I did then. It works.

A pastoral colleague of mine keeps a picture frame on his desk. It has no picture in it, nor does it have a glass cover on the front. It is just an empty frame. Whenever he receives some disappointing news or is processing regrets of the past, he holds the frame up to his face and asks himself, how might I reframe this experience so I remain positive and optimistic and not allow this negative thought to ruin my day and become an energy and confidence drain? He calls this "the reframe game."

I first learned about reframing in my studies of cognitive behavioral therapy (CBT). Let me illustrate how the reframe game is conceived. A few years ago, I failed at my second church plant effort. It hit me hard, and it shocked me to the core of my being, devastating my self-image and severely undermining the completeness of my confidence in God. The pain of it sidelined me in severe emotional torment for a couple of years. While in the agonizing throes, God challenged me to examine my thought life. He let me see that it was not acceptable for me to be emotionally down 75% of the time and up just 25% of the time. I could reflect upon happier seasons in my life when I was maybe 90% up and 10% down. I began to see that my new normal was not normal at all. Hence, I began a serious study of how to manage my thoughts and emotions.

It was during my research that I was introduced to the concept of reframing a negative event. I took a sheet of paper and drew a line down the middle of it. On the left side of the paper I wrote "setbacks," and on the right side of the paper I wrote "accomplishments." The event that evoked the most painful memories for me was that second failed church plant. That was debilitating. It evoked dreadful fears of the future. Therefore, I began the process of deliberately reframing it. I was sick and tired of being sick and tired. It wasn't fair to my God, my wife, and family, nor to those whom I was called to minister. My depression kept me pinned to a languid despair, flat on my back, unable to move, feeling trapped under an insuperable weight of grief and self-loathing. With pen in hand, I began the all-important reframing process. My extant defeated mentality made it all so horrible, but inasmuch as Romans 8:28 is virtuously edifying, God must have worked some aspect of this ever-unsatisfying recollection to my ultimate good. With this in mind, I wrote:

> **Don't let a dark past ruin a bright future.**

Setback	**Accomplishments**
Failed to sustain a church plant	1. Through the mild difficulties and challenges of ADD, by God's grace, I managed to remain focused enough to complete my doctoral dissertation — that ultimately became *The 21-Day Plan*.
	2. Saw God miraculously provide 3 plus years of free tuition to complete my doctoral studies.
	3. Humbled myself and allowed my professionally trained wife to become my personal therapist to help me process my grief.
	4. Successfully replaced worry with the word by memorizing a plethora of Scriptures and inspirational quotes (that I wrote down on 3x5 cards).
	5. Began hosting *Think Right Live Right Workshops* to help fellow strugglers (CCCR) deal with their negative thoughts.
	6. Co-founded a counseling center to help individuals become spiritually, emotionally, and mentally whole and healthy.
	7. Cultivated an increased mental toughness to withstand the turbulent storms in my life.

175

By reframing that painful memory, I came to view it as a setup for my comeback. Now, when Satan brings up the painful memory of that setback, I reflect upon those several accomplishments, thus arresting the negativity. I discovered that when the door was closed on the church plant effort, God opened a window to another area of ministry. It became apparent to me that failure can result in fruitful redirection. Over the ensuing days, months, and years, the dark, ominous clouds of melancholy lifted and optimism about my future began to fill my consciousness. Reframing the church plant experience took the disheartening sting out of it. There is nothing special about me; anyone can do it.

Concerning past hurts, Maya Angelou, a famous and admired African American poet once said, "Someone was hurt before you; wronged before you; yet, someone survived." Reframing is not lying. What we need to do is reflect more deeply and intently on other factors and other considerations that are at least equally true. There is no need to fabricate anything; additional truths suffice.

Questions for Reflection

1. Write down a painful memory that you would like to reframe. Choose just one. In the space provided below, begin processing your painful memories by precisely naming it under "Setback." (Remember, the longest journey begins with a single step.) Then, taking your time, write down--in as much detail as you want--several accomplishments that an objective viewpoint might commend.

Setback

_____

_____

Accomplishments

_____

_____

_____

2. To help you in remembering, fill in the words to the four-step thought management paradigm.

- Step 1. C_____it –to recognize it
- Step 2. C_____it –to resist and reject it
- Step 3. C_____it –to replace it
- Step 4. R_____it –to reevaluate it

3. List the "Filthy Five."

- F_____
- U_____
- R_____
- S_____
- T_____

A Closing Prayer

Dear God, I draw upon your strength to check, challenge and change my negative thoughts and bring them into alignment with your Word. God, I ask you to give me the insight and motivation I need to reframe painful emotional experiences that have wounded and discouraged me. Continue to heal me and make me whole. Help me to face the truth about myself and cease blaming people and circumstances for the way I think and feel. Please let me see more clearly the promise of a brighter future. Father, I know that everything that happened to me was not necessarily your will, but I take comfort in Your promise to work all things together for my good. In Jesus' name. Amen.

For an inspirational pick me up, I recommend:

- *Chain Breaker* by The Brooklyn Tabernacle Choir
- *Break Every Chain* by Tasha Cobbs
- *Running Back to You* by Fred Hammond
- *Glorious,* by Martha Munizzi

Until tomorrow, do this:

Memory Work

1. Continue memorizing The Filthy Five FURST acrostic.

2. Beginning today, and over the next few weeks, begin writing *The Filthy Five Memory Verses* (Figure 14.2, p. 242) on 3x5 cards and, if you want, also keep it in your smartphone. Daily begin to commit the verses to memory. Begin with only one verse at a time. I suggest you begin memorizing the one you are struggling with the most. To assist in your

memorization efforts, read *The 7 Keys to Memorizing Scripture* on pages 253-254.

3. Memorize the (**CCCR**) paradigm.

4. Practice your *I Am Significant* mantra (and repeat ten to twelve times per day, or every hour of the day).

I Am Significant. Why? (Because) God loves me and sent his Son to die upon the cross for my sins. He has adopted me into His family and has given me a new name. I am a born-again Christian, fearfully and wonderfully made in the image of God.

5. Practice your *My Spiritual Identity* acrostic.

My Spiritual Identity–N-O-W-M-O-V-E-F-O-R-W-A-R-D acrostic. If you haven't done so already, write the acrostic on a 3x5 card and carry it with you wherever you go. Are you now able to recite it from memory? Try to do so now. Good job! You are making progress. Keep practicing. *An example of the 3x5 cards is on page 138.*

Mind Games:
A Game-Winning Strategy for Defeating The Filthy Five

The secret of change is to focus all of your energy, not on fighting the old, but on building the new.

– Socrates

• **Brain Fact** "Neurons [brain cells] that fire together, wire together. And every time we do it, we make it easier to do tomorrow."[1]

• **Key Thoughts** Metaphorically, your thoughts, negative or positive, run grooves in your brain. The longer you dwell on those thoughts, the deeper the grooves become.

• **Scripture** "...taking up the shield of faith...you will be able to extinguish all the *flaming arrows* of the evil one. And take the helmet of salvation and the sword of the Spirit, which is the word of God" (Ephesians 6:16b-17).

Daily Reading

Welcome to Day 11. I am so glad that you decided to read today's lesson. I cannot know what difficult situations you may be facing today. It is possible your circumstances may be screaming in your face, telling you that you are not going to make it – maybe that you'll fail or humiliate yourself. Your social relationships may be out of control. Your finances may be a source of distress. Or, perhaps you are facing the disappointment of yet another door slammed in your face, or another opportunity missed, or another "no" when you so desperately hoped for a "yes."

If such is the case, why do you feel that your mind is being bombarded with so many negative thoughts? Let's face it. Sometimes we are involved in intense, deeply personal thought wars. These negative thoughts attack our minds and evoke all kinds of toxic thoughts and emotions. Like it or not, realize it or not, you and I are involved in a spiritual battle between God's kingdom of light and Satan's kingdom of darkness (Ephesians 6:1-17). The battle is so subtle and invisible that many believers are not even aware that they are in a war for control of their minds and feelings, and that unawareness is just the way Satan wants it. To the winner go the spoils, control of your spirit, soul (mind, will and emotions), and the body.

God desires that our minds be at rest so that we can experience the peace, joy and contentment that abiding in Christ's presence brings. However, Satan loves nothing more than to keep our minds stressed, overwhelmed, confounded and depressed. His strategy is spiritual warfare with a two-fold attack.

The first part of Satan's strategy is mental. He knows that if he can keep us discouraged by all the negative things we see, feel, hear and think, then we will be less inclined to pray, read the Bible, memorize Scripture, praise God, and/or read *The 21-Day Plan*.

A Brain Rut

The second part of Satan's strategy is neurological. Neurologically, his aim is to get your brain to settle into a permanent negative groove. Once in that negative groove, he will have you constantly thinking negative thoughts, engaging in negative self-talk, and suffering negative, distressing images of yourself in your mind's eye. Those thoughts and images spin around and around in our heads like a broken record. And often people get to a point where they consider it a normal aspect of living.

On this subject of broken records, how many of you are old enough to remember the old 45 black vinyl records and larger LP's? The vinyl records have a series of circular grooves into which the needle rests. When the needle is placed in that groove and the record spins, you can hear the music. However, every now and then the record would get a scratch on it, and much to the disappointment of listening ears, when the needle reached that part of the record where it was scratched, the record would skip and skip and skip. How frustrating! The record was ruined. Your only recourse was to buy another copy of the record, as the scratch was irreparable.

In like manner, your thoughts, negative or positive, along with their emotional memories, have etched grooves in your brain. The longer you remain muddled in those thoughts, the deeper the grooves become, metaphorically speaking. As we learned previously (Day 7), "left to its own devices, the brain will try to make almost any routine into a habit, because habits allow your mind to ramp down more often."[2] That's how you and I get stuck in a negative mental rut. Remember, you don't get stuck this way because you are a bad person or someone who has committed some misdeed. Resist succumbing to false guilt and shame. You get stuck because of Satan's influence and because of the basic wiring of your brain. Now let's move on to how you can interrupt this mental groove.

Thinking for a Change

From a neurological standpoint, that is what the CCCR thought management strategy is designed to do. When you check your thought, you are interrupting your mental recording. In essence, you are disrupting your brain's mental habit and forcing it to deal with additional information. When done deliberately and consistently, we retrain the brain to overcome chronic negative thinking patterns. Dr. O'Conner explains,

"When we do anything repeatedly, with focused attention, our nerve cells will physically grow new connections between, say, nerve center A... and nerve B [they] develop a stronger connection with more transmitting and receiving points, [the activity] becomes a habit with a physical embodiment in the brain. Neurons [brain cells] that fire together, wire together. And every time we do it, we make it easier to do tomorrow."[3]

For example, each day you get up and have your daily quiet time (QT), quote your *I Am* mantra, or read your *21-Day Plan*, you make it easier for your brain to do the same tomorrow.

In order to be successful in these difficult-to-manage mind games, you must face the fact that you are going to have to retrain your brain. Today, we are going to practice some rewiring. We are going to take A: The Filthy Five: FURST (Day 9; Figure 9:1) and rewire it with B: The Check, Challenge, Change, Reframe. (CCCR) (Day 10) and continue the process of rewiring your brain to overcome negative thinking. *When practiced consistently, taking your negative thoughts captive will become an automatic mental habit.* I refer to it as Thought Management 101. (See Figure 11.1).

> *When you check your thought, you are disrupting your brain's mental habit and forcing it to deal with additional information.*

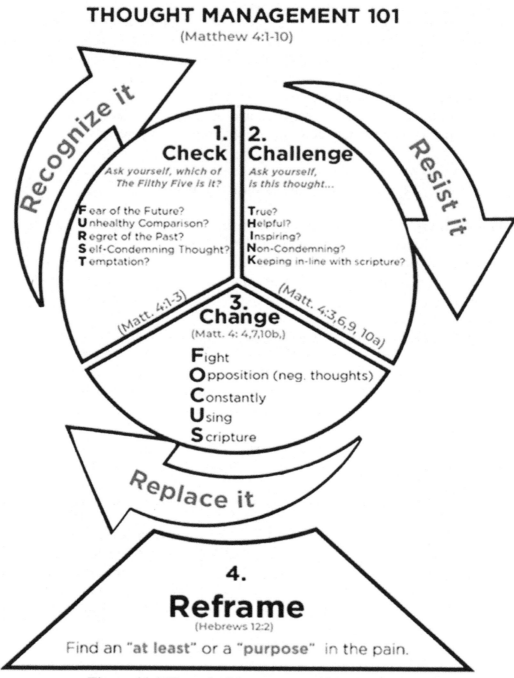

THOUGHT MANAGEMENT 101
(Matthew 4:1-10)

Recognize it

Resist it

1. Check
Ask yourself, which of The Filthy Five is it?

Fear of the Future?
Unhealthy Comparison?
Regret of the Past?
Self-Condemning Thought?
Temptation?

(Matt. 4:1-3)

2. Challenge
Ask yourself, is this thought...

True?
Helpful?
Inspiring?
Non-Condemning?
Keeping in-line with scripture?

(Matt. 4:3,6,9, 10a)

3. Change
(Matt. 4: 4,7,10b,)

Fight
Opposition (neg. thoughts)
Constantly
Using
Scripture

Replace it

4. Reframe
(Hebrews 12:2)
Find an "**at least**" or a "**purpose**" in the pain.

Figure 11.1 Thought Management 101

I use the term "mind games" here because our mind can play tricks on us making it hard for us to distinguish between truth and falsehood—reality and fiction. In these mind games, Satan's aim is to keep our minds tormented, confused and fearful. In light of Satan's MO, the Apostle Paul cautions believers to…

- Prepare your minds for action, be completely sober [in spirit—steadfast, self-disciplined, spiritually and morally alert] (1 Peter 1:13 AMP).

- Put on the full armor of God, so that you will be able to stand firm against the schemes of the devil…[take]up the shield of faith with which you will be able to extinguish all the flaming arrows of the evil one… (Ephesians 6:10-11, 16b-17).

Figuratively, Satan has in his quiver five arrows that he uses to harass and torment. These flaming arrows, once launched from Satan's bow, penetrate our psyche and inflame our negative thoughts, causing the release of negative chemicals to be released into the brain. These **flaming arrows** I have labeled **The Filthy Five.**

Spiritual Amor for Spiritual War

We shall now use the CCCR thought management strategy as the shield of faith. Each time Satan launches one of his 5 flaming arrows (FURST), to protect our mind, we are to symbolically put on the Helmet of Salvation (Ephesians 6:17). Next, we are to raise the Shield of Faith and use the Sword of the Spirit—which is the Word of God—to douse the arrows' flames. (See Figure 11.1).

Shield of Faith (Eph. 6:16)

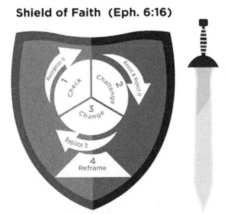

Sword of the Spirit—the Word (Eph. 6:17)
Figure 11.2 The CCCR Shield of Faith

Battlefield of the Mind: Protecting Your Mind Against The Filthy Five

⟫⟫ Fear of the Future ➤

(CCCR)

One of Satan's flaming arrows is fear of the future. You know that you have been shot by Satan's flaming arrow labeled 'fear of the future' when you find yourself *today* worried about tomorrow. Most fears of the future are likely to be contextualized as if they linguistically began with the words, "what if." "What if I don't pass my state boards?" or "What if I don't get that raise?" or "What if they don't give me a promotion?" "What if my child gets expelled from school?" When troubled by any negative thought, to win the battle, lift the Shield of Faith by employing your CCCR thought management strategy. Step 1: Check it. Recognize the thought. Which one of the Filthy Five describes it? Our answer here: It is fear of the future. By asking yourself this single question, you accomplish two things: First, you interrupt your brain's automatic negative thought pattern. Secondly, you prevent any additional negative thoughts from penetrating your frontal lobe because your brain is engaged in answering the question you posed to it.

Once you've checked the thought and identified it as a fear of the future, your next move is to Step 2: Challenge it. Whenever a thought pops into your head, remember to react quickly. Do not let negative thoughts ruminate. Remember the THINK acrostic and be prepared to ask yourself these questions:

Is this thought…

True?
Helpful?
Inspiring?
Non-condemning?
Keeping in line with Scripture?

The reason such questions are so effective in managing your thoughts is because neuroscience has revealed that:

Questions trigger a mental reflex that takes over the brain's thought processes. When the consciousness brain is focusing on finding an answer to the question, it is temporarily suspended in examining only that thought…The second you hear a question, you literally cannot think of anything else. For example, what is your job? After hearing that question, what were you thinking about? The obvious answer for most is their job. Consider what happened to your mind. The question momentarily took control of your thought process and focused it entirely on your occupation. You didn't consciously tell your brain to think about it; it just did so instinctively.[4] **Questions hijack the brain.**

By asking, the five THINK questions, you are literally taking control of your thought processes. After you check and challenge the thought and it fails the challenge (it is condemnable; it is unworthy), it is a flaming arrow come to life. You must feel yourself ready and justified in pulling it down and taking it captive. You next employ Step 3: Change it/Replace it! How, you ask? You discipline your mind by a deep familiarity with the FOCUS rubric. To FOCUS means to…

Fight
Opposition (negative, troublesome thoughts)
Constantly
Using
Scripture   *See page 242 (Figure 14.2) for replacement Scripture verses.*

By way of review (Day 10), this process of proactively identifying and attacking is what Jesus did when his mind was attacked by Satan in the wilderness. He countered every one of Satan's lies with the Truth of Scripture. Telling the devil to leave you alone is not going to achieve all you intend. You are going to have to FOCUS if you are going to win the thought wars. What are you to replace that fear of the future with? *The Word of God!* Concerning fear of the future, Jesus emphatically declares, "So don't be anxious about tomorrow. God will take care of your tomorrow too. Live one day at a time." (Mathew 6:34TLB). Jesus is encouraging you to trust him to meet tomorrow's needs tomorrow. Do not worry about tomorrow's needs today. Jesus wants you to live in the *now*. In the face of perceived lack, say to yourself, "TODAY, I have…." "TODAY, I have…." "TODAY, my needs are met." You may not have all that someone else has, but that would be engaging in unhealthy comparisons. Are your basic needs met <u>today</u>? Yes? Thank God for that!

In my counseling office, on the wall hangs a picture frame with the words "Don't be afraid of tomorrow; God is already there." I like to think of it that way. God has gone ahead and provided for your future. Now, He has returned to take you by your hand and walk you today into the future He has prepared for you. He's a good, good Father, as good as our knowledge of the Word, wisdom, faith, and humility allow. He promised to never leave or forsake you (Hebrews 13:5). He never leaves your side. How close is He, you ask? Well, if you are His child, He lives on the inside of you (John 14:16). That's very close!

FYI: Admittedly, this CCCR thought management strategy may seem a bit laborious. Don't sweat it. Once learned and practiced consistently, your brain will automatically begin to check, challenge and change your thoughts within seconds. Do not demand of yourself that you perfectly succeed in only a few days; success in *The 21-Day Plan* comes in weeks or months, not days. Don't feel that you need to implement all the questions at the same time. If you learn to check and challenge the thought, you are well on your way. One of the things I want you to get out of this program is an increased ability to think positively, to appreciate fully the small, incremental, and very personal successes that are yours each day.

The reason behind all the detailed analysis herein is because once you figure out Satan's strategy, he changes things up on you. This detailed Thought Management Strategy (Figure 11.1) accounts for Satan's subtle shifts in his manipulations of our views, impressions, and understandings. When Satan says to you, for example, "It's a hassle to try to remember all these steps and acrostics," remember this one unarguable fact: the more time you devote to memorizing the steps, the less time you will be thinking those negative, bothersome thoughts. Relax. Take your time. Everyone learns at his or her own pace. There is no rush. You will be thinking for the rest of your life, and that's plenty of time to achieve all your goals.

Questions for Reflection

1. What fears or concerns about tomorrow are robbing you of God's peace today? List the most prominent ones.

_____

_____

2. When you can, read Matthew 6:25-34 and jot down any phrases or verses that you could memorize to help you worry less about the future.

_____

_____

≫ Unhealthy Comparisons ►

(CCCR)

In the Mind Games, another flaming arrow that Satan fires at our minds is unhealthy comparisons. Concerning unhealthy comparisons, I once heard Dr. Hendricks, of Dallas Theological Seminary, say, "You were born an original. Don't die a copycat." Engaging in unhealthy comparisons is harmful to your self-esteem. Our consumer-driven society keeps us constantly comparing ourselves to the Joneses. In case you are wondering, who are the Joneses? These are the people in society, very often our neighbors, who we fashion in our minds as the more ideally affluent people. They are on practically every television commercial. The unhealthy comparison trap works in the following manner. After you finally figure out how to use the latest smartphone, Mac iPhone or iPad, companies come

186

out with an updated and more sophisticated product. And since the Joneses have it, you feel you ought to have it too. Ladies, our culture pressures you to constantly attend to and improve your appearance. Let me remark encouragingly: If you had four people working on you for four hours just to manage a brief photo shoot, you'd probably look just as marvelous.

Whenever you are tempted to compare yourself to others, raise the shield of faith to quench Satan's fiery arrow. **Step 1:** Check it. Recognize the thought. Often, just a bad feeling can serve as the necessary prompt to begin step one. Which of the Filthy Five is it? **Step 2:** Challenge it. Challenge it by asking several questions: Is it true? Is it helpful? Is it non-condemning? Is it keeping in line with Scripture? Remember to THINK fast; the challenge must be done quickly and reflexively, not the way we mull, for example, a philosophical proposition. Try to repeat the acrostic, recalling the gist of each step from memory. If you have difficulty, see Figure 11.1.

Satan, who desires that your mind stay aflame with feelings of sadness and insecurity, will be sure to keep tempting you to measure yourself against others, worsening your feelings of inadequacy and despondency. At the heart of unhealthy comparisons is a poor self-concept. Do not worry too much about excellently mastering this challenging process at this juncture. Building your self-concept will be discussed in greater detail in Day 16.

Change the automatic negative thoughts (ANTS) and replace them with a spiritual automatic thought (SATS).

After you check and challenge your thought, proceed directly to employ **Step 3:** Change it. (Replace it!)

Change the automatic negative thoughts (ANTS) and replace them with a spiritual automatic thought (SATS)—FOCUS. When tempted to compare yourself to others, instead say to yourself, "I will give thanks to Thee, for I am fearfully and wonderfully made; wonderful are Thy works, and my soul knows it very well" (Psalm 139:14). When circumstantially comparing yourself to others, say to yourself, "I like myself!" "I *really* like myself!" Perhaps, it feels a bit awkward saying that to yourself, but when we like ourselves more, we grow to love ourselves more, and that comes nearer to God's disposition. This uneasiness is because we are so used to pointing out all the things we don't like about ourselves. Push back on the push back. God loves you just the way you are—without changing a single thing. It isn't that we are somehow perfect and God loves perfection, but rather that God is the supreme expert in the practice of unconditional love. God does desire us to change, but His love is unconditional and not contingent on us changing. A smile appears on His face at the mention of your name. He loves you just as much as he loves Jesus (John 17:23). You were not and are not an afterthought. God designed you just the way you are. No matter what physical, mental, or behavioral distinctions make us each unique, God loves us with a fervency and assiduousness beyond our comprehension.

Questions for Reflection

1. On a scale from 1 to 10, (1 being the lowest and 10 the highest) how difficult is it for you to say, "I really like me"? Assign a number. ___

2. When you compare yourself with others, do you at times feel somewhat angry with God for not making you different than you are? Yes or No _____

The Apostles Paul and Peter give us the following sound advice:

- We won't dare compare ourselves with those who think so much of themselves. But they are foolish to compare themselves with themselves" (2 Corinthians 10:12 CEV).

- Be content with who you are, and don't put on airs. God's strong hand is on you; He'll promote you at the right time. Live carefree before God; He is most careful with you. (1Peter 5:6-7 MSG).

≫ Regrets of the Past ▶

(CCCR)

Satan has once again drawn his bow and is about to release another one of his flaming arrows. Perhaps it is this one that evokes the most painful response: regrets of the past. When was the last time you were watching television or engaged in conversation or heard a song or encountered an image that triggered a regret of the past? Automatically, as you ruminated upon it, the thalamus (the part of your brain that makes you generally conscious of your thoughts) directs the thought to your amygdala (that part of the brain responsible for ascribing feeling and emotions to your thoughts). The amygdala goes into your emotional memory bank and attaches that thought to the negative emotion you have stored up in your emotional library. The more you ruminate upon that regret of the past, the more emotional coloring it takes on, pictorially adding vivid reds, violets and other emotional "colors." Typically, the longer you reflect upon the experience, you begin to feel more remorseful and melancholy, and this is why we need to practice the several steps of the CCCR process by engaging each faster and faster; we need to immediately and reflexively treat these deviant flaming arrows as they arrive and not deliberate upon them. The faster you attend to your negative thoughts, the less emotional impact they will have on your feelings.

Remember, when the enemy of your soul shoots his fiery arrow into your frontal lobe, lift up the shield of faith to quench the fiery arrow. **Step 1**: Check it. Recognize the thought. Ask yourself, which one of the Filthy Five is it? Why the repetition herein, you ask? Because your brain is rewired through repetition. Rewiring is what we intend. **Step 2:** Challenge it—resist and reject the thought. If it doesn't pass the THINK test, reject it immediately. Satan uses our past regrets as part of his strategy to keep us mentally and emotionally enslaved to depressing thoughts and toxic mental images. With toxic chemicals surging through our brains, we may berate ourselves, for example, by asking for the 100th time, "If only I had not...? A parent full of guilt might lament, "If only I hadn't punished my child that way, he'd probably have a healthier self-concept." A twenty-something bemoans, "If only, I had not dropped out of school," or "If only I had not been so foolish and rebellious...," or "If only I had been more responsible...." A middle-aged man moans, "If I had not lost my job and fallen behind on my credit card payments...." Such "if only" laments will keep you in the doldrums. They only serve to generate negativity. Some of the thoughts may be **T**—true. However, they are not **H**—helpful, nor are they **I**—inspiring or **N**—non-condemning or **K**—keeping in line with Scripture. Your past does not determine your destiny. Hence, you need to reject all regrets of the past. All of them! If it's possible to right your previous wrongs and or indiscretions, do so. However, over 99% of the time it is useless to readdress past misfortunes. The past is gone! Treat negatives about the past with full awareness that Satan wants nothing more than to see us tied up in guilt, condemnation, and self-loathing, trying endlessly to rewrite the past. Do not doubt the enormity of God's grace. That's the message of the cross—FORGIVENESS. God chose not to hold your past mistakes against you. You get a do-over. Accept His forgiveness and move on.

Speaking from my personal experience, dealing with regrets of the past has been extremely challenging. But here are some things I learned to remind myself, and perhaps my telling here will bring to you some solace and peace of mind as you learn to forgive yourself, process and reframe some of your more painful regrets.

Work at *self-forgiveness* by repeating one or more of the following truths:

1. Since I believe that God has forgiven me, and I have asked the people affected for forgiveness, I choose now to forgive myself also and move on with my life. (Ps. 51:7; 103:1; Isa. 1:18; Jer. 31:3; Heb. 4:16;1 John 1:9)

2. I was mentally in a bad place at the time I made the decision to.... (I was stressed, under the influence, carnal, angry, desperate and/or depressed). If I had been in a better state of mind, I am confident I would have chosen differently. (Jonah 1-3:3; Ps. 27:10; 46:1; 119:71; Matthew 11:28)

3. God can work my past mistakes together for my good if I continue to trust Him by standing on his Word. (Isaiah 41:9-10; Romans 8:28)

4. God loves me, and despite my mess-ups He still has a wonderful plan for my life. Peter denied Christ in John 18:13-27. (Jer. 29:11; 2 Cor. 1:3-4)

5. I regret my decision, but I certainly cannot change it now; what's past is past. I can only learn from this and other mistakes. (Philippians 3:13b-14)

6. I honestly thought I was following God's direction, but it now appears I probably took the wrong road. However, I live and act anew, and I abide in faith that God is leading me in the right direction. (Proverbs 24:17)

7. I was then young and imprudent. If I had known better, I would have done better. (Proverbs 1:3-5; 7:7; Judges 16; Isaiah 49:15; Luke 15:11-32)

8. I was not following the Lord at that time in my life. God allows second chances. In fact, He welcomes them. (Jonah 1-3:3; Isaiah 1:18; 43:18-19)

The above lists are some things you can say to yourself to counter the enemy's stinging accusations. Be aware: once you decide upon one defense you like, for example #2, and shut Satan, the accuser, down, he will counter with another accusation against you. You will then need to counter with another defense, for example #6. Keep in mind that Satan is never finished, and the battle is ongoing. We must hit back again and again. That is how the mind games are won and lost. One thing I can say about Satan is that he is one persistent and pugnacious pest. But don't cave in under the pressure. Never let go of the knowledge and faith that God is incalculably more powerful than Satan- if we will only put our faith in Him. "Because greater is He who is in you than he who is in the world" (1 John 4:4). Satan loves nothing better than to hear you shout in frustration, "I'm tired of fighting." Because at that point he knows he's succeeding. We must learn to outlast the enemy in the thought wars. This is what the CCCR thought management 101 is designed to help you do – Win!

After you check and challenge the thought, next comes **Step 3**: Change it/Replace it. FOCUS. Observe how the Apostle Paul dealt with his regrets of the past. Paul had in his past harassed and murdered Christians directly and indirectly. As the chief prosecutor of the early church, Paul had blood on his hands. The Bible records how Paul – at the time named "Saul" –consented to the death of Stephen (Acts 7:54-58; 8:1-3) and many other Christians. However, when Satan would tempt Paul to hold on to regrets of the past, Paul refuted his accusations by boldly stating, "[I'm]Forgetting what lies behind and reaching forward to what lies ahead, I press on toward the goal for the prize of the upward call of God in Christ Jesus" (Philippians 3:13b-14).

Paul knew that if he were to hold onto his history (to fail to address his history) he was to do so at the expense of his destiny. He could not hold on to his past and embrace his future at the same time. He had to let go of one to embrace the other. Paul knew that he could not be pitiful and powerful at the same time. Hence, he chose to let go of his pitiful past, in order that he could embrace the powerful and unprecedented future that God had prepared for him. Talk about Amazing Grace, God used a former evildoer to write 13 of the 27 New Testament books.

Concerning my regrets of the past, the Lord also revealed to me that my unwillingness to forgive myself for past mistakes was nothing more than *pride* covering a false heart of humility. All have sinned and miss the mark (Romans 3:23). Who was I to think, just because I preached on Sundays, that I was somehow the single exception to the rule? He reminded me that Christian ministers are sinners too. In the final analysis, we are *all* a mess in our flesh. We *all* live in a fallen world misled by Satan. We are all bound to do things that we will sooner or later regret. Always remember, *God allows U-turns.* Your loving Heavenly Father has promised, "I will give you back what you lost…" (Joel 2:25GNT). Let go of your regrets of the past. God often gives double for your trouble (Job 41). A brighter future awaits you if you are willing to believe it and receive it (Mark 11:24). (To help process a loss or regret, see the Five Stages of Grief, p. 280).

Questions for Reflection

1. List one or more regrets of the past that you need to let go of in order to accept God's forgiveness

_____

_____

2. Which of the 8 steps above could best help you process your regrets so you can move on with life? Choose two or three, if necessary.

_____

_____

≫ Self-Condemning Thoughts ▸

(CCCR)

A fourth fiery arrow that Satan fires at our minds, concerns self-condemning thoughts. Self-condemning thoughts may be the results of regrets of the past, a perceived failure, negative self-talk, failure to meet our own expectations and/or the expectations of others. Such thoughts may also result from a tragic experience. And this was the case with King David's daughter Tamar after she was assaulted by her half-brother Amnon. As a result of this terrible incident in her life, the scripture records her reaction, "So Tamar, a broken woman, lived in her brother Absalom's house" (2 Samuel 13:20). Tamar never married. She didn't appear to flow in the social circles her royal status might have afforded her. Tamar can be considered an innocent casualty in Mind Games. Tamar's emotional and psychological pain is palpable. One can almost hear the torrent of self-condemning thoughts she dwelt upon. Maybe she said to herself, "I am such a fool, I should have known better than to trust Amnon? How could I have been so gullible? I am damaged goods. No man will ever want me. I feel so ashamed! I will never be able to show my face in public again." Tamar, in her quiet anguish, lived out the rest of her days as an isolated hermit in her brother Absalom's house. Self-condemning thoughts, if left unchecked, can lead a person down a slippery slope into self-deprecating self-talk, self-hatred, depression and suicidal ideation.

The thought wars are real. When a self-condemning thought pops into your head, it is necessary to immediately confront it. **Step 1**: Check it. Recognize the thought. Which one of the Filthy Five is it? **Step 2**: Challenge it. Ask yourself the THINK questions. If the thought does not pass the THINK test, we must resist and reject it. **Step 3**: Change it: replace Satan's lie with the truth of God's word. When self-condemning thoughts pop into your head, FOCUS by recalling: "Therefore there is now no condemnation for those who are in Christ Jesus" (Romans 8:1). Before God, no believer in Christ stands condemned. You stand clean before the Lord. Such is the infinite grace of God. God made it possible not through our good works, but through Christ's all-important suffering on the cross. "Christ was without sin, but for our sake God made him share our sin in order that in union with him we might share the righteousness of God" (2 Corinthians 5:21 GNT). Despite what the voices in your head may be telling you, the Bible declares, Jesus' shed blood has made you righteous and acceptable before God. God is not mad at you. He's mad about you.

As believers, we spend too much time listening to our thoughts and not enough time critically evaluating our thoughts. Talk back to your self-condemning thoughts. This is how you employ your **I Am** significant mantra and My Spiritual Identity–N-O-W-M-O-V-E-F-O-R-W-A-R-D acrostic. They will help you to fight the good fight of faith, by renewing your mind—one thought at a time. *In the near future, memorize the Scriptures associated with this acrostic.*

Questions for Reflection

1. Why is a deeper understanding of God's infinite love and grace necessary in the effort to counter discouraging and self-condemning ideas?

2. How effective has repeating your *I Am significant* mantra and *My Spiritual Identity* – N-O-W-M-O-V-E-F-O-R-W-A-R-D acrostic been in helping you to replace self-condemning thoughts?

_____

_____

≫ Temptations ➤

(CCCR)

Temptations are one of Satan's most familiar tricks. The enemy tempts believers in order to bring them under his evil control, that he might persuade them to sin against the commands of God (as he did with Adam and Eve in the Garden of Eden). The following verses illustrate diverse ways in which Satan manipulates the minds of believers and non-believers alike.

Satan tempted Peter to persuade Jesus to forego his trials and sufferings on the cross.

- "But He [Jesus] turned and said to Peter, 'Get behind Me, Satan! You are a stumbling block to Me; for you are not setting your mind on God's interests, but man's'" (Matthew 16:23).

Satan tempted Judas to betray Christ.

- "During supper, the devil having already put into the heart of Judas Iscariot...to betray Him [Jesus]" (John 13:2; Luke 22:3-4).

Satan incited Cain to kill his brother Abel.

- "God said to Cain: 'sin is crouching at the door; and its desire is for you, but you must master it'" (Genesis 4:7).

The sin crouching at the door of Cain's heart was the temptation to take offense. Cain took offense to what God told him to do, which was to bring God a sacrifice that was acceptable to Him. Next, he took offense toward his brother Abel because God accepted Abel's sacrifice but rejected Cain's. Taking offense is one of the commonest sins to which we fall prey. How many church members have changed churches because they took offense to something that the preacher or another church member said! How many marriages ended because one or both spouses took offense and refused to walk the path of forgiveness? How many opportunities have been foregone because of our pride?

Use your sanctified imagination to view offense in a different light. Imagine you are in a room full of large balls about the size of beach balls all around your feet. On each ball the word OFFENSE is written. As we interface with others, we are often tempted to take offense. When you and I take offense, it's like stopping to pick up one of those balls on the floor marked "offense" and holding onto it tightly. The danger in picking up the offense ball is you will be tempted to throw it back at the one that you feel offended you. And the fight is on as the ball goes back and forth, back and forth with greater velocity. Tired of playing that hurtful game? At this point, we need to pause – we really need to reconsider– the way we approach handling offense.

When faced with the choice of whether to continue in the mindset of offense or to challenge it and take it captive. **Step1:** Check it—recognize which one of the Filthy Five thoughts it is. Offense (the condition of feeling offended) is a temptation. **Step 2:** Challenge it—resist and reject it. THINK fast. **Step 3:** Change it. Replace the lie that you have the right to feel offended. Instead FOCUS. Speak back to the Devil who says to you that you're justified to take offense. Anyone, including God, would understand. But the Bible says, "The Lord knows how to rescue the godly from temptation" (2 Peter 2:9). No matter what temptation we are liable to succumb, the Bible assures us that we have both the strength to resist and the power to endure. "No temptation has overtaken you but such as is common to man; and God is faithful, who will not allow you to be tempted beyond what you are able, but with the temptation will provide the way of escape also, so that you will be able to endure it" (1 Corinthians 10:13). *See page 242 for all five replacement Scripture verses.* Temptation begins with a thought. If that thought is not challenged and brought into subjection to the will of God, it will culminate in sin (James 1:15).

Questions for Reflection

1. In what areas are you frequently tempted to take offense, worry, or seek revenge?

_____

_____

_____

2. What are some of the ways you have learned here in Day 11 to push back on Satan's temptations?

_____

_____

_____

Reframe It

(CCCR)

Because we are in a spiritual battle against an enemy who is armed with flaming arrows and dead set on destroying us (John 10:10), it's inevitable that we will get wounded. But instead of remaining wounded and disabled, God wants us to conquer. Hence, He's equipped us with spiritual armor (Ephesians 6:10-18). When severely wounded by our own mistakes or aversive circumstances, one of the best ways to nurse ourselves back to spiritual health is by reframing the negative experience that led to our feelings of woundedness and debilitation.

The ability to reframe past and present painful, despairing events is indispensable if we desire to keep our minds free from negative painful memories and images. These fictive mental fashionings lodge themselves in our emotional memory bank and release toxic emissions into our tripartite nature: our mind, heart, and body.[5] The concept of reframing, finding a purpose in one's pain, or finding an "at least" is a principle that is deeply-rooted in scripture.

"And we know [with great confidence] that God [who is deeply concerned about us] causes all things to work together [as a plan] for good for those who love God, to those who are called according to His plan and purpose" (Romans 8:28 AMP).

Note that this scripture does not say that everything that happens to us is good, only that God would work it to our good, providing we have the proper perspective that allows God to work the hardship to our benefit. And we must keep in mind that all is done in accord with His timing.

I once got fired from a job. Oh, did it hurt! And the way it was handled was totally humiliating! However, after much prayer, I determined that I was going to trust God. Don't you know God worked my firing for my good by extricating me from a three-year contract so that I would be available to accept my dream ministry job three months after my "unjustified" firing. I now praise God for the firing because I see that God used it as an opportunity to fulfill His plan, a superior plan, for my life. Finding some positive in every negative experience is critical in overcoming emotional pain, for it serves to rid the mind of negativity and in so doing strengthens the anterior cingulate (AC) so it can better maintain a healthy balance between the frontal lobe and limbic system.[6]

A classic Biblical example of reframing an event by finding a purpose in the pain is graphically illustrated by Joseph in the Book of Genesis (chapters 37,39-45, 50:17-20). Joseph, as a youth (age 17), is betrayed by his jealous brothers and sold into slavery. As a slave, he is accused of trying to rape his master's wife. But rather than being executed, he is thrown into prison to languish for many years. However, instead of languishing in prison, Joseph flourishes there and becomes overseer of the prison and ministers to his fellow inmates. By the miraculous superintendence of God, Joseph interprets a fellow inmate's dream and two years later is granted an audience before Pharaoh to interpret Pharaoh's dream. By doing so, Joseph is elevated to Prime Minster of Egypt, second only to Pharaoh.

Joseph, while in his mid-thirties, reining as the Prime Minister of Egypt, is in for the surprise of his lifetime. He is about to be reunited with his brothers, the same brothers that threw him into a pit and pulled him out of the pit only to sell him to slave traders for 20 pieces of silver (Genesis 37:28). His brothers come to Egypt to purchase food amid a widespread famine. Joseph recognized them, and after putting them through several tests to assess their true repentance, arranges a private audience with his brothers, at which time he reveals his identity. His brothers, fearing the worst, are mortally frightened; thinking their brother Joseph will exact vengeance and perhaps kill them all. But unbeknownst to his brothers, Joseph had reframed the entire gut-wrenching ordeal in his mind, and instead of killing his brothers as they expected, said to his brothers, "As for you, you meant evil against me, but God meant it for good in order to bring about this present result, to preserve many people alive. So therefore, do not be afraid… so he comforted them and spoke kindly to them" (Genesis 50:20-21). Overcome with emotion, Joseph and all his brothers embraced each other and began uncontrollably to weep, rejoicing that after all this time they were all alive and reunited. His brothers were overcome by Joseph's magnanimous display of unconditional love and forgiveness.

Questions for Reflection

1. How do you think Joseph kept himself from becoming angry at God and bitter toward his brothers?

_____

_____

2. In the left column, write another negative experience that you feel you need to reframe. In the right column, write some positive outcomes.

Negative Experience	**Positive Outcomes**
_____	1. _____
	2. _____
	3. _____
	4. _____

**A Closing Prayer**

Dear God, continue to help me to win my thought wars by learning to practice my (CCCR) thought management strategies. Please help me to routinely read and embrace your word so I can stand strong against the enemy's subtle attacks. Holy Spirit continue to remind me to quote my I Am significant mantras and re-frame negative experiences. As I interact with others, help me to not take offense, so that I can reflect Christ in all my relational spheres. In Jesus' Name. Amen.

For an inspirational pick me up, I recommend:

- *Bulletproof* by Citizen Way
- *Surrounded (Fight My Battles)* by Michael W. Smith
- *Fighting For Us* by Anthony Evans
- *No Weapon* by Fred Hammond

Until tomorrow, do this:

Memory Work

1. Repeat the *I Am Significant* mantra.

   Confession: **I Am Significant**. Why? (Because) God loves me and sent his Son to die upon the cross for my sins. He has adopted me into His family and has given me a new name. I am a born-again Christian, fearfully and wonderfully made in the image of God.

2. Confession: **My Spiritual Identity** –N-O-W-M-O-V-E-F-O-R-W-A-R-D acrostic. The corresponding Scriptures are found on pages 108-109.

3. Remember, repeat FOCUS.

4. Continue to write The Filthy Five Memory Verses (p. 242) on 3x5 cards.

5. Remember, repeat the (CCCR) paradigm.

6. Remember, repeat THINK.

Mood Swingers:
How to Turn Around a Bad Attitude—Fast

Progress is impossible without change.
--George Bernard Shaw

Daily Food for Thought

• **Brain Fact** A state of mind "is composed of a cluster of neural firing patterns that have embedded within them a certain behavior, a feeling, tone, and access to particular memories. A state of mind makes the brain work more efficiently, tying together relevant (and sometimes widely separated) functions with 'neural glue' that links them in the moment."[1]

• **Key Thoughts** You can change your state of mind (mood) within seconds if you choose to.

• **Scripture** "A joyful heart is good medicine, but depression drains one's strength" (Proverbs 17:22 GW).

Daily Reading

While there are many ways to shift one's mood, the following story illustrates a profoundly destructive way to do it. Our case in point: Elvis Presley. In Elvis's later years, he used a bevy of drugs to totally shift his mood. After a strenuous night of performing for his fans, most nights the king, in order to help himself sleep, would have his assistants pump him up with drugs, "a rainbow-colored assortment of barbiturates (Amytal, Carbrital, Nembutal or Seconal), Quaaludes, Valium, and Placidyl, followed by three shots of Demerol injected just below his bare shoulder blades."[2] Then, before falling asleep, he would often binge on cheeseburgers and banana splits. After a while, the drug abuse became so routinized that he would have assistants virtually force-feed his half-conscious body additional doses of the drugs.

Elvis called each administered batch (of drugs) an "attack." Eventually, drug abusers such as Elvis lose track of what they have taken and what might sanely be considered safe. The day Elvis died, apparently, he was given three batches of his drugs in close succession and it was too much for his body.

Virtually all of us want to get away from an unpleasant experience or mood from time to time. But the ways we each go about this deliberate detachment from unpleasant feeling is widely variable. The healthiest ways to do this are those which employ some activity or strategy (prayer, meditation, exercise, talking with a close friend) rather than resorting to antisocial behavior, destructive behavior, and drug and alcohol abuse.

Scripture informs us that Satan comes to steal, kill and destroy (John 10:10). That is precisely what Satan did to the life of the beloved entertainer Elvis Presley. David Stanley, who was Elvis's half-brother and was with him in his final days, stated that, Elvis "preferred being drugged and numb to being conscious and miserable."[3] In the last days of his life, Elvis had become accustomed to answering his emotional challenges with food and drugs rather than by other methods.

If you, like Elvis, occasionally find yourself depressed, disillusioned, emotionally drained or miserable, in a very dismal place, this lesson is designed to help you learn to swing your negative mood in a more positive direction and do so in a very healthy, wholesome, and intelligent way. We all at times struggle with negative mindsets, moods, and attitudes, primarily brought about by some sort of fear, worry, spiritual dissatisfaction or longing.

A few relevant statistics:

- As many as 40 million Americans suffer from various anxiety disorders.[4]
- The World Health Organization estimates that more than 350 million people worldwide suffer from depression, and that is the most common cause of disability.[5]
- Annually, about 12 million people in the U.K. visit general practitioners for mental and emotional illness treatment, ranging from anxiety to depression.[6]
- Government officials in Australia anticipate that 45 percent of their citizens will struggle with a mental health issue—most likely depression or anxiety—at some point in their lives.[7]

The statistics bear out the need for all of us to learn to better manage our emotions and fears. A drug prescription may curtail some of the anxiety, but it is not a cure-all; it is a temporary Band-Aid. You are still going to have to manage the ways you mentally process things. Today's lesson will offer some practical tips on how to swing a negative mood in a positive direction. *All the upcoming recommendations are to be coupled with and undergirded by fervent prayer.* Not a minute to waste. Let's get started!

Music

> *It's like the brain is on fire when you're listening to music.*

One of the best ways to cheer yourself up when you're in a poor mood is to play some inspirational music. Music has the ability to cheer up the melancholy soul. "Music hath charms to soothe the savage beast." However, we must account for musical taste: not everyone hears the same piece of music the same way. But music is uplifting. It inspires and refreshes. This is one of the reasons why you see so many people listening to music on their iPods, cellphones, or blasting on their car or home stereo. Music's ability to change a person's mood was demonstrated in the life of King Saul, who suffered from manic depressive episodes. When King Saul found himself depressed, he would call for David. The Bible states, "David got out his harp and played. That would calm Saul down, and he would feel better as the moodiness lifted" (1 Samuel 16:23 MSG). As evidenced in the life of King Saul, inspiring music refreshed his soul. Research indicates that "music has the capacity to both turn on and tone down neural activity in the brain."[8] For example, listening to slow music seems to lower heart rate and blood pressure. How is that possible, you ask? Neurological research has revealed that "music stimulates numerous regions of the brain all at once, including those responsible for emotion, memory, motor control, timing and language."[9] Music has been used to treat a wide array of emotional disorders including anxiety, depression and stress-related afflictions like post-traumatic stress disorder (PTSD).[10]

Neuroscientist Istvan Molnar-Szakacs, at the University of California Los Angeles, said, "It's like the brain is on fire when you're listening to music."[11] I am reminded now of an event that took place in the life of David that neurologically set David's brain on fire. After a long absence, the Ark of God, which represented the presence of God, was being returned to Jerusalem. That was a day of great celebration. The praise-filled singers were singing passionately, and jubilant citizens were shouting and cheering at the top of their lungs and worship bands were playing their musical instruments under a special Holy Spirit anointing. King David got so emotionally aroused in his worship that he began taking off the clothes that were obstructing his expression. He nearly danced himself out of his clothes, nearly stripping himself down to his undergarments (2 Samuel 6:14-15). Oh, the power of music!

Why is music so moving? Neuroscientists contend…

That music can activate so many brain systems at once is the reason it packs such a mental wallop. It exerts its most profound effect in the brain's emotional core, the limbic system. There, music changes virtually all areas of the brain responsible for regulating emotion. Music automatically engages areas essential to pleasure and reward. So much so, in fact, that the same pleasure centers in the brain light up whether you're listening to a favorite tune, eating chocolate or having sex.[12]

Do you now see why music is such an effective mood swinger? Neuroscientist Anna Blood and Robert Zatorre of McGill University in Montreal take it one step further to say music activates the brain's neural system in the same way that addictive drugs stimulate the brain.[13] Have you ever become hooked on a song? Everyone in the house is saying, "Enough already! We are sick and tired of listening to that song!" However, your brain is not sick of that song at all; it is still pumping you up! It's like your brain is addicted to it. Here's why:

Stefan Koelsch of Freje University Berlin, through his research, discovered that listening to one of your favorite songs will stimulate the release of one of the brain's feel good chemicals: dopamine. In fact, the more you listen to your favorite song or songs the more psyched you get.[14] When you play the same song over and over again you tend to become more and more emotionally aroused. Add clapping your hands, tapping your feet, dancing, picking up an instrument to play along with the song or singing out loud at the top of your lungs, and your mood is boosted and you climb emotionally even higher. When we, like King David, get our praise on, we are actually lowering our level of depression, anxiety and fatigue.[15] Imagine that! God is awesome! He can use a song to swing your mood. (God is the maker of all good things.)

Physical Exercise

As you are getting your praise on, make it doubly beneficial by moving your body. You can use any livening agent such as music to supercharge any exercise or activity.

In some Christian circles, exercise may be discounted. Sometimes Christians are somewhat disdainful of exercise because it is physical, "of the flesh." This attitude is extremely unfortunate because the benefits of a healthy life are always enhanced with routine exercise. In general, we all live healthier and happier and in the superior enjoyment of God's magnificent blessings when we live a well-rounded life. And this includes exercise.

201

It was the Apostle Paul who said, "Exercise is good for your body..." (1 Timothy 4:8 CEV). Evidence suggests that it is beneficial both neurologically and physically. These benefits were derived from such notable medical research institutions as the Mayo Clinic and the Anxiety and Depression Association of America.

The Benefits of Exercise[16]

1. During exercise, your brain releases endorphins, chemicals that leave you feeling happier and more energized (i.e. dopamine, norepinephrine and serotonin).
2. Physical activity helps to decrease muscle tension.
3. Exercise boosts your immune system while decreasing chemicals that cause feelings of depression and sadness.
4. Activity reduces fatigue and increases alertness.
5. When you combine exercise with being outdoors, you can get special health benefits – from oxygenated air and from sunshine (and the vitamin D in sunshine may decrease depression).
6. Rejuvenates the cardio-vascular system and boosts your immune system.

Since God made us trichotomous (three part) beings, consisting of spirit, soul and body, it stands to reason that exercise benefits the total you. Whatever form of exercise you choose, you will derive the most benefit if you do it consistently. Find an exercise that you can do without having to go out of your way. Don't overcomplicate it. Each day you develop the habit of exercise, your brain will make it easier to do in the future. This is because the habitual is the routine, and what was once an onerous task becomes something that is just done at a certain time of the waking day, and without much concentration or motivation; it becomes normal.

Talk to Yourself

I'm reminded of the preacher and author Martin Lloyd Jones, who once said, "The trouble with most believers is that they spend too much time listening to their thoughts and not enough time talking to their thoughts." The psalmist David found himself in a melancholy mood due to trying circumstances, but he didn't stay there. He talked himself right out of his bad mood. David lamented, "My tears have been my food day and night; while they say to me all day long, 'Where is your God?'" (Psalm 42:3). Have your troubling circumstances contributed to your negative mood? A divorce, a car accident, a troubling diagnosis, the loss of a job, relationship trouble, a failure, a humiliation: now the enemy is talking through your thoughts and asking you, (essentially) "Where is your

God?" You served Him, but what real difference has He made in your life? You've failed to achieve what you thought you would have at this point in your life. "Where is your God?" You lost or failed a test or contest. "Where is your God?" You have been answering responsibilities, but what has it gotten you? You are behind and you feel disrespected and/or underappreciated. "Where is your God?

Continually enduring a negative internal narrative will keep your emotions vacillating up and down like a seesaw rising up and down between hope and despair, faith and fear, joy and frustration. When your faith is about to collapse under the weight of all your fearful concerns, it's time to have a talk with yourself. That is what the psalmist did. He talked to himself and asked himself (soul) two questions: "Why am I so sad? Why am I so upset" (Psalm 42:5 ERV)? (Days 10-11). These two questions interrupted the flow of his ANTs and gave his anterior cingulate (AC) — a few moments to regulate his brain chemistry and tip his mental seesaw away from the emotion-laden limbic system toward the frontal lobe. Then, operating from his frontal lobe, the side of the brain where executive functioning resides, David began to talk to himself—to his soul (mind, will, and emotions):

> I tell myself, "Wait for God's help!
> You will again be able to praise him,
> Your God, the one who will save you" (Psalm 42:11 ERV).

By talking to himself, the psalmist made sure he got in the last word. When negative thoughts flood your mind, to swing your mood in a positive direction, you are going to have to get the last word. When your negative thoughts tell you that God has removed His favor from you, say (aloud)…

I am…Favored of God. *"For it is You who blesses the righteous man, O Lord, You surround him with **favor** as with a shield"* (Psalm 5:12).

When your negative thoughts tell you, your enemies are going to defeat you, say…

I am…Well protected. *"No weapon that is formed against you will prosper"* (Isaiah 54:17).

When fear of failure thoughts dominates your mind, talk to yourself and say…

I am…Assured of success. *"And in whatever [a righteous man] does, he prospers" (Psalm 1:3). Or "The God of heaven will give us success" (Nehemiah 2:20).*

When tempted to quit, tell yourself…

I am…Destined to win if I do not quit. *"But thanks be to God, who always leads us in* **triumph** *in Christ…" (2 Corinthians 2:14).*

In addition to Psalm 42, David spoke to himself in Ziklag – the town where his wife and children had been kidnapped – and upped his mood (1 Samuel 30). He showed us how to fight the good fight, how to take every negative thought captive. We must continue speaking to ourselves until we break through the hold of those negative thoughts.

Positive Energy People (PEPS)

When feeling down, the devil likes nothing more than to keep you isolated so he can continue his nonstop verbal assault on you. The best thing is an honest conversation with a trusted friend or confidant. Therefore, the next mood swinger is to surround yourself with positive energy people (PEPs).

My wife, Vonda, first introduced this term to me. She is a professional counselor. One day, as she was escorting a client out of her office, she told her client to be sure to surround himself with positive energy people (PEP). When I think of positive energy people, my mind takes me back to the Apostle Paul and Silas who were thrown into jail for preaching the Gospel. The local religious leaders sought to discourage them by locking them up in prison. However, they made one small mistake: they locked them up in the cell *together*. Paul and Silas had been preaching the Gospel before things took a turn for the worse.

> The crowd rose up together against them [Paul and Silas], and the chief magistrates tore their robes off them and proceeded to order them to be beaten with **rods.** When they had struck them with many blows, they threw them into prison, commanding the jailer to guard them securely; and he, having received such a command, threw them into the inner prison and fastened their feet in the stocks. But about midnight Paul and Silas were praying and singing hymns of praise to God, and the prisoners were listening to them; and suddenly there came a great earthquake, so that the foundations of the prison house were shaken; and immediately all the doors were opened and everyone's chains were unfastened (Acts 16:22-26).

Talk about a jailhouse rock. Understandably they might have been feeling a little down, but God swung their mood by giving them a song in their storm. In this text we discover how partnering with a positive energy person (PEP) can swing your negative mood in a positive direction. Paul and Silas were of kindred spirit; they were both positive energy people. They were badly beaten and bloodied, but instead of fretting about their predicament, they chose to *encourage one another* by singing praises to the Lord. Imagine Paul and Silas lying in the jail cell, when suddenly Paul belts out a verse of a hymn sung by first century believers (meeting in their house churches or hiding in the catacombs, for fear of persecution). Silas, inspired by the fervency of his companion's worship, recalls the second verse. They begin singing the second and third verses in unison, with a faith that may have surprised even themselves. The Spirit of God, moved by their heartfelt praise and worship, began to shake things up. Suddenly the earth quaked, and the prison doors swung open. God set them free!

To up your mood, seek out positive energy people (PEP).

Get Some Sleep

My son, Paul Chipman, II, a licensed professional counselor, is an ardent believer in sleep therapy. He recommends sleep for anyone in a bad mood or feeling overwhelmed after receiving some disturbing or heartbreaking news. The Bible (Psalm 4:18; 127:2), medical doctors and neuroscientists alike concur on the benefits of sleep. Research gathered from the National Institute of Health and the National Heart, Lung and Blood Institute extol the virtues of a good night's sleep.

The Benefits of Sleep on the Body[17]

1. Sleep restores your body by reducing inflammation.
2. Sleep boosts your immune system.
3. Sleep helps us maintain a healthy weight by regulating the hormones that cause hunger.
4. Sleep helps regulate blood sugar levels.

The Impact of Sleep on the Brain[18]

1. Sleep stimulates your brain and improves your mood and combats stress and anxiety.
2. Brain cells are repaired.
3. Experiences are processed into memories and stored in areas within the brain where they can be accessed more quickly.
4. Healthy growth hormones are released.
5. Connections between nerve cells multiply, increasing your brain's plasticity.

6. Decision-making skills, reaction time, and hand-eye-coordination are sharpened.
7. Sleep improves your memory as well as your ability to study, retain information and be more creative.

For those who have difficulty falling asleep, here are a few tips: [19]

1. Go to bed the same time every night. It helps to set your body clock.
2. Establish a bedtime routine so your brain can automatically begin to amp down. Your nighttime routine may include reading your Bible, journaling your thoughts, praying, or playing some soft music to help you wind down. Do this consistently, and your brain will make it into a habit.
3. Do not take work into your bedroom; it will either excite you or depress you and has the potential to negatively affect your mood in the morning.
4. Do not have a TV in your bedroom.
5. Never use your computer in your bed.
6. Strictly limit the use of your cellphone or any other electronic device that may cause you to recall scheduling, financial, health, employment, or other concerns or worries. Also, be aware that any internet use in the bedroom will not help in your efforts to get to sleep. The bedroom needs to be almost exclusively a place to depart from the stresses and agitations of the day and feel relaxed, so you can get to sleep.

After you get a good night's sleep, be sure to begin your new day with the fifth mood swinger: healthy food.

Eating Healthy Foods

While eating healthy foods may not seem to change your mood right away, consuming beverages high in caffeine and eating sugary foods will. Go for the long-term benefit, not the quick fix; have the healthy (fresh fruit, fresh vegetables, and nuts) foods available in your home when you awake each morning. Eating healthy foods can help promote emotional health and reduce stress and anxiety that can worsen feelings of sadness and make depressive mood swings more severe.

Several Foods to Eat in Abundance:[20]

1. Asparagus, broccoli, carrots, spinach
2. Avocado, garlic, sweet potatoes, mushrooms
3. Blueberries, raspberries, black berries
4. Cashews, walnuts, hazelnuts, pistachios, almonds
5. Apples, grapefruit, lemons, wheat germ, bee pollen
6. Legumes (beans),

7. Albacore tuna, and
8. Wild-caught salmon

Five Foods to Avoid:[21]

1. Caffeine
2. Sugar
3. Wheat
4. Dairy
5. Salt

Avoiding these food elements is important to the optimization of brain health. Paraphrasing a nutritionist: water cools, cleanses, lubricates and generally improves the body's condition. Fruits cleanse the body; vegetables build it; grains sustain it and herbs help to heal the human body.

Avoid a Sinful Lifestyle

To maintain a positive mindset, and to reach our optimum spiritual, emotional and mental health, it would be to our benefit to diligently avoid a sinful lifestyle. Seek to sin less and less each day. (1 John 1:9-10). Christians must seek to avoid practicing sin (i.e. adapting a sinful lifestyle). Sinful lifestyles – such as lying, gossiping, gambling, abusing alcohol and drugs, criminality, sexual immorality, etc. – result in greater overall stress, and they work counter to the purposes of this *21-Day Plan*. Perpetually living under the weight of guilt and condemnation will inevitably swing your mood in a negative direction.

Donnie McClurkin recorded a song entitled, *We Fall Down But We Get Up*, based on Proverbs 24:16; which states, "Though a righteous man falls seven times he will rise again." Because of the sinful nature of our flesh, in this earth, we will always struggle with sinful inclinations to fulfill our fleshly desires and craving. Therefore, we believers are admonished in scripture to "Throw off any extra baggage, get rid of the sin that trips us up" (Hebrews 12:1 CEB). What sin or sins are tripping you up in this season of your life? Is it a certain food, a certain drug, or a relationship that may have seemed off limits? It has been said, "Don't try to adjust the Word of God to fit your lifestyle; rather adjust your lifestyle to fit the Word." When you and I engage in sinful ideas, values, and behaviors we give our enemy a foothold into our thought life. The enemy knows that he can send your positive mood into a nosedive by reminding you of your private wickedness. As a believer, you actually have residing in you the same new life God gave Jesus when He raised him from the dead. The old sinner you once were has died. You've become a new creation on the inside. You are full of the resurrection life of God (Romans 6:4; 7:1-4)!

I've listed four essential reasons that God encourages His children to avoid living a sinful lifestyle:

1. Sin grieves the Holy Spirit.

The Apostle Paul warns us, "And do not bring sorrow to God's Holy Spirit by the way you live. Remember, he has identified you as his own..." (Ephesians 4:30 NLT).

2. Sin diminishes your joy.

A sin-sick sorrowful King David pleads with God to, "Restore to me the joy of your salvation..." (Psalm 51:1-2, 8).

3. Sin leads you into bondage.

The Apostle Peter reminds us, "Yes, people are slaves to anything that controls them" (2 Peter 2:19 ERV). As stated earlier, the brain will make a habit out of any behavior repeated consistently.

4. Sin separates you from your power source.

Jesus declares, "I am the vine, you are the branches; he who abides in Me and I in him, he bears much fruit, for apart from Me you can do nothing" (John 15:5).

The quicker you inculcate these mood swinging practices into your life, the easier it is to retrain your brain to overcome melancholy feelings and maintain a positive state of mind. Neurologically, a state of mind "is composed of a cluster of neural firing patterns that have [woven into them] a certain behavior, a feeling, tone, and access to particular memories. The state of mind makes the brain work more efficiently, tying together relevant (and sometimes widely separated) functions with 'neural glue' that links them in the moment."[22] Employing these mood swingers will help to lock your brain into a positive state of mind. In such a positive state, you'll spend more time praising rather than pouting or wallowing in self-pity and self-condemnation.

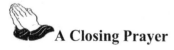 **A Closing Prayer**

Dear God, when I find myself in a negative place, may your Holy Spirit remind me to apply the truths in this lesson and swing my mood into a more positive direction. In addition, when I am sad, please remind me to not isolate myself and to reach out to others for encouragement and inspiration. In Jesus' name. Amen.

For an inspirational pick me up, I recommend:

- *Smile* by Kirk Franklin
- *A God Like You* by Kirk Franklin
- *Encourage Yourself in the Lord* by Donald Laurence
- *Shake* by Mercy Me
- *Peace in the Midst of the Storm* by Becky Fender

Until tomorrow, do this:

Memory Work

1. Continue memorizing The Filthy Five FURST acrostic as you continue learning to classify your thoughts.

2. Continue to write down The Filthy Five Memory Verses on 3x5 cards and practice verbalizing them (Figure 14. 2 p. 242).

3. Memorize to more successfully apply your (CCCR) Thought Management 101 strategy (p. 182).

4. Remember to THINK fast.

5. Memorize FOCUS.

6. Repeat the *I Am Significant* mantra. (Repeat10-12x's per day.)

Confession: **I Am Significant**. Why? (Because) God loves me and sent his Son to die upon the cross for my sins. He has adopted me into His family and has given me a new name. I am a born-again Christian, fearfully and wonderfully made in the image of God.

7. Confession: **My Spiritual Identity**–N-O-W-M-O-V-E-F-O-R-W-A-R-D acrostic. Write the acrostic on a 3x5 card and carry it with you wherever you go. The corresponding Scriptures are found on pages 108-109.

The Toxic Ten:
10 Distorted Patterns of Thinking (Part 1)

If error is corrected whenever it is recognized as such, the path of error is the path of truth.

--Hans Reichenbach

Daily Food for Thought

- **Brain Fact** Distorted patterns of thinking originate and participate in the limbic system of the brain. When the emotion-laden limbic system is frenetically charged, it inhibits the reasoning capacities of the frontal lobe.[1]

- **Key Thoughts** The Toxic Ten are ten distorted patterns of thinking and constitute a subcomponent of The Filthy Five. I consider The Toxic Ten as temptations, because we are "tempted" to engage in one or more of these distorted presumptions and reckonings.

- **Scripture** "Brothers, stop being childish in your thinking; but in your thinking be mature" (1 Corinthians 14:20).

Daily Reading

Today I am going to share a very personal story. The events of the story occurred at a time in my life when I was stressed, pressed and unknowingly depressed. I know that sharing such a personal struggle is a bit risky, but I figure if it can help someone avoid the mistakes I made, and as a result learn to save their most important relationships, it is worth the risk.

God blessed me to marry one of his favorite daughters. Some may view this statement as theologically incorrect. But, let's face it, I'm biased. My wife gave her life to Christ as a 9-year-old child in Sunday school, and apart from a few brief years as a depressed teenager, she has faithfully walked in close fellowship with God. I met her in Dallas, Texas in 1982. I had moved there after college in New Jersey to attend seminary. She moved there from Annapolis, Maryland for the sole purpose of finding a solid Bible teaching church. I was on staff at the church, serving as Director of Children's Education. As a director, it was my job to recruit several learning center teachers. She happened to be a public-school teacher with a heart for children, so I was interested. At the time, I needed a volunteer administrative assistant, and she fit the bill to a tee. As we spent time together, I was able to see her love for the Lord and her heart to serve people. The Holy Spirit spoke to me and urged me to add her name to my (fanciful) marriage prospect list. The decision to put her on my radar was made a whole lot easier by the fact that she was very pretty – a former model – and fairly tall for a woman. With the beauty as my foremost prospect, I went to confer with my three marriage mentors. I read to them the several names on my short list, and all three of my mentors chose her, Vonda, hands down. Then after securing my mentor's assent, I set out to win her heart. I wasn't handsome, but I had a sweet conversation, and I found I could make her laugh. She was (fortunately for me) a lonely girl a long way from home.

After several intense laughing sessions, we were engaged one year later and married six months after that. The first couple of years of marriage were great. I had been warned about the seven-year itch, but my marital itch came 4 years early. By year three, my interest in my wife began to wane and my marriage was in danger. I wanted out! However, walking away was made very difficult when I discovered my wife was pregnant with our first child.

As I wrestled for months with unwholesome torments in my head, (fueled by my unbeknown depression) the Lord allowed me a flash-back to a conversation I had with my father over a decade earlier. I was at that time about twelve years old. My father asked me to come outside so he could talk with me. Leaning against his classic 1955 Ford, with a full moon aglow in the night's sky, He said, "Son, there were many times I thought about leaving your mother, and all of you children, but I love you too much to do that."

As I pondered how to exit my marriage, inwardly, I heard the Spirit of the Lord speaking to me in a still small voice, saying, in essence, Your father may have had his reasons for wanting to leave your mother, you, and all twelve of your siblings, but he didn't. Here you are married to one of the prettiest and godliest of all my daughters, who happens to be pregnant with her first child. What's the matter with you? You are being deceived! Wake up!

Very suddenly, the gravity of my sinful ideas fell upon me. I felt so ashamed for wanting to abandon my pregnant wife and son. Overcome with remorse and regret, I cried out, *"Lord, please turn my heart toward home."* In only a brief few minutes the weight of my sin and guilt lifted from my shoulders. The next day I went to the seminary bookstore and picked up a few books on marriage and began the hard work of repairing what I had so long neglected and began working on the corrupt rationalizations that had so troubled my life. I had almost ruined a perfectly good marriage.

Dr. Norman Wright, in his book, *A Better Way to Think*, remarked,

When facing a problem or negative situation in your marriage, first look at your own thoughts. There's a good chance that by turning around your negative thoughts, you'll find your solution. Negative thoughts can kill the love in a marriage. They can escalate perceptions so much so that a neutral behavior can be seen as negative. Sadly, it's often the very qualities that attract two people to each other that later are seen by each other as negative. It's not that the attributes that each enjoyed or admired have disappeared. They're still there. But if self-talk about a spouse tends to be negative, it can seep into and affect one's perception even of the qualities once thought attractive.[2]

To me, it was crystal clear: my wife was not the problem—I was. The Apostle Paul told his young protégé, Timothy, "Keep a close watch on all you do and think..." (1Timothy 4:16 TLB). The problem was that I had not guarded my thoughts, and as a consequence was about to wreck a perfectly good marriage and wound my then-unborn son.

> *Negative thoughts can kill the love in a marriage.*

Today, I am eternally grateful to both my Heavenly Father and my earthly father for saving my marriage. I now realize that if my father had so many years earlier walked out on his family, in all probability, I would have done the same. Now, almost 35 years later with 3 adult sons, by God's grace, we are still happily married. To God be the glory! That's my testimony of gaining victory over distorted thinking patterns that would have led me to discount the most wonderful person in my life and would have caused me to ruin my most precious relationship. My words here are not intended to evoke feelings of guilt or condemnation. On the contrary, it is my prayer and intention that sharing my story may be insightful and instructive to those who are where I was mentally. To those readers: push back on those toxic regrets of the past, if you have not already, seek God's forgiveness, and practice living in the now.

Whether it is a present sense of confusion or guilt or something entirely in the past, the lesson is the same: the present is the only time in which we can proactively change our thinking and better our circumstances.

What's your story? How strong are your current relationships? Do you have a history of strained or broken relationships, perhaps in a romantic relationship, close relatives, co-workers, neighbors, fellow church members or social network correspondents? Are you on the verge of making a colossal mistake?

Over the next two days of this 21-Day Plan we are going to discuss ten ways that our thinking becomes polluted, impure, and distorted. A few of these are among the thought distortions that almost cost me my marriage – my shot at a truly blessed and fulfilling life. I have labeled these ten thought distortions, **"The Toxic Ten." The ten distorted patterns of thinking are a subcomponent of the Filthy Five (FURST). They fall under the category of <u>temptations</u>.** In unguarded moments, we are *tempted* to engage in these negative mental constructs.

These ten unhealthy thinking styles are the culmination of the research of Drs. Aaron Beck and David Burns. Dr. Beck is considered the founder of Cognitive Behavioral Therapy (CBT). CBT rose to prominence in the early 1960s.[3] Beck, a Freudian psychiatrist,[4] unlike Sigmund Freud, who believed the cause of depression "was anger turned on the self, "[5] Beck concluded, through his research in *1963*, that it was not "repressed anger" that was the sole cause of depression, but rather systematic distorted patterns in the thinking processes."[6] Years later, Dr. David Burns, a disciple of Beck, embraced and popularized Beck's unhealthy thinking paradigm and added several of his own to bring it to a grand total of ten types of twisted thinking.[7]

Now, without further delay, let us delve into The Toxic Ten. As you read along, consider how often *you* engage in these very same cogitative patterns. For a pictorial overview of these Toxic Ten, see Day 14, Figure 14.1 (p.238-239).

Emotional Reasoning[8]

According to Beck and Burns, with emotional reasoning, "you assume your negative emotions necessarily reflect the way things really are."[9] Feeling becomes its own justification. Why was my marriage in trouble? Because I felt unhappy. I felt I married too young. I felt trapped. So, I wanted out. Notice all the "I felts." That is what emotional reasoning does; it distorts the truth and stokes your fears. My wife, Vonda, a professional and spiritual counselor defines FEAR as…
Frightful **E**motions **A**ppearing **R**ational. That's a very accurate assessment of what unhealthy fear is. Because I perceived these frightful emotions as being real and rational, I felt trapped. Hence, I subscribed to a new acrostic of FEAR: **F**orget **E**verything **A**nd **R**un. When you rely on emotional reasoning, it will cause you to often think and do (essentially) irrational things.

For a Biblical example of emotional reasoning, we need to look no further than to the prophet Elijah. He went from the thrill of victory—defeating the 450 prophets of Baal (1Kings 18), to the agony of defeat when Queen Jezebel threatened his life. What did Elijah's emotions compel him to do?

Now Ahab [Jezebel's husband] told Jezebel all that Elijah had done, and how he had killed all the prophets with the sword. Then Jezebel sent a messenger to Elijah, saying, "So may the gods do to me and even more, if I do not make your life as the life of one of them by tomorrow about this time." And he was afraid and arose and ran for his life and came to Beersheba, which belongs to Judah, and left his servant there. But he himself went a day's journey into the wilderness, and came and sat down under a juniper tree; and he requested for himself that he might die, and said, "It is enough; now, O Lord, take my life, for I am not better than my father's"(I Kings 19:1-4).

A distraught Elijah, **F**orgot **E**verything **A**nd **R**an. In total, he ran over 115 miles[10] from the northern tip of the kingdom to the southernmost part of the kingdom. That is a whole lot of adrenaline surging through his system.

Neurologically speaking, Elijah's brain was in such a stressed and fearful state, that he was not able to properly access the rational side of his brain—the frontal lobe (Day 8). If he had engaged his frontal lobe, he would have reasoned that if God had just protected him from 450 false prophets, He could protect him from one mean-spirited antagonistic woman.

When the emotion-laden limbic system is fully activated it obstructs the logical reasoning capacities in the frontal lobe, rendering the doer a hapless pawn of his or her unbridled emotions.[11] Emotional reasoning distorts perception. Elijah is so discouraged that he asks God to kill him. Swept up in his emotions, Elijah has lost all soundness of mind. The text reveals still more distorted thinking. He swears to God that he is the last zealot standing for God: "I have been very zealous for the Lord, the God of hosts; for the sons of Israel have forsaken Your covenant, torn down Your altars and killed Your prophets with the sword. And I alone am left; and they seek my life, to take it away." (1 Kings 19:14). God both confronts and corrects Elijah's distorted thinking by assuring him that he is quite mistaken. God reminds Elijah, "I [have] 7,000 in Israel, all the knees that have not bowed to Baal and every mouth that has not kissed him" (1Kings 19:18). These verses attest that, though we "feel" a certain thing is true, such is often not the case.

Emotional reasoning is distorted because we cannot always trust our emotions; they are subject to change, like the weather. When our thoughts are driven by emotion, at one time you may feel one way and within minutes or an hour you may feel very differently. It is distorted thinking because you are thinking with only half your brain engaged.

Here are some examples of emotional reasoning:

* "I know that it doesn't make sense, but I feel…."
* "Of course, I know what the Bible says, but I feel the Lord is leading me to…."

- 'You make a sound rational argument, but I feel I know what is best."
- "But wouldn't anybody feel as I do?"
- "This time, I'm going to follow my heart and not my head."
- "I feel like a failure so I must be a failure."
- "I feel unloved; therefore, I must be unloved."
- "My head is telling me *no*, but my heart is telling me *yes!*"
- "It was love at first sight."
- "In my mind, I feel…"

Thinking for a Change

When you find yourself engaging in emotional reasoning, it is time for you to employ your check, challenge and change (CCCR) thought management strategy. 1) Check it. Ask yourself, "What kind of thought is it? It is a temptation. You are being "tempted" to engage in emotional reasoning. 2) Challenge it: THINK fast. Is it true? In the limbic-driven mindset the idea will feel true to you. Hence, it is important that you ask yourself the next several questions:

Is this thought…

True?
Helpful?
Inspiring?
Non-condemning?
Keeping in line with Scripture?

If the thought does not pass the THINK test, you are to resist and reject it, immediately.

3) Change it: FOCUS—Fight Opposition Constantly Using Scripture. Does God want you to make decisions based on your feelings and emotions exclusively? No! The Bible tells us to, "Trust in the Lord with all your heart and lean not on your own understanding; in all your ways submit to him, and he will make your paths straight" (Proverbs 3:5-6 NIV).

We have been told, scripturally, to submit to God and not our feelings. When you catch yourself being carried away by your emotions, pause, take a few deep breaths and begin counting slowly up to at least ten or twenty. In doing so, it will allow your anterior cingulate (AC) time to regulate your brain chemicals. Peter, one of the twelve apostles, a man given to much passion and emotion, told believers to "…brace your minds for action. Keep your balance" (1 Peter 1:13a TLV).

Keep your rational thoughts and emotions in proper balance. Do this by critically examining your emotions, especially the stronger emotions as they arise, and by delaying any action or expression. Generally, the stronger (upset, angry) emotion is also the least reliable.

Questions for Reflection

1. In what ways may you be engaging in emotional reasoning? What situations are likely to pose the greatest risks?

_____

_____

2. Based on this and previous lessons, do you now have faith that you will be better able to critically appraise present emotional challenges and use prayer when you are in a particularly vexing situation?

_____

_____

A second thought distortion is evident when we jump to conclusions.

Jumping to Conclusions[12]

There are two types of jumping to conclusions. They are referenced here as "mind reading" and "fortunetelling."[13]

Mind reading: "Arbitrarily believing you know what another person thinks, even though [he or she] has not told you"[14] and there is no strong proof. A mind reader may feel 100% certain that he or she knows what another person thinks. For example, after the job interview, the interviewee felt that he probably would not be called back for a second interview because he "felt" the interviewer did not like him. Mind readers do a lot of assuming. In my earlier years of marriage, I did a lot of mind reading and still suffer the fault. My wife would sometimes ask, "Where did you get that idea from? If you were not sure what I was thinking, why didn't you just ask me?" And my response was a typical mind reader's: "I thought...It looked to me that... or "I just assumed...." Are you sometimes doing the same thing?

Fortunetelling: You predict the future, and anticipate a negative or unfortunate, or aversive or undesirable outcome.[15] In such instances, we are often quick to assume a worst case scenario – a *no* rather than *yes*, a failure rather than a success.

A Biblical example of jumping to conclusions is demonstrated in the thought life of Jacob concerning the intentions of his twin brother Esau. Jacob had stolen Esau's birthright by disguising himself and pretending to appear to be Esau. Isaac, the father, knowing he would soon be transitioning from life to death, decided it was time to bestow his blessing upon his eldest son, Esau. However, while Esau was out hunting game, the youngest son, with the help of his mother Rebecca, deceived Isaac and instead of blessing Esau, blessed his youngest son Jacob. Once Esau is told by his Father, Isaac, what Jacob did, he becomes enraged and vowed to kill his brother Jacob. Jacob, to escape Esau's wrath, flees his homeland to stay with his uncle Laban (Genesis 27). After twenty years of living with and working for his uncle, the Lord commanded Jacob to go back home and reconcile with his brother whom he wronged twenty years earlier.

A fear-stricken Jacob begins to jump to conclusions, both mind reading and fortunetelling. He demonstrates mind reading by thinking his brother is still mad at him for defrauding him out of his birthright. (After twenty years, how would he know if Esau was still mad at him? He had never asked.) Secondly, as an example of fortunetelling, Jacob reasons that because Esau is so enraged, he is going to kill him and his entire family. Why else would he be approaching with four hundred men (Genesis 32:6-7)? Jumping to conclusions will often set our brain chemicals into a frenzy. As the plot thickens, Jacob scrambles to save his life and the lives of his family members. Jacob is so scared that he doesn't sleep a wink all night. When daylight breaks, Jacob is in for a surprise. "Then Jacob lifted his eyes and looked, and behold, Esau was coming, and four hundred men with him...Then Esau ran to meet him and embraced him, and fell on his neck and kissed him, and they wept" (Genesis 33:1,4).

Do you now see how unhealthy jumping to conclusions is; all that debilitating stress, pressure, anxiety and worry for nothing? God had, over those many years, performed a miraculous work of forgiveness in the heart of Esau toward his manipulative brother, Jacob.

How often do you engage in jumping to conclusions without being conscious of it?

Examples of mind reading:

- "Well, I thought...."
- "Everyone else liked it. I just thought you would too."
- "No, I didn't ask you, but you never seemed to complain before."
- "Based on the way she looked at me, I don't think she likes me."
- "I just assumed...."
- "She probably doesn't like that."
- "I didn't ask you because I didn't think I needed to."

Examples of fortunetelling:

- "I'll probably get fired!"
- "I don't see this working out."

- "No, I have not considered that, because I didn't think it would do me any good."
- "You'll never change."
- "I'll probably fail again."
- "Things will never improve."
- "People don't change!"

Thinking for a Change

When you find yourself jumping to conclusions, stop mid-thought or mid-sentence and employ your check, challenge and change (CCCR) thought management strategy.

Scriptural advisement against jumping to conclusions:

- "…How stupid! —to decide before knowing the facts!" (Proverbs 18:13 TLB)

- "The first person to speak always seems right until someone comes and asks the right questions" (Proverbs 18:17 ERV).

Questions for Reflection

1. On a scale from 1 to 5, (1 being the lowest, 5 being the highest) how often do you engage in jumping to conclusions?

Mind reading: 1-2-3-4-5 (Circle one.)
Fortunetelling: 1-2-3-4-5 (Circle one.)

2. Reflecting upon what you just read, in what ways might jumping to conclusions be damaging your relationships with those close to you?

_____

_____

3. Do you think people sometimes engage in fortunetelling as a way of guarding themselves against being overly disappointed?

_____

_____

The reason that jumping to conclusions is a thought distortion is because healthy mental processes help us to become aware that we cannot know what others are thinking unless we ask them. Even asking sometimes does not yield or reveal the truth we would like to hear.

218

A third thought distortion that we need to consider is the propensity to engage in negative mental filtering. This can also sometimes be understood as fault finding.

(Negative) Mental Filtering[16]

Beck and Burns maintain that we engage in negative mental filtering when we "pick out a single negative detail and dwell on it… to the point that the rest of our world is darkened." Burns likens this to a "drop of ink that discolors a beaker of water."[17] For example, if a woman makes a presentation at school, and her classmates complement her on it, but one classmate remarks on the poor quality of one component or aspect of the presentation, she would filter out all the positive, affirming, praiseworthy feedback and obsess on that one comment. The considerable weight of what she hears is only the negative, only the critical. In such instances she bypasses virtually all the positives.[18] In such an instance, the person notices her failures but not her successes.[19]Are you the kind of person that will dismiss six compliments and focus on the one lone negative comment? These habits are not conducive to personal fulfillment because a person who is excessively focused on his or her own (supposed) imperfections and flaws is not able to see his or her potentiality as she might. Do you see now why negative mental filtering is hurtful to our favorable end?

The healthy mentality hears both compliments and criticism and rather even-handedly evaluates failures and successes.[20] That is why my marriage was at one-point teetering on the brink of destruction. My distorted thinking had me focusing exclusively on the negative aspects of my spouse and ignoring all her positive qualities. Negative mental filtering evokes and nurtures negative emotions, and the result is that this is done to the exclusion of important and illuminating aspects and references.

For an exceptional Biblical example of negative mental filtering, read the story of Moses sending the ten spies to check out the Promised Land and report their findings. The entire story is recorded in Numbers 13. In the final analysis, 10 of the 12 spies gave Moses a negative report because they chose to focus on the negative aspects of the land (mainly the giants) to the exclusion of a myriad of positive aspects of the Promised Land. Like a large ink drop, their negative mental filtering obscured their perception of the entire expanse. The 10 spies' negative reports so poisoned the minds of the children of Israel that they refused to enter the territory out of fear of the reported oversized inhabitants.

Examples of negative mental filtering:

- "I can't see anything good coming out of this."
- "The odds are stacked against us."

- "There is no way we can win."
- "This is hopeless."
- "God may be all powerful, but He's powerless to change that person's ways.
- "It's impossible!"
- "We are never going to get the help we need."

Like the children of Israel, we become discouraged when we engage in negative mental filtering. Some of you are on a job you can't stand. Could it be that you are engaging in negative mental filtering – seeing only what is wrong, guessing at limitations and others' intransigence?

Thinking for a Change

When you find yourself thinking and seeing only the negative things around you, you are engaging in negative mental filtering. To shift your focus, employ your check, challenge and change (CCCR) thought management strategy.

The Bible informs us to attend to positive things (among them, God Himself).

- "Finally, brothers and sisters, whatever is true, whatever is noble, whatever is right, whatever is pure, whatever is lovely, whatever is admirable—if anything is excellent or praiseworthy—think about such things" (Philippians 4:8 NIV).

God wants us to shift our attention away from the negative and focus instead on all the good things He provides.

Questions for Reflection

1. Identify one situation in your life in which you may be engaging in negative mental filtering.

_____

_____

2. Based on the verse above (Philippians 4:8) name several positive things that you can think about each day?

_____

_____

Discounting the Positive

When we engage in discounting the positive, we tend to reject positive experiences by insisting they somehow "don't count." If one does a good job, one may think it wasn't good enough or that "anyone could have done as well."[21] For example, a person who is given a promotion may say, "I don't think I deserve this." The enlightened, mature, and healthy functional mind receives compliments and praise, and sees them as only occasions to say thank you.

The contributions my wife was making to the marriage were ill-considered. I discounted the fact that she worked tirelessly every day as a schoolteacher, so I could pursue my seminary studies full-time. I discounted the positive contributions she made to the ministry I oversaw. I discounted the fact that she cooked dinner every evening and, in an effort to please and satisfy me, did her best to adjust her schedule to accommodate me. However, my attitude was she's *supposed* to do such things; it's a wife's job. After all, she's my helpmate (Genesis 2:18). Steadily discounting all the positives, I focused on the few negative things. Discounting her positives was definitely a stupid thinking thought distortion.

Another biblical illustration of discounting the positive: regarding the ten spies aforementioned, the two who came back with a positive report, were discredited and scoffed by the other ten and ultimately by the whole congregation. These are the positives the other ten spies discounted: 1) rich soil (Numbers 13:27); 2) large fruit in abundance (Numbers 13:23); 3) God's promise to fight for and with them in any potential contest with the giants (Numbers 13:6-8).

Examples of discounting the positive are exemplified in the following:

- "I appreciate all you do, but it's overshadowed by this one thing...."
- "Yeah, you may have cleaned the entire house, but you neglected...."
- "I am pleased you got mostly A's, but that B is unacceptable.
- "Am I supposed to commend you for doing what any responsible person would do?"
- "Sure, you do a lot of chores, but they are easy for you; you're used to them."
- "Yes, you support the family financially, but you should do more."

Thinking for a Change

When you find yourself disparaging positive contributions and qualities, know that you are engaging in a kind of distorted thinking; it's time to employ your check, challenge and change (CCCR) thought management strategy.

The Bible instructs us to well-consider positive elements and virtues rather than contrary, discouraging, woeful negatives. The Apostle Paul wrote the following words while languishing in a prison cell:

- "Summing it all up, friends, I'd say you'll do best by filling your minds and meditating on things true, noble, reputable, authentic, compelling, gracious—the best, not the worst; the beautiful, not the ugly; things to praise, not things to curse" (Philippians 4:8 MSG).

If we observe, consider, and weigh the most beautiful and praiseworthy things, the Bible promises that...

- "[God] will keep in perfect peace all those who trust in him, whose thoughts turn often to the Lord" (Isaiah 26:3 TLB)!

Questions for Reflection

1. When you find yourself disparaging your own positive contributions and qualities, what should you do?

_____

_____

2. What are some examples of a person discounting the positives of others?

_____

_____

As I desisted engaging in these thought distortions, I began seeing my marriage improve. Therefore, if you change your thought distortions, things will change for you, too. How can I say this? It is because, although while I don't know you, I do know God, and I know that His Word is true. He loves you and only desires the best for you. He may disapprove of what you have done, but totally approves of *you* and your potential.

As we close today's lesson, praise God and thank Him for revealing to you a strategy to repair relationships and difficulties that might have ruined you had you not been edified by the concepts revealed in The Toxic Ten. As long as we live in this body of clay, we will always struggle in many areas of our lives. Sometimes, it may honestly seem like you are taking two steps forward and three steps back. My goal in writing *The 21-Day Plan* has been to help you to learn to win most of your mental and behavioral challenges. You may not win EVERY battle nor should that be your expectation. Every life has its setbacks, dissatisfactions, and disappointments, but if you can grow to maintain a 75% ratio of positive thoughts, to 25% negative, you should consider that a major victory. Thought management is a lifelong process that includes many successes and failures. Stick with it! You'll be glad you did.

A Closing Prayer

Dear God, help me to become more and more aware of when I am engaging in distorted thinking. When I am thus encumbered, Holy Spirit, bring to my awareness the "check, challenge and change" thought management paradigm. Lord, help me to envision the positive things, increase in appreciation of my brothers and sisters, and renew my faith in your promise. In Jesus' name. Amen.

 For an inspirational pick me up, I recommend:

- *Tell Your Heart to Beat Again* by Danny Gokey
- *Press On* by Selah
- *Brighter Day* by Kirk Franklin

Until tomorrow, do this:

Memory Work

1. Continue to write down The Filthy Five Memory Verses on 3x5 cards and practice memorizing them (Figure 14. 2, p. 242).

2. Memorize the (CCCR) paradigm (p.182).

3. Remember to THINK fast.

4. Memorize FOCUS.

5. Repeat the *I Am Significant* mantra. (Repeat 10-12x's per day.)

6. Confession: **I Am Significant**. Why? (Because) God loves me and sent his Son to die upon the cross for my sins. He has adopted me into His family and has given me a new name. I am a born-again Christian, fearfully and wonderfully made in the image of God.

7. Confession: **My Spiritual Identity** –N-O-W-M-O-V-E-F-O-R-W-A-R-D acrostic. Write the acrostic on a 3x5 card and carry it with you wherever you go. Corresponding Scriptures are found on pages 108-109.

The Toxic Ten:
10 Distorted Patterns of Thinking (Part 2)

Men must not only know, they must act...
--W.E.B. DuBois

• **Brain Fact** "Negative thoughts secrete 'downer' chemicals (i.e. cortisol and adrenaline) in the brain which cause people to feel depressed, anxious, worried, stressed, or fearful, etc." [1]

• **Key Thoughts** Dr. Aaron Beck, considered the originator of Cognitive Behavioral Therapy (CBT),[2] argued that depression is a consequence of engaging in systematic distorted patterns of thinking.[3] The Toxic Ten are reflective of those thought distortions. The Toxic Ten are ten distorted patterns of thinking that will likely result in depression if consistently engaged.

• **Scripture** "I can't bear to even think such thoughts. My insides churn in protest" (Hosea 11:8 MSG).

Daily Reading

Today's lesson is a continuation of The Toxic Ten thought distortions begun in our last lesson. The Toxic Ten have the potential to ruin your most valued rela-

224

tionships. These thought distortions almost cost me my young marriage (Day 13). These forms of unhealthy thinking patterns may be adversely affecting your relationships as well. If you are experiencing difficulties effectively communicating with your spouse, fiancée, children or significant others, a supervisor, coworkers, church members or, closest friends, it may be due in part to forms of unhealthy thinking. Yesterday (Day 13), we discussed four of the ten: emotional reasoning, jumping to conclusions, negative mental filtering, and disqualifying the positive. Today, we shall fully explain the remaining six. First, let us talk about all or nothing thinking – ways we sometimes frame things in absolutist terms.

All or Nothing Thinking[4]

My all or nothing thinking was what got my marriage into hot water from the outset. I was in my mid-twenties and didn't know how detrimental my thought patterns could become. Hence, when my wife and I had a difference of opinion, I thought she should just submit and fall in line. It was my all or nothing thinking, which I sometimes reference as one-way thinking, which developed into serious communication problems. The major reason that all or nothing thinking is a major relationship buster is that the person thus engaged tends to see things in black and white, either-or conceptions, with no gray area. Consequently, he or she becomes more judgmental and dismissive of other people's contrasting feelings and opinions. Additionally, all or nothing thinkers view compromise as a weakness or as having already lost.

For Biblical examples of all or nothing thinking, one need look no further than the religious leaders of Jesus' disciples and Saul of Taurus.

The religious authorities (i.e. Pharisees, and Sadducees) out of fear of Jesus' popularity, sought to intimidate their fellow Jews with the following edict. "…whoever confessed Jesus to be the Christ would be expelled from the synagogue (John 9:22 CEB). Most all or nothing thinkers view compromise as a weakness/softness.

Jesus' disciples were also guilty of engaging in all or nothing thinking. Observe John's report to Jesus. "Master, we saw a man using your name to expel demons and we *stopped* him because he wasn't of our group." Jesus said, "Don't stop him. If he's not an enemy, he's an ally" (Luke 9:49-50 MSG). All or nothing thinkers tend to feel that they are right, and everybody else is wrong.

Saul of Taurus, an ardent Pharisee, prior to his conversion, viewed all followers of Christ (Christians) as a threat to Judaism. In his zeal, he sought to destroy this new religious sect. We read in the Books of Acts, "[Saul], threatening with every breath and eager to destroy every Christian, went to the High Priest in Jerusalem. He requested a letter addressed to synagogues in Damascus, requiring their cooperation in the persecution of any believers he found there, both men and women, so that he could bring them in chains to Jerusalem." (Acts 9:1-2 TLB). All or nothing thinkers are often very rigid in their thinking and legalistic in their behavior.

Consider now how entrenched in all or nothing thinking you might be. Here are a few examples of all or nothing constructions:

- "It's my way or the highway!"
- "It's now or never."
- "I'm right, you're wrong."
- "If I can't do it perfectly, I won't do it at all."
- "If I can't have you, no one will."
- "It isn't over until I win!"

Some inherent problems with all or nothing thinking, or as I refer to it as one-way thinking, are as follows. It stifles two-way communication, shows one's lack of objectivity and leads one down a dead-end street. Unless abandoned, this type of thinking will cause loving relationships to die prematurely and job opportunities will be filled with potential to crash and burn. The inability to respect another's opinions will often lead one into isolation resulting in relational death in many spheres and sometimes even lead to violence. See this thought distortion illustrated in Figure 14.1 The Toxic Ten (pp. 238-239).

Thinking for a Change

When you find yourself thinking in all or nothing terms, it is useful to employ your check, challenge and change (CCCR) thought management strategy. And in so doing, ask yourself these very incisive questions: Is it (the idea, notion, memory, etc.) …

True?
Helpful?
Inspiring?
Non-condemning?
Keeping in line with Scripture?

If the thought does not pass the THINK test, you are to resist and reject it, immediately. It is always necessary to change the troublesome ideation proactively and FOCUS —Fight Opposition Constantly Using Scripture. On all or nothing thinking, the Bible states,

- "Pride is the first step toward destruction. Proud thoughts will lead you to defeat" (Proverbs 16:17 ERV).

226

- "There is a way that seems right to a man and appears straight before him, but at the end of it is the way of death" (Prov. 16:25 AMPC).

The next two types of thought distortion: magnification and minimization.

Magnification (Catastrophizing) and Minimization

The concept of magnification, when extrapolated, may include, "blowing things out of proportion (catastrophizing)." This concept of catastrophizing is epitomized in the statement, "making a mountain out of a mole hill." The thought distortion of minimization involves "inappropriately shrinking [discounting] something to make it seem less important."[5]

The concepts of magnification and minimization are both vividly illustrated for us in the Book of Numbers Chapter 13. The Children of Israel after their miraculous deliverance from the land of Egypt, in which God parted the Red Sea with a mighty wind, causing the water to stand erect, could walk through the Red Sea on dry land. But when Pharaoh and his mighty army pursued them into the water, to kill them, God released the waters and drowned the Egyptians. (Read the story in the Book of Exodus chapter 14.) The estimated 1.5 to 2 million Hebrew slaves are now free and are marching toward the Promised Land, the land promised to them by God.

After weeks of traveling, the multitude is now camped out on the border of the Promised Land. Before entering that land, Moses, their esteemed leader, chooses 12 leaders and sends them into the land on a recognizance mission to spy out the land and give an account of the land to the people. Forty days later the 12 spies return and report their findings. Ten (10) of the twelve (12) spies give the congregation a negative report saying,

- "We are *not* able to go up against the people, for they are too strong for us." [32] "The land... is a land that devours its inhabitants; and all the people whom we saw in it are men of *great* size (Numbers 13:31-32).

The 10 spies concluded the two negatives outweighed the positive aspects of the land.

However, two of the spies (Caleb and Joshua) gave the congregation a positive report of the land saying,

We should by all means go up and take possession of it, for we will surely overcome it. The land which we passed through to spy out is an exceedingly good land. If the Lord is pleased with us, then He will bring us into this land and give it to us—a land which flows with milk and honey. Only do not rebel against the Lord; and do not fear the people of the land, for they will be our prey.

Their protection has been removed from them, and the Lord is with us; do not fear them." But all the congregation said to stone them with stones (Numbers 13:30; 14:6, 8-10).

Faced with these two diametrically opposing perspectives of the Promised Land, the children of Israel were forced to decide. Whose report were they going to believe? Would they believe the negative report of the ten spies or the positive report of the two spies? Moses, their leader, and his brother Aaron embraced Caleb and Joshua's positive assessment. Thus, they encouraged the people to trust God and believe that the same God who had delivered them from the mighty hand of Pharaoh was more than able to defeat the giants living in the Promised Land. The people's response:

Then all the congregation lifted up their voices and cried, and the people wept that night. All the sons of Israel grumbled against Moses and Aaron; and the whole congregation said to them, "Would that we had died in the land of Egypt! Or would that we had died in this wilderness! Why is the Lord bringing us into this land, to fall by the sword? Our wives and our little ones will become plunder; would it not be better for us to return to Egypt?" So, they said to one another, "Let us appoint a leader and return to Egypt (Numbers 14:1-4).

In the final analysis, much to Moses' chagrin, the Children of Israel *magnified* the behemoth inhabitants and *minimized* the power of their great God. Because of their *catastrophizing*, and discounting the power of God, God prohibited them from entering the Promised Land. So, they spent the next forty years wandering in circles in the wilderness.

Study the examples below and decide which category of statements are examples of magnification or minimization. Fill in the blank below with the word magnification or minimization.

The following statements are examples of _____.

- "That one decision has ruined my entire life! I will never be able to recover."
- "I promised myself I would never forgive you for hurting me!"
- "Nothing's as bad as this!"
- "I don't think I can live without it!"

The following statements are examples of _____.

- "He has a bit of a temper, but he only gets physical with me when he's been drinking."
- "Sure, she has more than a few red flags, but...."

228

- "I only drink on weekends, so I don't have a drinking problem."
- "Overall, he's a pretty honest guy. He only lies when he gets in a pinch."
- "Yes, I slept with her, but it was only sex."
- "You should be over that breakup by now."

Questions for Reflection

1. Try to reflect upon a recent incident in which you engaged in one or both thought distortions. What was the result?

_____

_____

2. Knowing yourself as you do, which of the spies' report would you have most likely believed? The report of the 10 or the report of the 2? I probably would have sided with the report of

_____

_____

Labeling

Labeling involves "attaching a negative label to [oneself] or others."[6] Burns argues that "labels are just useless abstractions that lead to anger, anxiety, frustration, and low self-esteem."[7] He goes on to say that when we label others, we need to know that the problem is not with others, it is probably with our thinking, brought on by certain expectations that we held.

Perhaps the most dramatic and most consequential Biblical example of labeling is found in our earlier story recorded in Numbers 13. Recall the children of Israel about to enter the Promised Land. God had sworn to give them that land when he freed them from Egyptian bondage. However, the people refused to enter the territory, due to their fear of the "giant" inhabitants there. Hence, the 10 spies negatively labeled themselves, saying, we, "became like grasshoppers in our own sight, and so we were in their sight" (Numbers 13:33). They had a grasshopper mentality.

"When we are so anxious, we lose touch with the wise part of our brain [frontal lobe] and act on impulse [limbic system], often to our regret." [8] Regrettably, they talked themselves out of the Promised Land by engaging in five of the thought distortions of the Toxic Ten: (1) Emotional reasoning (we're afraid of the giants); (2) Jumping to conclusions (We will never be able to defeat the giants); (3) Negative mental filtering (It's a good land, but...); (4) Disqualifying the positive (the fruit is big, but the giants are bigger), and finally (5) Labeling (we're grasshoppers, too small and too insignificant to defeat them).

Examples of labeling by others:

- "You are academically slow; a C student at best."
- "They're slobs!"
- "They're ignorant and they'll never learn!"
- "You're a loser and will never amount to anything."
- "You're a mess up. You've made too many mistakes."
- "You're all washed up. Your best days are behind you."
- "She's ugly. I don't know why anyone would date her."
- "Why would you get a tattoo like that if you weren't an idiot?"

Examples of personalizing those labels:

You're right…
- "I am stupid."
- "I'm a slob."
- "I'll never learn this."
- "I am a loser just like my father."
- "I'm such an awful screw up!"
- "I feel like a 'has been.' My best is behind me."

The healthy thinking person avoids labeling. You may have failed, but you are not a failure. If it were true that a failure made the person "a failure," all humankind would have to be thus categorized. A healthy-minded person knows to separate his/her "who" from his/her "do." You are not the same as what you do. We must practice distinguishing between actions and conditions. Failure is an event—not a person.

Questions for Reflection

1. You have many positive attributes. What are some of the labels (terms) you and others have given these positive attributes? For example, "I always thought I was…"

_____

_____

_____

2. Who were some of the people who positively labeled you?

_____

_____

3. As an adult, what positive labels do you think you warrant?

_____

_____

Thinking for a Change

When you find you're negatively labeling yourself, it would be to your advantage to employ your check, challenge, change and reframe (CCCR) thought management strategy. And repeat your *I Am Significant* mantra and your *My Spiritual Identity* –N-O-W-M-O-V-E-F-O-R-W-A-R-D acrostic. Remember these three things: (1) God declares, "There is no condemnation for those who are in Christ Jesus; (2) Since God is your creator, only God has the ultimate right to name (label) you; (3) The only power a label holds is the power you give it."

Overgeneralization[9]

The person who engages in this form of twisted thinking (overgeneralization) will see a single negative event, such as "a romantic rejection or a career reversal, as a never ending pattern of defeat by using such words as 'always' or 'never'."[10] Our twisted thinking causes us to draw across-the-board conclusions from very little evidence.[11] For example, a young man shows romantic interest in a young girl and she gives him the cold shoulder. He concludes, "I'm always being rejected." A healthy-thinking person will draw a conclusion only after weighing all the evidence and considering the full scope of potentiality.

For a Biblical example of overgeneralization, let us reflect upon the words King David spoke about a person or persons who had disappointed him. He said, "All men are liars" (Psalm 116:11). Surely, not *all* men are liars! He said it when he was emotionally upset. Now, let's examine the verse in its entirety, "I said in my alarm, 'All men are liars'" (Psalm 116:11).

Like King David, in times of frustration we've all probably made similar statements. For example,

- "My prayers are never answered."
- "I never catch a break."
- "I always get speeding tickets."

231

- "All guys are dogs. You can't trust them."
- "All women are gold-diggers."
- "All Christians are hypocrites."

> *A healthy-thinking person will draw a conclusion only after weighing all the evidence.*

Thinking for a Change

Making such overgeneralizations will support the creation of a lot of toxic emotions by increasing unhealthy chemicals in the brain. Whenever you find yourself thinking or speaking in overgeneralized terms, it is helpful to catch yourself and employ your check, challenge, change and reframe (CCCR) thought management strategy. The Bible encourages us to think more maturely:

- "Brothers, stop being childish in your thinking; but in your thinking be mature" (1 Corinthians 14:20).

- "When I was a child, I spoke like a child, I thought like a child, I reasoned like a child. When I became a man, I gave up childish ways" (1 Corinthians 13:11 ESV).

Overgeneralizing statements cause more communication problems than they solve. Each of us is better than any single mistake we have made, and the mistake made does not the person make.

Questions for Reflection

1. Do you sometimes hear yourself saying "always" or "never" (maybe in your head)?

_____

_____

_____

2. Might you be able to sometimes stop yourself and say, "Wait a minute. This is just one occurrence, and I am wrong to judge the whole person based on this?"

_____

_____

_____

232

Should Statements[12]

Dr. Burns contends that by using *should, must* or *ought* statements about ourselves, we are setting ourselves up for disappointment if we do not follow through. Such statements, when not followed by constructive actions, often lead to feelings of guilt and self-condemnation.

When we apply "should statements toward other people, the result is often frustration."[13] When we word our frustrations, tacitly or otherwise, we deepen our belief in them. While it may be in a sense true, it is unhelpful cognitively or socially to think and act in terms of "should." Isn't it true that you *should* exercise every day? Yes, it is. But you don't. Is it not fair then to accommodate others when they too violate the "should" rubric? We know, of course, our own reasons for doing what we do, and we use those reasons for blame-removing purposes. Others' actions draw our judgement and anger. We need, as sincere Christians, to be much more restrained in taking the attitude that another person or other people should have acted differently. "Judge not that you will be not judged" (Matthew 7:1-3). Burns points out that we use "should," "must" and "ought" with others when we feel frustrated that they fail to follow through. And frustration was never, of course, the goal.

By way of a Biblical example, the Scribes and Pharisees with all their legalistic practices and customs were masters of using "should," "must" and "ought". They often expressed what they felt Jesus should do and what he ought not do. He shouldn't eat with tax collectors and sinners, they claimed. He and his disciples ought to always wash their hands before eating, and he must never heal anyone on the Sabbath, etc., so they alleged (Matthew 9:11; 12:2).

Personally, I've intentionally tried to stop using terms of expectation. I have been able to replace the words *should, must*, and *ought* with the phrase "It would be to my advantage/benefit to...." Quoting myself: "It would be to my advantage:

- "to pray and read my Bible every day."
- "to obey God in all things."
- "to be less judgmental."
- "to not make excuses for my sins and mistakes."

You may not have noticed, but throughout the writing of this book I've tried my best to avoid telling you what you ought to do. Rather, I word my advisement, "It would be to your advantage to...." After my suggestion, I often end the sentence with a phrase like, "You'll be glad you did!" Try your hand at replacing the 'should', 'must' and 'ought' with the phrase, "It would be to my advantage to...."

As we hasten to discuss the final two couplets of thought distortion – personalization and blame – I must admit that these two distortions have been my unfortunate undoing for decades. I'm not sure, but it may be a part of an ordinary person's desire to want to fix things.

Personalization

"Personalization occurs when a person holds [him- or herself] personally responsible for an event that isn't entirely under [his or her] control...personalization leads to guilt, shame, and feelings of inadequacy."[14] For example, a working mother blames herself for her child's disruptive behavior in school or a husband holds himself personally responsible for his wife's extramarital affair. Or, a child feels personally responsible for his or her parents' divorce. A healthy-thinking person knows what she or he cannot control and therefore will not feel buried under a load of guilt and self-condemnation, nor will she or he blame others for those things he or she may have failed to do (and is now suffering the consequences of).

For a Biblical example of personalization, read Matthew 16:21-23 and John 18:10-11. Jesus foretells his death to his disciples, but Peter is adamantly against it. In fact, he takes personal responsibility to prevent Christ's arrest and ultimate crucifixion. Consequently, the Great Prophet rebukes Peter saying, "Get behind Me, Satan! You are a stumbling block to Me; for you are not setting your mind on God's interests, but man's" (Matthew16: 21-23). However, Peter dismissed His words. And, on the night the Roman soldiers came to arrest Jesus at Gethsemane, Peter sprang into action to defend his teacher.

> Simon Peter then, having a sword, drew it and struck the high priest's slave, and cut off his right ear.... So, Jesus said to Peter, "Put the sword into the sheath; the cup which the Father has given Me, shall I not drink it?" (John 18:10-11).

The loyal disciple failed to realize that the circumstances he faced were beyond his control. Try as he might, he could not prevent Christ from ultimately suffering on the cross. Why did Peter feel personally responsible for preventing Christ from capture? First, Peter loved Jesus, and as a disciple, he sought to prove his loyalty and devotion to his rabbi. Second, he was engaging in precisely this sort of distorted thinking: personalization. Other examples of distorted thinking are evident in the following questionable statements:

- "I'm going to make you love me!"
- "It's my fault my parents divorced!"
- "I'll make him change for the better."
- "She won't succeed without me."
- "I'll grow this little [organization, business, enterprise] into something great."

- "Nobody can do what I am doing."
- "No, he's not spiritually inclined now, but I'll make him more interested in spiritual things."

It was exactly this kind of distorted thinking that led to my feelings of dejection, low self-esteem and depression when things did not work out as I had planned. I was trying to control things that were outside my control. This overestimation of my "powers" caused me to feel like a failure. It was all very humbling. When we take responsibility for things, we have no control over, we are setting ourselves up for disappointment.

Questions for Reflection

1. In what areas of your life might you be taking responsibility for things outside of your control? Think broadly.

_____

_____

2. Is it more important to change yourself or change those around you? Why?

_____

_____

3. In what affairs of your present life could recognizing your own limitations afford you greater peace of mind?

_____

_____

Blame

Unlike personalization, those who play the blame game fault others for their problems and misfortunes in life, while overlooking the ways that they may have contributed to their own unenviable circumstances.[15] The originator of the blame game was Adam. When God asked him why he had eaten the forbidden fruit, Adam responded, "The woman that you gave me, gave me the fruit and I did eat" (Genesis 3:12). Adam, in his one statement, blamed both God and his wife, Eve, for his decision to eat from the tree of the knowledge of good and evil (Genesis 2:17): God, it's your fault. If you had not given me this woman, we would not be having this discussion. Eve, for her part, not wanting to be the fall girl, blamed the serpent (Genesis 3:13).

A New Testament example of someone playing the blame game is found in John 5. There we find a man sitting on a porch for 38 years waiting for someone to put him into the pool so he could be healed. "When Jesus saw him lying there and knew that he had already been a long time in that condition, He said to him, "Do you wish to get well?" The sick man answered Him, "Sir, I have no man to put me into the pool when the water is stirred up, but while I am coming, another steps down before me" (John 5:2-3, 5-7).

Like the needy man in this story, today you may be discouraged because you're feeling you didn't get the personal support you felt you needed (at some time in the past). Perhaps a specific friend let you down. You may even feel God has let you down. I have only one question for you. How long do you plan to play the blame game? Playing the blame game is a major thought distortion because it deceives you into thinking that you are a victim. But you are not a victim; you are a victor. Hence, Jesus commanded the man to, "Get up, pick up your pallet and walk." Immediately the man began to walk (John 5:8-9). In essence, Jesus was commanding the man to take personal responsibility for his own life. He is saying the same thing to each one of us. Stop looking to others and stop blaming others for your present state of affairs. You can rise up, with Jesus' help.

None of this is to suggest that everyone has treated you with complete respect and righteousness. The foregoing discussion is only intended to bring to your attention that many of us give the slight, insult, offense, injury, etc. far greater power than is necessary. To play the blame game is to forfeit a measure of control over your own fortunes.

> *No one drives us crazy unless we give them the keys.*

Here are some examples of blaming:

- "I punched you because you made me angry!"
- "Sure, I was unfaithful in our marriage, but it was only because you were not meeting my needs."
- "If you had only treated me better, I probably would have stayed."
- "You took away my dreams."
- "The drugs made me do it."
- "My grades are poor in that subject because the teacher does not like me."
- "I'm an emotional mess because of my parents."

Thinking for a Change

When you find yourself playing the blame game, immediately check, challenge, change and reframe (CCCR) your thought management strategy. 1. Check it.

What kind of thought is it? In this case it is a temptation. You are being tempted to blame someone or something for your problems. 2. Challenge it: THINK fast. Is it true? Perhaps not. If it doesn't pass the THINK test, you are to resist and reject it straightaway. 3. Change it. FOCUS—Fight Opposition Constantly Using Scripture. Concerning blaming others, the Bible instructs:

- For every person will have to bear [with patience] his own burden [of faults and shortcomings for which he alone is responsible]. (Galatians 6:5 AMP)

A more modern translation renders the verse:

- Each person has his or her own burden to bear and story to write (Galatians 6:5 VOICE).

How do you envision your story ending?

Instead of pointing the finger, use that same finger to turn the page and start writing a whole new chapter in your life. You can start the chapter with these words, "Beginning today, I am taking personal responsibility for my life story. No more excuses! It was the great American basketball player Michael Jordan, who said, "There are a million excuses for not paying the price." Are you willing to begin paying the price, or will you put if off another day? The lame man lay at the side of the pool for 38 long years. Are you ready to pick up your mat of personal responsibility—TODAY? Or are you of the mindset of the Scottish poet, Thomas Campbell, who said, "Tomorrow let us do or die." Today, Jesus is asking you what He asked the man at the pool, "Do you wish to get well?" The American activist and educator W.E.B. Du Bois had an answer to this question: "Men must not only know, they must act." *Act* on the information that was presented to you over the past two days and begin to rid your mind of toxic thoughts and emotions. Don't be just a hearer. Stephen Covey, author of *The 7 Habits of Highly Effective People*, maintains *"To learn and not to do is really not to learn. To know and not to do is really not to know."* Please apply these truths. The riddance is supremely empowering! You will be glad you did! For a pictorial overview of these Toxic Ten, see Figure 14.1.

> *"To learn and not to do is really not to learn. To know and not to do is really not to know."*
> *--Stephen Covey*

The Toxic Ten

10 Forms of Unhealthy Thinking

1. Jumping to Conclusions

1) Mind Reading
(assuming you know what someone is thinking)
2) Fortune Telling
(predicting the future with a negative outcome)

- "I don't think she likes me."
- "I predict their relationship will not last."

2. All-or-Nothing Thinking

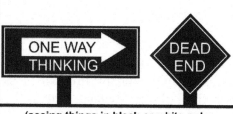

(seeing things in black or white only,
allowing no gray area)

- "It's my way or the highway!"
- "If I can't do it perfectly, I have failed."
- "That thing is hopeless!"

3. Mental Filtering (Negative)

(viewing matters through a negative lens)
**You notice your failures, but not your
successes.**

- "This is not going to work."
- "They'll never change."

4. Emotional Reasoning

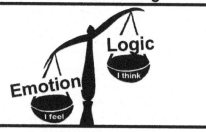

**Because you feel a certain way,
you think your feelings must be true.**

- "I feel like a failure so I must be a failure."
- "It may not make sense, but I feel..."
- "It was love at first sight."

5. Should Statements

**Using judgmental words like "should",
"must" and "ought" can make you feel guilty.
When applying "should" statements to
others, the result is often frustration.**

- "I should be further along by now."
- "You ought to know better."

Figure 14.1 The Toxic Ten

6. Personalization & Blame

"It's all my fault." "It's all your fault."

You hold yourself responsible for things that are not your responsibilty.

- "It's my fault my parents divorced!"

You blame others for things that are your responsibility.

- "I punched you because you made me angry!"

7. Discounting the Positive

See no positive. Hear no positive. Speak no positive.

You discount the positive things that have happened to you and/or disregard your accomplishments.

- "Oh, that was nothing. Anyone could have done that."
- "They were just trying to be nice."
- "That doesn't count."

8. Magnification & Minimization

You blow things out of proportion. (catastrophising)

- "That one decision has ruined my entire life."

You inappropriately shrink something to make it seem less important.

- "It's not that big of a deal."

9. Overgeneralizing

You **never** listen to me!

Because you are **always** fussin' !

You tend to draw exaggerated conclusions from very little evidence; using such words as 'always' or 'never'.

- "God seems to never answer my prayers."
- "I'm always a day late and a dollar short."
- "I never catch a break."

10. Labeling

I am... stupid lazy unworthy idiot
You are... a loser

You assign negative labels to yourself or others.

- "I am "ugly", "unloveable", "inadequate", "unworthy", etc."
- "You are such an idiot and a real screw up."

The Toxic Ten

10 Forms of Unhealthy Thinking

Figure 14.1 The Toxic Ten

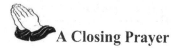 **A Closing Prayer**

Dear God, I open my heart to allowing your Holy Spirit to instruct my conscious mind when I am engaging in any form of distorted thinking. Lord, help me to learn The Toxic Ten thought distortions. In Jesus' name. Amen.

 For an inspirational pick me up, I recommend:

- *Let Revival Come* by People and Songs
- *Reckless Love* by Cory Asbury
- *My Help* by The Brooklyn Tabernacle Choir

Until tomorrow, do this:

Memory Work

1. Continue memorizing The Filthy Five FURST acrostic.

2. Continue to write down The Filthy Five Memory Verses (p. 242).

3. Memorize the CCCR paradigm, THINK and FOCUS acrostics.

4. *I Am Significant* mantra (Repeat 10-12x's per day—p. 65).

5. **My Spiritual Identity** –N-O-W-M-O-V-E-F-O-R-W-A-R-D acrostic. Write the acrostic on a 3x5 card and carry it with you wherever you go.

6. Review Conflict Resolution: Rules of Engagement on the next page.

7. Become familiar with The Toxic Ten thought distortions graphic.

FYI: Your brain can remember anything if you consistently review the information and provide your brain with the necessary mental hangers. *Most of us don't have a memory problem, we have a recall problem.* The following acrostic is just such a mental hanger to help you remember The Toxic Ten: **JAMES** is a **PD** (Police Department) **MOL.**

Jumping to conclusions
All or nothing thinking
Mental filtering (negative)
Emotional reasoning
Should, must, and ought thinking
(is a...)
Personalization and Blame
Disqualifying the Positive

Magnification and Minimization
Overgeneralizing
Labeling

Conflict Resolution: Rules of Engagement

The Toxic Ten are often the root cause of relational conflict. Conflict is an inevitable part of most relationships. See Appendix D: Conflict Resolution (p. 380).

Assertiveness

Assertiveness is the "ability to express your feelings and ask for what you want in any relationship."[16] We must never assume our partner is capable of mind reading. Many of our relationships are mired in negativity and conflict because we fail to ask for what we really want, settling instead to go along to get along. *Assertiveness* is learning to make **"I"** statements (in a positive, respectful manner) instead of saying "you". Here's an example of a typical **non-assertive** "you" question: *"You want to go shopping?"*

Examples of Assertiveness:
- "I plan to go shopping within the hour. Would you like to come?"
- "I'm tired. I'm not going to cook tonight. Take me out to dinner!"

Active Listening

Active listening is the ability to let the other know that you understand, often by restating or rephrasing their idea, assertion, or intention.[17]

Examples of Active Listening:
- "I *understand* that while you appreciate the times we spend together, you still enjoy spending time alone. *Is that what you meant just now?"*
- "If I *understand* what you said, you would like to see an action adventure movie, but you believe maybe I would prefer a comedy. *Did I get you?"*

The Filthy Five Memory Verses

When Satan attacks your mind with The Filthy Five, use these Scriptures to check, challenge, change and *reframe* (CCCR) the negative thoughts with the Word of God. This is what it means to FOCUS (**F**ight **O**pposition **C**onstantly **U**sing **S**cripture and "take every thought captive" (2 Corinthians 10:5). Write the five verses on 3x5 cards or keep in your smartphone, and commit them to memory—one at a time. Begin memorizing the verse you are struggling with the most. You'll be glad you did! To aide you in your efforts, read The 7 Keys to Memorizing Scripture found on pages 253-254.

Topic: Fear of the Future	Topic: Unhealthy Comparisons
Address: Mathew 6:34 (TLB) **Verse:** So don't be anxious about tomorrow. God will take care of your tomorrow too. Live one day at a time. **Address:** Mathew 6:34 (TLB) *Other verses: Jer. 29:11; Matt. 6:25-26; Phil. 4:6-7*	**Address:** 1 Peter 5:6-7a (MSG) **Verse:** Be content with who you are, and don't put on airs. God's strong hand is on you; He'll promote you at the right time. **Address**: 1 Peter 5:6-7a (MSG) *Other verses: Psalm 139:14; 2 Cor. 10:12*

Topic: Regrets of the Past
Address: Isaiah 43:18-19a (NIV) **Verse:** Forget the former things; do not dwell on the past. See, I am doing a new thing! **Address:** Isaiah 43:18-19a (NIV) *Other verses: Philippians 3:13b-14a; 1 John 1:9*

Topic: Self-condemning Thoughts	Topic: Temptations
Address: Romans 8:1 (NASB) **Verse:** Therefore there is now no condemnation for those who are in Christ Jesus. **Address:** Romans 8:1 (NASB) *Other verses: 2 Cor. 5:21; 1 Peter 2:9*	**Address:** 1 Corinthians 10:13 (NIV) **Verse:** No temptation has overtaken you except what is common to mankind. And God is faithful; he will not let you be tempted beyond what you can bear. **Address:** 1 Corinthians 10:13 (NIV) *Other verses: 2 Peter 2:9; James 1:13-14*

Figure 14.2 The Filthy Five Memory Verses

FYI: At the bottom of each card, other verses are listed. Should you choose to memorize these verses, it is important you choose a verse that resonates with you; thus you'll be more motivated to memorize it.

Week 3
Thought Replacement (Days 15-21)

Where there is doubt, faith;
Where there is despair, hope;
Where there is darkness, light;
Where there is sadness, joy.

-- St. Francis of Assisi

Day 15

Replacing Unforgiveness with Forgiveness

Forgiveness is a great attribute to have, but it is only afforded to the strong. The weak can never forgive.

--Anonymous

Daily Food for Thought

- **Brain Fact** "Patterns that are repeated over time become wired in the brain and body."[1] "The brain will take whatever data you give it consistently and make it into a habit and create its very own neurological craving to perpetuate the habit."[2]

- **Key Thoughts** "It isn't difficult to replace lies with God's truth. It just takes intentional and consistent effort...it takes the time and energy to find statements of God's truth and apply them to life's [untruths]."[3]

- **Scripture** "Be kind to one another, tender-hearted, forgiving each other, just as God in Christ also has forgiven you" (Ephesians 4:32).

Daily Reading

It has been said, "Harboring unforgiveness is like drinking poison and hoping your enemy dies." We've all been hurt before. You may have been hurt by someone who lied to you or lied about you, or verbally, physically or emotionally abused you. You wear emotional scars in the aftermath of a divorce, a breakup, or some other insult, or other transgression, or betrayal. And because you were hurt so deeply, you have vowed to never forgive the transgressor for the pain and suffering he, she, or they caused you. I feel your pain. But let me tell you some-thing: of all the poisonous thoughts that enter our minds, perhaps the most vicious and most damaging is unforgiveness; it eats away at us psychologically, damaging our total being – spirit, soul and body. Lest you think I'm just writing about things I've never experienced; I want to take a minute to share with you a personal story of betrayal by a dear friend of more than 20 years.

One of the many times I was tempted to harbor unforgiveness occurred when I was fired from a church staff position. The senior pastor apparently feared that I wanted his job. One Sunday morning he handed me a resignation letter that he himself wrote. He even signed my name at the bottom. In hindsight, it seems funny, but at the time I was devastated. Initially, I was shocked and hurt, but my hurt quickly turned into anger as I questioned how a man of God could act in such a dastardly way toward a friend he had known for over twenty years.

Well, it is longstanding in my personality that I do not take mistreatment ly-ing down. Instead of going to sleep as usual, I stayed up practically all that night strategizing my next move, enlisting allies and mounting my defense. By dawn, I had my rebuttal all typed up in an email and was about to hit the send button to all parties involved as well as a Christian reconciliation ministry in our area. In my mind, this was a slam dunk case. As I sat in front of my computer, having reread the document laced with countless Bible references, eager to press the send button, the Lord reminded me that I had not had my morning devotions (QT) and that I should do so before sending off my email. Hence, I opened my Bible, which happened to reveal the Book of Exodus, chapter 14. As I began reading, the following words seemed to jump off the page: "Stand still and see the salvation of the Lord" (v.14). When I read those words, my heart sank. I knew the Lord was telling me to hold off on sending my email and launching a campaign to clear my name. Instead, I was to wait on Him to fight this battle for me.

As I waited upon God to right what I per-ceived as a terrible wrong, I was battling in my mind whether to forgive my longtime friend and fellow pastor. This mental battle of re-sentment and umbrage went on for weeks.

> *Forgiveness is a 3-step pro-cess: Forgive, Forgiving, Forgiven*

Each time I rehearsed my unjust firing in my mind, I could feel myself becoming more bitter and enraged. All the while the Holy Spirit was cautioning me, "Watch out that no poisonous root of bitterness grows up to trouble you, corrupting many" (Hebrews 12:15 NLT). Still, I resisted the Holy Spirit with all my might. Believing I had a right to be mad, and in addition being concerned that to forgive him would be the same as allowing him to think that I was some sort of nothing he could push around, my pride responded - oh no! He was going to pay for his vileness. However, my attitude underwent a major shift after I reflected on the words of Jesus, who said,

If you forgive others for the wrong things they have done, then your Father in heaven will forgive you. But if you do not forgive others, your Father will not forgive you for the wrong things you have done (Matthew 6:14-15 MSG).

That jerked the slack out of my chain; it was like smelling salts to my nostrils. It was clear as day: if I were expecting Jesus to forgive me of my sins, I would have to forgive my brother who had sinned against me. This verse, along with the encouragement of my wonderful spouse, added to my desire not to be a hypocrite, eventually caused me to yield to the Holy Spirit and begin a healing journey of forgiveness. As I was processing just how to forgive him, the Lord, in his grace, led me upon a statement made by a former classmate of mine and well-known Bible teacher named, Chip Ingram. He mentioned in one of his sermons that someone had told him that forgiveness is a 3-step process: *Forgive, Forgiving, Forgiven.* Chip just made this three second statement and went on preaching, oblivious to how deeply his words had impacted me. God used those words – Forgive, Forgiving, Forgiven – to help me forgive my longtime friend and brother.

Step 1: Forgive

The first step to forgiving someone who hurt you involves making the volitional decision to forgive. This is done in the frontal lobe, very separate from the emotions of the limbic system. It is a decision you make with your head and *not* your heart. You might not feel any different toward the person at all. I know in my case I felt worse in the belief that I was letting him off the hook. But that is what true forgiveness is; it is letting the offending party off the hook. You are making the choice to no longer hold their offense against them.

What we are attempting when we try to forgive, especially egregious transgressions, is far profounder than you may at first realize. What I am referring to is Christ's unparalleled sacrifice on the cross. Forgiveness is part of God's plan, and we must understand that it is also a demonstration of Christ's transforming love. It is exactly the same thing Jesus did for you (Matthew 6:14-15).

Step 2: Forgiving

The second step involves actively forgiving. The forgiving stage is the hardest. Forgiving is the daily process of checking, challenging and changing (CCCR) the thoughts that tempt you to dwell resentfully upon the harmful experience with all its emotional fetters. In order to overcome the angry and vengeful feelings that arrive consequent to the wrong done to you, you will need to take those thoughts and images captive by employing your CCCR thought management strategy (Day 10 and Day 11).

When images and feelings pertaining to the offense come to mind, you remind yourself, "No, I have already made the volitional choice to forgive." This is the hardest step in the forgiveness process, and it thus requires the most earnestness and attention. When those raw emotions of the offense pop into your mind, you will have to repeatedly forgive your offender(s) time and time again. This is what I believe Jesus was referring to when Peter asked him, "Lord, how often shall my brother sin against me and I forgive him? Up to seven times?" (Matthew 18:21). I believe Peter expected to receive a major complement from Jesus. Instead, Jesus said to him, "I do not say to you, up to seven times, but up to seventy times seven" (Matthew 18:21-22). Now do you see why the forgiving stage is the hardest step in the forgiveness process? Because in the early stages of forgiving a person, that person's name or face may come to your mind seventy plus times in a given day. In fact, some of your best friends may also be friends of your offender(s). They may innocently mention the person(s) you are struggling to forgive. At that very moment, you need to take your negative thought captive. Again, it may take innumerable distinct efforts to take all those negative thoughts captive. But, as you daily rely upon the Holy Spirit's enabling power, by the grace of God it gets easier with each passing day.

FYI: Whether you realize it or not, each thought has an emotional memory associated with it stored in your amygdala. The more you think and meditate upon the experience and play it over and over again on the screen of the mind, the darker and melancholier your feelings are very likely to become. Meditate upon it long enough, and your amygdala will re-create the exact feelings as though the offense had just occurred, although it occurred quite a long time ago. Why? The amygdala cannot tell the difference between past and present; everything is neurologically treated as occurring in the present. [4] When the emotionally impactful imagery comes, "the amygdala… sends the message to the pituitary and adrenal glands to produce the chemicals the body needs to respond to the emergency. The chemicals (adrenaline and cortisone) are released into the bloodstream, causing stress…. This is essentially what happens when someone has an anxiety or panic attack."[5] Although it is a perceived danger, not an actual and immediate physical threat, the body still responds as though it were real.

My own unawareness of exactly how the amygdala works kept me stuck in my pain and unforgiveness and may be keeping you stuck also. Because I was fired on the spot and asked not to come again onto the church property, I didn't get the chance to say my goodbyes to anyone. Hence, church members were calling me and asking me where I was and what happened. Hurt, I told my sad side of the story, regurgitating the facts as best I could. But remember, *no matter how flat the pancake, there are always two sides.* Let me acknowledge that this (telling) is where I sinned. I desperately wanted to clear my name. However, unbeknown to me, each time I told my sad story, I was reactivating the old memories stored in my amygdala, all the while wondering why I was having so much trouble forgiving my ole friend. I've heard it said, *Stick with your story, and your story will stick with you.*

> ***Stick with your story, and your story will stick with you.***

With my wife's encouragement, I one day decided that I wasn't going to tell my sad story anymore. Hence, when church leaders and laity called, I referred them to the senior pastor and asked them to pray for me. When thoughts and mental pictures popped into my head, I shut them down immediately and instead of ruminating upon them, I began replacing them by praying for my friend. As I stopped hating him and instead began praying for him, the Lord began to afford me feelings of sympathy for my friend. I realized he fired me not because he hated me, but because he felt threatened by me. His conscious and subconscious fears and insecurities were the catalyst that moved him to fire me. The Lord, over time, helped me to see that just like me, he too struggled with his insecurities. In addition, the Lord helped me to realize the truth behind the oft-quoted adage: "Hurt people hurt people." This led me to stop vilifying him and instead pray more sympathetically for his healing and wholeness. As I continued to pray for him, a strange thing happened: I slipped into the third stage.

Step 3: Forgiven
One day, someone mentioned the offender's name, and the name no longer evoked feelings of anger, but compassion. That is when I knew I had forgiven my ole friend from my heart. What seems impossible with sinful human minds is the commonest routine with God.

Why Satan Opposes Forgiving Anyone

The primary reason Satan wants us to harbor unforgiveness toward perceived offender(s) is because he desires to keep you tethered to the toxic thoughts and deadly emotions associated with the hurtful offense. As we constantly ruminate upon the upsetting and cutting details of the offense, we are, giving mouth to mouth resuscitation to the offense.[6] We are breathing life into the hurtful wrongdoing. When we do so, metaphorically, we are peeling the scab off the wound; it can never heal that way. Consequently, we sink deeper and deeper into the quagmire of negativity as we marinade in the noxious juices of anger, self-pity, pessimism and bitterness. For this reason, the Bible cautions us to, "Watch out that no bitterness takes root among you, for as it springs up it causes deep trouble, hurting many in their spiritual lives" (Hebrews 12:15 TLB). Satan's hand in instigating the wrongdoing is to stunt your emotional, relational and spiritual growth. So, instead of going through the painful experience and coming out better, he wants it to make us bitter and resentful. The Devil plots to keep you stuck in your pain by harboring *unforgiveness*. His goal is to keep the negative experience forever playing on the movie screen of your mind to keep you in a state of perpetual anguish. When I contemplate the phrase *a state of perpetual*

> *Don't be held in bondage to people who don't know they are holding you captive.*

anguish, I am reminded of an experience I had many years ago in college. Allow me to explain.

During my college days, I befriended a young man studying to become an Anglican priest. As a token of his friendship, he gave me a large crucifix, 12-14 inches long. A crucifix is the Christian cross with a dying Jesus affixed to it. Initially, I proudly displayed the cross on my dormitory wall, but eventually I tired of continually seeing Jesus suffering in anguish nailed to a cross. I knew the crucifix told only half the story. So, I took it off the wall and returned it to my friend, Eddie. Decades later, while working on today's lesson, the Lord brought the image of that crucifix to my mind. He reminded me that just as Christ was affixed to the cross by the nine inch spikes in his hands and feet, in like manner, metaphorically speaking, we affix ourselves to our cross – the offense—the deep hurt with nine-inch spikes of unforgiveness as we perpetually suffer emotionally, relationally and spiritually; that is until and unless we make the quality decision to forgive our transgressor. *I caution you; don't be held in bondage to people who don't know they are holding you captive.*

As Christians, we are called to be like Christ. Christ bore his cross. He went through the painful events of his unjust trial, torturers flogging and the ultimate humiliation crucifixion upon a Roman cross. There affixed to the cross, he forgave his offenders and came through the ordeal whole and healed by finding a purpose in his pain. Observe Jesus' perspective: "Because his heart was focused on the joy of knowing that you would be his, he endured the agony of the cross and conquered its humiliation, and now sits exalted at the right hand of the throne of God"(Hebrews 12:2 TPT)! God expects you to bear your cross — personal offenses and injuries—and work through your pain, job loss, relationship issues, test failure, traumatic accident, etc., without getting stuck, trapped, or bogged down in it. For some, this may require professional counseling; it depends upon your coping skills and the severity of the personal injury. The healthier you are, the more people you can help.

From God's perspective, suffering is intended to be a phase of life, not a life sentence. Jesus, because he worked through his suffering, transformed the most hideous symbol of hate—the Roman cross—into a symbol of love. The cross, once a symbol of death, is now perceived the world over as a symbol of life— eternal life. The cross, once a representation of hopelessness, is now an emblem of hope. The cross, once a symbol of defeat, is now a symbol of victory! That's why the Protestant symbol of faith is an empty cross—not a crucifix. Jesus' suffering has ended. He is now seated at the right hand of the Father in heaven interceding for you and me (Romans 8:27, 34) and encouraging us to press through our pain because there's a blessing in the pressing (Mark 5:25-34).

Several concluding thoughts: 1) Cease defining yourself by that traumatic event. It would be to your advantage to stop referring to yourself as a divorcee, an ex-con, sickly, etc. That may be what happened to you, but that's not who you are. Instead, talk to yourself and remind yourself you are the child of the most-high God; that makes you a *victor* not a victim. 2) Stop allowing your frail feelings to control you. Stop waiting on a feeling. For those who are constantly manipulated by their feelings, Apostle Paul observed, *"Their own emotions are their god..."* (Philippians 3:19 GW). Instead of being controlled by your emotions, *control* your emotions. You can because the Spirit living in you is far stronger than your fickle feelings (1 John 4:4). Step up! In real time, start applying the thought management principles that you were taught throughout *The 21-Day Plan.* 3) I've observed that a good number of Christians desire to have a glorious triumphant testimony, without going through a *test.* You can't have one without the other. Impossible! *The 21-Day Plan* is the by-product of my personal test. It's my testimony of God's healing and delivering power. Commit to gaining the victory in your test. So, once you come through on the other side, you can sing the praises of the Almighty God who brought you out! I challenge you, don't just tell your story. Write it down. It will prove to be a very cathartic experience. Perhaps even consider publishing it so that countless others can be encouraged by your testimony. By so doing, God will receive greater glory. 4) Finally, stop holding yourself responsible to exact your own self-contrived vengeance. God says, "Vengeance is mine, I shall repay" (Romans 12:19). Let it go! Surrender it to God. Let God handle it in his own time, and in his own way. Forgive and forget. I know what you're thinking; easier said than done. Well, I'm now going to explain neurologically how you can both forgive and forget.

Rewiring Your Brain to Forgive

On Day 7, I explained that the brain is a creature of habit. Anything we do consistently, whether good or bad, the brain will make into a habit. Harboring unforgiveness is nothing more than a bad habit. Each time you dwell upon the negative experience and replay the mental images, it becomes more deeply entrenched neurologically in your brain. That is how it becomes a habit. Charles Duhigg, author of *The Power of Habit*, argues that habit formation within the brain is "a three-step [process] beginning with a cue, routine, reward. When it becomes more and more automatic, a habit is born."[7]

Applying Duhigg's habit formation analysis to our discussion of unforgiveness works in the following manner: The recollection of the offense is the cue or "trigger." The routine involves the behaviors you engage in once the offense is again triggered in your mind. The "reward" (albeit negative) is the (conceptual) satisfaction you estimate you'd feel if the offender or offenders received their comeuppance.

The key to breaking any bad habit, including harboring unforgiveness, is to change your routine. To break the old mental habit of harboring ill-feeling toward a transgressor, Jesus provides us with a new routine. Concerning enemies, Jesus encourages us to, "Love your enemies, do good to those who hate you, bless those who curse you, pray for those who mistreat you" (Matthew 5:44). Neurologically, by replacing hate with love, and replacing evil actions with good deeds, replacing curse words and words of condemnation with words of blessing and affirmation, we disrupt our habit of unforgiveness and begin the process of developing a new brain habit: forgiveness. (See Figure 15:1).

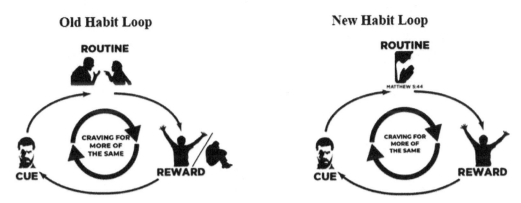

Figure 15.1 Habit Loop of Forgiveness

By changing your routine, you are rewiring your brain to forgive. That is exactly what happened to me when I stopped berating my friend and began praying for him and wishing him and his ministry well. I was delivered from my toxic mental habit loop by my own practice of forgiveness. At this point, some of my readers may be wondering, "Well, now that you have forgiven him, do you still socially interact with one another?" No! *When people show you who they are, believe them.* Secondly, part of the forgiveness process is completely revamping the mental process. Often encountering the same person will surely make the forgiver recall the offense. Do not assume that a disinterest in engaging further with the individual or individuals is a symptom of continuing to hold a grudge. The undesirable of grudge holding isn't necessarily so. However, at times it may be. Pray: ask God to reveal your true motives (Psalm 139:23-24).

However, in such cases of a spouse, parent, or family member, etc., where such avoidance may not be available, interactions should be Spirit led, keeping in mind other biblical injunctions to forgive: "When you are angry, don't let that anger make you sin, and don't stay angry all day" (Ephesians 4:26ERV). The severity of the offense forgiven corresponds directly to how steadfastly you will adhere to the aforementioned statement. Avoidance, in my case, still seems the best way to have facilitated the forgiveness of an extreme offense. Godly David distanced himself from fitful, morose King Saul (1 Samuel 24:16-22; 26: 21-25).

What about repentance? What if you learn that the transgressor is remorseful and desirous of some sort of reconciliation (and continued involvement)? This is a risky proposition. I cannot know what each offense is and cannot make recommendations. However, you must consider both the harshness of the offense, and the personality of the person you have forgiven (or are still trying to forgive). It may be unsafe to expose yourself to a circumstance where you are likely to get hurt again. Whenever appropriate, simply forgive and move on.

As you learn to break old habit loops and establish a new routine, something interesting happens to the old thoughts that used to compel the old negative habit.

Dr. Caroline Leaf reminds us that we can empower our positive thoughts by dwelling and meditating upon them and starving our negative thoughts to death, by ceasing to roil continually in them? The dendrites begin to deteriorate and die. We literally have the power to starve our unforgiveness to death.[8] (Figure 5.1) If Jesus lives in you, you have the power to forgive anyone—including yourself. *Love yourself enough to forgive yourself.* We've *all* made mistakes. We *all* have regrets. How to forgive yourself? (See 1-8 on pages 189-190.)

Thought Replacement

In order to starve your automatic negative thoughts (ANTS) to death and over-come unforgiveness, you must replace them with spiritual automatic thoughts (SATS) that are conducive to forgiveness. Therefore, memorizing Scripture and obedience to the Word plays such a crucial role in the mind-renewal process. Dr. Don Colbert, author of *Deadly Emotions* remarked, "It isn't difficult to replace lies with God's truth. It just takes intentional and consistent effort…it takes the time and energy to find statements of God's truth and apply them to life's lies."[9] Should you find yourself today struggling with an on-going inability to forgive, here are two verses that you can memorize to replace your nega-tive thoughts:

> *It isn't difficult to replace lies with God's truth. It just takes intentional and con-sistent effort.*

- "Be kind to one another, tender-hearted, forgiving each other, just as God in Christ also has forgiven you" (Ephesians 4:32).

- "If we confess our sins, He is faithful and righteous to forgive us our sins and to cleanse us from all unrighteousness" (1 John 1:9).

How to Ask for Forgiveness

When we're offended, we can work to build the habit of "forgiving each other" (Ephesians 4:23). Below is a three-step process my spouse and I have used when seeking to forgive and reconcile with each other. Right after we individually pray with a humble heart, one of us begins by saying,

Step 1: "I am sorry. I was wrong for…" _____ *(state the offense)*

Step 2: "Please forgive me."

Step 3: "I love you."
(Or whatever is appropriate – i.e. I really appreciate you/your friendship.)

How to Memorize Scripture

Verbatim memorization of scriptural texts is indispensable to Biblical mind-renewal. Biblical mind-renewal is the lifelong process of exchanging our perspective (our thoughts, opinions and beliefs for God's perspective (Day 4). This type of mind-renewal is accomplished in part by scripture memorization and obedience to the Word. In Day 3, (p. 69), I gave you some pointers on how to memorize your *I Am Significant* mantra and your N-O-W-M-O-V-E-F-O-R-W-A-R-D acrostic. Today, I want to share with you how best to format your 3x5 card to help create a new routine to help your brain best accomplish this. You brain thrives on consistency. Consistently doing the same thing the very same way every time makes it easier for the brain to form a habit. Once the brain can form it into a habit, it puts the process (essentially) on autopilot. I've used this technique for years to help me memorize dozens and dozens of passages. Follow this format and you're bound to experience similar results.

Topic: Motivation for Forgiveness
Address: Ephesians 4:32 (NASB)
Verse: Be kind to one another, tender-hearted, forgiving each other, just as God in Christ also has forgiven you.
Address: Ephesians 4:32

Topic: Assurance of Forgiveness
Address: 1 John 1:9 (NASB)
Verse: If we confess our sins, He is faithful and righteous to forgive us our sins and to cleanse us from all unrighteousness.
Address: 1 John 1:9

FYI: This is the same format that you use when you begin to memorize the scriptures that coincide with your N-O-W-M-O-V-E-F-O-R-W-A-R-D acrostic. Begin memorizing those scriptures at your own pace.

As you begin a structured plan to memorize your scriptures, here are a few helpful pointers:

The 7 Keys to Memorizing Scripture

1. Pick a translation you like and stick with it.
2. In every instance, give the topic a short title.
3. Every time give the location/reference ("address").
4. After reading the verse several times to fully apprehend its meaning and usefulness, begin to memorize by the time-honored practice of repeated verbalization. Once you have memorized the first phrase, go on to the second phrase, and then to the third phrase.

5. PRACTICE, PRACTICE, PRACTICE. Enlist a friend or family member to quiz you (if it is convenient to do so).

6. Do not move onto a different Bible verse until you can quote the verse flawlessly. If you fail to do so, all your half-memorized verses will become scrambled in your mind and they will prove ineffective in the all-important mind renewal process.

7. Review the pertinent verse several times daily. Do this even after initial "memorization" has been achieved. The more you practice, the faster the teaching will become steeped in your mind and hasten the mind renewal process.

I can hear someone perhaps puzzling over a problem: I would love to memorize edifying scripture, but my life is so busy, and my mind is so crowded with things I have to do that I doubt I can find the time and self-discipline to memorize them.

How to Cue Your Brain to Remember

Normally, for your brain to remember something new, it needs a cue—a trigger, a reminder. Listed below are eight brain cues to help you remember to do your memory work. Choose whichever cues work the best for you.

1. **Your Daily Prayer Time, Quiet Time (QT) and Meal Times**
   The best way to start a new habit is to couple it with an existing habit. If you have a daily prayer time or QT, as soon as you finish your morning devotional, review your 3x5 cards also. Since you eat 2 to 3 times daily, before or after each meal refer to your cards.

2. **Your 3x5 Cards**
   Each time you look at your 3x5 cards, they serve as a cue to remind your brain to memorize your Scripture verses. Push back on any thought that says, "Not now, I'll do it later."

3. **Your Inner Witness**
   The Holy Spirit, living on the inside of you, will consistently remind you to pull out your 3x5 cards and review your verses. Don't procrastinate.

4. **Your Downtime**
   One thing we all have is downtime (relaxed periods or times of inactivity). Use your downtime to review your memory work. For an exhaustive list of downtime moments, see Day 3 (p. 69).

254

5. **Your Car or Commute Time**

   I have memorized the bulk of my scriptures during my morning and evening commutes in my car. Every time I see my car, it serves as a cue to begin reciting my verses.

6. **Your ANTS**

   Your automatic negative thoughts (ANTS) are a major cue to begin to memorize your verses, to quote them aloud and thereby replace them with spiritual automatic thoughts (SATS). Don't let the devil have the last word.

7. **Your Bedtime**

   Each night, before going to bed, read over your memorization verses before you fall asleep. You may also review them first thing in the morning.

8. **Your Accountability Partner**

   If you selected an accountability partner, remind one another to stay on task. If you didn't select a partner previously, do so now. (See My Covenant page 18).

Real Life Testimonies to Help Build Your Faith

Wesley's Story: The Power of Forgiveness

In 1989, I was a man on the run. I shot the man who shot me and killed my brother. After shooting him, I sought shelter in a hotel room in Virginia Beach. The police had shown my picture on local TV. I was alleged to be "armed and dangerous." Indeed, I was. I had a .45 on one side and a 357 Magnum on the other. The police were told to shoot on sight and ask questions later. While sitting in a hotel room, grappling with my fate, considering death by cop or life in prison, I opened the nightstand drawer beside my bed. I discovered the Gideon's Bible there. My initial thought was: *What's a Bible doing in a place like this?* Perhaps out of curiosity or just out of desperation, I randomly opened it and my eyes fell upon the following verse, "If you confess your sins, He is faithful and just to forgive you of your sins and to cleanse you from all unrighteousness" (1 John 1:9). I then said to myself almost audibly, "God, do you know what I have done? Do you know the people I shot and the lives that have been lost? My own brother has gotten killed. And you are going to tell me that you can forgive me? Okay! God, I will give you one shot. I will give you one chance. If you can change my life, do it! I have nothing to lose. You either change it, or I go back to my former life of drug dealing." I knelt on my knees beside the bed, not really knowing what to say in such a dramatic and perilous circumstance as mine. So, I prayed with the mere words, *"Lord just do it!"*

After that simple petition, I called my attorney and the police to inform them each that I had decided to turn myself in without incident. The policemen came promptly and arrested me. Once behind bars, I continued to read my Bible and pray. On the day of sentencing in 1999, the judge dealt me 59 years in prison. Upon hearing my sentence, the next voice I heard was the voice of the Lord, saying, "We walk by faith and not by sight" (2 Corinthians 5:7). According to the judge's sentencing, I was not to be released until 2038. As I endeavored to adjust to prison life, I told Jesus that I'd rather be here incarcerated than out on the streets living the life I used to live. As I read my Bible and prayed each day, the Lord began moving my heart to forgive the man who shot me and killed my brother. He revealed to me through the Lord's Prayer that unless I was willing to forgive the man, He would not forgive me. This ultimately turned out to be a set up for the next thing that would happen to me.

Over time, I was transferred to a second correctional facility. Once again, the Lord began moving me to forgive the man who killed my brother. One day, while in this new prison environment, I saw the man who had testified against me at trial. The other prisoners, who were with me, edged me on to kill the man for being a snitch. Lifting their shirts, exposing their knives and other weapons, they shouted, "Get him! Get him!" I walked up to the man, reached in my pocket, pulled out a Bible tract, and handed it to the young man. I told him that I was not seeking vengeance, that I was now "rolling with Jesus," and I walked away. Shortly after that incident, I was due back in court. Little did I know that God was already working on my redemption. Remarkably, the judge took thirty years off my original sentence.

God began to move again. I was transferred to another facility, King Mountain. Once there, I encountered the man who shot me and killed my brother. God said, unambiguously, "Forgive him." Again, proximate inmates lifted their shirts and said, "Let's kill him." I said, as I had before, "No, I'm rolling with Jesus." The Warden, having heard about the disturbance, locked me up, asserting that she didn't care about any jailhouse religion and put me in "the hole" (solitary confinement) for 40 days. While suffering that peculiar terribleness, I was only allowed out one hour per day. Determined not to mentally break, as I had seen others do, I decided to make my experience into a spiritual pilgrimage. I took my Bible with me and some gospel music. I read my Bible and played the recordings continuously. I fasted 3 days, and then ate. I fasted 5 days and then ate. I fasted 7 days and then ate. On the 39th day, another warden heard about me and commented, "I believe you are for real," and he let me out of the hole. Liberated from my ordeal, I went immediately to the man who shot my brother and handed him a Bible tract.

God was about to move in my life again. I was transferred to yet another facility. There, I received a letter informing me that, remarkably, 7 more years had been taken off my sentence. In this new facility, I saw another man that I had shot in the head from point blank range. He was confined to a wheelchair as a result of what I had done to him. The Lord told me to go to him and humbly ask his forgiveness. However, I felt I could not readily do this because we were in different sections of the prison facility. Again, God was miraculously working; somehow, the doors opened as I walked in the direction of the man's holding cell. I saw him sitting there in his wheelchair. Our eyes met. He was shocked to see me. I asked him if I could speak to him. He agreed. I told him that I was a born-again Christian. He told me that he was also. I asked him to please forgive me for shooting him. I had no right to try to play God in deciding who should live or die. I assured him that I was not after him and wished him God's protection and blessings. My request was well received.

After serving a total of 12 years, I was sent back to Petersburg, Virginia to stand before the same judge who sentenced me to 59 years. Standing in court, dressed in my prison uniform and shackled hand and foot, I looked at the judge as he said, Mr. Nicholas, "I remember your case very well. Somehow your paperwork got mixed up. You are supposed to do 7 more years, but today I am going to dismiss all your charges."

I was released in 2001. Upon my release, as I continued to walk with Jesus, He enabled me to reconnect with my two daughters. One day, while I was cutting hair in a barber shop, a little boy climbed up in my chair, and as we conversed, I discovered to my wonder and delight that he was my son. Eventually, by God's grace, I was blessed with a wife, two beauty salons, and a beauty school. The building that we now own and use for the business is valued at over $500,000. We purchased it for only $60,000. God is a magnificent miracle worker! Apart from a divine intervention in my life, I'd probably be dead—gunned down in the streets—another statistic in the unending drug wars of American cities. But, by the grace of God, I'm alive today. When I called on Jesus, He forgave me, turned my life around and encouraged me to forgive others who had hurt me. Jesus is so good. He saved me in ways that surely no human being ever could.

* * *

Although Christians sometimes think of forgiveness as something mysterious that they are obliged to do for God and without any personal benefit, the reality is that forgiveness brings mental and emotional liberation, and this gift to ourselves is what God so graciously intends. Face it. Forgive it. Forget it.

Wesley's heart was unshackled and transformed by the power of forgiveness. His was no jailhouse conversion. The police had previously penned his name on their roll call of the most wanted criminals, but now it appears in the heavenly roll call—the Lamb's book of life (Revelation 21:27).

* * *

A Closing Prayer

Dear God, lead me to choose the best cues that will remind me to do my memory work. Father, also please help me to be quiet and still enough to follow the prompting of Your Holy Spirit as He reminds me to pull out my 3x5 cards. Lord, I draw upon the Holy Spirit's power to enable me to write down my memory scripture, so I can learn to find SATS to replace my ANTS. Father, I partner with You to renew my mind one thought at a time and see my thought life transformed to Your glory and honor. In Jesus' name. Amen.

For an inspirational pick me up, I recommend:

- *A Heart That Forgives* by Kevin LeVar
- *Too Hard Not To* by Tiny Campbell
- *Yesterday* by Mary Mary

Until tomorrow, do this:

- Look over The Toxic Ten (pp. 238-239); reflect upon which thought distortions you may be entertaining. (Where there is relational conflict, somebody is most likely engaging in one or more of The Toxic Ten.)

![elephant]

Memory Work

1. Continue memorizing The Filthy Five FURST acrostic as you practice categorizing your daily thoughts.

2. Continue to write down The Filthy Five Memory Verses on 3x5 cards and practice memorizing them (Figure 14. 2, p. 242).

3. Continue repeating your *I Am Significant* mantra (p.65).

Confession: I Am Significant. *Can you repeat it from memory?*

4. Repeat your N-O-W-M-O-V-E-F-O-R-W-A-R-D acrostic. In the future, memorize the Scriptures associated with the acrostic. The Scriptures are found on pages 108-109.

Day 16

Replacing Negative Thoughts and Images of God: *God, Why Did You Do That? (Part 1)*

You can't get over anything that hurt you until you first give up what you had in mind.

--TD Jakes

Daily Food for Thought

- **Brain Fact** "As we start to understand how a thought forms and impacts our emotions and bodies, we have two choices: we can let our thoughts become toxic and poisonous, or we can detox our negative thoughts, which will improve our emotional wholeness and even recover our physical health".[1]

- **Key Thought** God is not the problem. He is the solution to the problem. As we mature in our thinking and grow in our understanding of the five causes of pain and suffering, we learn to stop blaming God for every negative thing that happens to us.

- **Scripture** "In spite of everything that had happened, Job did not sin by blaming God" (Job 1:22 GNT).

Daily Reading

Have you ever felt that God disappointed you or that He let you down big time? Have you asked, "God, what did you do that for?" I have personally felt that God has disappointed me. You probably have also. Many Christians are uncomfortable admitting that they sometimes harbor negative, resentful notions about God. Your disappointment with God could be rooted in a heartfelt prayer that went seemingly unanswered. Maybe you prayed your spouse wouldn't leave you, but he/she ultimately walked out. Maybe you prayed that a loved one wouldn't die, but despite your earnest entreaties the cherished person died anyway. Or, perhaps you prayed for a mate or intense friendship or relationship but you're still single and blue at 42. Worse yet, perhaps a clergyman, presumably representing God, grossly mistreated you or behaved in a way that wasn't even marginally decent or respectful. Now, most of us wouldn't confess that we are mad at God, for that kind of conduct is often considered taboo. However, your actions speak louder than your words—giving voice to the inner secrets of your heart.

You may be mad at God if you avoid reading God's Word consequent to some disappointment or disillusionment. Maybe you neglected praying or refused to allow anyone else to pray for you. You may be mad at God if you avoided going to church, and, when facing challenges, trouble or pain in your life, instead of turning to God and His Word, you looked for other ways to help alleviate the emotional distress. You're not alone. As a Christian pastor, I've been angry at God more times than I'd like to admit. So, if you think I am in these pages going to scold you and insist you shouldn't feel the way you do, think again. I am sure, in your own mind, you have perfect justifications for the way you think and feel. This is natural. However, I would like to share with you several conclusions that I have drawn from my many personal experiences of being angry with God.

First, I discovered that all the times I was mad at God, He was never once mad at me. Secondly, God is not intimidated when, we question his existence, his promises, his goodness and his love. He knows it's only human to question him in times of disappointment and grief. So, feel free to ask God whatever you desire. I'm of the belief it's healthier to get it all out, than it is to keep it all bottled up on the inside. God is all-knowing; therefore, he already knows what you're thinking, whether you choose to verbalize your thoughts or not (Psalm 94:11; 139:23). He can handle it!

God knows that life can be devastatingly hard and difficult. Don't let people guilt trip you into thinking you've somehow disappointed God because you're questioning his judgment, fairness or his love. Truth be told, we probably all have from time to time. Even Jesus, while dying upon the cross, questioned his Father's judgement; in anguish, he cried out, "My God, my God, why have you forsaken me?" (Matthew 27:46; Mark 15:34). However, it's equally important to remember Jesus' final words, "Father, I place my life in your hands!" (Luke 23:46 MSG). Like Jesus get it all out, but afterwards, will yourself to remember your loving heavenly Father's promises (Hebrews 13:5; 1 Peter 5:7 TPT). I find immense joy in knowing that God loves us unconditionally. Therefore, our indifference and decreased interest in him does not diminish His love for us. It was Pastor Max Lucado who said, "God's love is spontaneous; it generates from within Himself, not from what He sees in us."

Finally, I discovered that giving up on life and giving up on God is not going to take away the pain. In fact, over time, neurologically, the pain becomes more entrenched in the mind, causing more tormenting thoughts and oppressive, irksome emotions. In one painful trial, at a time I was not speaking to God, the Holy Spirit posed his very own question to me. In a still small voice, he posed the following question: "If *you get mad at and stop speaking to the God of heaven, who in Hell is going to help you?* The profundity of that question really jarred me. After pondering that question, I knew it was time I truly humbled myself and asked God's forgiveness and began to take greater responsibility for my situation rather than blame God. It was time to let go of my arbitrary expectations and ask God to help me try to see the situation from His perspective: top down, His perspective, rather than bottom up from my vantage. Taking these mental steps, over time, helped me get over my personal disappointment and misplaced blame.

> *If you get mad at and stop speaking to the God of heaven, who in Hell is going to help you?*

Admittedly, during a somewhat immature stage of my life, I blamed God for every negative thing that happened to me. *"God, what did you do that for?"* became my constant refrain. I played the blame game. However, as I matured spiritually and became more biblically literate, I came to discover that God was not to be blamed for my personal pain and suffering or for the much more substantial suffering of the world's people. After much study and consultation with other learned believers, I discovered that there were at least five primary reasons for all the endless trouble, tragedy, and tribulation of this world affecting both believers and nonbelievers (Matthew 5:45).

God, Why Didn't You Do It My Way?

Now, before I launch into the practical aspects of how to replace negative blaming (of God) with wisdom and positivity, I feel I need, at the very outset herein, to caution you and downplay two expectations you might have. First, neither I nor any other serious-minded and sagacious person (or theologian, for that matter) can answer all your, *"Why, God"* questions. Some, *"Why, God"* questions you may take with you to your grave (Deuteronomy 29:29). Secondly, if you are the type of individual who subscribes to the belief that for God to be (considered) *good*, He must answer all your most earnest supplications with an affirming *Yes*. With such an attitude, I can assure you that you will become disillusioned with God. God does not exist to be your personal *bellhop*. God is not ever to be understood as ignorant, careless, toady, or subordinate. God is sovereign; He sees the whole picture, not just the tiny missing puzzle piece you are staring at so intently. The quicker you internalize this elemental spiritual ethic, the better off you will be. I remind you; these self-centered perspectives are rooted in The Toxic Ten thought distortions which we discussed in detail on Day 13 and Day 14. (In the future, commit them to memory.) The Apostle Paul, remarking about this kind of errant mindset, intoned, "Brothers, stop being childish in your thinking; but in your thinking be mature" (1 Corinthians 14:20).

Today, my aim is four-fold. First, I want to help nurture your understanding of the causes of your personal anguish. Secondly, I intend to challenge you to stop blaming God for the negative things that happen in your life. In so doing, hopefully, *you will learn to run to God in your pain rather than run away from God.* Third, it is necessary to help you find a purpose in your pain, broadening your perspective, so you can reframe painful experiences and bring closure. Finally, I endeavor to equip believers with plausible explanations (of divine inscrutabilities) so they can minister to others who are going through similar struggles and similarly looking for answers.

So, buckle your seat belt. You are in for a roller coaster ride. In addition, like most roller coasters, there are some parts of the ride that thrill and other parts that sicken. I encourage you to just hold on. Holler if you must, cry if you must, but just keep holding on tightly. Don't close the book in the frustration that arrives when we don't get all the answers neatly delivered to us. Ride it out to the end. You will be glad you did!

> *Will you continue blaming God for the negative things that happen in your life?*

The Several Reasons for Our Troubles

The reason that you and I experience troublesome pain and suffering in this world is a consequence of five causal factors. The five primary reasons bad things happen to both good and bad people alike are because of...

1. a sinful fallen world (Genesis 2:16-17; 6:5-6)
2. sinful personal choices (Genesis 3:7)
3. sinful choices of others (Genesis 4:6-8)
4. Satan is the ruler of this world and is intent on destroying man (Genesis 3; John 12:31; John 10:10)
5. the sovereign will of God (Genesis 3:16; Deuteronomy 29:29; Job 1-3; Isaiah 55: 8; Romans 8:28)

#1 – A Sinful, Fallen World

The first reason there is so much suffering in this world is because we live in a sin-cursed and fallen world. How did our world become so full of sin and corruption? Because of something that happened long before any of us were born. You've probably heard the story of our most distant forbearers, Adam and Eve. Their story is in the Book of Genesis. Long story short, God gave Adam the following command: "From any tree of the garden you may eat freely, but from the tree of the knowledge of good and evil you shall not eat, for in the day that you eat from it you will surely die" (Genesis 2:16-17). All was an idyll until Satan, speaking through a snake-like creature, duped Eve into eating the forbidden fruit of that fateful tree. Adam, when offered the fruit by his wife, ate of it as well (Genesis 3:6-7). This, in purely theological terms, is referred to as "the Fall" (Day 3), meaning mankind "fell" from his righteous, sinless standing with God. From the moment they ate (that apple of legend), Adam and Eve died spiritually, and because of their sin, all the earth was cursed (Genesis 3:17-19). Proof of a cursed (i.e. the earth is not functioning as God originally designed it) earth was initially manifested in the ground hardening, making it more of a struggle for Adam to cultivate the soil. Additionally, perfect trees and bushes began growing thorns and thistles and other mutations. There were thunderstorms, hurricanes, floods and droughts and other climatic and meteorological afflictions.

The entrance of sin did not just affect the earth environmentally, but it adversely affected mankind relationally and socially as well. Case in point: Adam and Eve, after eating the fruit (sinning) for the first time, experienced the negative emotions of fear, anxiety, stress, shame, guilt and self-condemnation. The emergence of these fear-based emotions changed the dynamic of their relationship forever as Adam and Eve, no longer living in blissful harmony, sought to control and dominate one another. "[Eve] your desire will be for your husband, and he will rule over you" (Genesis 3:16). The deadliness of sin, having been released, infected all of humanity. God's commentary on his creation after sin was introduced into the world: "The Lord saw that humanity had become thoroughly evil on the earth and that every idea their minds thought up was always completely evil. The Lord regretted making human beings on the earth, and he was heartbroken" (Genesis 6:5-6 CEB). The sin of disobedience unleashed pain and suffering into a once peaceful and sin-free world.

Finally, the most dramatic impact of sin on humankind was spiritual and physical death.

- "You will eat bread by the sweat of your brow until you return to the ground, since you were taken from it. For you are dust, and you will return to dust" Genesis 3:19 CSB).

God created man to live forever. Interestingly, it was never God's intention that humans die physically, but with sin came sickness, disease, genetic defects, cancers, and ultimately physical death. God was not caught off guard (taken by surprise) by Satan tempting Adam and Eve to sin. It was all part of God's plan. God knew what would happen and prepared ahead of time for it (1 Peter 1:18-20). But humankind must still be held accountable for its sins. Each of us can choose to sin, but we can't choose the consequences.

#2 – Sinful Personal Choices

The second reason that bad things happen to you and me is because of *our own sinful personal choices.* Because God did not want a bunch of mindless robots in a relationship with him, God made angels and man free moral agents. This means that man has the freedom to do as he/she pleases—both good and evil. It is important to note that while Eve may have been deceived (Genesis 3: 3-6; 2 Corinthians 11:3) by the serpent to eat from the Tree of the Knowledge of Good and Evil, Adam ate with his eyes wide open and freely choosing to disobey God (Genesis 3:7).

You may ask why God did not just stop Adam and Eve from eating the forbidden fruit. To do so would have been to violate this concept of free will. How would you like it if God took away your right to choose—your free will? Free will is so important to God that he didn't stop Lucifer (Satan) from leading one third of the angels in heaven to rebel against Him (Isaiah 14:12). Satan and his minion-demons (fallen angels) were kicked out of heaven into the unformed earth realm. Those demons are in partnership with the devil in wreaking havoc and destruction in this world by tempting us to make sinful choices that we often live to regret (Revelation 20:9-10). The reason you and I make sinful personal choices is because we have inherited a sinful nature from our forefather Adam (Romans 5:12).

This point about free will is at the foundation of our access to happiness. God is infinitely more insightful, and intelligent and generous than we are. This being so, God arranged our existence from the very outset to afford us unhindered free agency; our happiness and fulfillment depends on our continuing opportunity to choose from an infinite array of possibilities. God wants us to choose the right and moral path, but He knows (since the Fall) that we will often choose wrongly and sinfully. But God knows in his infinite wisdom that our happiness cannot be achieved while we are subjugated, virtually enslaved. Hence, it is extremely important that we achieve a basic understanding of this free will matter. Without this understanding, we are much more likely to mistakenly charge God with all the awfulness of the world.

#3 – Sinful Choices of Others

The third reason that bad things happen to all of us is because of the *sinful choices of others.*

Because man is inherently sinful and has the right to exercise his free will, in so doing, at times he chooses to exercise his free will in such a way that it negatively impacts the lives of others. Case in point: Adam and Eve's son, Cain, chose to kill his brother Abel.

The Lord asked Cain, "Why are you angry? Why does your face look sad? You know that if you do what is right, I will accept you. But if you don't, sin is ready to attack you. That sin will want to control you, but you must control it." Cain said to his brother Abel, "Let's go out to the field." So, they went to the field. Then Cain attacked his brother Abel and killed him (Genesis 4:6-8 ERV).

Concerning free will, I can hear someone perhaps saying, "Man's free will is good, but God should limit it when it comes to infringing upon someone else's free will." Cain had absolutely no right to kill his brother. That is true. But free will is free will—the freedom to choose whatever you want to do, right or wrong. Perhaps, you see more clearly the impact of your own choices and the impact of living in a fallen, sinful world. And the ledgers of misdeed are infinitely long; hurt people hurt people. Just watch your local and national news and see that this is true. The drama of sinfulness plays out daily in our own personal lives. As I stated at the outset, there will be parts of this roller coaster ride you will not enjoy, but ride it out, nonetheless.

For those who may be thinking, Pastor, are you telling me the God of the Bible is deistic—meaning, He got the world started and has taken his hands off, exerting no controlling influence?

No! God intervenes at a time of His own choosing. He will ultimately intervene and put an end to all pain and suffering, but that time is not now (Revelation 21:4). (Concerning God's spiritual laws of the universe, my mentor, Dr. Tony Evans, used to say, tongue in cheek, if you don't like God's rules, when you become big and bad enough to create your own universe, you can make your own rules. Until then, His rules remain unimpeachable.)

#4 – Satan is the Ruler of This World

The fourth and most significant reason for evil, pain and suffering in this world is because Satan—the Destroyer—is out to kill and destroy all humanity, you and me (John 10:10). (However, God has placed severe limits on Satan's destructive aims.) Satan is regarded as "the ruler of this world" (John 12:31) and also "the god of this world" who keeps people blinded to the truth of the gospel (2 Corinthians 4:4).

God made this earth for man to rule and reign. The psalmist declares,

- "You [God] have made him [man] rule what your hands created. You have put everything under his control" (Psalm 8:6 GW).

- "The heavens are the heavens of the Lord, but the earth He has given to the sons of men" (Psalm 115:16).

God has placed mankind as a steward of this earth. However, when Adam fell into sin, he delivered control of this world into Satan's hands (Luke 4: 6). As ruler of this world, Satan has been raining death and destruction upon humanity from biblical times until the present day. Satan's ownership of this world is evidenced by the fact that he offered to give Jesus the kingdoms of the world if Jesus was willing to fall down and worship him (Matthew 4:8-10). Satan could not give away something he didn't already believe he had a claim on.

As ruler of this world, "Satan comes to steal, kill and destroy" (John 10:10). Why? Because he hates God and is jealous of God's crown of creation: man. Hence, Satan and his demons are out to destroy every one of us. My friend, whether you realize it or not, you are engaged in a spiritual battle of good (God) versus evil (Satan).

Why did Cain kill Abel? It was because he was influenced to do so by Satan. Why did a relative or friend betray you or abuse you? It was because they were influenced by Satan, who is set on destroying your life. Why did someone so close to you, somebody you wholly trusted and respected, so egregiously offend and disappoint you (or otherwise horribly transgress)? Make no mistake: it was because she/he was influenced to do so by Satan.

Satan is also the diabolical force behind the world wars, the Civil War, the Holocaust, and all sorts of terrorism and pandemics. He is the wicked impetus behind poverty, slavery, racism, sexism, atheism, and all the other negative "isms." He and his demons are the influencing spirits behind drug addiction, sex trafficking, human trafficking, prostitution, confusion or discontent over basic identity, domestic violence, pornography, and all forms of sexual and other exploitation. He is also behind all forms and genres of lewd and profane music, movies, and entertainments. His goal is to oppress, distress, depress, and destroy mankind. He is the influence behind the pernicious emotions of hopelessness, despair, depression, low self-esteem, debilitating pessimism, sexual perversions and all sorts of obsessive and/or suicidal ideas and feelings.

Satan is also behind the so-called "acts of God"—the hurricanes, tornadoes, earthquakes and tsunamis which extinguish thousands of innocent lives (Job 1:13-2:7). The Bible informs us that Satan rained fire down from heaven and destroyed Job's crops (Job 1:17). If Satan is behind all this horror and tragedy, then why are they so often called acts of God? A lot of this confusion stems from sev-

266

eral Old Testament passages illustrating how God would manipulate nature at various times: for example, the flood and God's plagues upon pharaonic Egypt. In these instances, God did these things apparently to establish the Nation of Israel, correct His errant people or His wayward prophets and kings or to punish sinful heathen nations. There are at least 93 Old Testament references to the "anger of God." Based on these numerous examples, it may be easy for one to conclude that God is livid, angrily standing by ready and willing to extinguish errant mankind without a moment's notice. But that was under the Old Covenant (Testament) based on the Law when the consequences of men's sins were atoned for through the sacrificial system (elucidated in Leviticus). The Old Law's underlying rubric was *do good, get good—do bad, get bad* (Deuteronomy 28:15-68).

God's Not Mad At You

That's the bad news. Here's the good news: We now live under a new and better covenant—the New Covenant (Testament) of grace (Hebrews 9:15; 12:24). "For the law was given through Moses, *but* the grace and the truth *of God* came through Jesus, the Christ" (John 1:17 JUB). Under this dispensation of Grace, [2] Jesus, through his death on the cross, paid for *all* of mankind's sins, past, present and future. Jesus took the wrath of God upon himself, so God is no longer disposed to condemn and punish. Through the atoning crucifixion, man would no longer have to pay for his own sins – so long as the person individually turns to Christ for forgiveness (Romans 10:9-10; 1 John 1:9). Because Christ took our punishment for us, God is no longer manipulating nature, nor intending to punish or judge us for our wrongdoings. He already judged and treated man's sin in Christ. If we are in Christ, we are free from all condemnation (Romans 8:1). No matter what you've done, don't believe Satan's lie that God is mad at you and punishing you for your sins. While there are natural consequences for our unwise choices and self-destructive and sinful behavior, don't confuse that with *God* punishing you. To set the record straight, God is not mad at you; He's mad about you (loves you unconditionally).

> This is how much God loved the world: He gave his Son, His one and only Son. And this is why: so that no one need be destroyed; by believing in him, anyone can have a whole and lasting life. God didn't go to all the trouble of sending his Son merely to point an accusing finger, telling the world how bad it was. He came to help, to put the world right again. Anyone who trusts in him is acquitted… (John 3:16-17 MSG).

Because God loves you, you can trust Him to see you through literally every trial, every vexation, every suffering and every test.

Double Indemnity

In US jurisprudence, there is a law which states that a person cannot be charged for the same crime twice. This is referred to as *double indemnity*. This same concept applies in the 'courtroom' of heaven. Christ's stead in the place of man (substitutionary atonement) was judged once (by God) and divinely deemed a repository for man's sins (Isaiah 53:6; Romans 3:25). He was accursed, sentenced to death; his was an atonement for all on the cross. His body was placed in a tomb, but on the third day, he rose again, demonstrating his power over sin, hell and the grave. Christ, through his death, paid for man's sins (1 Corinthians 15:1-4). Hence, God would be unjust to convict us again for the same offenses (sins). It would constitute a kind of eschatological double indemnity.

The Apostle Paul explained it this way:

In this is love, not that we loved God, but that He loved us and sent His Son *to be* the *propitiation* for our sins" (1 John 4:10).

The word propitiate means to satisfy, appease or please. Theologically speaking, Jesus, on the cross, satisfied His Father's anger towards sin (not the sinner) and the need to judge and condemn sin, once and for all time. Hence, Jesus offered himself as the perfect sinless sacrifice acceptable to God (John 1:29). While dying on the cross, Jesus uttered the words, "It is finished," signifying that man's sin debt had been paid in full (John 19:30). This pleased God's holy demand for justice (John 2:2; Hebrews 2:17).

Adam's one sin brings condemnation for everyone, but Christ's one act of righteousness brings a right relationship with God and new life for everyone. Because one-person disobeyed God, many became sinners. But because one other person obeyed God, many will be made righteous (Romans 5:18-19 NLT).

To be made righteous means to come into right standing with God. As man has been freed from the penalty of sin, by the shed blood of Christ, he now stands acquitted before God.

Questions for Reflection

1. In your own personal circumstance, how do you reason that you no longer need to feel or fear that God is mad at you?

_____

_____

2. Now, knowing that God is not out to get you (i.e. punish you), how does that make you feel?

_____

_____

A Learning Activity: Identifying the Root Causes of Pain and Suffering

Now that you are more aware of the four reasons for pain and suffering in the world, here is an exercise to help reinforce these truths. We are going to use the chart below to help us identify the root causes of our own personal torments. Take the time to now write the initials beside the experience to point out its origin. Chose the category (cat.). Some may have more than one originating source. While Satan (S) is the spirit influencing all the evil actions and activities in this world, try to resist labeling all of experiences with an (S). If you remain ignorant of the devil's schemes, he will repeatedly use your hurt and pain as a wedge to drive you apart from God. This exercise is designed to help you break that habit of blaming God for every undesirable thing. As an assist to you, the first four are done for you. (Review the answer key following Questions for Reflection below when you have finished.)

The Sources of Our Suffering

- Sinful, Fallen World (SFW)
- Sinful Personal Choices (SPC)
- Satan (S)
- Sinful Choices of Others (SCO)

Experience	Category	Experience	Category
You got a DUI ticket	SPC	Your child was born with a birth deformity, died from SIDS, or a rare blood disease.	SFW
You are continually fearful and worried about your mental health.	S	Someone is hit and killed by a drunk driver.	SCO
1. As a child, you experienced physical abuse.		6. Your parents divorced.	
2. A tornado/hurricane (etc.) destroys homes and kills 100's.		7. Your child committed suicide.	
3. Your brother was shot and is now paralyzed.		8. I can't conceive and have a baby.	
4. Your grandfather died from brain cancer.		9. The thoughts that cross your mind are extremely frightening.	
5. A gunman walked into the school and just started shooting!		10. People, especially in developing countries, are starving and dying from curable diseases.	

*Answers will vary: 10. SCO/SPC/SFW 9. SFW/S/SPC 8. SFW/SPC/SCO 7. SPC/S 6. SPC 5. SPC/SFW 4. SFW 3. SCO/SPC 2. SFW/S 1. SCO/SFW

Questions for Reflection

1. How would you categorize the sources of the major struggles in your current life?

_____

_____

2. Is there any way you can permanently eliminate Satan's influence (temptations, etc.) in your life?

_____

_____

It's All God's Fault

Why are we so inclined to blame God for things He's not responsible for? Our propensity to blame God, in large part, is because we are ignorant of Satan's schemes (2 Corinthians 2:11). Satan is cited in scripture as being "the accuser of the brethren" (Revelations 12:9), meaning he tells God bad things about God's children (us) (Job 1:11; 2:5). However, he doesn't stop there. He also accuses God to us. He plants negative thoughts (in our mind) about God (Genesis 3:4-5). That is one of the prevailing reasons you think God is mad at you. How Satan plants negative thoughts in our minds about God is vividly illustrated for us in the story of Job's wife.

When Job was attacked by Satan, Job's wife, upon hearing the devastating news of their children's demise, demanded that Job, "curse God and die" (Job 2:9). She was directly blaming God for something God did not do. Her grieving state of mind probably made her more susceptible to listen to Satan's lies. Satan probably told her the same things he tells us, for example: *God doesn't love you. God doesn't care about you. If He did, such bad things would not be happening to you and your loved ones. God must be punishing you for something.* These are the exact accusations Job's three friends leveled against him (Job 4).

During your trials, setbacks, troubles, challenges and tragedies, it is important that you check, challenge, change and reframe (CCCR) all the inciting thoughts running through your head. Challenge each one discriminatingly. Don't allow Satan to trick you into blaming God for the things he himself is doing. James, the half-brother of Jesus, cautions followers against attributing evil actions to God:

My dear brothers and sisters do not be fooled about this. Every good action and every perfect gift is from God. These good gifts come down from the Creator of the sun, moon, and stars, who does not change like their shifting shadows (James 1:16-17 NCV).

The text affirms that only good things emanate from God. If it isn't for our *overall good*, it is not from God. "There is nothing deceitful in God, nothing two-faced, nothing fickle" (James 1:17 MSG). I believe the primary reason many people have distorted notions of God is because (in their minds) Satan has been accusing God, and they are not cognizant of it. (To discover more of Satan's accusations, see pages 306-308). The goal of this writing is to disarm the enemy.

Now on to the fifth and final cause of pain and suffering:

#5 – The Sovereign Will of God

God is always in charge, but He doesn't always take charge. So, why does our loving God allow pain and suffering? Consider the way a loving father allows his infant child to suffer the doctor's needle. Let me explain. When my hyperactive middle son was between the ages of 5 and 10 years old, he was always running about and falling on hard sharp objects which required him to be taken to the hospital for stitches in his face and head.

As was our custom, we'd enter through the emergency room, be questioned by a nurse and interviewed by a social worker before being permitted to see the doctor. My son would squeeze my hand tightly as we walked down

> *God is not indifferent to our suffering; that is why Jesus wept. (John 11:35).*

the hall toward the doctor's examination room. Once inside, the doctor and I would take a good look at my son's most recent injury. The final time I took him to the emergency room he had sustained a ½-inch long laceration nearly down to the bone. The doctor engaged some small talk with my son as he turned his back to prepare his syringe. His needle looked to be at least three inches long. As he strode toward my son exposing the syringe, my boy looked up at me with his tearful dark brown eyes as if to say, "Daddy, are you going to allow him to stick the needle in my head again?" before burying his head in my chest. The doctor would say to me, "Mr. Chipman, hold him down securely. This is going to sting a little." Pushing back my own tears, I would watch the doctor inject the syringe into the open wound. My son let out a yelp so stentorian that I felt it could be heard three floors above. The wound anesthetized, I would continue to hold my son down as the doctor on that occasion administered over a dozen stitches into his scalp.

Was I a neglectful father for allowing my son to go through some short-term pain for long-term gain? Was I somehow insufficiently loving? Although my son, in the moment, may have questioned my motives (love), the doctor and I knew some things my youthful son didn't know. As his father, I knew the injection would benefit him in the long run. I knew I was acting out of love, although my son may have not seen it in the moment. I knew that the pain was short, and it was insubstantial in comparison to the long life he would live and enjoy.

In like manner, our loving heavenly Father also thinks on a higher, long-term goodness level. God told us (in His Word), "My thoughts are not your thoughts, nor are your ways My ways" (Isaiah 55:8). God sees, "thinks" and acts on a level totally different from ours. We see in part; He sees the entire picture all at once. Thus, I often remind myself when I experience frustrations, disappointments, and travails (instead of blaming God), *when I can't see God's hand, I can always trust God's heart.* If God allowed it (this trial, test, or hardship) to pass through His sovereign hand down to me, He is going to use it just as He used Job's trials and tragedies ultimately to bless him (Job 1:1-3; 42:12-17).

Viewing things from God's perspective can prove challenging at times. Take death, for example. Many of us view the death of a loved one as supremely devastating. However, God, who sees the big picture, perceives the death of His children as a celebration, and that is very different.

- Precious in the sight of the LORD is the death of his godly ones (Psalm 116:15).

- We take delight in the thought of leaving our bodies behind to be at home with the Lord (2 Corinthians 5:8 TPT).

- Our time on earth is brief; the number of our days is already decided by you, God (Job 14:5 CEV).

Many of us casually expect that we will live to age 90, die without pain or ordeal, and soon thereafter behold the loving face of Jesus. However, as the full number of our days is predetermined, some of us will live to 90 or beyond, while others die earlier and unexpectedly, but God views our temporal demise as the door to a kind of reunion. Death, premature or otherwise, is then something rather to be celebrated.

We can use the thought management strategies to push back on the errant notion that death is not fair. It's not fair, but that's our fate in a fallen world. Our fretting serves no purpose. We would be wise to instead celebrate the time we have, no matter how brief. And in cases of untimely death, we rightly perceive the positive. Celebrate the fact that God blessed your love one to be in your life.

By renewing our minds to take on a greater closeness to God's perspective, we can learn to change our old habit loop (routine) of blaming God and create a new habit loop of trusting God during life's most distressing and woeful circumstances (Days 7 and 15). What you are going through is a test of your faith. Resolve to prevail through the test. *Have faith even when you don't have answers.*

If it pleased God, the Father, to allow His Son, Jesus, to suffer the pain of the torture-flogging and crucifixion for a higher purpose – the saving of mankind (Isaiah 53:10) – surely, He's not opposed to His earthly children suffering a little to accomplish His divine eternal purposes. If Jesus suffered, why should we think we should be exempt from suffering? Jesus forewarned us, saying, "While you are in the world, you will have to suffer. But cheer up! I have defeated the world" (John 16:33 CEV). "[Jesus] left us an example to follow" (1 Peter 2:21). The fact that we live in a fallen, sinful world should cause us to expect some pain and suffering.

What should be our perspective? The Apostle Paul, who arguably suffered more persecution at the hands of his enemies than all the original twelve apostles (2 Corinthians 11:23-29), shared his perspective: "These hard times are small potatoes compared to the coming good times... There's far more here than meets the eye" (2 Corinthians 4:17 MSG). This verse encourages us to view our trials, although painful, as short-lived, yet beneficial in the long run. Often, the pain of our suffering blinds us to the spiritual character development that God is working in us, which, for His omniscient reasons, allows us at times to undergo intense sorrow and suffering (James 1:2-4; I Peter 2:21).

Seven Biblical Reasons God Allows Suffering

1. Suffering equips us for ministry. The Apostle Paul writes that God "comforts us in all our affliction, so that we may be able to comfort those who are in any affliction, with the comfort with which we ourselves are comforted by God" (2 Corinthians 1:4).

2. Suffering brings mature minded believers into a deeper relationship with Christ and a deeper revelation into His Word (2 Corinthians 12:7; Philippians 3:10).

3. Believers suffer as a testimony of their faith – to other believers as well as nonbelievers (Hebrews 11).

4. God often allows people to suffer to get their attention or to bring them to repentance (discipline) or keep them from perishing eternally (Jonah 1-3; Psalm 119:67,71; Luke 13:1-4; Acts 5:1-8; Hebrews 12:6,10).

5. Suffering helps keep our pride in check. Paul the Apostle said, "Because of the surpassing greatness of the revelations, for this reason, to keep me from exalting myself, there was given me a thorn in the flesh, a messenger of Satan to torment me—to keep me from exalting myself!" (2 Corinthians 12:7).

6. Christians suffer so they can be conformed more closely to the character of Christ (Romans 8:28-30, James 1:2-4).

7. Suffering prepares us for greater glory, promotion and fruitfulness. Job received double for all his trouble (Job 42:12-16). And Joseph was ele-

vated from being a prisoner to being Prime Minister of Egypt (Genesis 37-50:20). To make us more fruitful, Jesus prunes us (John 15:1-2).

See how God may be using painful circumstances to accomplish His divine work of sanctification (conforming you into the likeness of His Son Jesus) in your life? God allowing pain and suffering is not to be confused with God causing (being the source or originator of) pain. That is Satan's role. *If you ever suspect that God is the source of your misfortunes, you won't be able to believe Him for your deliverance from them.* Jesus said He came to earth with a purpose "to destroy the works of the devil" (1 John 3:8). God will ultimately put an end to all sorrow, pain and suffering. But that time is not now (Revelations 21:4).

Standing on the Promises of God

The Apostle Paul reminded first century believers that "through many tribulations we must enter the kingdom of God" (Acts 14:22). Trouble and trials are a part of life and we believers are not exempt from them. If God, in His infinite wisdom, has allowed the trials and tests to pass through to us, rest assured that He, the good Shepherd, our loving Father, has made us several promises to help sustain and strengthen us so that we don't lose *hope* in the midst of the storm. It was Dr. Martin Luther King, Jr. who said, "We must accept finite disappointment, but never lose infinite hope."

> *Think to yourself, "This isn't happening to me. It's happening for me."*

To keep hope alive, let us now direct our attention to at least three of God's sacred promises when we are confronted with the inevitable sadness, disillusionment, immense grief, insults, and tribulations of this world. We would do well to adapt the confident perspective of David the psalmist who when reflecting on his troubles, confesses to God saying, "My troubles turned out all for the best— they forced me to learn from your textbook." (Psalm 119:71 MSG)

Promise #1: God Promises to Protect You

God has protected you by placing a limit on the severity of the pain He allows you to endure. Make no mistake, your pain can be *much, much* worse than it is! God has promised not to push you beyond your limits. In your suffering, surrender to the *is* that is God's supreme, infinitely seeing design. Perhaps right now you may be walking through a kind of fog, trying to make sense of your present challenges. Yet, draw strength from knowing,

No test or temptation that comes your way is beyond the course of what others have had to face. All you need to remember is that God will never let you down; he'll never let you be *pushed past your limit*; he'll always be there to help you come through it (1 Corinthians 10:13 MSG).

Your feeling of most extreme distress is not a cue to falsely conclude that God either has no power in your life or is trying to harm you. Your distress is a cue for you to more earnestly entreat God in prayer and meditate upon His power-packed promises found in the Bible.

Once again, observe the fact that God placed a limit on all of Paul's suffering. Just as God placed limits on Job's suffering, He has also placed a wall of protection around you and me (Job 1:9-12). By way of illustration, let me explain that as I travel up and down Interstate 95 near where I live, I often see weigh stations. These stations are designed mostly to weigh those massive 18-wheelers. The tractor trailer has been designed to carry a specific maximum weight. The weigh stations are staffed with inspectors to ensure that each tractor trailer is carrying no more weight than is permissible, no more than each was designed to carry. God, our heavenly Father, functions like a highway inspector. As you travel down life's figurative highways, God makes sure that you will never be carrying too heavy a load.

During sufferance of any kind, know that you are living in a controlled environment. Avoid telling yourself that you can't take it and stop telling God you can't take it anymore. None of us know what we can take. Only God knows what we can take. In contrast, the biblical David said, "It was good that I had to suffer..." (Psalm 119;71 GW). If you persevere through the direst trial, you will almost certainly emerge averring:

--"Lord, I didn't know I was so strong!"
--"Lord, I didn't know I could do it!"
--"I didn't know the extent of God's grace!"
--"Lord, I didn't know I could survive this!"

> *Stop telling God you can't take it anymore. Only God knows what we can take.*

Of course, you survived it. You were in a controlled environment!

The Apostle Paul knew much about God constantly limiting what we each must endure. On his own suffering, he makes these observations:

We are hard pressed on every side, but *not* crushed; perplexed, but *not* in despair; persecuted, but *not* abandoned; struck down, but *not* destroyed" (2 Corinthians 4:8-9 NIV).

In these two verses, Paul lists several types of suffering — mental, physical, emotional, and spiritual. Each of these are different ways that we can suffer, but I want to direct your attention to the four *"but not"* statements. Read the verse from the Apostle Paul once again, this time more slowly and deliberately, paying closer attention to the italicized *"not."* Paul is alluding to this fact that there is a limit to the suffering God allows us to endure. Whatever lack, loss, trouble, anxiety, grief or vexation you may be experiencing, God has given you the grace to endure it. Whether we realize it or not in any specific moment, we are in a controlled environment.

Promise #2: God Promises to Comfort You

God has promised to comfort you in your pain when you choose to turn to Him, to appeal to Him in your pain, instead of following a sort of "I can do this myself" path, separate from Him. How many of you can hark back to a time when you were playing as a child (away from home) and you hurt yourself? Do you remember how you reflexively sought remedy? Perhaps you ran home or to an adult. Well, in like manner, God wants you to come running to Him when you are discouraged, distraught, despairing or otherwise in need. If you run to Him, He promises to comfort and strengthen you. (He comforts according to His superior wisdom. And He knows what you need far better than you do.)

> Blessed be the God and Father of our Lord Jesus Christ, the Father of mercies and God of all comfort, *who comforts us in all our affliction* so that we will be able to comfort those who are in any affliction with the comfort with which we ourselves are comforted by God (2 Corinthians 1:1-3).

Three observations about God's comfort: First, God's comfort is *personal.* "He comforts us." Second, His comfort is *perpetual.* He comforts us endlessly in "all our affliction." Finally, His comfort is *purposeful.* He comforts us "so that we will be able to comfort [others]." By this process, God turns your misery into a sort of potential ministry and turns your test into testimony. *The 21-Day Plan* is my ministry to you, born out of my personal struggles with all sorts of negative, distorted and self-defeating thoughts that held me in bondage for far too many years. When I turned to God in my pain, He comforted me in my misery, and I believe also that His additional purpose was to prepare me to comfort and help guide you.

Promise #3: God Promises to Prepare You

God has promised to use our hardships to prepare us for a brighter future. He's made this promise:

276

And we know [with great confidence] that God [who is deeply concerned about us] causes all things to work together [as a plan] for good for those who love God, to those who are called according to His plan and purpose (Romans 8:28 AMP).

This verse from Romans underscores the fact that God has a predetermined plan for each of our lives. His plan does not infringe upon our free will but takes into consideration all our (variable) personal choices. You and I were created by God for a specific God-ordained purpose. Thus, all our experiences, good, bad and unwholesome, irrespective of their origin, God, in His infinite wisdom, ties together to ensure that we fulfill His divine purpose (if we perseveringly prevail upon Him for His guidance). God says,

I alone know the plans I have for you, plans to bring you prosperity and not disaster, plans to bring about the future you hope for" (Jeremiah 29:11 GNT).

God wants to direct us to that which he has beforehand prepared. An example of this can be seen in the life of the Bible character Joseph. He was heartlessly betrayed by his brothers. They threw him into a pit to die. Perhaps guilt-ridden and stressed by his cries from the pit, his brothers pulled him out and sold him to slave traders. Unfortunate Joseph found himself bound and chained in a slave market in Egypt. He was purchased by a rich Egyptian officer whose wife would much later accuse Joseph of attempted rape. He was thence thrown into prison, but he was not alone… God was with him. Miraculously, after years in a dingy prison cell, he was given an audience before Pharaoh to interpret one of Pharaoh's troubling dreams. Literally overnight, Joseph was elevated from inmate to Prime Minister of Egypt, second only to Pharaoh himself. God used Joseph's fiery trials as a test to prepare him for God's divine purposes – foremost, in retrospect, to preserve the Nation of Israel. In the end, Joseph said to his brothers, "You thought it for evil, but God meant it for my good" (Genesis 50:18-20).

In like manner, God is using your difficulties, failures and challenges to prepare you for His divine purposes. You may not be able to see it right now, because the pain is so severe, but I know that God is molding you and shaping you for the future He has prepared for you. That's why He is cutting off little things to prepare you. He's teaching you something. He's teaching you (just perhaps) some special etiquette, how to be wise, that you cannot always walk in your emotions and in your flesh. Inasmuch as you are attuned to His omniscient voice, He's teaching you how to control your mind, moods and attitudes. He's teaching you to trust Him. He wouldn't be teaching you those things if He didn't have a place prepared for you. God reminded the prophet Jeremiah, just as He reminds each of us, "Before I made you in your mother's womb, I knew you. Before you were born, I chose you for a special work" (Jeremiah 1:5 ERV). Believe in faith that God has a special work for you and that your trials and tests have been a preparation for you.

God has made us what we are. In Christ Jesus, God made us new people so that we would spend our lives doing the good things he had already planned for us to do. (Ephesians 2:10 ERV).

Another verse that kept me hopeful and moving forward during my darkest times was Psalm 27:13-14.

I would have despaired unless
I had believed that I would see the good-
ness of the LORD
In the land of the living.
Wait for the LORD;
Be strong and let your heart take courage;
Yes, wait for the LORD.

> *Just because you can't see a way, doesn't mean there is no way.*

As you are going through your preparation process, don't believe the Devil's lie that your best days are behind you. No! Your best days are still in front of you. I declare, your best life is yet to come! The Bible declares, "Eye has not seen, nor ear heard, nor have entered into the heart of man the things which God has prepared for those who love Him" (1 Corinthians 2:9 NKJV). This means that our sincere faith paves the way to a closer relationship with God and that "best life" still in front of us. Don't focus on what you're going through—focus on what you're going to. Don't focus excessively on your current circumstances. Just because you can't see a way, doesn't mean there is no way. Time and faith avail all things. God has already made a way—just believe! Don't be an 'unbelieving believer.' As believers, we are encouraged by Scripture to "walk by faith, not by sight" (2 Corinthians 5:7).

Finding Purpose in the Pain

As we are rational thinking beings, we seek to find a rational explanation for the things we are going through or have gone through. We desire an explanation for why we were betrayed, why we were abandoned, why we were rejected and unloved, why we were so harshly treated, and why we have been made to suffer so much injustice. Finding a purpose for your pain is essential if you are to emerge from your painful circumstances wiser and more mature. Some people remain stuck in their pain for many years or, worse yet, for their entire lives. I remember talking to a discouraged woman who was lamenting the death of her husband. I, out of curiosity, asked her how long ago her husband died? She paused briefly, breathed deeply, dropped her head and said meekly, "I'm undergoing a protracted grief process. My husband died ten years ago."

That grieving widow got stuck in her pain. People who ride above the storm are people who have learned to go through the storm without allowing the storm to go through them. Finding a purpose in your pain allows you to go through life's storms without them going through you.

When the past remains unresolved, it retains enormous power in the present. To keep from becoming embittered and paralyzed, stuck in your pain, it is imperative that you process your pain. One way to do that is to believe wholeheartedly, although it may not make sense in the moment of experience, God will, over time orchestrate all the unpleasantness together for your good and His ultimate glory, just as he did for Joseph, King David, the Apostle Paul, and Jesus himself. That's what God promises in Romans 8:28. This is what it means to find a purpose in your pain. Failure to identify a purpose for one's pain will frequently cause a person to adopt a victim's mentality. But you are not a victim, you are a victor! Once you discover a useful purpose for your pain, you will be able to bring a kind of closure to the bitter experience. Once you achieve closure, you will be able to move on and experience a more positive, purposeful, and fulfilling life.

> **When the past remains unresolved, it retains enormous power in the present.**

Reframing Your Pain

Finding a purpose for your pain is a process – days for some, many years for others. As a starting point, earlier in today's lesson, I articulated 7 reasons God allows pain and suffering. Prayerfully reread the seven and see which ones might be applicable to your current situation. You might write them down as I have done. In my case, God used my ministry failures and financial struggles to draw me closer to Him (#2), to build up my faith (#3), to humble me (#5), to prepare me for promotion (#7), and most importantly, to equip me for the new ministry He had been preparing me for (#1). Sharing the thought management principles of *The 21-Day Plan* with fellow Christian brothers and sisters via the sale of this book, traveling and preaching weekly in different churches, and hosting *Think Right Live Right* seminars are interconnected approaches to the same end – to help people control their negative thoughts rather than be controlled by them.

> **Don't just go through your pain, grow through your pain.**

When dealing with a particularly trying situation or dilemma, it is essential to reframe it. When you (positively) reframe a negative experience, you define the experience as opposed to the experience defining you. (By way of a reminder, you can revisit your (CCCR) thought management strategy, Day 10 and Day 11).

Discovering God's purpose in allowing my pain enabled me to cease being angry with God and helped me to bring closure to a very painful chapter in my life. God used my failure to redirect my life. Thence, I was ready to walk forward on the new path God had been preparing me for. David reminds us, "A person's *steps* are directed by the Lord..." (Psalm 37:23 GW).

Getting Through What You Can't Get Over

God said to the Prophet Samuel, "You have mourned long enough for [King] Saul" (1 Samuel 16:1 NLT). He was essentially saying, *Enough with your depressing pity parties over Saul.* King Saul persisted in making his sinful choices, and therefore, I (God) have made mine. A very wise man once said, *"You can't get over anything that hurt you until you first give up what you had in mind."* Samuel had in mind that God should continue to use disobedient King Saul to lead the Nation of Israel, but God had another king in mind: a young, steadfastly faithful shepherd boy named David. Hence, for Samuel to get over his hurt, (God's rejection of Saul) and move on with God's purpose and plan, (anointing David as the next king) he had to first be willing to give up what he had in mind. Samuel had to give up his expectation.

God is saying the same thing to you and me. Give up your (original) expectation. Your situation isn't really all that bad when compared to the horrors others have lived through and are living through. It's just not what you had in mind. Your marriage isn't all that bad. It's just not what you had in mind; it isn't your idealized imagining of things; it is non-perfect reality. Your job isn't all that bad. It's just not what you had in mind; it's reality. You may be an adult who has suffered numerous adverse childhood experiences (ACE) or a devastating betrayal, the destruction of your marriage, the death of a loved one, the loss of financial stability, the loss of job or career, or damage to your reputation. The Bible allows for a period of mourning. But God objects to a lifestyle of virtually continuous mourning (Deuteronomy 34:6). It's time to move on. Learn to accept your new reality, your 'new normal.' It's called *acceptance therapy.* The sooner you accept it, the sooner you can begin the healing process. Acceptance is the final stage of the grieving process. Recall the Five Stages of Grief: *1) denial, 2) anger, 3) bargaining, 4) depression, and 5) acceptance.*[3] (The stages are fluid, not static; experiences vary.) Jesus in the Garden of Gethsemane agonizingly prayed three times to the Father, beseeching Him to assess if there was another way to pay for mankind's sins apart from His being tortured and crucified. God, his Father, assured Him there was no other way. Jesus responded, "Father, not my will, but your will be done" (Matthew 26:39). Jesus accepted his circumstances. In so doing, he allowed himself to be arrested by the Roman soldiers without the slightest resistance. For the sake of our mental and emotional well-being, it is imperative that we not get stuck in the previous stages. Acceptance is the stage where genuine healing and finding *meaning/ purpose in your pain* becomes possible. When in grief, ask God to reveal to you its purpose? Reframe your misery and make it your new ministry—your *cause.* After her 13-year-old daughter was tragically killed by a drunken driver, Candy Lightner found *meaning* in her pain by founding the organization **MADD** (Mothers Against Drunk Driving).

Resist becoming enmeshed in anger. God knows that all of us will get angry at times. In fact, Christ got angry (Matthew 21:12-13). God is not opposed to our being angry. God is not angry at you because you are angry at Him for feeling He let you down. Do not confuse the ways and dispositions of humans with the way God considers things. God knows that anger is a necessary part of the grieving process. Concerning anger, God said, "Go ahead and be angry. You do well to be angry—but don't use your anger as fuel for revenge. And don't stay angry… Don't give the Devil that kind of foothold in your life" (Ephesians 4:26 MSG). It is permissible to get angry at sin, injustices and gross victimization, but don't stay angry for long. The longer the bout of anger, the unhealthier it is. The key to getting over your anger is courageously choosing to forgive. Give your peculiar burden to God to treat or remedy. Forgive the person. Forgive yourself. Again, don't fault God for the awfulness of the world. God is not the problem; God is the solution. There can be no genuine healing where one harbors unforgiveness. Don't get stuck in your anger.

The enemy will attempt to keep you locked in (stuck in the grieving process) your pain and tempt you to dwell continually in sadness and unproductiveness, as we always prefer the same and the familiar, and Satan knows this very well. Why does the enemy enjoy enticing you to engage in self-pity? Because each time you dwell on the pain and disappointment, it's like pulling the scab off the wound, making it impossible to heal. Each time you contemplate and meditate upon that negative experience, you release toxic chemicals into your brain, throwing off its chemical balance and leaving you to roil in the self-imposed dungeon of apathy, and hopelessness.[4] As we repeatedly give in to bleak, unhelpful, distressing feelings, they take deeper root neurologically, and Satan tightens his grip on our thoughts and emotions. It is helpful to recognize that there is a brighter future for us if we would only accept that the thing is past (and useless to dwell on), and God is with us in our mindful and emphatic venturing forward.

If you have tried to move forward on your own and have not been successful, pick up the phone and call for help. There are many government agencies and faith-based organizations that offer, at no charge, sound, caring advice to people in every sort of need, every trial and every emergency. Reach out to your pastor or any trusted minister for help. Find a good Christian counselor or join a support group meeting at a nearby church. Call a 1-800 help line if necessary, and there are many! (In any time of extreme need or distress, when other options are not appropriate or haven't worked, you may contact my ministry: Think Right Live Right Ministries. That contact information appears at the end of this book.)

Move on, so you can embrace the things that God has prepared for you and is preparing you for. Don't waste another day! Stop your "why God" refrain and learn to sing a new song. Rejoice! God has promised to protect you, to comfort you and to prepare you for His preordained work.

Real Life Testimonies to Help Build Your Faith

We can all gain strength and inspiration from the true stories of others' triumphs. And such is the testimony of a Virginia minister, Juanita. This godly woman refused to get stuck in her pain. She, with the help of God and others ministering to her, processed her pain, discovered its spiritual purpose, and is now comforting many others. With her personal testimony, she shares with us the same comfort she received from the God of all comfort (2 Corinthians 1:4).

Juanita's Story: It Hurt So Bad!

Many years ago, I experienced what was perhaps the darkest period of my life. Major facets of my life changed overnight, flooding my life with heartache, devastation, and loss. I kept thinking inwardly: "I'm a Christian—this isn't supposed to be happening to me." My marriage of 25 years ended in divorce, and its snowball effect impacted the church that my spouse and I founded and pastored for eight years. My husband, despite being a highly anointed preacher and psalmist, was a broken man who harbored many dark secrets. Unbeknown to me, he struggled with same sex attraction, he was a cross-dresser, and used drugs. His secret life began to unravel like a ball of yarn when he was arrested in an airport with drugs in his pocket. In shock and disbelief, I was left to salvage my personal life as well as stabilize the church. Once the church leaders and the members found out about my spouse's secret life, they began leaving the church one by one until there was hardly anyone left.

During this crisis, I spent many days trying to process what had happened because the events seemed surreal. As problems escalated, I hardly knew which one to tackle first. I was overwhelmed as I came face-to-face with my spouse's secret life, about which he was in total denial. I experienced a paralyzing fear as I learned of the immense debt we were in, having relied upon him completely to manage the household budget throughout our marriage. I was 48 years old—not the ideal age for re-entering the workforce. Yet, I had to quickly find a means of supporting myself. I had an additional challenge to keeping focused, due to the prescription medication I was taking for chronic pain from a previous injury from an auto accident. These were just a fraction of the problems for which I had no solutions.

The mental oppression and spiritual warfare I experienced during this time—especially at the onset of the crisis—was more than I can describe. It was as though an unseen wrecking ball was rolling through my life crushing everything within its path. A "what if" motion picture drama would begin to play in my mind when I went to bed at night, and as soon as my eyes opened the next morning the nightmarish saga would continue. I knew that I had to believe God was with me no matter what, and to trust Him daily to help me work through the fallout. Yet, there were days when God was quiet and not saying much. But, as I cried out to Him in despair, He not only allowed me to see another side of His love for me, but He also began to give me the following coping tools to practice daily.[5] These were all within my power to do with His help. They required an open heart toward God, determination, and discipline. What He did for me, He can do for you.

1. The first thing I had to do was to take control of my thought life. I had to take negative toxic thoughts captive. I asked God to show me how I was engaging in distorted and twisted thinking and to help me replace them with His life-giving Word.

2. I resisted the temptation to blame God. My husband out of his brokenness made a series of bad choices that ruined the ministry and ultimately cost him his life.

3. I started a journal that I named "My Gratitude Journal." Regardless of the challenges of any given day, I would only write in the journal the things for which I was thankful. Everything I was praying for God to do in my life, I would thank Him for in advance. If something negative occurred, I would thank Him for causing it to work for my good. I was amazed as I witnessed how this simple posture of gratitude changed my environment and lifted me out of despair by changing how I felt.

4. I went to counseling to help me process my tremendous grief. In that safe and caring environment, I was able to see how damaged I was and how that had fed into my tolerance of verbal and emotional abuse within my marriage for so many years. In the context of counseling, the Holy Spirit ministered healing peace and a joy which I cannot even begin to describe.

5. I committed to grow closer to God. Romans 12:2 says, "Be transformed by the renewing of our minds." It became my "go to" scripture as God was rebuilding my life. Along with spending time in His Word and being still and quiet in His Presence to allow Him to talk to me, I played worship music and sometimes sermons on CDs throughout the night as I slept. This allowed me to download what was positive and uplifting to my spirit as I slept so that I could face the new day with the peace of God and great expectation. When I experienced waves of anxiety, I would speak His peace over my spirit until I felt His peace cover me like a blanket. When commuting in my car, I would listen to inspiring sermons—the same ones, over and over. Daily, I had to feed my spirit with the written and spoken Word and surround myself with people who spoke life into my spirit. This is how I grew closer to God and achieved deliverance.

* * *

To learn the rest of Juanita Adam's inspiring story, read her fascinating book, *Yes, You Can Begin Again.*

* * *

**A Closing Prayer**

Thank You, Lord, for giving me insights into troubling questions. Dear God, I commit to turn to You when I am in pain and to stop allowing pain to drive a wedge between myself and you my loving Father. In Jesus' name. Amen.

For an inspirational pick me up, I recommend:

- *Stronger (What Doesn't Kill You)* by Kelly Clarkson
- *Haven't Seen It Yet* by Danny Gokey
- *He Is With You* by Mandisa
- *Praise the Lord* by Russ Taff

Until tomorrow, do this:

- Look over The Toxic Ten (pp. 238-239); reflect upon which thought distortions you may be entertaining. (Where there is relational conflict, somebody is most likely engaging in one or more of The Toxic Ten.)

 **Memory Work**

1. Repeat the *I Am Significant* mantra. Why? (Because) God loves me and sent his Son to die upon the cross for my sins. He has adopted me into His family and has given me a new name. I am a born-again Christian, fearfully and wonderfully made in the image of God.

2. Repeat your *My Spiritual Identity*: N-O-W-M-O-V-E-F-O-R-W-A-R-D acrostic. In the future, memorize the Scriptures associated with this acrostic. The Scriptures are found on pages 108-109.

3. Continue to write down The Filthy Five Memory Verses on 3x5 cards and practice memorizing them (Figure 14. 2, p. 242).

4. Daily employ your (CCCR) Thought Management 101 strategy (p. 182).

Replacing Negative Thoughts and Images of God: *How to Feel God's Love (Part 2)*

Live out of your imagination, not your history.
--Stephen Covey

Daily Food for Thought

- **Brain Facts**: "The imagination has the power of making the things we picture real and effective."[1] "The longer you focus on your goal, the more real it begins to feel, and if you stay focused long enough you'll alter the neural circuitry in your brain. *Focus on God long enough, and God becomes neurologically real.* Focus on peace, and your body becomes relaxed and serene."[2]

- **Key Thoughts:** The only way to do away with negative thoughts and images of God is to replace them with positive thoughts and images of God.

- **Scripture**: "Casting down imaginations, and every high thing that exalted itself against the knowledge of God and bringing into captivity every thought to the obedience of Christ" (2 Corinthians 10:5 KJV).

Daily Reading

Welcome to Day 17. If you are a follower of Christ but find it difficult to emotionally connect with God on a consistent basis, you've come to the right place. If you know that you are not harboring animosity toward God (blaming Him for a painful experience, etc.) and are not now or in the past guilty of identifiable sin or moral transgression, this lesson offers you a possible explanation.

Dr. David Eckman, author of the book, *Becoming Who God Intended*, wrestled with not feeling loved by God. In his search for answers, Eckman, a professor at Western Seminary in California, in working with thousands of college students for several years, discovered that family background plays a major role in determining whether you feel God loves you. He discovered that the more dysfunctional your home life was or is, generally, the less you feel God loves you. Christians fall into three categories of dysfunctionality in family of origin (FOO).

> *Family background plays a major role in determining whether you feel God loves you.*

Family Group One: healthy family background. These individuals grew up in homes in which they experienced love and affection on a consistent basis. "They felt loved and accepted whether they performed well or not."[3] The result: they felt an emotional connection with their parents, and they transferred those feelings to God. Hence, they felt loved by God.

Family Group Two: confused family background. They are labeled "confused" because they were given confusing signals growing up. They have positive memories of growing up, felt love and affection was meted out freely, but as time went on, they felt they had to earn their parents' love and affection by their performance. This Eckman labels the "yo-yo of affection."[4] This group felt loved sometimes, while at other times they did not.

Family Group Three: considerably dysfunctional family background. "Rarely have they experienced pure, [non-merit-based] affection."[5] They were denied proper (ideal) love and affection as children and as adults therefore have an underlying suspicion about God,[6] questioning the appropriateness of trusting God, and often they feel little to no emotional connection with God. Eckman cautions, if you are in this third group, emotional resonance with God will be harder to realize. However, these feelings can be cultivated by simply exerting more effort than those who fall into family groups one and two. For those coming out of a dysfunctional background, the extra work you are charged with concerns the exacting use of your imagination. To get the loving feelings that avail a closer emotional connection to God you must meditate upon new pictures of God's love. Because these pictures were not in your home, you are going to have to invoke them mentally. Many believers have accomplished this, and you can too.

Questions for Reflection

1. Do you think Eckman's separation of all persons here into three categories works, or do you think four or more catergories should be elucidated?

_____

_____

2. Which family category do you fall into? Explain

_____

_____

Dr. Jerry Mungadze, a leading neuropsychologist, makes the following observation concerning one's family of origin (FOO) and one's feelings about and images of God.

We may believe that God is distant, especially if our own fathers were distant. If our fathers didn't care, we may believe that God doesn't care. If our fathers were punitive, we may believe that God is punitive. If our fathers were performance-oriented, we may believe that God is performance-oriented. These beliefs can be resolved by first processing the experiences on which they're founded, and then by learning the truth about God.[7]

Those of us from especially dysfunctional homes are tasked with nurturing those loving feelings that bring a closer and deeper connection to God. I am one of 13 children, reared in a very dysfunctional home with an ADHD and alcoholic father. My family put the D in dysfunctional! I can swap dysfunctional anecdotes with the best of them and usually come out on top. However, only in recent years did I discover the correlation between my struggles to connect emotionally with my heavenly Father stemming substantially from my having an emotionally distant father myself. The insights I acquired from Dr. Eckman have benefited me tremendously. I pray it does the same for you.

Questions for Reflection

1. Take the time now to assess your relationship to your parents and your relationship with God. For you, do you believe such a correlation exists?

Yes/No?

2. Candidly describe your father's personality.

_____

_____

3. Candidly describe your mother's personality.

_____

_____

4. How may their personalities and parenting styles have contributed to both your positive and negative conceptions of God?

Positive:

_____

_____

Negative:

_____

_____

5. Do you feel that God has difficulty loving you sometimes? Explain.

_____

_____

According to Dr. Eckman, to get the loving feelings you desire, it would be greatly beneficial to meditate upon new pictures of God's love. By way of example, if your earthly father failed to verbally affirm you, imagine yourself standing in the place of Christ at his own baptism. The clouds roll back, the sky opens up and you hear the voice of your loving heavenly Father saying, "You (insert your name) are my beloved child in whom I am well pleased" (Matthew 3:17). Throughout each day, meditate on this exquisite image.

Information Versus Integration

In the past, people came to me who were struggling with negative thoughts and images of God. Like a good pastor, I would prescribe a couple of God-centered Bible verses for them to memorize. However, Dr. Eckman maintains, for some to feel God's love, it is going to require more than the mere accretion of knowledge. Christians are routinely (every Sunday) presented with truthful information, but realize very little change in their thought lives, emotions, attitudes, and resulting behaviors. Dr. Eckman goes on to say it is important to be able to distinguish between gaining new information and integrating that new information to bring about change in our thought life and all that results. "With information, the conscious mind has simply placed data into the memory. With integration, the conscious mind has taken a picture formed in the imagination and placed it [into] the subconscious, where it will affect emotions."[8] He contends that for this reason the Bible is mostly ineffective in the lives of many Christians. Dr. Eckman goes on to relate that as you begin to conceive new Bible-centered images of God in place of the negative images derived from your childhood, adolescence and adulthood, your emotions will begin to change and you will begin to feel a greater closeness to the loving, omnipresent God who thinks continuously about you. There is not a nanosecond in a day in which He is not thinking loving thoughts about you. In fact, when Christ was dying on the cross, you were, in a sense, on his mind. Can you imagine that?

By "integration," Eckman is describing what the Bible refers to as meditation. To meditate connotes the idea of pondering a particular scripture in your mind, ingesting it and regurgitating it and chewing on it some more, just as a cow regurgitates the cud and re-chews it over and over again until it extracts all the nutrients from it. Integration/meditation also includes using your imagination to picture yourself in the scripture. For example, have you ever wondered how David came to write Psalm 23—The Lord is my Shepherd? I imagine that while David was out in the pasture caring for his sheep, after watering them and leading them to greener pastures where they could contentedly graze, as they rested, he too rested, took out his stringed instrument and began singing in praise of the Lord. And just perhaps, David, while reflecting upon his responsibility to protect his sheep, was allowed by God to begin to see a parallel between the ways God cared for him and the way he himself cared for his sheep. I imagine, as he kept meditating upon that image, the joy of the Lord began to well up in his heart. David might have then realized; *the Lord is my shepherd... I shall not want!* That's how I often imagine David received the inspiration to initially sing and write Psalm 23. David saw himself as a lowly sheep and God as a loving shepherd. That's the difference between information and integration. The latter requires that we spend quality time in God's presence meditating upon God's word. It's not that God is hiding from us, but to feel his loving presence, He requires that we seek him in prayer, worship, and listen to hear His "still small voice" (Jeremiah 29:12 and James 4:8).

From a neurological standpoint, the human brain is hard-wired to experience a deep and intimate relationship with God. For this reason, God is widely worshiped all over the world. Therefore, all humanity is born with a "God Attachment."[9] But to better connect with God, you will need to habitually meditate upon positive mental pictures of God.

> *To better connect with God, you will need to habitually meditate upon positive mental pictures of God.*

Rewiring Your Brain to Feel God's Love

The brain does not discriminate in the ilk of our opining, positive or negative. It will take whatever conceptual or ideational approach you give it consistently and make it into a habit. Not only will the brain's functioning make it into a habit, it will create its very own neurological tendentiousness – to perpetuate the habit. [10]"The longer you focus on your goal, the more real it begins to feel, and if you stay focused long enough, you'll alter the neural circuitry in your brain. The same is true for any principle in life. Focus on God long enough, and God becomes neurologically more real,[11] more authentic.

That's What God Is Like

To gather more positive thoughts and images of God, Eckman points out that we need not restrict ourselves to scripture alone. He encourages us to go outside the Bible and look for expressions of love that mirror God's love for us. When you see a father, for example, affectionately carrying his tired children in his arms after a long day at a theme park or some other recreational setting, you might take a mental snapshot of that image as an edifying prompt for future use – saying, essentially, *"That's what God is like!"*

It would be a gain for us all to also look for images of God's love in movies, stories, testimonies, the majesty of the natural world God has created, ordinary providence, the benevolence of others, and artistic genius. Occasionally, I will listen to a secular love song and imagine God is singing that song to me. Did you know that the famous Simon and Garfunkel song "Bridge Over Troubled Water" is sung from God's perspective? When the lyric intones, "I will lay me down," it is God giving His all to the children He loves. The Bible states that God sings, "Joyfully because of you" (Zephaniah 3:17 NABRE). God's immutable love for us is represented in a song written and performed by the legendary American musician Stevie Wonder, titled "As." Wonder may be singing about his wife, but I hear God singing that song to me, assuring me that despite my hindrances and hang-ups, He's committed to always loving me just as I am.

Questions for Reflection

1. Can you think of a love song that you could modify the lyrics to and imagine it's a song Jesus might sing to you or about you?

_____

_____

_____

2. Are there movies or scenes in movies that remind you of God's love for you or some other attribute of God? What is it exactly in the scene or movie that gives it this potential to religiously instruct?

_____

_____

BFF (Best Friend Forever)

As you contemplate what God is like, picture in your mind one of your best friends. Next, think about the things that person does or has done that would cause you to hold him or her in such high esteem. What are some of the characteristics that person possesses that make you consider him or her one of your best friends? With that person's image in mind, along with those positive characteristics, I want you to use your sanctified imagination to view Jesus—for our purposes here, God in human form— in that same positive light. Jesus already calls you his friend. Jesus said to his followers, "Greater love has no one than this: to lay down one's life for one's friends. You are my friends... I no longer call you servants, because a servant does not know his master's business. Instead, I have called you friends..." (John 15:13-14a, 15 NIV). Reciprocate and call him your friend! The songwriter Joseph Scriven alluded to his friendship with Jesus by penning one of the most beloved hymns of Western Christianity, "What a Friend We Have in Jesus."

Jesus is a friend like no other! We can feel God's love by consistently meditating upon a positive image of God. Repeat to yourself multiple times each day: "Jesus is my best friend forever."

Jesus is a **F.R.I.E.N.D.** who (is):
- **F**aithful to me
- **R**ejoices over me
- **I**ntercedes for me
- **E**mpowers me
- **N**ever stops loving me
- **D**efends me

Jesus is a **F.R.I.E.N.D.** who is ...
Faithful to Me (Lamentations 3:23)

When I think of faithfulness, I think of my father who seemingly worked around the clock at the local steel mill to support our family of over 13 members. Often, I would see him only on weekends (or whenever I was in trouble), but he was a tirelessly faithful man. He never gave up on any of us and never walked away. He stayed the course and remained married to my mother until the day of his death. In a practical sense, he worked himself to death. My parents were married for over 40 years. That's faithfulness.

That's what God is like! Despite our unfaithfulness, Jesus is ever faithful; irrespective of our ups and downs, our frailties, idiosyncrasies and inconsistencies, Jesus remains faithful to us. He faithfully forgives us every time we entreat Him with absolute sincerity (1 John 1:9). He blesses us outside and beyond the context of familiar merit. When friends walk away (perhaps due to some failing or transgression), He faithfully remains our steadfast advocate. "Great is [God's] faithfulness" (Lamentations 3:23). Give God some praise now for His unwavering faithfulness!

Jesus is a **F.R.I.E.N.D.** who ...
Rejoices Over Me (Zephaniah 3:17)

Anecdotally: when I would return home from the church after a long day at work, just in time for dinner, my three toddling sons, Paul, Allan and Mark-Anthony, would run out of the apartment, with big smiles and excitement in their eyes, reaching up for me to lovingly pick up and embrace them. I'd reach down and scoop all three of them up at the same time. Holding them in my arms, I'd begin to smother them with butterfly kisses and tickle them. They could barely control their enthusiasm. What a delight! *That's what God is like!* How do I know that? The Prophet Zephaniah provides us a window into the heart of God.

> ... A mighty Savior! He will delight over you with joy. He will quiet you with His love. He will dance for joy over you with singing" (Zephaniah 3:17 TLV).

Imagine that! ...God dancing with joy over you – He's your number one fan. Try to imagine God watching over you all night, and as you open your eyes to the dawn of a new day, a smile appears on His face as He says, "I've got an extraordinary day planned for you. God rejoices over you because you are made in His image. He (figuratively) dances for joy because you bear His name. He sings you a song to quiet your heart as he walks by your side at work, at play, and at your times of need. Focus worshipfully on that characterization throughout the day and you will begin to feel God's loving presence.

Jesus is a **F.R.I.E.N.D.** who ...
Intercedes For Me (Hebrews 7:25)

Again anecdotally: When I think of an intercessor, I cannot help but think of my wife, Vonda. She was praying for me before she even knew me. She prayed that I would see that she was the one I ought to marry. She prayed that we should have sons (instead of the daughters I desired). God heard her prayers and gave us three sons. When I, like a lost sheep, wondered away from the side of my Good Shepherd, she prayed me back into sublime and lasting fellowship with Jesus. I don't know where I would be or what I would be if she had not so faithfully interceded on my behalf. *That's what God is like!* Whenever you see a unilateral confidence, a surpassing love, a devout faith, you must also see the hand of God. The Bible informs us, "He [Jesus] is able also to save forever those who draw near to God through Him, since He always lives to make intercession for them" (Hebrews 7:25).

He prays for you, too. When you lose faith in the midst of a battle, Jesus prays to the Father to revive your faith. When you were battling with thoughts of walking away from your ministry, your marriage, your job, or your schooling, and you *didn't* walk out, it was because Jesus was praying for you. His prayers sustained you. When you cried yourself to sleep at night but woke up with joy in your heart in the morning, you endured because Jesus prayed for you all through the night, for He never sleeps or slumbers (Psalm 121:3-4). Whatever your sigh-filled laments and frustrations and torments, know that Jesus is praying for you. The Apostle Paul reminds us, "Christ Jesus is He who died, yes, rather who was raised, who is at the right hand of God, who also intercedes for us (Romans 8:34). The Holy Spirit is also speaking to God on your behalf (Romans 8:26). We're going to make it through because we've got friends in high places!

Jesus is a **F.R.I.E.N.D.** who …
Empowers Me (Philippians 4:13)

When I think of someone who empowered me to trust God and to believe in my abilities, I cannot help but think of Reverend Eddie Lane. He was my academic adviser and spiritual mentor while I was a student at Dallas Theological Seminary (DTS) in the 1980s. During my second year in seminary, I was burnt out from the tedium of studying Greek and Hebrew. So, I made an appointment to go see him and inform him of my plan to drop out for a semester or two. Apprising him of my intentions one day, he paused for a moment, leaned forward in his chair and said, "Son, you don't have the right to quit. You've been called by God. You'd better pull your head together, and make sure you are in class the first thing Monday morning. There are people waiting for you and the gifts God has placed in you." His remarkable faith in God and faith in me empowered me to press on. And three years later, I graduated. *That's just like God!* God empowers us through His Holy Spirit to press on and to fight the good fight of faith. The sustaining power of God is real. I know that, "I can do all things through Christ who strengthens me" (Philippians 4:13 WEB).

When you were weak, He exchanged your weakness for His divine strength and made you strong. When you were going to give in to that temptation, He empowered you to resist. When you were desperate and discouraged, He filled you with hope. The sustaining power of God is real. He will hold us up and never leave us or forsake us (Hebrews 13:5).

Jesus is a **F.R.I.E.N.D.** who ...
Never Stops Loving Me (Romans 8:35, 38-39)

After my wife and I had been married for about 15 years, I felt there was a grow-ing distance between the two of us. I felt this was perhaps due to the fact that I had been keeping several secrets from my wife. Wanting to take our marriage to a level of greater intimacy, I decided to tell my wife some of the darker secrets that I held deep in my heart. So, one night I decided to unpack some of the 'junk in my trunk,' so to speak. We got into bed. I turned off all the lights, pulled the curtains tight so my neighbors' light could not shine into my bedroom, and I be-gan to reveal the secrets that I had held in my heart, beginning with the smaller and working my way up. When I finished, she turned toward me, kissed me on the forehead, embraced me and said, "I already knew that. I love you uncondi-tionally. Always know, I'll love you forever; I'll like you for always." She's never afterward brought up my past shames and indiscretions. *That's what God is like!* God says to his children, "I've loved you with an everlasting love, there-fore I've drawn you with gracious love" (Jeremiah 31:3 ISV). The Apostle Paul asked, "Who will separate us from the love of Christ (Romans 8:35)? The an-swer: "I'm absolutely convinced that nothing—nothing living or dead, angelic or demonic, today or tomorrow, high or low, thinkable or unthinkable—absolutely nothing can get between us and God's love because of the way that Jesus our Master has embraced us" (Romans 8:39 MSG). The only one who will ever love you unconditionally is God. Jesus proved that magnificence on the cross. Sure, you may have broken many promises to God, but His loving mercy is mightier than any mistake you will ever make. He loves you just the way you are, but He loves you too much to allow you to remain as you are.

FYI: I used to come down on myself quite critically when I felt I'd "disap-pointed God." However, it occurred to me one day that if God is sovereign and omniscient – and He is – then He knows my behavior beforehand. So, in a purely philosophical sense, we cannot disappoint (surprise) God. Profoundly omnisci-ent, He already knew that we were going to mess up before we messed up. In the final analysis, we may disappoint ourselves with our laxity, moral compromise and outright sin, but still not surprise God. God loves us unconditionally; He is ever mindful that we are "dust," always tempted and given to moral transgression (Psalm 103:14). Shake off your discouragement. Cheer up! Put a smile on your face! Why? Because God is smiling back at you! He loves you unconditionally.

Jesus is a **F.R.I.E.N.D.** who...
Defends Me (Romans 8:1, 33; Revelations 12:9)

One mental image of a defender that is etched in the corridors of my mind is rooted in a childhood experience. My Father was a harsh disciplinarian. If you disobeyed his commands, you were in for a world of trouble. He was "old school," and he used a thick leather belt to discipline us, but when he wasn't wearing his belt, anything in arm's reach would work just as well. As children, we were rarely allowed to venture anywhere far from home. However, on one occasion, my three older sisters asked my father's permission to go to a school-sponsored party. Surprisingly, my Father said *yes*. My sisters enthusiastically got dressed and scurried into the car. My mother and I dropped them off at the school around 7:00 pm and later returned. I must have been between the ages of 8 and 10 at that time, but I was old enough to know that my sisters were acting strange. They were staggering, laughing and acting uncharacteristically giddy. As my Mom put one sister in the car, the other climbed out—making strange utterances. After a struggle, Mom secured them in the back seat of the car. Mom jumped in the front seat, slammed the door and said disapprovingly, "Paul, they're drunk." The first thought that came to my mind was, "Dad is going to kill them. Daddy is going to kill them." My heart was palpitating. Mother and I drove home in dead silence, anticipating what frightful tortures awaited them.

As Mom slowly pulled into the driveway, she sat in the car for a long time. We both foresaw the awful violence that was seemingly only moments away. After a while, dad stuck his head outside the front door. Upon seeing him, my mom quickly jumped out of the car to run some sort of interference. She hastily walked toward my father. They huddled for several minutes as she attempted to brace him for what he was about to encounter. Defending her daughters, she explained to her husband how someone spiked the punch at the school party and the girls drank it, and as a consequence all three were obviously drunk. Mom pleaded for mercy, making the case that it wasn't their fault and that they didn't know what they were doing. Remaining dread-stalled in the car with my sisters, I saw my dad slowly walk up to the car. My heart once again began to thump in foreboding. Slowly he opened the car door and for a brief moment gazed upon his three daughters fast asleep. He tenderly picked them up one by one and carried them in his arms into their bedrooms. Once inside, he took off their shoes and tucked them into bed, each fully dressed. He turned off the light and turned to me and said, *"Don't mention this to the girls in the morning. We'll act as though this never happened."* I was shocked! No whippings; no verbal thrashings; no punishment of any kind! Unbeknown to me that night, I had been given my first glimpse of what grace and mercy looks like. That was uncharacteristic of my father. But *that's just like God!* Because of His immense love, He doesn't give us what we deserve. "As far as east is from west— that's how far God has removed our sin from us" (Psalm 103:12 CEB). When Jesus was being crucified on the cross, he cried out to His Father in our defense, pleading our case, "Father, forgive them, for they do not know what they do" (Luke 23:34 KJV).

Jesus ran interference for us. He is our defender against Satan and all other accusers. The Apostle Paul posed the question, "Who will bring a charge against God's elect?" (Romans 8:33). Christ died to save us from the (eternal damnation) consequences of our sins (Romans 8:34). You may have convinced yourself that God is mad at you or that you are unworthy of God's love. You may even be mad at God for past hurts. Although you may be mad at God, He's not mad at you. He loves you and calls you his friend. Jesus said, "Greater love has no one than this: to lay down one's life for one's friends. You are my friends…" (John 15:13-14 NIV). Jesus loved you so much that he was willing to die on the cross to secure your friendship for all eternity. Jesus, through his death on the cross, was saying He'd rather die than to spend his life in eternal bliss without you. Imagine that! Christ dying on the cross, just for you. Christ made the first move. Now it is your move. Jesus invites you to have a personal relationship with him. But you need to believe what he did on the cross He did just for you. He invites you to be his personal guest.

> **God loves you simply because he has chosen to do so.**

Once, after an Andrae Crouch concert, I took it upon myself to meet the gospel artist backstage in his dressing room. I snuck through the door. Andrae was startled to see me at first, but knowing I was star struck fan, he smiled and invited me to sit down and dine with him as his impromptu guest. Oh, what a night! I left there with his autograph, humming one of his many hits. *That's just like God!* God's always welcoming – eagerly desiring to advocate for us and assist us.

Jesus said, "Behold, I stand at the door of your heart and knock… if anyone hears My voice and opens the door, I will come into him and will dine with him, and he with Me" (Revelation 3:20). Just as Andrae Crouch invited me to sit down and have a meal with him, Jesus extends the same invitation to you. Could it be that one of the reasons that you are feeling far from God and not experiencing Him as your closest friend is because you have never invited Him to come into your life? Will you at this very moment make the decision to come to know your Creator in a personal way? Close your eyes and imagine Jesus knocking at the door of your heart, waiting for you to open the door and invite him in to be your personal friend, Lord and Savior. The Bible relates, "Whoever calls upon the name of the Lord shall be saved" (Romans 10:9-10). Metaphorically speaking, you open the door of your heart by praying from your heart the following prayer:

Lord Jesus, I know that you love me. You died to prove it. I admit that I have failed to live up to your standards. I ask you to forgive me of my sins and come into my life. I acknowledge you as my Lord and Savior. Thank you for saving me, forgiving me, and adopting me into your family. I freely declare that I am now your child and friend forever. Amen.

If you sincerely prayed this prayer, I believe you were born again. Becoming a friend of God is just that simple. As a friend of God, find a good Bible-teaching church where you can learn to grow spiritually. Read your Bible daily. I strongly recommend that you begin with the New Testament, The Gospel of Saint John or Saint Luke. God is committed to transforming your life from the inside out. Keep Jesus first in your life, and He will do things in your life that you never imagined possible.

Real Life Testimonies to Help Build Your Faith

Read the testimony of a man named Bobby whose father severely marred his image of God. He fought back to reclaim that which was taken from him as he learned to replace his earthly father's image with the image of his loving heavenly Father.

Bobby's Story: I Had a Dad, But Now I Have a Father

My earthly father was my first image of God, authority, and masculinity. My relationship with him was nothing short of a horror that I desperately wanted to escape. The fact that he was also my pastor and later bishop made the damage worse. Dad was larger than life to me, but not in the way a boy admires his dad as his hero. He was narcissistic and emotionally, verbally, physically, and spiritually abusive. I never knew what emotional channel he was on. Consequently, I walked on eggshells around him for fear that the slightest mistake would set him off. When angry with me, he would either go into a physical rage, threatening to throw me out of the house, or punish me by refusing to speak to me for days. He maintained control over his house through fear, intimidation, secrecy, and manipulation. When my father showed affection, I thought I was the most important person in the world. When I angered him, he withheld it to the same degree that he gave it. Additionally, my father was addicted to various types of pornography for as long as I could remember. I watched him abuse cocaine and alcohol. What baffled me most was that I saw firsthand how God allowed him considerable influence in the areas of preaching and the prophetic ministry. The incongruity between his home and church personas was like seeing two different people trapped inside one body. My observations were later somewhat corroborated when he was diagnosed with bipolar disorder.

As I journeyed through life, I came to believe Satan's lies – that the God I could not see was like the father I could see. I viewed God as psychotic, unpredictable, and waiting to cast me into hell if I did not pray and serve Him earnestly enough. I learned that you could hide and be dysfunctional so long as your gifts and talents still "worked."

I also developed a very warped view of marriage relationships. What I saw my mother endure with my father and how she struggled to exit a toxic relationship deepened my belief that marriage was a trap to be avoided at all costs.

Because my father was already effeminate in his mannerisms, I naturally modeled myself after him. My gestures and my general behavior were often unmanly. My peers in school called me "faggot" so much until I thought it was my middle name. I began to think, well, if every person I meet is saying this about me, then maybe it's true. Since I knew about hell and about sexually transmitted diseases before I knew about a loving accepting God, I was afraid to act out sexually. I already believed in my heart that I was trash.

Shortly after my parents' divorce, I took all my unresolved issues into my own heterosexual marriage. I married for all the wrong reasons: to escape my father's influence and for selfish sexual gratification. *Essentially, I ran into what I was running from and became what I wouldn't forgive.* My ex-wife became the target of my unforgiveness toward my father. My unwillingness to release the past, coupled with an unabated porn addiction rooted in rejection, was one of the major reasons why I failed miserably at marriage. It took this kind of crisis to wake me up to the urgency of change. Pain has a purpose in that it can make us desperate enough to cry out to God – not to rescue us for a quick fix, but to partner with Him in the infinitely worthy project of lifelong healing.

I have been working out my own healing for almost four years now, since the marriage ended. I had to submit myself to accountability, therapy, and prayer counseling. I had to open my Pandora's box to a community of believers who God said were safe and I could trust. In that seven-month period I was introduced to my heavenly Father's nourishing power. It was fleshed out in group therapy sessions through the testimonies of people who had suffered in even worse ways. They managed through God's persistent grace reflected in a healing community. They found the True Father's voice, a divine edification that had been muffled by years of the enemy's lies.

Most days the past feels like it happened yesterday. Every day, I ask God to grace me to be connected with my heart and to live with Him from that place. When I say that, I mean living moment by moment, so that I'm aware of what I'm really thinking and feeling in real time. Next, I ask myself, "Is this from my True Father or my inferior self?" If it's a lie from my past that I'm believing, I go to the one or two scriptures or prescriptions that the Lord has given me to stand on, and I recite it aloud. I do this until God's peace washes over me. Then I identify something life-giving to do to change my focus.

My relationship with my biological father in my youth brought about a chronic undercurrent of anxiety in the core of my being. It manifested itself in various acts of commission and omission that resulted ultimately in self-harm. There were even several acts of physical self-mutilation. Additionally, I felt driven and never at peace. Some days I feel like my emotions are stronger than the potentiality-filled truths of my Father in heaven. I talk out loud to myself a lot to remind my spirit that what I am presently feeling is not my truest, most empowering reality. I must consistently fight the urge to isolate myself from community. That I have been rejected in the past doesn't mean I am accursed! I have people in my life that still keep me accountable when I'm "missing in action." I maintain accountability filters on my computer devices, and I'm still opening my life to the people God has placed in it. I've had relapses, but the quicker I got back up and kept moving, the rarer and less severe they became.

The key for me was realizing that God was not angry with me, that his anger was satisfied through Jesus on Calvary. I understood that God's forgiveness didn't give me a license to continue to willfully sin. I realize that God doesn't give me the supernatural ability to overcome until I partner with Him and decide to obey Him in simple ways every day.

In closing, my own desperate need for Jesus' healing and cleansing allowed me to see my earthly father in his raw humanity with compassion. Although I don't make excuses for his choices, nor mine, I had to consider the toxic home and church environments that produced the broken boy inside his adult self. I later discovered that he was sexually abused multiple times by his uncles and cousins. Therefore, he was so fiercely and obsessively protective where my safety was concerned. Had it not been for him, I could have been violated in the same way. Unfortunately, when he finally worked up the courage to tell his parents, they called him a liar. Part of my healing has been in allowing God to sift through my false perceptions of Dad, to give me a clearer and fairer perspective on my dad and to know it could have been much worse, to celebrate the many and lasting good things he was to me and to many others. Dad is finally at peace, no longer split, no longer at war with himself. I ask God to grant me a substantial portion of that peace too. Great is Your faithfulness, Father, unto me!

* * *

Bobby had a Dad but now he has a Father, a heavenly Father who loves him unconditionally. One who is capable of looking beyond all his faults to see his deepest needs. Your experiences or the experiences of others may have marred your image and perception of God, but you now have the knowledge and the skills to change that. God says, "You will seek me and find me when you seek me with all your heart" (Jeremiah 29:13). Decide today to begin replacing your negative images of God with the images portrayed in today's lesson, the Bible, creation, and the goodness of God on display in the lives of loving, helpful people all around you. John did it, and so can you. Seek Him. He longs to be found by you. God made the first move toward you by sending his Son—Jesus. Now it's your move. You use your imagination to imagine a host of other things. Now use it to imagine your friendship with God.

* * *

A Closing Prayer

Lord Jesus, thank You for helping me to see the many ways that You have been such a good and loyal friend to me. Thank You for revealing to me the specific ways I can use my imagination to replace my negative images of You with positive images of You. Thank You for loving me so much that You were willing to surrender Your very self, so I could become Your best friend forever. Amen.

For an inspirational pick me up, I recommend:

- *Reckless Love* by Steffany Gretzinger
- *How He Loves Us* by Anthony Evans
- *I Am a Friend of God* by Israel Houghton
- *You're a Good Good Father* by Chris Tomblin
- *He Knows My Name* by Tysha Cobbs

Until tomorrow, do this:

1. Throughout the day, think about songs, movies, and people that may bring to mind: "That's what God is like."

2. Familiarize yourself with the Jesus is my FRIEND acrostic by reading it aloud. Perhaps even write it down on a 3x5 card. Repeat it to yourself whenever the enemy seeks to trick you by reminding you of your faults and possibly also tries to convince you that God could never love anybody like you.

3. Look over The Toxic Ten (pp. 238-239); reflect upon which thought distortions you may be entertaining. (Where there is relational conflict, somebody is most likely engaging in one or more of The Toxic Ten.)

Memory Work

4. Repeat the *I Am Significant* mantra. Why? (Because) God loves me and sent his Son to die upon the cross for my sins. He has adopted me into His family and has given me a new name. I am a born-again Christian, fearfully and wonderfully made in the image of God.

5. Repeat *My Spiritual Identity*: N-O-W-M-O-V-E-F-O-R-W-A-R-D acrostic. In the future, memorize the Scriptures associated with this acrostic. The Scriptures are found on pages 108-109.

6. Continue to write down The Filthy Five Memory Verses on 3x5 cards and practice memorizing them (Figure 14. 2, p. 242).

7. Apply your (CCCR) Thought Management 101 strategy (p. 182).

Replacing a Negative Self-Image,
Building a Healthy Self-Image

Next to a knowledge of God, a knowledge of who you are is by far the most important truth you can possess.

--Dr. Neil Anderson

Daily Food for Thought

- **Brain Fact** A negative self-image will perpetuate negative self-talk, which will generate more negative thoughts and overstimulate the limbic system, causing your glands to release chemicals that result in toxic emotions which in turn negatively impact your overall physical, emotional, and yes, spiritual health.

- **Key Thought** A healthy self-image involves learning to "see yourself as God sees you—no more and no less."

- **Scripture** "I say to every man among you not to think more highly of himself than he ought to think, but to think so as to have sound judgment..." (Romans 12:3).

Daily Reading

Welcome to Day 18. Let's begin with a story. In between ministry assignments, the Lord opened a door for me to teach life skills at a workforce development program at a local community college. One day in class, during a break, a student confided in me that she had just recently purchased a mirror for her house. Noting my quizzical expression, she told me her story. For years she struggled with a life-threatening cocaine addiction. During her protracted struggle she grew to loathe the person she had become. In her own words, she "could not stand to look at [herself] in the mirror," so she smashed them all and removed them from her home, including the one in her bathroom.

> *Your self-image is a lot like the cruise control in your car. Once set, it will lock you into a set speed.*

However, after overcoming her addiction, she felt comfortable seeing reflections of herself. She had emerged from a religion-based 12 step program that worked excellently to her benefit. In that experience, God's beneficent love for her was revealed, and she regained a wholesome image of herself.

Is Having a Healthy Self-Image Important?

You may believe possessing a healthy self-image is good, but not all that essential to one's overall emotional health and wellbeing. However, the preceding story proves something quite different. How one views oneself has a significant impact on one's social, psychological and spiritual outlook. Having a healthy self-image is important for a least these several reasons:

1. A *poor self-concept.* What you think about yourself plays a critical role in generating either positive or negative thoughts and self-talk.
2. *Low self-esteem.* Distressing feelings about yourself (failing to adequately love and accept yourself) makes it hard for you to feel God's love and acceptance.[1]
3. *Abject self-worth.* How much you *value* yourself will cause you to attract people of a similar spirit, who will only reinforce what you initially project.
4. A *poor self-image.* How you see yourself will potentially hinder the ability to achieve your dreams in life. A poor self-image may cause you to give up and flee instead of fighting or accepting a failure or degradation as somehow "fitting." A poor self-image, a "grasshopper mentality," is what in scripture prevented the children of Israel from possessing the Promised Land (Numbers 13:33).

Your self-image is a lot like the cruise control in your car. Once set, it will lock your car into a set speed. However, depending on the road's terrain, it may surpass or fall below the set speed – but not for very long. The cruise control will bring the car back into sync with the locked-in speed. In like manner, your self-image may at times rise somewhat higher depending on your successes and achievements, but eventually it will recalibrate to its more normal setting due in large part to your most enduring beliefs about yourself.

For faith-based and experiential reasons, some Christians are uneasy about the concept of a "healthy self-image," thinking it leads to some sort of pride or egoism. However, upon a review of pertinent scripture, we are told to love ourselves in at least several discreet passages (Leviticus 19:18; Matthew19:19; Mark 12:31; Luke 10:27; Romans 13:9). The Apostle Paul told husbands to "love their wives as they love themselves" (Ephesians 5:28-29). In the Scriptures, a natural self-love is affirmed. The Scriptures never tell you to hate yourself; Scripture assumes that you will care for yourself and have a concern for your own well-being. To be in possession of a nourishing and enriching self-worth is to have a conviction that you have fundamental value because you were created by God in His image for His specific purpose (Genesis 1:26; Psalm 139:14; Jeremiah 1:5). If your creator says you are worthwhile and valuable, you mustn't allow distorted thinking, nor other people's opinions, nor your personal negative experiences to render null what God has ordained.

Striving to Maintain a Biblical Self-Image

Christian apologist Josh McDowell, in his book *Building Your Self- Image*, defines a healthy self-image as "seeing yourself as God sees you, no more and no less."[2] His definition is based on the words of the Apostle Paul who said, "I say to every man among you not to think more highly of himself than he ought to think; but to think so as to have sound judgment..." (Romans 12:3). Most of us do not see ourselves at all the way God sees us, and this is because our minds have not been renewed sufficiently. Romans 12:2 says, "be transformed by the renewing of your mind." As we spend time praying, reading, meditating, visualizing, memorizing and obeying the Word, gradually we begin to see ourselves more the way God sees us. As a reminder, Biblical mind renewal is the lifelong process of replacing our perspective (thoughts, opinions and beliefs) with God's perspective – as stated in His Word. Only as our minds are renewed and transformed will we begin to see ourselves as God sees us.

How Healthy is Your Self-Image?

According to McDowell, no matter how confident and poised others may appear, we all struggle with self-image issues to varying degrees.[3] Listed below are some beliefs and attitudes characteristic of people suffering from issues of low self-esteem.

(1) Pessimistic outlook on life; (2) Extreme sensitivity to the opinions of other people; (3) Self-consciousness about appearance, performance, or status; (4) Striving to become something or somebody instead of relaxing and enjoying

who they are; (5) Fear of God or belief that He is uninterested or angry with them; (6) A problem in believing or accepting God's love or the love of another person.[4]

Questions for Reflection

1. Which of the 6 identifiers relate most to your current life? Feel free to choose several.

_____

_____

2. Has a poor self-image caused you to neglect or alter your dreams? Explain.

_____

_____

Perceived Identity vs True Identity

Concerning one's identity, Dr. Jerry Mungadze, maintains:

Most of what we call identity is perceived identity. Perceived identity is heavily influenced by how we were raised and our circumstances. Therefore, the [pertinent] area of the brain varies from person to person. True identity, on the other hand, doesn't change and has nothing to do with our experiences or our perceptions…true identity rests with God. God has the final say on who you are. But if you are like most people, you have let your upbringing and your experience tell you who you are, and these things do not and cannot define your identity. In fact, God has already declared who you are… because we were created in His image. This means that questions of value and purpose tied to identity rest with God, not us. God made us before we did any -thing; therefore, what we do, how we were raised, and all our experiences throughout our lives have no bearing on who we are. So, if you want to improve your self-image, you will do yourself a great service by paying attention to what God says about you.[5]

Viewing ourselves based on our perceived identity is virtually automatic. To retrain our brain to embrace our truer identity is going to take some time, but due to the brain's changeable nature, it is doable only providing that you are willing to do the required work.

> *To retrain your brain to embrace your truer identity is doable providing you are willing to do the required work.*

304

Perceived Identity

A graphic Biblical example of one's perceived identity is demonstrated in the life of Gideon who finds himself literally buried with the burdens of his circumstances. Let me explain. The Nation of Israel was once again repeating its sin cycle. As a consequence, God allowed an ungodly nation to oppress and enslave them. In response, they cried out to God for deliverance. God, in his mercy, sends them a deliverer. God's human deliverer is an unsuspecting farmer by the name of Gideon, on the verge of starvation and annihilation. An angel speaks to Gideon, directing him:

> But one day the Angel of the Lord came and sat beneath the oak tree at Ophrah, on the farm of Joash…Gideon, had been threshing wheat by hand in the bottom of a grape press—a pit where grapes were pressed to make wine—for he was hiding from the Midianites. The Angel of the Lord appeared to him and said, "Mighty soldier, the Lord is with you!" (Judges 6:11-12 TLB).

Picture Gideon hiding underground, sifting his wheat in the bottom of the press because if he were to do it in the open in front of the Midianites, they would come and steal it. His actions seem cowardly, but observe what God calls him: "Mighty soldier" (v.12); that's Gideon's true identity. However, observe Gideon instead attaching himself more to his perceived identity, one based on his family of origin (FOO), his dismal, humble circumstances and life experiences.

> But Gideon replied, "Sir, how can I save Israel? My family is the poorest in the whole tribe of Manasseh, and I am the least thought of in the entire family!" (Judges 6:15 TLB).

Observe that last phrase: "I am the least thought of in the entire family."

Gideon definitely suffered with a negative self-image. What labels have you ascribed to yourself? Do you think of yourself as the least or among "the least" because you were born and grew to adulthood suffering various degradations and disappointments? Do you feel you have not achieved enough or established enough to deserve the confidence and respect of others?

You are not a mistake in God's eyes. Perhaps you wear the label of being a "bad seed" because you have been frequently in trouble or do unusual or "unacceptable" things. How long are you going to wear that label? "The only power that a label has over you is the power you give it."[6]

This is exactly the state of mind in which God found Gideon, but God wasn't going to allow him to perpetually remain in his sad helplessness. To motivate Gideon to look outside of himself for the confidence he needed, God encouragingly him said, "I'll be with you. *Believe me*; you'll defeat Midian as one man"

(Judges 6:16 MSG). Gideon's reaction was not to come to him in the form of familiar self-confidence. Instead, his confidence was grounded in his awareness that God was with him. God would fight his battle for him – if he would receive His help and believe it in faith. Gideon had a decision to make. He could choose to cling to and hold tightly to his perceived identity (after all that was what he was most familiar with), or he could choose to trust God and accept God's superior assessment of his (true) identity and begin the mind renewal process of beginning to see himself as God saw him. Fortunately, for Gideon, he chose the latter.

Hindrances to Accepting Your True Identity

Have you ever wondered why it is so difficult for you to embrace your true identity? As one who has struggled with self-image throughout my life, I've concluded that there are basically three primary reasons it is such a struggle to see ourselves as capable, purposeful and dignified as God sees us. Firstly, our family of origin (FOO) and negative life experiences have so etched their impressions on our psyche that unless we purposefully renew our minds according to Romans 12:2, our self-image will not appreciably change.

Secondly, we struggle to accept our true identity because of our propensity to engage in emotional reasoning. We reason within ourselves that because we don't feel like a new creation in Christ, we *must not* be. 'Since I don't feel like an overcomer, I must not be one,' goes the reasoning. As believers, we are to walk by faith, and not by sight (2 Corinthians 5:7). Yet, emotional reasoning is a thought distortion (Days 13 & 14).

Finally, and by far the most compelling reason we struggle to embrace our true identity, is because of the intense spiritual attacks leveled against our minds by Satan. Satan's arch goal is to keep us confused about our true identity, so we won't accomplish and fulfill the plan God has for our lives. Hence, he daily assaults our minds (often, the mind games) with a barrage of half-truths, full blown lies and sorted accusations (Revelation 12:9).

Satan's Five Accusations [7]

Years ago, the comedic actor Jim Carey starred in a motion picture called *Liar Liar*. In the movie, he played an attorney who was a compulsive liar. He lied to his fellow colleagues, his boss, the judges in the courtroom, his neighbors, his ex-wife, and his son... everyone! By his very nature he was a compulsive liar. The Bible says of Satan that whenever he speaks, he speaks a lie (John 8:44). He goes about spreading his lies to any individual gullible enough to believe him. Hence, the Bible says, "Be on your guard and stay awake. Your enemy, the devil, is like a roaring lion, sneaking around to find someone to attack" (1 Peter 5:8 CEV). Satan's accusations are one of his major weapons. Invading your inmost psychology, he's out to attack your true, God-intended identity. He does so by employing a five-fold strategy:

1. **He accuses us to ourselves.** He tells us negative things about ourselves. This is evidenced by our negative self-talk and the negative labels we ascribe to ourselves. The prodigal son said of himself, "I am no longer worthy to be called a son" (Luke 15:19, 21). He causes us to use sad, insulting, degrading and dehumanizing experiences in our past to appraise our current selves.

2. **He accuses us to others**. He puts negative thoughts in other people's minds about us, and those people relay those thoughts to us. If internalized, these labels become integral to our perceived identity. For this reason, our family of origin (FOO) and life experiences play such a major role in forming our self-image—be they positive or negative. The Scribes and Pharisees loathed Jesus (Luke 20:20; John 5:16-18; 8:39-41).

3. **He accuses others to us.** He puts negative thoughts in our minds about other people. Not only do others label us, we also label others based on various preconceptions, ignorance, prejudices and biases. We end up thinking or saying to ourselves that because someone is very different (in appearance, social standing, or values) he or she is unworthy or somehow otherwise condemnable. Satan uses such unspiritual ideas to contaminate our minds, and the ease with which we form negative views of others is an extreme and enduring problem. Satan put negative thoughts in Judas mind about Jesus which resulted in Judas betraying Jesus (Luke 22:3).

4. **He accuses God to us.** He puts negative thoughts in our minds about God. Observe what Gideon said about God, "If the Lord is with us, why has all this happened to us?" (Judges 6:13). Gideon was inferring that the nation was in dire straits because God had abandoned them. Israel was on the brink of destruction as a result of their many sins. Satan, the accuser, will accuse God by whispering in your ear, for example, "The reason that bad things keep happening to you is because God is punishing you for your sins!" Job's distraught wife told him to "curse God and die" (2:9).

5. **He accuses us to God.** Satan points out our failures and shortcomings to God. Satan tells God, for example, that we who claim Christianity do so for selfish and unwholesome reasons, such as the receipt of blessings. He also tries to direct God's attention to our almost unlimited capacity for sin. Satan doesn't succeed in his effort to reduce or sully God's view of

us, but that does not mean that Satan stops trying. It is one of the characteristics of Satan that he, the Great Liar, seems almost inexhaustible in energy or interest in deception. Satan accuses us to God every time we mess up. Satan says, essentially, God, they call themselves Christians, but look at the things they say and do. They act more like my children than yours (Revelation 12:9).

Objection Overruled

Concerning Satan's role as our chief accuser, Dr. Tony Evans in his book, *Theology You Can Count On*, makes the following observation:

> The idea of an accuser suggests a legal setting, a court scene. We need to understand that God operates His universe like a court. He gave Israel his law, and throughout the Old Testament we find God bringing a charge against His people when they broke that law. Lucifer himself was brought into the court of heaven, charged with rebellion, found guilty, and sentenced to the lake of fire (Revelation 20:9-11). His fellow rebellious angels were also sentenced to eternal fire. The Devil is on death row, even though he is being allowed to operate for a period of time. He has taken the role of prosecutor, bringing charges against us before God, accusing us of all sorts of things, slandering us and God. The great thing is that we have a 'defense attorney,' Jesus Christ, to defend us by pleading His blood (1 John 2:1).[8]

Jesus' role as our defense attorney is explained, "My little children, I am writing these things to you so that you may not sin. And if anyone sins, we have an Advocate with the Father, Jesus Christ the righteous" (1 John 2:1). The Greek word for advocate is *paracletos*; it refers to one called alongside to help. So, while Satan the prosecutor accuses us, Jesus our defense attorney helps to defend us against Satan's accusations.

The Apostle Paul reassures us, "If God is for us, who is against us" (Romans 8:31)? Continuing with the courtroom analogy, Paul, well versed in the Law of Moses, poses the question, "Who will bring a charge against God's elect" (Romans 8:33 NKJV)? The elect is a reference to every ultimately saved child of God. Satan can bring a charge against us each time we sin. However, his accusation is overturned because of Jesus' work of redemptive forgiveness upon the cross. The Bible assures us, "If we confess our sins, God will forgive us. We can trust God to do this. He always does what is right. He will make us clean from all the wrong things we have done" (1 John 1:9ERV). We have the assurance of forgiveness not just for our past and present sins, but for our future sins as well.

Jesus is not just our advocate, but also our Great High Priest (Hebrews 10:21) who offered Himself once and for all time as the final sacrifice for our sins. Jesus, while on earth, never ministered in the temple by way of offering sacrifices; His ministry was far superior. He entered into heaven itself. The following text explains this in further detail.

Under the old covenant, the priest *stands* and ministers before the altar day after day, offering the same sacrifices again and again, which can never take away sins. But our High Priest offered himself to God as a single sacrifice for sins, good for all time. Then he *sat down* in the place of honor at God's right hand (Hebrews 10:11-12 NLT).

The Good News Bible, translates verse 14,

"With one sacrifice, then, he [Jesus] has made perfect forever those who are purified from sin" (Hebrews 10:14 GNT).

We've been purified and made perfect by the shed blood of Jesus. It is important to note the above text emphasizes the point that the priest stood (v.11) as they daily offered sacrifices for sins. They never sat down because their work was never complete, never finished. In juxtaposition, Jesus, knowing that the blood of bulls and goats could never take away the sins of men, offered himself as the *final sacrifice*, by shedding his precious blood upon the cross of Calvary. After his crucifixion, he was taken down from the cross and placed in a tomb late one mournful Friday evening. But he rose early Sunday morning with all power in his hands and ascended into heaven. Once in heaven, Jesus our Great High Priest, sat down at the right hand of God. Jesus sat because His work was complete. Man's "sin debt" was paid in full. Jesus *sat down* because his mission was accomplished.

-- Christ sat down so that you and I could stand—*forgiven!*
-- Christ sat down so that you and I could stand—free of *guilt and shame!*
-- Christ sat down so that we could stand—*Righteous*—right with God!
-- He sat down so that we could stand—*Justified!*
-- Christ sat down so that we could stand—*friends of God!*

How was that possible?
God dropped the charges!

"But now, in union with Christ Jesus, you, who used to be far away, have been brought near by the blood of Christ" (Ephesians 2:13 GNT).

Satan's accusations can't touch us. We stand clean before the Lord. Objection overruled! The primary reason believers need not give in to feelings of self-condemnation and fearing that God will not accept them is because our self-esteem and our acceptance before God is based on God's acceptance of Christ's finished work on the cross and not our half-hearted efforts. We may personalize this by stating it in the first person: My acceptance before God is based on...

Christ's:

--Special importance and my position in Christ, and not my own (Philippians 2:7-11; Ephesians 1:3-11).
--Accomplishments, and not my own (1 Corinthians 5:21; 8:9).
--Victories, and not my own (Romans 5:8, 17-19; Revelation 1:5).
--Earnest Love of the Father, and not my own (Mark 12:30; John 8:42; Ephesians 5:2)
--Perfect Obedience, and not my own (John 1:29; Hebrews 5:9; 7:28; 10:14).

You and I bring nothing to the table. We receive *everything* as a gracious gift of God the Father. You have got to find your self-image in Christ—alone. Declare to yourself: in Christ I am made perfect. Jesus did it all! You just have to believe it and receive it by faith. This is the kind of truth that sets a person free from feelings of unworthiness, low self-esteem and a poor self-image. Very carefully write this on a 3x5 card and trounce the Great Liar's deceit the next time

> *"It [Jesus' death] was a perfect sacrifice by a perfect person to perfect some very imperfect people" (Hebrews 10:14 MSG).*

he accuses you of being an unworthy sinner.

JD Grier in his book entitled, *Gospel*, has framed perhaps one of the best definitions of the Gospel that I've seen. He writes:

In Christ, there is nothing I can do that would make You [God] love me more, and nothing I have done that makes You love me less. Your presence and approval are all I need for everlasting joy. As You have been to me, so I will be to others. As I pray, I'll measure Your compassion [love] by the cross and Your power by the resurrection.[9]

The next time Satan accuses you of being a pitiful, unworthy wretch, citing something you've done or failed to do, tell Satan forthrightly, "Yes, I blew it, and in and of myself I am unworthy, but *my worthiness is not based on my performance*! As a born-again, blood-bought Child of the living God, my worthiness is found in my *position* (in Christ) and not my *practice*. God qualified me to participate in Christ-worthiness. I am a divine partaker in His righteous, holiness, favor, and excellent standing with God."

Run the devil off; tell him to sell his trash talk to someone else. You now know who you are! Your mind is steadily becoming renewed and attuned to your true identity. As you consistently renew your mind to these divine truths, you are retraining your brain to accept your new identity predicated on the finished work of Christ.

310

How to Build up Your Self-Image

In addition to praying and spending quality time in God's presence, Josh McDowell offers some practical things we can do to enhance our self-image[10]:

(1) Do not label yourself negatively (i.e. "I am clumsy," and so on). We tend to become the label we give ourselves.

(2) Behave assertively (but not aggressively) even in threatening situations, particularly when you experience contrary impulses.

(3) When you fail, admit it to yourself and confess it to God your Father, and then take the vital step of refusing to condemn yourself. "Therefore, there is no condemnation for those who are in Christ Jesus" (Romans 8:1). Remember, you are in the process of becoming like Christ. Growth takes time. *Be as kind to yourself as you would be (or would hope to be) to any other person.*

(4) Do not compare yourself with others. You are a unique person. God understands and enjoys you in your uniqueness.

(5) Be positive (Philippians 4:8). We all, of course occupy an existence overflowing with imperfections, disappointments, insults and degradations, but it is not necessary that we focus on these; the good, decent, nurturing and hopeful are there always, and they await our observance.

For those interested in a more in-depth discussion of this topic, I recommend McDowell's book *How to Build Your Self-Image.* It is one of the best resources on the subject. If you apply its principles, I assure you that it will benefit you greatly.

A word of caution: Do not allow the devil to dupe you into thinking that you cannot fulfill the dreams of your heart, or that you cannot be used significantly by God unless you have an ironclad positive self-image. This is an untruth. Consider Moses. He was a man who suffered with a poor self-image at times, but indubitably God used him mightily! When God first approached Moses and told him to go to Egypt and tell Pharaoh to let God's people go, the insecure and fear-riddled Moses replied, stammering, "Who am I that I should go to Pharaoh?" God replied, "Certainly, I will be with thee" (Exodus 3:11-12 KJV). You see, it really didn't matter who Moses was; it only mattered that Almighty God was with him. The same is true of you today.

Seek to improve your self-image and self-concept, but be aware of the fact that all you need for success is the presence of the living God with you who is backing and supporting you one hundred percent!

Wearing Your Designer's Label

In certain circles, there is much ado made about designer labels and all the clothes and accessories (etc.) of famous designers such as Givenchy, Yves Saint Laurent, Dior, Vera Wang, FUBU, Sean John, Prada, GUCCI and Chanel. Inside their apparel, they affix their name and logo. The other day, while scanning the internet for men's dress shirts, I happened upon an unfamiliar designer label: Un-Bathed Ape. I thought to myself what a silly name that was, but then I was reminded that it didn't matter what I thought of the name. It was none of my business. The designer maintained the exclusive right to name his product whatever he wanted. In like manner, God, by virtue of being your "designer," maintains exclusive rights to name you as He pleases, and no one else.

And the only way we can approximate God's fine and unchallengeable (highest truth) assessment of us is to see ourselves in a steadily more and more righteous and redemptive light.

Your Creator breathed His life into you. He has crowned you with His favor and affixed His designer label upon you. God knows how powerful labels are. So, wear your designer's label confidently.

(God) your **Designer** says,
> You are...
> Significant... Why?
> Because God loves you.... Can you recite the acrostic from memory?

> *Don't let other people define your worth.*

Your **Designer** says,
> You are (a)...
> **N**ew creation in Christ Jesus (2 Corinthians 5:17)
> **O**rdained and chosen by God to fulfill His purpose for your life (Jeremiah 1:5; 29:11).
(And you...)
> **W**alk in the power of the Holy Spirit (Acts 1:8; Ephesians 5:18).

(And because you walk in the power of the Holy Spirit...)

Your **Designer** says,
> You are (a/an) ...
> **M**ore than a conqueror (Romans 8:37).
> **O**vercomer (1 John 5:4).
> **V**ictor, not a victim (1 Corinthians 15:57).
> **E**ternally loved (Romans 8:35, 38-39).

> *God, by virtue of being your "designer," maintains exclusive rights to name you as He pleases, and no one else.*

312

Your **Designer** says,
> You are (the)…
> **F**avored of God (Psalm 5:12).
> **O**h, so bold, confident and courageous (Proverbs 28:1; 2 Timothy 1:7).
> **R**econciled to be a reconciler (2 Corinthians 5:18-20).
> **W**ell protected (Isaiah 54:17; Psalm 23:4-6).
> **A**ssured of success (Psalm 1:3; Nehemiah 2:20; Joshua 1:8).
> **R**ighteousness of God in Christ Jesus (2 Corinthians 5:21; 1 Peter 2:9).
> **D**estined to win if you do not quit (2 Corinthians 2:14; Romans 8:31; Isaiah 41:9-10; 43:1-4).

But what do you say about yourself? Will you wear your Designer's label? If so, repeat your spiritual identity N-O-W-M-O-V-E-F-O-R-W-A-R-D acrostic to yourself multiple times a day in the first person, enthusiastically declaring, *I Am…!* It's not enough that you just say it; you must believe it. You must visualize it, memorize it, and integrate it into all your thoughts. The more you repeat it and meditate upon it, the quicker it will become wired into your brain and create a new neuropathway toward formulating your new spiritual identity. This will help to cultivate a far healthier self-image. "The wiring in the brain contains our beliefs and assumptions. With enough deliberate practice, we can rewire ourselves."[11] Yet, practice makes perfect!

Concerning your true identify in Christ, Neil T. Anderson, author of *Piercing the Darkness*, affirms, "Because you are in Christ, every one of [the statements in the acrostics] characteristics is completely true of you, and there's nothing you can do to make them more true. But you can make these traits more meaningful and productive in your life by simply choosing to believe what God has said about you."[12]

Gideon Prevails

Fortunately, for Gideon, he decided to receive in faith his designer's label – *mighty warrior*. As a mighty warrior, Gideon gathers an army of 33,000 fighting men and presents them to God. God, viewing this vast assemblage of soldiers, told Gideon that he had too many men because if they fought and won, they would take credit for the victory. So, God told Gideon to allow any man who was afraid to fight to go home. Much to Gideon's dismay, 23,000 men turned and went home, leaving Gideon with only 10,000 fighting men. God told Gideon he still had too many men. Hence, God thinned the ranks of Gideon's army even more by putting the remaining 10,000 men through a final test. After the concluding test, 9,700 men failed the test and were sent home. Gideon was now left with only 300 soldiers. God says to Gideon, (as the New Street Version tells us), "Let's get ready to rumble!"

Gideon's mind, attuned to his new spiritual identity, backed by a 300-man ragtag army, witnessed God's awesomeness in the vanquishing of an estimated

150,000 Midianite soldiers without any of Gideon's soldiers having to raise their swords in their defense. (Read this amazing story in Judges 7:19-25 and 8:28-34.)

After this miraculous victory, Gideon was elected to an elevated judgeship and reigned over Israel for the next forty years in peace, and this was the same guy who maintained that he was "the least thought of." Had Gideon allowed his perceived identity to blind him to his true spiritual identity, he likely would have died an impoverished farmer barricaded in a hole in the ground and feeling sorry for himself.

As was the case with Gideon, God knows all the raw talent and untapped potential that He has placed in you. God will never ask you for anything you do not already have. He sees the mighty warrior down on the inside of you that you presently do not see. However, to reach your full potential, you are going to have to shake off those old negative self-fettering beliefs and labels just like Gideon had to do. Don't you dare die in the shadows of your dreams! God would not have put the dream in your heart if he had not intended to bring it to pass. Don't allow a wanting self-image to keep you from fulfilling your goals and dreams. Push back on those negative thoughts and images proactively. Boldly wear your Designer's label. Let Satan and your critics know that God made you the right size, the right color, of the right intelligence, the right sex, the right personality, the right emotional disposition, and the right mix of other gifts to fulfill your destiny. The Bible informs us, "God has made us what we are. In Christ Jesus, God made us new people so that we would spend our lives doing the good things he had already planned for us to do" (Ephesians 2:10 ERV). Step up into your new identity and begin this very instant. N-O-W-M-O-V-E-F-O-R-W-A-R-D!

Real Life Testimonies to Help Build Your Faith

A hapless, once-hopeless drug addict became a new creation in Christ when his mind and heart were unshackled as he renewed his mind to see himself as His divine Designer saw him.

Tony's Story: I Now Know Who I Am

My name is Tony. It is said that our lives are marked by defining moments, and what we choose to do in those moments decides the course of our lives. I got off to a very good start. I was raised in a two-parent home. My father was hardworking and owned his own trucking business and a sawmill where he cut and sold lumber. Therefore, they were able to provide us with many things other children growing in Montpelier, Virginia couldn't afford. However, the propitious trajectory my life was on was about to change forever by two defining moments, the first of which occurred when I was 12 years old. My parents moved our family into a bad neighborhood, and I made friends with some of the failure-destined kids. Secondly, my parents divorced when I was in high school. With the security of my home life shattered, and my father no longer in the picture, I began cutting classes, drinking, and hanging out with the bad crowd, which resulted in my getting busted for drug possession in high school. As a consequence, I was expelled. Having been reared to work hard, I got a job and moved into an apartment in Richmond, Virginia, with my girlfriend. To help pay the bills, I started selling marijuana.

A third defining moment came when my younger cousin came by the apartment with a sandwich bag full of cocaine. I had never experienced a high like that in my entire life! The next decade or more of my life I spent chasing that high, and that dissolute pursuit included selling drugs, which ultimately resulted in numerous criminal convictions and jail sentences.

At my lowest point, I was sitting in Richmond City jail, not caring whether I lived or died, but I had a praying mother. After spending about 2 years in jail, I got out and went directly to a bar. This is where my next defining moment occurred, one that would alter the trajectory of my life forever. I was sitting at the bar when I had a religious experience, an epiphany; an angel approached me and whispered three words in my ear: "Read Psalm 27." I know you're probably thinking it was the liquor talking, but very strangely, I noticed a Bible right beside me. I opened the Bible and turned to Psalm 27 and read the following words:

The Lord is my light and my salvation;
Whom shall I fear?
The Lord is the defense of my life;
Whom shall I dread? (v.1)

As I read, hope filled my heart. I thought to myself, there is someone who can help me. Suddenly, I heard a still small voice speak to me. I had heard it before, but I never knew it was the voice of the Lord. From then on, I started reading the Bible and talking with Him. I would laugh and joke with Him about things. Through our dialog and reading His Word, He revealed to me that He loved me and wasn't mad at me or out to get me because of my past indiscretions and present predicament.

While God had forgiven me, the criminal justice system had not, and I was sentenced to four years in jail for earlier crimes. I was turned down for parole three times. After the second rejection, I stopped worrying about getting out of jail and started focusing on preparing myself to stay out of jail. It was here that my final defining moment occurred. As I chased hard after God and sought to get insight into my addiction, I began attending Narcotics Anonymous (NA). In all NA meetings, each participant is taught to introduce him-or herself by stating his/her name, followed by the words, "I am an addict." After introducing myself in this manner for about 6 months, I became very uncomfortable identifying myself as an addict, because in the Bible study I was attending, I discovered that the Bible said I was a "new creation." After months of going back and forth, the Lord finally spoke to my spirit, and He told me, "You are not a drug addict. You are a new creation; the old things have passed away and all things have become new" (2 Corinthians 5:17). Thereafter, I refused to confess (refer to myself) that I was an addict. From that moment, I never took another drug. I knew that I had been delivered. God took the cravings for cigarettes away from me as well. All the negative things that I had previously believed about myself were lies. This was my new reality. Right before my eyes, God was renewing my mind and transforming me into the God-fearing man He said that I was in His word.

Finally, I made parole in 1999 and returned home. Within a year, God blessed me with my own trucking business. I am now married to a godly Christian woman who loves me and loves Jesus. We have three daughters, six grandchildren, and one great-granddaughter. At church, I serve in several ministries, including the prison and substance abuse ministries. As of mid-2017, I have a total of three trucks and several employees. To God be the Glory for the things He has done! Learning to accept my true spiritual identity has proven to be, in retrospect, the crucial psychological adjustment of my life.

* * *

As God transformed Tony's self-image, He awaits to do the same for you and me. Apply the principles of *The 21-Day Plan* and watch your mind be daily transformed into the mind of Christ.

* * *

 **A Closing Prayer**

Dear God, I thank You for seeing the very best in me. Holy Spirit, I draw upon Your power to enable me to push back on any negative self-labeling and confidently wear my infinitely superior Designer's label. In Jesus' name. Amen.

For an inspirational pick me up, I recommend:

- *Worthy* by Anthony Brown
- *Redeemed* by Big Daddy Weave
- *Just for Me* by Donnie McClurkin
- *Thank You* by Walter Hawkins (featuring Donnie McClurkin)

Until tomorrow, do this:

- Look over The Toxic Ten (pp. 238-239); reflect upon which thought distortions you may be entertaining.

Memory Work

1. Continue repeating your *I Am Significant* mantra & *My Spiritual Identity*: N-O-W-M-O-V-E-F-O-R-W-A-R-D acrostic from memory.

2. Continue to write down The Filthy Five Memory Verses on 3x5 cards and practice memorizing them (Figure 14. 2, p. 242).

3. Apply your (CCCR) Thought Management 101 strategy on page182.

Day 19

Replacing Fear with Faith:
The Four Levels of Faith

Faith is taking the first step even when you don't see the whole staircase.
                    --Dr. Martin Luther King, Jr.

Daily Food for Thought

• **Brain Fact** "Despite our... negativity, the human brain has a bias toward optimism...If not, we would be prone to increased anxiety and depression"[1]

• **Key Thought** The best way to exercise your brain is through exercising faith.[2]

• **Scripture** "We hope that your faith will continue to grow" (2 Corinthians 10:15 ERV).

Daily Reading

We've come a long way together on this mind renewal journey. I hope you have found the journey both enlightening and transforming. Today I am going to discuss fear and its polar opposite—faith. Why discuss fear? It is because fear is at the root of almost all our toxic thoughts and emotions.

Fear can be such a powerful and intimidating emotion that it can paralyze us. Despite having renewed our minds in most areas, we still struggle at times with certain kinds of fears. Some of us are fearful of getting sick, fearful of dying,

318

worried about losing a job, anxious about the possibility of not being able to pay bills, or being put out of the home, dreading the circumstance where you might be embarrassed, or apprehensive concerning the prospect of being rejected. Alas, fear, if not contained, can become like a raging wildfire, consuming all our positivity along with our physical and emotional health. Dr. Ken Nichols, author of *Untie the Fear Knots of Your Heart*, provides us with some neurological insights into the destructive effects of long-term fear on our physical bodies.

When we are faced with a threat, fear triggers the production of adrenaline and other stress hormones that prepare the body to fight or flee the impending danger. This defensive reaction increases the blood sugar, heart rate, blood pressure and muscle tension, all of which provide the extra energy required for emergency actions. But if the sensation of fear persists once the emergency has passed, this extra energy remains. Our heart rate, blood pressure and muscle tension continue on an elevated plane, which begins to cause harm to the body. Constant tension raises the risk of illness.[3]

Some of these afflictions are migraine headaches, hypertension, stroke, cancer, skin problems, diabetes, infections, and allergies, just to name a few."[4] With this in mind, it is easy to understand why Jesus warned us, "You must not let yourselves be distressed—you must hold on to your faith in God and to your faith in me" (John 14:1 PHILLIPS). It has been said that worry is nothing more than low-grade fear in disguise. One thing we know for certain is that debilitating (inhibiting, paralyzing, superstition-or ignorance-founded) fear is not from God. The Bible informs us that "God has not given us a spirit of fear and timidity, but of power, love, and self-

> **Worry is nothing more than low-grade fear in disguise.**

discipline" (1 Timothy 1:7 NLT). So, how are we to deal with such "manipulating" fears? God desires that we replace our fears with faith in His Word. The goal of today's lesson is to attack fear on two fronts: neurologically and spiritually.

How to Strengthen Your Brain to Fight Fear

If you sometimes find that your mind is tangled up in fear knots, it is likely indicative of at least three things:

First, if you are suffering or have suffered under the oppressive weight of various fears, you have to increase your mindfulness and guard against The Filthy Five (FURST). As a consequence, the worries and concerns of your outer world have begun to seep into the inner recesses of your mind, negatively impacting your attitudes. Analogously, as long as water remains on the outside of the boat the boat is fine. However, once massive amounts of water begin seeping into the boat, it will begin to sink. You may be sinking emotionally because "worry waters" are leaking into your ship, causing your dispositional boat to list and at most sink.

Secondly, when we are overrun with negative emotions, it is a telltale sign that our spirit is weak. The Word of God is to the spirit as bread is to the body. When the body feeds on physical food, it produces a physical power: energy. When the spirit feeds on the nutriment of the Word, it produces the spiritual power of *faith*. When we fail to feed our spirit through our religious rituals and practices, it becomes too weak to push back on negative thoughts, making us more vulnerable to Satan's onslaught (Galatians 5:16-17). We are engaged in an interminable spiritual battle, and the battle is for mastery of the mind.

Finally, neurologically speaking, if your mind is being overrun with negative, fear-based (sometimes subconscious) thoughts, this is ultimately producing a chemical imbalance in your brain. If you are under a doctor's care and taking medications to correct a chemical imbalance, that is potentially remedying. However, for those seeking to adjust their brain chemicals naturally, Dr. Newberg introduces us to the brain's thought manager – the anterior cingulate (Day 8). By way of review, "the anterior cingulate acts as a kind of fulcrum that controls and balances the activity between the frontal lobe and limbic system."[5] (See Figure 8.1, p. 142).

When the limbic system is overcome with debilitating fears, it can severely impede all logical and reasoning capacities in the frontal lobe, rendering you subordinate to a painful and unproductive emotional loop.[6] (See Figure 8.2).To bring brain chemistry back into proper balance, you must strengthen your anterior cingulate, and this is what meditation and spiritual practices do."[7] Such spiritually nurturing and facilitative practices include Bible reading, prayer, Scripture memorization, and positive faith-based affirmations, and meditation.

Eight Brain Exercises

To further strengthen your anterior cingulate, neuroscientist Drs. Newberg and Waldman, authors of *How God Changes Your Brain,* compiled a list of the top eight brain exercises, listed here in reverse order.

8. Smile as often as possible.[8]
7. Exercise your brain by continuing to learn; it keeps your brain intellectually active.[9]
6. Incorporate into your daily routine a time to "consciously relax."[10]
5. Intentionally yawn at least 12 times in succession. This releases positive chemicals into your brain and helps wake you up.[11]
4. Practice meditating upon the Word of God and other inspirational things.[12]
3. Exercise your brain by [fun] aerobic exercise.[13]

2. Exercise your brain through dialog with others.[14]

1. Exercise faith.[15]

The very best way to exercise your brain is via exercising your faith.

The Power of Faith

Dr. Newberg defines faith as intrepid trust in your beliefs.[16] It is imperative that believers trust their instincts regarding their beliefs. To have doubt puts the brain in a very precarious state. "Faith is equivalent with hope, optimism, and the belief that a positive future awaits the believer. Faith can also be defined as the ability to trust beliefs, even when there is no proof that such beliefs are accurate or true."[17] Another researcher pointed out that, "despite our... negativity, the human brain has a bias toward optimism...If not, we would be prone to increased anxiety and depression."[18] Therefore, cultivating your faith is far more significant than you may have realized. Perhaps that is why Jesus admonishes us to, "Have faith in God" (Mark 11:22). The Bible emphatically states, "Without faith it is impossible to please Him" (Hebrews 11:6). To please God, it is essential that we maintain faith and hope amidst all adverse circumstances and not succumb to manipulating fears.

> *There are no hopeless situations; there are only people who have grown hopeless about them.*

"There are no hopeless situations; there are only people who have grown hopeless about them".[19] My motto: *Believe Yes until God says No.*

The Four Levels of Faith

Paul, speaking to the believers in Corinth, said, "We hope that your faith will continue to grow" (2 Corinthians 10:15 ERV). Elsewhere in the New Testament Paul went on to say, "For in it the righteousness of God is revealed from faith to faith." The phrase "from faith to faith" references the idea of there being disparate levels of faith (elucidated below). It is written, "But the righteous man shall live by faith." (Romans 1:17).

Saving Faith

The first level of faith is *saving* faith. The Bible states, "For by grace you have been saved through faith, and that not of yourselves; it is the gift of God, not as a result of works, so that no one may boast" (Ephesians 2:8-9). This gift of saving faith is afforded to all humanity by God. He desires that all men and women come to know Him personally (1 Timothy 2:4). Saving Faith is the most elementary form of faith, and is characterized by...

1. The acknowledgement of personal sin and Jesus' offer of forgiveness (Romans 3:23).

2. The acceptance of Christ as your personal Lord and Savior (Romans 5:8; 10:9-10).

Questions for Reflection

1. Have you personally made the decision to accept Jesus into your life as Lord and Savior? Yes/No (If you have not made this profession of faith, consider moving deliberately toward a greater appreciation of God's promise.)

2. Do any fears prevent you from making this declaration of faith? If so, explain.

_____

_____

Will you invite Jesus into your life today? You can do so by bowing your head and sincerely praying the following prayer:

Dear God, I know that I have not always pleased you. Please forgive me of my mistakes and wrongdoings. I repent of them. I now invite Jesus into my life to become my personal Lord and Savior. Jesus, I know that you love me and died so that I might have the opportunity to experience new life in you. Amen!

Do not get hung up on specific wording. All sincere prayer is good.

Simple Faith

The second level of this process is simple faith which grows out of saving faith. As the term (simple) implies, it is an immature or weak faith. Jesus would at times rebuke his disciples by calling them, "Men of little faith" (Matthew 6:30-32).

Simple faith is...

1. **Feeling Focused:** This is believing what one sees and feels, and not what God says. For example, I don't see God working behind the scenes to improve my situation; therefore, He must not be working. Or, I don't feel saved; therefore, I must not be saved. Simple faith seeks to validate the Word by *feelings*. It doesn't stand on the Word of God and is easily intimidated by a faith challenge and tends to back down.

322

2. **Outcome Focused:**[20] Simple faith prays for specific outcomes (things), and if those outcomes are not immediate and observable, the simple faith believer is prone to become disappointed with God and give up on his/her faith. For example, I prayed to get accepted into a certain college and was not accepted. I prayed that my loved one would not die, but she died anyway. The specific prayer doesn't seem to work. The person of simple faith becomes disillusioned with God, stops praying and ceases other religious and spiritual activities and behaviors, such as reading the Bible and attending church services.

Strong Faith

The third level of faith is strong faith, and it is characterized by being…

1. **Word Focused:** The Word-focused believer accepts what God says, not what he or she sees or feels. Strong faith is rooted in the Word of God, rather than one's fickle feelings. Strong faith declares, "God said it; I believe it; and that settles it." A strong faith walks by faith and not by sight – not by any of the physical senses (2 Corinthians 5:7).

2. **Outlook Focused:**[21] A strong faith is one that has matured to the degree that it is no longer exclusively outcome focused, but now has the power of perspective to see the big picture: top-down (God's perspective) versus bottom-up (personal perspective). The Bible makes it clear that God's thoughts and ways are higher than our thoughts and ways (Isaiah 55:9). A strong faith is able to trust God when praying and a contrary result seems apparent. Because they have a top-down perspective, such persons know that God has the right to exercise His divine prerogative anytime He chooses. Hence, a strong faith readjusts perspective without getting bummed out and disappointed for hours, days, weeks, or more. Instead, it dries its eyes, trusting in its heart, knowing, 1) God can work all things together for my good, even the things I do not understand, and 2) God must have something better in store; the best is yet to come (Jeremiah 29:11; Zechariah 9:12; Psalm 103:12). The strong faith's motto might be understood as: God, I will trust in You despite all appearances.

Supernatural Faith

The highest level of faith is supernatural faith, characterized by a…

1. **Supernatural Word from God**: You know with utmost confidence that God has spoken to you. One is assured, much as Abraham, Moses and Mary were when they received a communication from God (Genesis 12:1-3; Exodus 3:4-10; Luke 1:26-38).

2. **Supernatural Swagger**: a suppression of fear, giving rise to an out-of-your-natural-mind confidence in God's ability to do the impossible, based on your previous (welcome) faith experiences (1 Samuel 17:34-37 Isaiah 50:7; Luke 1:26-38).

3. **Supernatural Manifestation**: Your confidence and intrepid faith in God is based on tangible evidence of God's miraculous providence and favor (Exodus 14 13-16; 21-22; Psalm 77:14). In other words, you know that there are many things in your life that can only be explained as the divine supernatural intervention of God.

Questions for Reflection

1. Based on the four levels of faith and their characteristics, on which level are you? Explain.

_____

_____

2. What is the value of being able to see things form a top-down versus a bottom-up perspective?

_____

_____

Moving From One Level of Faith to the Next

> *Your faith will never grow beyond your knowledge of the Word of God.*

After reading about the levels of faith, some of you may be saying, "Lord, increase my faith." Likewise, Jesus' disciples asked Jesus to increase their faith (Luke 17:5). For those who may be asking, "How can I grow my faith?" There are two ways to increase your level of faith. First, know that your faith will never grow beyond your knowledge of the Word of God. Thus, the Bible asserts, "Faith comes from hearing, and hearing by the word of Christ" (Romans 10:17). As you hear the word, and continue hearing it, speak the word, and keep speaking it; meditate upon the word, and keep meditating upon it; obey the word and keep obeying it. Your faith will increase in concert with your level of spiritual maturity.

The second way God increases our faith is by allowing us to undergo strengthening and emboldening spiritual faith experiences. Sandwiched between each level of faith are what I call stretchy faith experiences (SFE)—ordained and destined to move believers from one level of faith to the next. I did not remark here that God caused or designed *all* these stretchy faith experiences... only that He uses adverse circumstances to elevate us, however mysteriously or incrementally, to the next level of faith.

They are called stretchy faith experiences (SFE) because they stretch you like a rubber band in two different directions. First, they stretch you upward to the next level of faith, while paradoxically stretching you downward to your knees in humble dependence upon God, which tends to be both scary and emotionally troubling. Let's examine a stretchy faith experience in the life of King Saul, a shepherd boy named David, and a nine-foot giant named Goliath. For King Saul, his encounter with Goliath was designed to move him from simple faith to strong faith. For David, his encounter with the mighty Goliath was designed to move him from strong faith into supernatural faith. In 1 Samuel 17 we see the remaining three levels of faith and their characteristics.

Stretchy Faith Experiences: Simple Faith

King Saul was supposed to fight Goliath. After all, he was the reigning King of Israel, an accomplished warrior and leader of his nation who just so happened to stand a remarkable seven-feet tall (1Samuel 10:23). Saul, albeit tall in stature, was short on faith. King Saul possessed a simple faith which was feeling-focused. Saul looked at himself and then looked at the size of Goliath and immediately felt within him that there was no way he could defeat Goliath. Therefore, he didn't even try. Fear stricken, he backed down to Goliath's daily challenges to send a warrior from Israel to fight him (1 Samuel 17:8-11). Simple faith is easily intimidated when facing a challenge and almost always produces the behavior of backing down.

Questions for Reflection

What might be some stretchy faith examples in your own life? Were you able in those instances to identify how they were moving you to the next level of faith? How hard was it to not back down? Explain.

_____

_____

_____

_____

Stretchy Faith Experiences: Strong Faith

Since King Saul's simple faith, caused him to back down from Goliath, God went in search of someone who would not back down. God found that person in a teenage shepherd boy named David. Our figurative biblical dossier on David describes him as "a skillful musician, a mighty man of valor, a warrior, one prudent in speech, and a handsome man; and the Lord is with him" (1 Samuel 16:18). The most important of all these praiseworthy attributes is revealed in the last phrase, "the Lord is with him." Day by day, David tended his sheep and cultivated a splendid friendship with God. God, desirous that David's strong faith grow to the next level (supernatural faith), was about to introduce David to his most challenging "stretchy faith" experience (SFE): mortal combat with a 9-foot-tall fighting machine, Goliath.

Having identified David as His champion, God employs a plan to get David away from pristine pastures and onto the battlefield in earshot of the boastful, overconfident behemoth. Hence, God prevailed on Jesse, who was David's father, to send David to the battlefield to take food to his brothers, who were enlisted in King Saul's (Israelite) army. The Israelite army was engaged in an ongoing battle against their longtime rival, the Philistines. In an effort to curtail bloodshed, the Philistines proposed that instead of all the soldiers battling that the Israelites choose one of their number to fight the Philistines' proxy, Goliath of Gath. As David was delivering his brothers' lunch, he witnesses Goliath's challenge to the armies of Israel. In response to Goliath's bluster, David asks, "'Who is this uncircumcised Philistine that he should taunt the armies of the living God?'… the words which David spoke were heard… they told them to Saul, and [King Saul] sent for [David] (1 Samuel 17:31).

The foremost characteristic of a strong faith is that it is Word-focused; it follows from a belief in what God says and not what is seen or felt. Surely, David saw how formidable Goliath was, but David knew that His God was superior. For it was David who wrote, "Even though I walk through the valley of the shadow of death, I fear no evil, for You are with me; Your rod and Your staff, they comfort me. You prepare a table before me in the presence of my enemies (Psalm 23:4-5). Goliath was an enemy of God, and therefore David stood on the Word of God that assured him that God would assist in the fight against his enemies. A strong faith is not feeling-focused, but Word-focused. The Bible informs us to "Walk by faith, not by sight" (2 Corinthians 5:7).

That is a tall order when you are staring at a turn off notice, or an overdue mortgage bill, or legal troubles. A strong faith doesn't back down. If the Word says, "My God will supply all of my needs" (Philippians 4:19), a strong faith will take hold of the Word of God with a resolute tenacity and won't relent until victory is won.

What "giant" are you facing today? Say no to fear and yes to faith! Obliterate fear by replacing it with the faith promise that is the Word of God. A strong faith says, *God said it. I believe it. And that settles it.*

Secondly, a strong faith is also outlook focused. David wasn't concerned over the manner in which God chose to kill Goliath. David left those details up

326

to God. David just wanted to cooperate and flow with God to take this unbowed adversary down. David saw in his mind's eye the ultimate victory. Trusting his Lord in his stretchy faith experience, David stretched upward to the next level of faith – supernatural faith.

Stretchy Faith Experiences: Supernatural Faith

The Supernatural level of faith is the highest level of faith. Few Christians attain this level, although a larger number may visit it momentarily. For example, Peter exercised supernatural faith when he briefly walked on water before taking his eyes off Jesus, and he sank. Supernatural faith is exemplified by robust adherence to the supernatural Word of God. Just as Peter heard Jesus say, "Come!" (Matthew 14:29), David heard God say to him, essentially, "You are the one I have chosen to respond to Goliath's challenge." I can only imagine that David paused to make sure he had in fact heard from God rather than his experiencing an imagining; then he pushed back on his fears. After all, he was human. He swallowed gravely, quoted the latter part of Psalm 23:4 – "I will fear no evil because you are with me…," swallowed hard once again, and consented. That supernatural Word from God gave David an otherworldly inspiration and confidence, a supernatural swagger.

Here is a sampling of the faith-abounding words David spoke to King Saul.

"Your Majesty," David said, "I take care of my father's sheep. Any time a lion or a bear carries off a lamb, I go after it, attack it, and rescue the lamb. And if the lion or bear turns on me, I grab it by the throat and beat it to death. I have killed lions and bears, and I will do the same to this heathen Philistine, who has defied the army of the living God. The Lord has saved me from lions and bears; he will save me from this Philistine." "All right," Saul answered, "Go, and the Lord be with you" (1 Samuel 17:34-37 GNT).

Convinced by David's supernatural swagger, King Saul readied David for battle by clothing him in conventional armor. But David insisted…

I cannot go with these [Saul's armor], for I have not tested them. And David took them off. He took his stick in his hand and chose for himself five smooth stones from the brook and put them in the shepherd's bag which he had, even in his pouch, and his sling was in his hand; and he approached the Philistine (1 Samuel 17:38-40).

I imagine that as David was walking toward the giant, he was probably praying and thinking this battle is not mine, it's yours, Lord, my great shepherd and defender. David didn't need Saul's armor, because he was able to sense within his spirit that his was going to be an unconventional victory.

327

God doesn't always work through conventional means. God can get you a car without taking on a conventional auto loan. He can pay off your mortgage before the conventional 30-year term, if it is His divine will. With His nonpareil omnipotence, He can cancel your student loans and wipe out your credit card debt. He can heal you of cancer without known medical interventions, such as chemotherapy and surgery.

As David is now walking toward Goliath, he demonstrates the third characteristic of supernatural faith: supernatural manifestation.

> Then it happened when the Philistine rose and came and drew near to meet David, that David ran quickly toward the battle line to meet the Philistine. And David put his hand into his bag and took from it a stone and slung it and struck the Philistine on his forehead. And the stone sank into his forehead, so that he fell on his face to the ground (1 Samuel 17:48-49).

Before Goliath could insult David or his God again, the trash-talking giant was down for the count. The text notes that Goliath fell to the ground face down. He could have fallen backward having been hit in his forehead, but he fell forward, face down. Les Brown, the motivational speaker, said, when you fall down, always try to land on your back; because if you can look up, you can get up. That the overgrown warrior couldn't look up meant that he wasn't getting up. David would make sure of that! David had a supernatural word, a supernatural swagger, and now he was going to experience a supernatural manifestation.

> Then David ran and stood over the Philistine and took [Goliath's] sword and drew it out of its sheath and killed him and cut off his head with it. When the Philistines saw that their champion was dead, they fled (1 Samuel 17:51).

David's faith in God grew exponentially that day. The supernatural manifestation was evident in the fact that David was then in possession of (both) Goliath's sword and his very crest. Just as he had with the testimony regarding the killing of the lion and the bear, he could now add to his souvenir exploits the sword of Goliath. David's accomplishment in vanquishing a foe so formidable, one who ordinarily would have seemed a prohibitive favorite in this sort of martial contest, places it solidly in the category of a supernatural manifestation. Such a result was concrete evidence that God had spoken to him.

Questions for Reflection

Are there things in your life that cannot be explained in any way apart from God's intercession or favor? Think hard – are there any things that proved exceptionally beneficial but are not easily explained?

How to Replace Fear with Faith

Are you being stretched today? I've used the term stretchy faith experiences and have allowed the letters (SFE) to represent it. However, if you insert the letter (A) in between the S and F it spells the word **S(A)FE**. As you are going through your SFE experiences, know that you are **SAFE** in the arms of your loving heavenly Father. The Bible assures us, "The eternal God is your refuge, and underneath you are [His] everlasting arms (Deuteronomy 33:27 MEV). You may feel that your life is in a freefall today, but through all tribulation you must maintain faith that the loving arms of God are there to catch you! You will not fall to your destruction, but He'll catch you. Just as you would hold a frightened child tightly in your protecting arms, so, too, you are being held safely in the arms of your heavenly Father. Do not depend on fleeting experience or "proof" for this to be so; God is our surest and sincerest advocate, even when there seems little or no evidence of it.

Do not be dismayed or befuddled by God's silence. You may be going through a test, and just as the teacher is silent during a test, so, too, at times is your loving heavenly Father. His silence does not equate to His absence. Endure through the silence. Persevere.

The reason you have big challenges is because you have a big destiny. Trouble is not hindering you; not unlike David, trouble is very likely preparing you. It is not going to defeat you; it's going to promote you. However, to be victorious in your fight against fear-based thoughts, spiritually you are going to have to depend upon God's supernatural strength. You can't gain ultimate victory in your life depending upon your own strength. Hence, the Bible informs us to…

Be strong in the Lord and in the strength of His might. Put on the full armor of God, that you may be able to stand firm against the schemes of the devil. For our struggle is not against flesh and blood, but against the rulers, against the powers, against the world forces of this darkness, against the spiritual forces of wickedness in the heavenly places. Therefore, take up the full armor of God, that you may be able to resist in the evil day, and having done everything, to stand firm… (Ephesians 6:10-13).

> *Fear is an evil, manipulating spirit from the enemy, Satan.*

The reason we must stand firm against fear is because fear is an evil, manipulating spirit from the enemy, Satan (2 Timothy 1:7). To replace fear with faith, it is necessary to incorporate the following seven principles to help guide your daily routine.

329

1. When manipulating fear-based thoughts come to your mind, be sure to check them at the outset, using your check, challenge, change and re-frame paradigm (Days 9-12). You mustn't allow one of those fear-based thoughts inside your peaceful mental habitation. If you do, they will overstay unwelcomely.

2. To grow your faith, it is imperative that you "stretch" in courageous faith and stop backing down to your SFE. You can memorize all the faith scripture you want, but until you're committed to applying those scriptures to the figurative giants in your life, they will do little to propel you to the next level of faith. David knew a lot of scriptures; after all he is credited with writing over 70 of the 150 Psalms. However, to grow from simple faith to a strong faith, and then to progress into supernatural faith, he had to apply God's Word just as he did with the lion, the bear, and ultimately Goliath. King Saul, on the other hand, refused to step up to his stretchy faith experience (SFE), and as a consequence remained on the level of simple faith through the remainder his life. If you've read his story, you know his life was plagued by fear and inured in people pleasing, insecurity, worry, depression and bouts of compromised sanity. Whom will you serve—fear or faith?

3. Consistently meditate upon and begin memorizing faith Scriptures. As you work toward memorizing them, be sure to quote them also each time a manipulating fear pops into your frontal lobe. Listed below are some faith scriptures. You might find some of them inspiring. I wrote the following verses on 3x5 cards myself (and carry them with me almost every place I go).

   - 2 Corinthians 2:14
   - Romans 4:17-21; 8:31
   - Hebrews 10:35-36, 38; 13:5; 11:1,6
   - Isaiah 50:7: 41:9-10; 12:2; 43:1-4, 18-19
   - Mark 7:7-8,11; 9:23;11:22-24
   - Matthew 9:29; 9:21-22
   - Luke 1:37; 18:27

   > *Everything you want is on the other side of fear.*

I highly recommend a scripture promise book. This resource is also available as an app for smartphones and tablets.

4. Replace fear by embracing a Pauline perspective on trials and tests. Instead of viewing them as a nuisance, reframe them as stretchy faith experiences

(SFE) designed to propel you upward to the next level of faith and stretch you downward to your knees in humble dependence upon God. It is all in how we treat adversity and refusing to be daunted by how frequent the encounter.

5. Learn to persevere in the experience of fear. Fear is not an indication that you are somehow deficient or unworthy. Fear is the unending experience of the courageous. Habitually push back on your fearful thoughts that impede action and maintain faith that your positive and righteous intentions will prevail. It is said, "Courage is fear that has said its prayers."[22] Mark Twain once wrote, "Courage is resistance to fear, it is the mastery of fear, not absence of fear."[23] Resist your temptation to accept the negative voice that says you are not equal to the task (only God can know that). The peace of God may or may not come at the onset of the challenge, but as you move in supernatural faith, take a deep breath (or as many breaths as the pertinent chore requires), say a quick prayer, and enjoin the battle just like David did so very long ago.

6. Recognize that your inhibiting, paralyzing, pessimism-fueled fear is ultimately rooted in an incomplete understanding of God's love. The Bible declares, "Where God's love is, there is no fear, because God's perfect love takes away fear..." (1 John 4:18 ERV). When you know confidently that God loves you, is not angry with you, is not out to punish you, and will never forsake you, manipulating fears will have little opportunity to take root in your mind. Your heartfelt knowledge of God's unconditional love for you will drive out fear as you consistently meditate upon and memorize the Word of God. Some examples of scriptures declaring God's love for you: Jeremiah 31:3; John 3:16; 13:34; 15:9; Romans 8:35: 38-39.

7. To grow your faith, you may also find faith mentors. Expose yourself to people who are or seem to be on a higher level of faith than you are. (Do not confuse some special or refined quality in them with moral excellence; your purpose is to learn from them, not to idolize them.) They may be men and women of faith that you listen to on the radio, on podcasts or see on television or encounter on the Internet. And of course, it is all the better if you know such people personally. If you know them personally and they are willing, begin to find opportunities to converse with, learn from, or work with them. Ask them how they attained their level of faith and what they endured to get there. God is no respecter of personality! He promises to reward all who diligently seek him (Hebrews 11:6). In addition to this, read books about men and women of great faith who accomplished mightily for God (Daniel 11:32). Reading such stories will

inspire your faith. "Faith comes by hearing" (Romans 10:17). This is how you face off against your fears and prevail.

Real Life Testimonies to Help Build Your Faith

We close today's lesson with the stretchy faith experience (SFE) of a woman we'll refer to simply as "SJ."

SJ's Story: Lord, Do What?

God, you want me to do what? So, what do you do when God Himself seems to instruct you to leap off a figurative cliff? Do you proceed trusting He'll be there to catch you? Or do you provide Him with a litany of reasons why the timing is bad, you don't have the resources, or that it's simply too onerous or painful or awkward for you to comply?

In the year 2000, life was good – better yet, life was great! I was living (born and raised) in South Carolina. One year earlier I had gotten married, and my husband and I were blessed with a baby boy. My husband and I were involved in a church that we really enjoyed attending. The Lord had blessed us to build a brand-new home, and I had a dream management job in which I only had a few years left to be eligible to fully retire…with immediate payment of benefits. Did I say life was great? It was, until one day I heard the Lord say to me to leave it all and move to Richmond, Virginia. Dismayed, I began to give God the reasons I couldn't possibly make such a move. Foremost, I am definitely not going to forfeit my retirement! Secondly, my daughter is getting ready to enter middle school and puberty, and my husband, just out of the military, is now a bank manager. My final reason was intended to open God's "eyes" to see why His calling for me to relocate was impossible. My mother's health had taken a turn for the worse, and I felt I needed to stay in South Carolina to help my dad and my siblings take care of her. However, God wasn't hearing any of these excuses. Hence, I, like the biblical Jacob, began to in a sense wrestle with God. However, for six months God pestered my conscience, and I finally relented. In retrospect, how stupid I had been to even think for a moment that I could separate myself from His will. After all, God had called Abraham to "get thee out of thy country, and from thy kindred, and from thy father's house…"(Genesis 12). So, who was I to question His calling me to comply similarly?

I told God that if He'd open the doors, I'd go through them. Immediately, the doors began not just to open, but God seemed to tear the doors off their hinges, so I would have no doubt about exactly which doors I should then proceed through. Apparently, to keep me from changing my mind, eerily, doors began closing in South Carolina. Was this His work? I then knew I couldn't turn around or change my mind. God made it clear there was no going back!

If I had known then all that my family and I would have enjoyed (in increase, favor and promotion), I would have moved on God's instructions from day one rather than delaying for six months. I have seen God do things that only He can do, set up connections, and bring me to the front of the line time and time again. For example, how do you leave a nearly six-figure job and go to zero dollars and never skip a beat? In fact, He blessed us to buy multiple investment properties and go on more vacations than when I was in the 9 to 5 routine. How do you buy over a half-million-dollar house and fully decorate it and not sell your existing over quarter-million-dollar home? Apart from God's favor, how can you explain the builder of our house calling us up after signing the contract and giving us over $90,000 off the contract price? Furthermore, how do you start a real estate business in the middle of a recession, and, years later, become a top producer in the industry? How? No explanation but God! I could go on and on and on about the many miracles, signs and wonders He's been able to do for me and through me. It's all been as a direct result of taking that leap of faith many years ago – to say, in essence, God, I trust you (Proverbs 3:5-6). The Bible declares, "If you be willing and obedient, you'll eat the good of the land" (Isaiah 1:19 KJV). The key to it all is simply being "willing and obedient." Listen ever so carefully to His still small voice and do exactly what He instructs you to do! And, never forget to let others know that, God did it! Glory be to God for all the marvelous things He has done!

A Closing Prayer

Dear God, I thank You for helping me to see my trials and tests as stretchy faith experiences (SFE) designed to pull me upward to the next level of faith, and downward to my knees, too, in dependence upon You. God, I will trust You to work all things together for my good. In my weakness, I draw upon Your power to strengthen me to fight the good fight of faith by taking hold of and standing on Your precious promises. In Jesus' name. Amen!

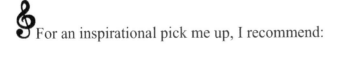

For an inspirational pick me up, I recommend:

- *Trust in You* by Anthony Brown
- *The Breakup Song* by Francesca Battistelli
- *Trust in You* by Lauren Daigle
- *In the Middle* by Smokie Norful
- *Hills and Valleys* by Tauren Wells
- *I Need You Now* by Smokie Norful

Until tomorrow, do this:

- Look over The Toxic Ten (pp. 238-239); reflect upon which thought distortions you may be entertaining. (Where there is relational conflict, somebody is most likely engaging in one or more of The Toxic Ten.)

Memory Work

1. Continue repeating your *I Am Significant* mantra.

    Repeat *My Spiritual Identity*: N-O-W-M-O-V-E-F-O-R-W-A-R-D acrostic. In the future, memorize the Scriptures associated with this acrostic. The Scriptures are found on pages 108-109.

2. Continue to write down The Filthy Five Memory Verses on 3x5 cards and practice memorizing them (Figure 14. 2, p. 242).

3. Daily employ your (CCCR) Thought Management 101 strategy (p. 182).

Replacing Weakness:
Building Mental Toughness to
Withstand Life's Storms

Don't wait until everything is just right. It will never be perfect. There will always be challenges, obstacles, and less than perfect conditions. So what? Get started now. With each step you take, you will grow stronger and stronger, more and more skilled, more and more self-confident, and more and more successful.

--Mark Victor Hansen

Daily Food for Thought

- **Brain Fact** Choosing to meditate on "positive thoughts strengthens positive reaction chains and releases [neuro] chemicals, such as endorphins and serotonin, from the brain's natural pharmacy. Bathed in these positive environments, intellect flourishes, and with it mental and physical health."[1]

- **Key Thought** The key to overcoming negative thoughts is to keep them God-centered by erecting mental walls to insulate your mind from fear, anxiety, and worry.

- **Scripture** "Set your minds *and* keep them set on what is above (the higher things), not on the things that are on the earth" (Colossians 3:23 AMPC).

Daily Reading

In the final days of August 2005, Hurricane Katrina's ferocious winds wreaked havoc upon the residents of the Gulf Coast of Louisiana, causing raging flood waters to rise as high as fifteen to thirty feet in some areas, forcing residents to seek higher ground, often on rooftops. From there they could be dramatically airlifted to nearby hospitals, shelters and other safe places. The reason the waters in the flooded areas rose to record highs was because the levies broke. They had not been designed to withstand such pressure; thus, under such tremendous physical force, they gave way. Sections of the levies that were originally designed to protect the city crumbled and were washed away, affording locals no protection from the powerful storm. The death toll from that awful week exceeded 1,800.[2]

Spiritually speaking, much like the raging floodwaters that engulfed Gulf coast residents, your enemy, Satan, aims to create stress storms that flood your mind with fear, anxiety, and worry, causing you to become imperiled by the figurative floodwaters of fear, hopelessness, and despair. However, our Protector declares through His Word, "When the enemy comes in like a flood, the Spirit of the Lord will lift up a standard against him" (Isaiah 59:19). As our minds are the battlefield upon which Satan wages spiritual warfare, it is imperative that believers maintain a solid defense against his attacks. So, here I'm going to show you how you can prepare your mind in advance of the thought wars brought on by the unending stresses and pressures of life. Stress, for example, can be brought about by discovering your spouse has had an affair, or finding out that your child was arrested, or another check bounced. Such stress typically has the effect of momentarily (or transiently) stealing our peace of mind. If you are to protect your mind and heart from being inundated by toxic emotions, it is necessary that you develop proactive strategies to fortify your mind against such perturbations before they happen.

Today, I am going to show you how you can erect mental walls (levies, if you will) to help you weather the storms of life. These "walls" are not physical but designed to protect your mind against the enemy's thought attacks. Envision them as an invisible force shield like the one Captain Kirk and Mr. Spock hid behind in one particular episode when they found themselves under fire. If that is perhaps a little too "spacey" for you, the concept of four mental walls can be viewed as analogous to the "helmet of salvation" mentioned in Ephesians 6:17, which was intended to protect the believer's mind. Picture yourself standing in front of a mirror each morning, or before you rise from your bed, erecting mental walls to protect your mind against Satan's detriments (accusations, lies, half-truths and instigation to fear). Be on guard to not let anyone or anything get behind your walls. As you learn to erect these mental barriers, you will be, in essence, developing a superior mental toughness. These four walls are alluded to in Philippians 4:4-9, 13. Should you choose to memorize these verses, review *How to Memorize Scripture* (pp. 253-254).

The Wall of Praise

The first wall is the *Wall of Praise*. Despite whatever irksome, daunting winds may be troubling your life, Paul tells you to, "Rejoice in the Lord always; again, I will say, rejoice" (Philippians 4:4)! The theme of the book of Philippians is joy. "Joy (Greek *chara*) is used four times there (Philippians 1:4, 25; 2:2; 4:1); and rejoice (*chairo*) eight times (1:8; 2:17-18; 3:1; 4:4)."[3] But you may be saying to yourself, "How can I make the choice to rejoice and maintain an attitude of gratitude when troubles are pressing in on every side?" Certainly, Paul isn't telling me to rejoice over my troubles and sorrows? No, he's not. Paul says exactly, "Rejoice in the Lord." There is a big difference. That subtle shift in focus is what enabled Paul to be joyful even through his fretful circumstances. Paul's love for Jesus and his calling to be a preacher of the Gospel fueled his conviction and gave him the strength to overcome all challenges.

We often quote Paul's words: "Rejoice in the Lord always, again I say rejoice" (Philippians 4:4), but I wonder how many people realize that Paul penned these words while sitting in a jail cell, perhaps even chained to two Roman centurions, not knowing whether he was going to live or be executed. It was Paul's perspective that fueled his faith and extinguished his fears. Furthermore, Paul viewed prison as a God-ordained season for writing. Why? Because while in prison Paul wrote four letters, commonly referred to as the prison epistles: The New Testament books of Ephesians, Philippians, Colossians and Philemon. I once read a quote that imparted, "Perspective is not what we see, but the way we see it." That was most certainly true of Paul. To erect the mental wall of praise is to take an intrepid leap: to rejoice. So, when someone or something proves upsetting, instead of resorting to reproach, or insults, or pouting, it's time to erect your mental wall of praise: remind yourself, *I've got my Wall of Praise; I'd better utilize it.* Despite my circumstances, I make the choice to rejoice in the goodness of the Lord. I chose to rejoice in God's magnanimous grace: the fact that God loves me and accepts me when others shun and reject me.

> **Perspective is not what we see, but the way we see it.**

Neurologically, making the choice to rejoice has the capacity to change your mental state of mind by releasing "feel good" chemicals into your brain, which strengthen your anterior cingulate (AC), thus beginning the process of turning around a negative mindset. Dr. Amen, a neuro-psychiatrist, advises that when people are caught in a negative rut, in order to break free from the negative thought pattern, they should do at least two things: (1) Sing a favorite song. (2) Listen to music that makes you feel positive.[4] Praising and thanking God for his goodness to you is another way you can find peace in the midst of woeful personal storms. The Bible affirms, "The joy of the Lord is your strength" (Nehemiah 8:10).

Questions for Reflection

1. Are there any situations or problems in your life that are robbing you of your peace of mind? Is God powerful enough to treat these problems?

_____

_____

2. What are you thankful for?

_____

_____

The Wall of Patience

After making the choice to rejoice, Paul directs our attention to the second mental wall, described in verse 5: "Let your gentle spirit be known to all men. The Lord is near" (Philippians 4:5). The Greek term _epieikes_, translated "gentle spirit" by the New American Standard Bible has another meaning: to be patient, forbearing, and longsuffering.[5] Why is patience so important?

We live with a constant attitude of doing and getting on our timetable, inadequately appreciating God's infinitely superior understanding and timing. Patience is that subtle quality that fundamentally enables the wise purpose of apprehending the will of God.

We all need to improve our level of patience because things are going to take longer than we think. The benefits of marriage counseling, weight loss efforts, career change efforts, smoking cessation efforts, and other agendas will inevitably frequently require more time and effort than we initially estimated. Say to yourself, "This may take a minute." Patience is that all-too-rare capacity to conform to a world of competing values and interests. Weight loss, for example, competes with the real-time want of tempting foods and physical leisure. Marriage or relationship counseling must navigate the problem of different and individual personalities. Wealth accrual takes much, much longer than we'd like. Remind yourself, "This may take a minute."

Neurologically, we need to erect a wall of patience because exercising patience helps the anterior cingulate to balance the frontal lobe and limbic system (Day 8). Balance is key. Impatience, and its frequent accompanying emotions of anger, frustration and anxiety, overstimulate the amygdala, and this emotionally charges the limbic system, inhibiting the anterior cingulate and frontal lobe. Erecting a wall of patience is germane to keeping a healthy chemical balance in your brain. Often times, prayer functions as an incidental practicing of patience. This is because prayer is an implicit reliance upon God, and this presupposes

338

God's sense of timing. Deferring to His timing is directing ourselves in paths of greater patience.

Now for the million-dollar question: Why does God make us wait? There are many reasons: 1) God makes us wait to test and mature our faith (James 1:1-4; Hebrews 6:12; 10:35-36, 38). For this reason, God usually seems to avail things at the last minute, and we respond emotionally to apparent peril. God parting the Rea Sea (Exodus 14) or delivering Paul and Silas out of jail hours before they were going to be executed (Acts 12:9-17), these are examples of God's interventions at the last minute. When God knows your rent was due the first of the month, why does He not come though until the 30th? He tends (from our perspective) to afford things at the last minute; 2) He's orchestrating things behind the scenes (Genesis 37-57); 3) He makes us wait to give us a fuller appreciation that ours is a receipt of His blessing. "Therefore, the Lord will wait, that He may be gracious to you; And therefore, He will be exalted, that He may have mercy on you…. Blessed are all those who wait for Him" (Isaiah 30:18 NKJV).

Another reason God makes us wait is that He may be seeking to purify our motives. My mind takes me back to my early twenties when I would come home from college during the summers and work with my father at the steel plant. My Dad had a pretty dangerous job. He was a furnace operator. He would dress up in an astronaut-ish asbestos suit, and, as the alloys (the raw materials that make up titanium steel) were dumped inside of a massive cast iron cauldron-furnace, my Father would heat up the temperature of the mobile furnace to thousands of degrees Fahrenheit until all the alloys would turn into a molten lake of fire. Father would stand on his platform overlooking this red orange cistern and use a long spoon-like device to skim off the slag at the surface. If it were not removed, the impurities of the slag would weaken the titanium. In like manner, the fiery trials of life cause our impurities to rise to the top, where the Holy Spirit can take his sanctifying ladle and remove our spiritual slag (anger, impatience, jealousy, envy, unhealthy comparisons, impure motives, etc.) The sanctification process is not completed in a day. No, that takes time. God, through the process, is trying to show us things about ourselves.

> *My desire to pastor a mega-church was a vain attempt to prop up my sagging self-image.*

For example, from the time I graduated from seminary, my dream was to pastor a megachurch. Why a megachurch (2000 + congregants)? Oh, I told myself, because I wanted to do a great work for God. Hence, the bigger the church I pastor the more resources we would have at our disposal to reach even more people and ultimately the entire world for Jesus Christ. It all sounded good. But it wasn't until many years later, and especially as I began working through the concepts in *The 21-Day Plan*, I discovered my true motivation – my desire to pastor a megachurch had little to do with Jesus or winning the world for Him. Truthfully, my desire to pastor a megachurch was a vain attempt *to prop up my sagging self-image.* You see, because I didn't really like myself, I reasoned that if I became well known, rich and famous, then people would like me, and then perhaps I would begin to like myself. Now, I don't want to put anybody on a guilt trip. My point is simply this: my heart and your heart are each like an onion; an onion has many layers, and God the Holy Spirit is daily peeling off the outer layers of our hearts to reveal to us our true motives. Facing the truth is painful! But Jesus said, "Then you will know the truth, and the truth will set you free" (John 8:32 NIV). In order for God to conform us into the image of his Son Jesus, He has to purify our motives, and that takes time, and plenty of it. David, a man who loved God, dearly prayed:

Search me, O God, and know my heart;
Try me and know my anxious thoughts;
And see if there be any hurtful way in me,
And lead me in the everlasting way (Psalm 139:23-24).

The man who underwent the longest spiritual development process in the Bible was Moses. It took God 40 years to prepare him to become Israel's grand deliverer. Yet, even after that 40-year process Moses still had some anger and impatience issues.

Be patient, God is not through with you yet. We are all works in progress (WIPs). The main reason we need to erect the mental Wall of Patience is so we won't be tempted to give up on ourselves, on God, and other people before He completes His work upon us. We need faith and patience so we can receive everything God has promised us (Hebrews 6:12). As I was once reminded while demonstrating impatience, *"God does not wear a wristwatch."*

On those days when my journey seems long and hard, and I become impatient with myself and God, I erect the Wall of Patience by pushing back on my automatic negative thoughts (ANTS) and replace them with spiritual automatic thoughts (SATS). I reach into my pocket and take out my 3x5 cards and read to myself. I call these several declarations the "G-6 Summit" because each day I wake up I face an uphill climb to overcome my habitual negativity and ascend to a kind of summit – a higher plane of faith and the path to greater positivity. With every faith affirmation, I'm getting closer and closer to the top of that summit— God's perspective (The Mind of Christ) on my situation. Despite my challenges, I choose to persevere through the journey, being assured of the following truths:

--God loves me. (Romans 8:35, 38-39; Jeremiah 31:3)
--God knows what He is doing. (Isaiah 55:8-9)
--God has a plan that is intended for my good. (Jeremiah 29:11)
--God knows how to make everything work out. (Romans 8:28)
--God is in complete control. (Psalm 103:19)
--God in His perfect time will bring me out bigger, better, and stronger.
  (Genesis 41:25-56)

I repeat these over and over and over again until my soul is quieted, as the Holy Spirit ministers to me. As I meditate upon these crucial acknowledgements, and by applying them to my situation, a smile arrives; God gives me strength to keep walking by faith and not by sight. Try it for yourself. Do it multiple times and feel the power of God's growing presence in your life.

Question for Reflection

Professor Howard Hendricks of Dallas Seminary used to say, "The process (God takes you through) is more important than the end product." What are your thoughts on this idea?

_____

_____

The Wall of Prayer

The Apostle Paul sat in a prison cell, not sure whether he would be released, beaten or tortured, or sentenced to death; how could he have the presence of mind to write an inspired letter as he did with the Book of Philippians? Paul knew how to erect the mental Wall of Prayer. Paul's prescription for managing his thoughts and regulating his emotions is related in verses 6 and 7 in Philippians: "Be anxious for nothing, but in everything by prayer and supplication with thanksgiving let your requests be made known to God" (Philippians 4:6). Paul's secret? *Pray* instead of panic.

The Greek word that translates "anxious" in Philippians 4:6 means "to be pulled in different directions." God's Word pulls us in one direction, and our worries pull us in another; hence, we are being pulled apart. The reason we are told not to be anxious and worry is because worry has definite physical consequences: headaches, neck pains, ulcers, even back pain and nausea. Worry can affect our thinking, our digestion, and even our coordination. From a spiritual point of view, worry is among the most preponderant thieves of joy.[6]

Learning to pray effectively is a safeguard against the manipulating fear and anxieties that would interfere with our peace and joy. For those of you who maintain you don't know how to pray, and for those who desire to spend more time in prayer, I present here a prayer strategy that I learned from the Navigators Discipleship Ministries. It utilizes the "ACTS" prayer model.[7] It is in large part based on the verses we have already referenced above: Philippians 4:6. In addition to praying, Paul also mentions supplications and thanksgiving, which is extremely relevant to the Wall of Praise.

Practically, this is how it is used: Instead of rushing into God's presence and stating your laundry list of needs; you rather enter into His presence employing the ACTS prayer model. You begin this prayer with...

Adoration—You acknowledge and repeat to God His attributes. For example, God, you are holy. Hence, I along with the angels in heaven, cry out to you, "Holy, Holy, Holy, is the Lord of hosts; the whole earth is full of His ["Your"] glory" (Isaiah 6:3). Other attributes would include God's eternal love, His kindness, mercy, righteousness, wisdom, and His power (omnipotence). These attributes are found in Psalm 68:35; Daniel 2:20; Matt. 22:29; Luke 1:78; Ephesians 2:4; 2 Corinthians 13:14. Next, you move to confession.

Confession—You acknowledge your personal sins and ask God's forgiveness. After confessing your sins, you refer to God's promise in 1 John 1:9: "If we confess our sins, He is faithful and righteous to forgive us our sins and to cleanse us from all unrighteousness." No matter what you may have done, God no longer holds it against you once you ask His forgiveness. This time of confession is designed to help us learn to come before God with clean hands and a pure heart (James 4:8). After a time of confession, you transition into a disposition of thanksgiving.

Thanksgiving—You express your thankfulness to God for His goodness to you. "Let us continually offer up a sacrifice of praise to God, that is, the fruit of lips that give thanks to His name" (Hebrews 13:15). Father God, I thank you for loving me, forgiving me, guiding me, protecting me and granting me so much extraordinary favor. I thank you for my social connectedness, my health, and my access to so much opportunity and self-betterment. After, you have ascribed to God His worth, confessed your sins, and thanked Him, you will be ready to bring to Him your prayer request, your supplications.

Supplication—You ask God to attend to your needs and wants. God, I humbly ask that you would_____. Lord, I ask your blessing and your guiding hand as I deal with the many difficulties that I am certain to face. And we don't need to feel limited in our mode of petition. Jesus, in the Lord's prayer, taught us to pray, Father, "Give us this day our daily bread..." (Luke 11:3 KJV).

Note: See today's closing prayer as an example of the ACTS prayer model. You may also change the acrostic so that it reads CATS, whichever works best for you. Or, you may use them interchangeably, depending upon the condition of your heart and mind at the time you feel led to pray. An added benefit of using the ACTS/CATS format is that it adds some much-needed variety to your prayer time with God; it shifts your focus away from a "give me, give me" attitude. Praying, instead of panicking, will help build the mental toughness to guard your mind against the storms of life. (Storms are inevitable.)

In verses 6 and 7, we learn that if we focus our minds on God's promises rather than our problems, our anxiety will be replaced with His peace, "And the

342

peace of God, which surpasses all comprehension, will guard your hearts and your minds in Christ Jesus" (Philippians 4:7). The peace of God is neurologically like a chemical surge in your brain that impacts your emotions, attitude and behavior. This peace of God guards your heart (emotions) and your mind (thoughts, ideas), for these are the two areas that cause worry and mental turmoil. The peace of God (POG) neutralizes fear and worry so that your emotions and thoughts remain healthy and God-centered. (See Figure 20.1) The peace of God takes fear-based thoughts captive to the obedience of Christ as we earnestly pray and remain in His presence.

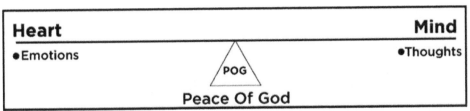

Figure 20.1 Peace of God

The Wall of Positive Thoughts

Having erected the Wall of Praise, the Wall of Patience, and the Wall of Prayer, the final wall to be erected is the Wall of Positive Thoughts. Consistently attending to positive thoughts to replace negative thoughts is the key to renewing your mind and (figuratively) starving your negative thoughts to death. Be mindful: It is not enough to simply stop thinking negative thoughts; you *must* replace your negative thoughts with the positive thoughts so now apply verse 8: "Finally, brethren, whatever is true, whatever is honorable, whatever is right, whatever is pure, whatever is lovely, whatever is of good repute, if there is any excellence and if anything worthy of praise, dwell [think deeply and habitually] on these things" (Philippians 4:8).

> *Peace and joy can be yours!*
> *How bad do you want it?*

As we routinely think and meditate upon positive, faith-filled ideas and perspectives, they penetrate into our born-again spirit and begin renewing our minds and transforming us from the inside out. As our minds become saturated with positive, Word-based sensibility, our negative, fear-based thoughts are deprived of the think time needed to nourish their growth and they begin to die off. The actual dendrites begin to deteriorate and die. You literally have the power to starve a thought to death (Day 6, 16).[8] Taking advantage of opportunities to meditate on the positive to the exclusion of all contrary ideas and notions is absolutely essential to our success. "Positive thoughts strengthen positive reaction chains and release [neuro] chemicals, such as endorphins and serotonin, from the brain's natural pharmacy. Bathed in these positive environments, intellect flourishes and with it mental and physical health."[9] Simply stated, positive thoughts gain (energize) your brain and negative thoughts drain your brain. You are not just thinking positive thoughts; you are renewing your mind (Romans 12:2) and rewiring your brain.

Speaking from personal experience, many times I have observed that often we are not able to think positive thoughts because our minds are flooded with The Filthy Five (FURST). Using myself as an example, upon reflection, my melancholy during a time in my life stemmed from regrets of the past, which consequently fueled my fear of the future. My biggest regret centered on my decision to leave the church that I had pastored for ten years to nurture the development of two new churches, both of which failed over the ensuing ten years. These back to back failures devastated my self-esteem as well as my personal finances and caused my family extreme hardship. I feared that I had missed God and wondered if I would ever recover, ministerially and financially. Such preponderance of negativity (self-loathing) released a toxic cocktail into my brain, which led to my thinking in even more abjectly depressive ways. In my darkest moments, I wished that I could just somehow fall asleep and wake up in the presence of the Lord. The only two things that were clear to me were that I was a "failure" and that God had once again abandoned me. Have your thoughts ever taken you to this unenviable low?

But unknown to me, a reckless love of God was quietly working behind the scenes to expose me to some truths that would impact my view of God, my perception of failure, and deliver a major victory over my tormenting regrets of the past.

One day, while sitting in a doctoral class and feeling like a "total failure," I was handed an article by my professor with a title that piqued my interest. It was entitled, *Developing a Theology of Failure*. What did he see in me that made him hand me that article? The co-authors' premise was that "the biggest problem with many of us is that we are soft from too much success. While we still don't like to fail, we increasingly realize that nothing teaches us more than failure."[10] The gravity of those two statements shot straight to my heart and with cutting conviction. All I could do was to hang my head in shame and clandestinely wipe away the tears that filled my eyes and descended down my checks. Indeed, I had grown soft from too much early success, which in turn had caused me to become mentally soft (spoiled). While this was a bitter pill to swallow, I was desperate to rid my mind of the tormenting thoughts that had kept me in a vortex of negativity off and on for well over a decade. I read that article several times. I came away with several mind-transforming insights:

Overcoming the Fear of Failure: A Theology of Failure

1. Failure is not evidence that God has removed his hand of favor and blessing from your life. Through failure God purifies our motive(s). He wants

to know whether we are prepared to serve in failure, or only in success. "Failure separates the quitters from the servants."[11]

2. "When success becomes the be-all and end-all in ministry, it becomes an idol that God must throw down. Note that failure may come in an area other than our ministry, but it will surely come."[12] I had been worshiping at the feet of the false idols of success, achievement and recognition for as long as I could remember.

3. Through failure we are humbled (our egos crushed), and we learn dependence upon God, not our own narrow capacities, nor our status ("charisma", etc.), but our standing in Christ alone (John 15:7). Now, humbled, we are forced to conclude that God alone can bring us ultimate spiritual success (2 Corinthians 11:30-33).

4. "Failure separates the quitters from the servants. God wants to know whether we are prepared to serve in failure, or only in success."[13] I was forced to admit that my motives were convoluted and self-serving. That was one of the reasons I quit when times got hard, things did not turn out as planned or took longer than expected. Such actions rendered me a quitter and not a servant. When frustrated, my tendency was to ask, God, what's taking so long? You are blessing others! What about me? Lacking the faith and mental toughness, I would capitulate. Failing to heed the Apostle Paul's warning, "When troubles come, accept them,...Do all the duties of a servant of God" (II Timothy 4:5ERV).

5. "Leaders thus broken through failure become suitable tools in the hands of the Lord. But unbroken leaders pose a threat to themselves..."[14] and the people they have been called to lead. Painful as it was, God was breaking me. As if I were on the potter's wheel, God, the master potter, was smoothing out my rough edges, removing impurities from my heart and humbling me through "failures". In love, He was reshaping me into a vessel fit for His divine use. In retrospect, on the potter's wheel is a good place to be! (Jeremiah 18:2-4) I concluded, "It was *good* for me to be afflicted so that I might learn your decrees" (Psalms 119:71NIV).

After reading this article, for the first time in a long time I saw my failures from a top-down (God's perspective) versus a bottom-up (personal) perspective. The Lord helped me to realize that all my failures were a part of His preparation process for my life, and that as long as I didn't quit in my discouragement I was, in a sense, *"failing"* my way to success. *"Failures" are learning opportunities.*

My mind renewed, I felt an indignation welling up on the inside of me. I said, "Enough is enough! Satan! No longer are you going to keep me bound to my regrets of the past. I am breaking free – *today!* I could almost literally hear those chains braking and falling to the ground. Immediately, I felt the Holy Spirit telling me to do three things:

Redefining Success

First, I had to redefine success. The enemy kept telling me I was a failure because of my *past* failures, and I would agree with him. Downward I would descend into a cesspool of self-pity which can become addictive, crutch-like. However, the Lord allowed me to see that failure is an event, not a person. And my wife helped me by sharing her definition of success: True success, in her estimation, is…

> Becoming who God created you to be;
> Doing the works God created you to do; and
> Blessing as many people as God empowers you to bless.

I wrote this three-part definition on a 3x5 card and carried it with me most of the time. When the evil liar levels his accusations against me, (pp. 306-308) calling me the biggest loser of all time, I take out the card and read it several times until I silence the enemy's voice. Satan is nothing more than a big bully! Boldly confront him with the Word, and he'll turn tail and run—every time (James 4:7). This is what Paul means when he says, "Fight the good fight of faith" (1 Timothy 6:12). We are fighting against fear, anxiety and hopelessness, and replacing these with *faith, confidence* and *hope.*

Another definition of success that resonates:

> Success is…
> Knowing what you want, and…
> Becoming what you want, and…
> Refusing to take no for an answer. (or until God redirects you)

The phrase 'becoming what you want' challenges each of us to take self-improvement and the development of greater optimism more seriously, to figuratively "take ourselves on" as a project. We all have areas (aspects, agendas) in our lives that we need to intently sacrifice for, to "die to," in order to live the abundant life Christ died to give us. Edifyingly, the Apostle Paul said, "I die daily" (1 Corinthians 15:31 KJV). For me personally, I had to "die" to negate distorted thinking and stress-induced eating.

Our born-again spirit loves God and wants to be completely obedient to God. Your spirit doesn't want to sin, but the submissiveness-averse soul (mind, will

346

and emotions) and the weakness of the flesh causes us to fall victim to any of the myriad temptations around us. Taking yourself on as a project necessitates being willing to address the areas in your life that only God can bring to mind, such as to afford the focus of attention in order to become the kind of person He wants you to be (in order to achieve the things both He and you want). Our wants and God's wants do not need to always be viewed as disparate; God is there to show the way to the achievement of the things you want (Psalm 37:4).

Secondly, I had to become a "spin doctor." Much like those news commentators who with their words spin a loss verbally into a win, as a newly self-proclaimed spin doctor, I began reframing my past regrets. Concerning the church, I had left, I told myself if I were still there then I wouldn't be here engaged in my present ministry. Concerning the prior failed church plants, I learned that I should not be mad at the things I went through, because in addition to humbling me, they built my spiritual and mental fortitude. Now I'm stronger than I've ever been. Furthermore, God used the failed church plants to redirect my life into another aspect of ministry. God had given me the motivation to share my story and use it to help others similarly vexed. Instead of preaching in a single pulpit each week, I was to begin traveling and sharing the truths embodied within *The 21-Day Plan* with the broader Body of Christ. Hence, He launched me into a new ministry called Think Right Live Right Ministries. The ministry's mission is to equip and empower the broader Body of Christ with the thought management skills necessary to rewire believers' brains to overcome negativity and all its destructive consequences.

> *For some, failure is a tombstone. For others, failure is a steppingstone.*

In addition to ministerial regrets, I had marital, parental, and other relational regrets. In these matters, I called the people I felt I had offended or otherwise wronged or disserved (beginning with my wife, sons and siblings) and sincerely asked their forgiveness. In certain cases, I did so more than once. If the offended individual refused to forgive me, I prayed that God would, over time, afford that person the grace to do so. In the meantime, I would not allow the experience of not enjoying another's forgiveness to hold me in a kind of bondage to guilt and self-condemnation. The other might have had a psychological or spiritual impediment to forgiveness. As far as I was concerned, thenceforward, it was in God's hands.

Lastly, I had to begin looking for success in other areas of my life. Often, people construe "success" using outward, material, and status-based criteria. Successes need to be understood far more broadly. While failing "miserably" on the ministry side, I was excelling in my marriage and family life. My health was perfect, and I had many friends who genuinely loved and cared for me, numerous endowments and enjoyments that money couldn't buy!

Academically, I also seemed to be excelling; I was mere months away from earning the doctoral degree. At that time, I was pleased with my becoming continually more and more positive and hopeful. I had learned to somewhat manage my thoughts as I sedulously applied the skills to rewire my brain to overcome much of my negative thinking. As this happened my former negative mental narrative began to change, and it was replaced by something vastly more positive. As I turned the page and redirected my self-story, from negative to positive, I gradually, with the indispensable help of the Holy Spirit, transformed my thought life.

Until we learn to answer Satan's accusations with our higher, deeper, more powerful and godly truth, the evil liar will continue to torment us. One of the goals of *The 21-Day Plan* is to provide you, the believer who is already empowered by faith, the strategies you need to quill the enemies voice—to shut him down!

Questions for Reflection

1. Though there may be many of them, what single recollection or mental construction (i.e. regret of the past) might you be relieved of by your becoming a "spin doctor" and reframing that experience? In other words, how shall you go about finding purpose in the pain?

_____

_____

2. Are there any areas of your life (however "small" or large) that you presently feel you need to take on or the Lord is challenging you to address?

_____

_____

If you should need professional help in this effort, I strongly encourage you to do all that is prudent and necessary in your current situation to obtain that help. It may be necessary to consult with more than one therapist, counselor or minister, etc. Continue until you make substantial progress.

A Firm Foundation

A house is only as strong as the foundation it rests upon. The same applies to the four spiritual walls that we've been discussing here. The more we avail the lessons woven within them, the stronger our spiritual foundation becomes. Paul explains how the foundation is built in verse 9: "The things you have learned and received and heard and seen in me, practice these things…" (Philippians 4:9). The word "practice" therein means to perform something repeatedly or habitually.

Figure 20.2 Erecting Mental Walls

As you consistently practice praising instead of complaining, mindfully demonstrating patience instead of impatience, praying instead of panicking, and focusing your concentration upon the best instead of the worrisome and disheartening, you are laying the foundation for two important things to occur.

Firstly, as you continue to practice the methods of erecting the walls, consider that Apostle Paul affirms, "the God of peace will be with you" (v.9). Making these kinds of choices and proactively developing your resilience will lead you into the very presence of the God of peace. How many of us can attest that in the middle of a stress storm we began to praise God, pray to God and think on the positive. Then, as you patiently waited upon Him, He gave you peace in the midst of the storm. (This is the blessing available to *all* of us!) The Bible declares, "You [God will] keep [any individual] in perfect peace whose mind is stayed on you, because he trusts in you (Isaiah 26:3 ESV). We are hardwired to experience God's presence and power; it's part of our spiritual DNA. [15]

Second, neurologically, each time you push back on your negative thoughts and instead elect to erect these mental walls, you are creating a new neuropathway in your brain. Each time you rejoice (in the awareness of God), wait on God, and pray (with an emphasis on the positive) you rewire your brain, and additional repetition of the same works to establish a new mental habit. "Patterns that are repeated over time become wired in the brain and body."[16] "The brain changes, adapts because of the development of new circuitry, and induces more and more of the...behavior."[17] Neurologically, this is how our minds are renewed and our lives transformed from the inside out. And this is all fully within our ability to accomplish.

> *The best driver of neuro-plastic change in your brain is your behavior.*

Neuroscientist Dr. Laura Boyd of the University of British Columbia maintains, "Nothing is more effective than practice in changing and rewiring your brain... Your brain is very plastic, and it is being shaped both structurally and functionally by everything you do, and by everything you fail to do. The best driver of neuroplastic change in your brain is your behavior."[18]

Malcolm Gladwell, author of the book, *Outliers*, argues that to master a skill like painting a portrait, learning to play the piano or some other instrument, becoming a skilled vocalist, or pitching a fastball takes about 10,000 hours of diligent practice.[19] While experts argue about the actual number of hours it takes, the fact is the more you practice the better you become (at the work, art, skill, etc. being practiced). What is my point? The more you and I practice the CCCR thought management strategy, and the more times you consistently repeat your I AM Significant mantra and the N-O-W-M-O-V-E-F-O-R-W-A-R-D-my spiritual identity acrostic, you become better at rewiring your brain and building strength of memory. Practice long enough, and your brain will begin to filter your negative thoughts without much conscious effort on your part. It will identify the negative thought and push back against it before you have time to work through your CCCR thought management strategy. Like a burglar alarm that is tripped, it can automatically notify you that an intruder (a negative thought) has entered your mind. Your brain will begin to develop the capacity to detect and replace negative thoughts.

It is extremely important that we not get hung up on the "10,000 hours" notion. Focus on the present moment to the exclusion of anything that smacks of ambition or even a long-term goal. Pray with utmost earnestness and practice the mantras and corresponding scriptures and do so with only a sincere focus on the authenticity of your present moment actions. Also, take care not to compare yourself with anyone else. (We are all more unique than we realize.) Work at your own pace and have faith that future episodes of practice will take care of themselves.

The Power to Renew Your Mind

Where do we get the power to practice the techniques necessary to renew our minds? Philippians reminds us, "I can do all things through [Christ] who strengthens me" (Philippians 4:13). The spiritual empowerment that facilitates mind renewal is not willpower or determination, because God knew that we would at times fall miserably short of these unreliables. The true source of power derives from the Holy Spirit which dwells within each believer (Acts 1:8). As spiritual beings made in the image of God, we are empowered from the inside out. Hence, we are reminded in Scripture, greater is He who is within me than he who is in the world (I John 4:4). But Holy Spirit doesn't do all the work alone. We have to really want it! There is no substitute for passion. This is where willpower, drive and determination come into play. Our job is to set our minds and keep them set on the things of God by taking captive contrary, deceiving, energy-sapping men-

350

tal constructions. However, this will prove challenging, because "the Spirit is willing, but the flesh is weak" (Matthew 26:41). As you battle with your negative thoughts, pray to God for His profoundest strength. He'll empower you to shut the door of your mind and lock the devil out. Satan will keep knocking, but once he witnesses that you've developed the mental toughness to resist him, he will flee (but momentarily) and go looking for another victim to trick and harass and torment.

A secondary power source is hardwired into our brain. Neurologically, anything we do consistently, the brain's neurocircuitry facilitates a kind of "craving" to produce more of the same behavior, good or bad (Day 7), useful or useless, health or unhealthy, wise or unwise.[20] The more you practice erecting the four mental walls, the more your brain 'craves' repeating the behavior.

Building Mental Toughness

Replacing relative mental weakness with greater mental toughness occurs over time as we consistently develop the ability to …

1. Praise rather than complain. (The Wall of Praise)
2. Patiently wait on God's timing. (The Wall of Patience)
3. Pray instead of panic. (The Wall of Prayer)
4. Positively think the best rather than the worst. (The Wall of Positive Thoughts)

Practicing the thought management principles outlined in this book is the key to success. As we seek to develop new habits, we follow a kind of paradox: we work with a focus on the present intending to achieve a (non-present, long-term) future goal.

No one can do it for you. Say to yourself, *"If it's going to be, it's up to me!"*

Each night before retiring, my wife asks me to check that all the doors are locked. A short time later, she comes behind me and checks what I've done. Why? Because she wants to make sure our house is safe, and no intruders steal into our house while we are asleep. That is the same way we need to be with our cogitative processes. We need to consistently lock out fear, doubt and unbelief. Shut the door. Lock out the devil with the proactive strategies you have learned by reading this book.

Real Life Testimonies to Help Build Your Faith

We close today's lesson by sharing a personal story of how I, through prayer and practice, had to erect mental walls to keep my mind from crumbling when calamity struck.

My Story: I Almost Lost It!

In *The Purpose Driven Life*, the author, Rick Warren, contended that with every truth comes a test. Having conceptualized and practiced the truths about the four mental walls, my test came in a very sudden, dramatic way.

I was in my den working on the final draft of this manuscript. After months of wrestling with a title for my book, I found one I really liked. I jotted it down on my laptop and sprinted up the stairs to get my wife's opinion on it. She offered a few ideas, and I hurried back downstairs to write her suggestions down before forgetting them. As I turned the corner to enter my den, my stride was broken as the strap on my flash drive had gotten caught on my den's doorknob, and the mishap jerked me backward. I stopped and detached it from the knob and sat down at my desk and began jotting down the thoughts from my very recent conversation with my wife. I then pressed save, but the document failed to save. I tried this repeatedly. Upon closer scrutiny, I noticed the skewed angle of my drive in the USB port and that the flashing red signal on the flash drive had disappeared. This was very, very scary. My heart began palpitating, and the thought came to my mind that I might have broken the tiny device. It was really obvious that I had. I took a few deep breaths to calm myself and thought about how the Holy Spirit had been prompting me for weeks to back up these extremely important documents, but in my lamentable procrastination, I had failed to do that.

In a loud, almost audible voice, I heard the evil liar gleefully exclaim, "Your flash drive is broken, and you didn't store any of your work in the Google drive like you were supposed to. It's all gone! You're such a fool! Four years of work down the drain! The book is gone! Lost forever! What do you think of your God now?"

While my heart was pounding, my head was relatively poised. It was as if my mind was being guarded, shielded by an invisible spiritual force. Everything appeared to move in slow motion. Pushing back against the panic that inundated me, I had the presence of mind to call on God for help and wisdom. Erecting a wall of prayer, I entreated God for His help. The Lord then enabled me to compose myself and begin to call a few computer technicians. After speaking to two such experts ("geeks"), both of whom told me there was "no way" to retrieve data from a damaged flash drive, a foreboding pessimism engulfed me. Pushing back, I took those thoughts captive, breathed deeply three times, and I called a third expert. This computer specialist told me there might be a possibility of retrieving the data, but I would have to mail my flash drive to his shop in Dayton, Ohio along with a deposit of $300.00 with a promise to pay a total of $1,000.00 if they succeeded in rescuing the data. This was not entirely good news, because my accident with the doorknob was apparently going to cost me $1,300.00.

In those first few moments after damaging the flash drive, I needed to keep a cool head. My fields of study – counseling and theology – in addition to behavior modification strategies, came in very handy at this time of great concern about my data. I was able to immediately apply several of the thought management strategies that I had been designing (and practicing) for years. In a kind of shock, I stood up, walked about, out of my den, and into the bathroom. As I caught a glimpse of my reflection in the mirror, I heard Satan say, "Ok, Mr. Think Right Live Right, what are you going to do now?" Staring at my image in the mirror, at the cusp of breaking into tears, I felt an inner toughness begin to well up inside me. In that moment, the Holy Spirit brought to my mind the Biblical Job who, after receiving the devastating news that he had lost all his wealth and all his children in a violent storm, dropped to the ground and worshiped his Maker. Staring at my sad and pensive reflection, I squared my shoulders, and I told Satan flatly, "This is what I am going to do: lift both my hands heavenward and praise God." I thanked God for his magnificent, indispensable grace and mercy.

I thanked Him for choosing me to reveal the thought management truths of *The 21-Day Plan*. After all, He could have revealed them to anyone. Tears of joy streamed down my face as I thanked Him for the unconditional love that brought Him to my aid when I was at my worst. As I worshiped God, I felt a supernatural strength welling up inside me. I told the Lord that I didn't believe He had brought me this far to leave me in such dire circumstances. "Lord, the book is yours," I confessed. "Father, although I can't see a remedy myself, I know you have a way of retrieving the lost information on my flash drive. Show me what you want me to do to restore this flash drive," I pleaded. As I prayed, the Holy Spirit reminded me of a Scripture I had memorized: "…God who gives life to the dead…" (Romans 4:17). I meditated upon that phrase. Suddenly, it hit me: God, my flash drive is dead, and *I need you to bring it back to life*. With a scriptural promise undergirding my faith, I felt exhilarated, and continued to praise His Holy name, more confident than ever that my flash drive or its contents would somehow be restored. I began to thank God proleptically for the restoration. By faith I believed and received it repaired. I even envisioned myself once again engaged in typing on my laptop with the fully functioning flash drive plugged in the USB port. As I extolled the many virtues of the Lord, He brought to my mind the face and name of my computer repairman. I had initially guessed that he didn't have the expertise to solve such an extreme problem (disaster). He only repairs computers, I reasoned, but I eventually pushed back on that faithless notion and hurriedly picked up my cellphone. I explained the situation to him, and his first words met my ears like one stranded in the desert meets a lake of fresh water: out of his mouth, "I've fixed flash drives before. Bring it to my shop and I will take a look and tell you whether I can repair it." Faith filled my heart as I began to think of all the miraculous possibilities that God affords His children. I experienced an eerie and inexplicable confidence that God would give this man the capacity to repair what no one else was able to do. I imagined myself driving to the shop and seeing the flash drive supernaturally restored. I saw myself at my computer clicking on the tab, scrolling down to weeks 1, 2, and 3, and seeing them in their untainted original condition.

It was time to erect a wall of patience when the impaired device was out of my hands and in the hands of experts. I would have to wait as long as this peculiar miracle would require.

Eleven days after the technician received my flash drive, I received a text from him. It read, "It is FINISHED!" "It is ALL RESTORED!" I cried tears of joy and shouted—PRAISE the LORD!"

Once I arrived at his shop, he confided that it took him and his partner 13 hours to repair the drive. Indeed, the Lord who restores life to the dead restored four years of hard work.

Questions for Reflection

Are there any dead things in your life that you need restored? Is your marriage or other significant relationship dead? Is your hope in the future dead? Based on today's lesson, what do you need to do to turn things …renew your hope and confidence in God's ability to give life to the dead?

Today's closing prayer is an illustration of the ACTS prayer model.

A Closing Prayer

(A) Heavenly Father, I come before You today acknowledging Your omnipotence, omniscience and Your omnipresence. (C) I confess my sins in not being sufficiently grateful for all that You have done and continue to do for me. (T) I pause now to thank You, Father, for never giving up on me. I thank You for your tireless love that constantly pursues and woos me back to You at those crucial times when I become distracted and stray. (S) Lord, help me to daily practice these thought management strategies, so I can grow mentally tougher and passionately pursue Your plan for my life. In Jesus' name. Amen.

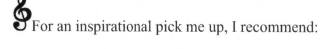

For an inspirational pick me up, I recommend:

- *Stronger* by *Mandisa*
- *Stand* by Donnie McClurkin
- *More Than Wonderful* by Laurnelle Harris and Sandi Patty
- *For Every Mountain* by The Brooklyn Tabernacle Choir

Memory Work—Follow instructions 1-3 for Day 20 (p. 334)

Day 21

I Think Myself Happy!

"Happiness (like winning) is a matter of right thinking, not intelligence, age or position."

--Charles Swindoll

Daily Food for Thought

- **Brain Fact** "Deep in the brain there are colonies of rapidly dividing cells which can migrate outward and replace any specialized cell in the brain... learning stimulates this cell division. *Practicing* what we've learned seals the connections between the new cells and the existing ones."[1]

- **Key Thought** The brain is rewired through repetitive practice.[2] Therefore, happy and joyful thoughts can be wired into the brain through practice.

- **Scripture** "I think myself happy..." (Acts 26:2 NKJV).

Daily Reading

Surely, most people desire to be happy. Often, they just don't know the means to its achievement. We want to experience what Bobby McFerrin encouraged them to do in his song, *Don't Worry, Be Happy*! Many people are looking for a pick me up, something to put a little smile on their faces and a little pep in their steps. This unabashed positivity was more recently exemplified with the song "Happy" by Pharrell Williams. That music video has been viewed over 1 billion times. Impressive! The video's popularity attests to the desire of most people to be happy. Today's lesson focuses specifically on the techniques and skills necessary for each of us to make ourselves happy, so to speak, in any situation, and this lesson is especially concerned with deliberate practice and how practicing can work to our long-term benefit. This is going to require two things: practice and perspective.

Practice

God designed us in such a way that our thoughts affect our emotions, attitudes and behavior. Just as worry has been hardwired into our brains through happenstance, happiness can also be hardwired into our brains through deliberate practice (repetition). Little practice is very likely to produce little happiness. Much practice is likely to afford much happiness. It's that simple. The brain is rewired though repetitive practice.[3] People who are disciplined have practiced being disciplined. In like manner, people who are positive are thus because they (very fortunately for them) practice being positive. If you practice taking every thought captive, by utilizing your (CCCR) thought management strategy, and consistently practice replacing negative thoughts with positive, I can assure you that you'll become a more joyful, contented and happy person. But don't take my word for it. The Bible expressly states, "As a man *thinks,* so he will become" (Proverbs 23:7). Intentionally directing ourselves toward positive, faith-filled ideas and attitudes will help us to become more constructive in our thinking. Becoming a happier person also requires perspective.

Perspective

Perspective is not what you "see," but how you see it. *The following* is an instructive story about the power of perspective. A college student wrote her parents a letter telling about college experiences. She wrote:

"Dear Mom and Dad: There was a riot on campus. There was smoke in the air. From the smoke I inhaled, I developed a lung disease. At the hospital, I met a parking lot attendant, and we fell in love. We became very involved in each other's lives, and now we have a baby on the way. Importantly, he has been in trouble with the Law. Soon his term of probation will end. One month after he gets off of probation, I intend to drop out of college. We plan to move to Alaska and get married. – Your loving daughter."

At the bottom appeared a P.S.: It read,

"None of this is true, but I did fail chemistry."

She wanted to enable her parents to gain greater perspective on her academic setback. Could it be that your present worries, concerns, and vexations, in the bigger picture, are really not all that terrible and/or insurmountable, but are essentially as bad as you think them to be? No matter how bad your current situation, somebody else is very probably winning with that same hand. No matter how strange this idea at first seems, many of us are practiced in that fortuitous art of "making lemonade." (Recall the folk wisdom that "When life gives you a lemon, make lemonade?") Pastor Chuck Swindoll asserts, "Life is 10% what happens to you and 90% of how you react to it."

Someone else would love to be in your shoes! It all boils down to *perspective*. And this becomes possible because of the depth and sincerity of our faith in God. Up to now, you may have been using your thoughts maladroitly, inviting the worst by tapping into misfortunate mental habits, but it is actually possible to very deliberately design our thinking for the best. Here I will explain how each of us can think ourselves out of sadness and into gladness.

A Biblical Perspective on Positivity

It seems the Apostle Paul had the mental discipline and toughness of personality to think himself happy in any situation. For example, on one occasion, the Jewish religious leaders had Apostle Paul arrested for preaching the Gospel. Consequently, Paul was also bound in chains and brought before King Agrippa to defend himself against their trumped-up charges. We might reflexively assume that in such a situation Paul must have been downcast and depressed. Think again. Paul's day in court opens with King Agrippa calling Paul, a Roman citizen, to approach the bar and plead his defense. Observe Paul's opening statement: "I think myself happy "King Agrippa." Paul said, "because today I shall answer for myself before you concerning all the things of which I am accused..." (Acts 26:2 NKJV). How was Paul able to think himself happy whilst not knowing whether he was going to live or be executed? Paul was able to respond in this way because he had, through practice, learned to control his negative thoughts and had developed a spiritual perspective that was out of this world. Paul feared neither death nor life. This attitude may be rare, but it is no less achievable for its rarity. In fact, we are all capable of attaining this perspective and attitude as a consequence of enlightened instruction. Paul, in his confident defense, was able to think himself happy because he practiced focusing on these three essential realities:

1. God's promises instead of his problems.
2. God's purposes instead of his pain.
3. God's gracious provision instead of his perceived ("glass half empty") lack.

In like manner, in order to think yourself happy, you are going to have to mentally force yourself to think on Christ rather than your crisis. Think on God's promise instead of your problem. This is not as easy as it may initially seem.

Focusing on God's Promises Instead of Your Problems

In the midst of Paul's dire troubles, God made him a promise, "I will deliver you from the Jewish people, as well as from the Gentiles, to whom I now send you" (Acts 26:17 NKJV). In order to think himself happy (optimistic), Paul had to push back against his fear and meditate upon God's promise of protection. Just as God promised to protect Paul, He has also promised to protect you and me as well. God promises, "Do not fear or be dismayed because of this great multitude, for the battle is not yours but [Mine]" (2 Chronicles 20:15). Memorize this verse. When extreme challenges rise up against the more positive developments, or seem to, you can rest in peace, knowing God has your back. You need not fear the taunts of the enemies and detractors, the possibility of failure, nor the prospect of calamity. God's will is all that counts. This is what it means to think on God's promises instead of your problem.

I once read that there are well over 3,000 promises in the Bible. That's a whole lot of promises, made by the chief Promise Keeper Himself—God Almighty. When fear and anxiety overtake our minds, we must zero in on one or more of His promises and meditate thereupon. To meditate means to think about something over and over again. You may find meditating upon the Word of God difficult. But you are already meditating on your problem. It's called *worry*. The problem is that worry almost never solves your problem; it just opens the door of your mind and heart to more manipulating fears, anxieties, and doubts, etc. These may manifest in the form of panic attacks, migraine headaches, ulcers, or other maladies. However, meditating upon the promises of God produces peace of mind, even in the midst of the storm (Isaiah 26:3), and confidence where there was fear. Below are some promises God has made to His children.

When you're facing a problem and you don't know what to do, God wants you to have faith in His Word, even when you don't have the answer, or your answers seem to fall short.

- God promises: "Call to me and I will answer you. I'll tell you marvelous and wondrous things that you could never figure out on your own" (Jeremiah 33:3 MSG).

When faced with the problem of people falsely accusing you and slandering you, or otherwise discrediting or criticizing you,

- God promises: "Weapons made to attack you won't be successful; words spoken against you won't hurt at all… I, the LORD, promise to bless you with victory" (Isaiah 54:17 CEV).

358

When the month is long and your money is short,

- God promises: "[I] shall supply every need of yours according to his riches in glory in Christ Jesus" (Philippians 4:19 ASV).

At such times when you are tempted to stress out over your problems, push back on those negative thoughts by meditating upon the promises of God. As you practice spending time with God and meditating upon God's promises, you will begin to experience God's peace (Philippians 4:6-7; Isaiah 26:3).

> *When you are tempted to stress out over your problems, push back on those negative thoughts by meditating upon the promises of God.*

How to Keep from Stressing Out

1. Inhale deeply. Get out of your emotions. Be still before God (Psalm 37:7, 46:10).
2. Speak directly to God, and make sure you understand that you are taking instructions from God and not giving God instructions. Allow God to work as He chooses. Pray humbly and listen.
3. Know that all crises eventually pass, and the challenge is not as horrible and devastating as it presently seems. Look for an *"at least."*
4. Remind yourself that "because He Who lives in you is greater (mightier) than he who is in the world," you are strong enough to handle any challenge/crisis (1 John 4:4 AMPC).
5. Reflect on past victories, blessings, and deliverances and situations that God brought you through. (1 Samuel 17:37)
6. When possible, call upon mature-minded, spiritual individuals for guidance (Proverbs 11:14).

Questions for Reflection

1. I heard it said, most people (most of us) are either heading into a trial, in the middle of a trial or coming out of a trial. Where do you find yourself today?

_____

_____

2. If you are in a storm, based on today's lesson, what are some steps you can take to refocus on God's promises instead of your problem?

_____

_____

Focus on God's Purpose Instead of Your Pain

Paul, having been encouraged by God's promise to protect him from his accusers, now boldly shares his testimony. Standing before such royal dignitaries as King Agrippa, his wife the queen, and Festus the Governor, Paul shares how he was confronted by Jesus on the Damascus Road. Having been knocked off his horse and blinded, Paul heard the voice of Jesus say to him:

"Paul, Paul, why are you persecuting Me?' So, I said, 'Who are You, Lord?' And He said, 'I am Jesus, whom you are persecuting. But rise and stand on your feet; for I have appeared to you for this purpose, to make you a minister [to both Jew and Gentiles] to whom I now send you, to open their eyes, in order to turn them from darkness to light, and from the power of Satan to God, that they may receive forgiveness of sins and an inheritance among those who are sanctified by faith in Me.' (Acts 26:14a-16, 18 NKJV)

In order for Paul to think himself happy, he chose to think about God's purpose instead of his pain. What pain? The pain of being constantly harassed and jailed by the Jews. Paul, however, willingly endured it because he kept in mind God's purpose for his life—to preach the Gospel. Paul realized that the pain he had to endure was not for his sake exclusively, but for the good of others. Paul said, in another prison epistle, "Now I am full of joy to be suffering for you. (Colossians 1:24 NLV). Just as Jesus willingly suffered (Hebrews 12:2), Paul knew he, too, was going to have to suffer (Acts 9:16). Now, let me make a clarifying statement. When I encourage you to meditate upon God's purposes instead of your pain, I do not mean to imply that God is the cause of the pain we suffer in this world. No, my point is that God uses pain to fulfill his overall plan and purposes for our lives. Such was evidenced in Paul's imprisonment by the Jews and Christ's crucifixion by the Roman authorities.

Pain enters our lives, by our own doing, the actions of others, the consequences of living in a sinful world or Satan himself (Day 16). To prevent the pain from robbing us from our joy, it would be to our benefit to have the mental discipline of Paul to be able to see the pain but not see the pain. But you ask, how can I see the pain and at the same time not see the pain? I suggest to you that you do it all the time. For example, you walk into a room and see the one person you can't stand to be around. What do you do? You act like you don't see them; being careful to avoid them as you mingle and socialize with all your other friends and associates. You see them but you act like you don't see them. The one whose mind has been trained through practice is able to see the blessings and not see the burdens. Oh, you know they are there, but you don't allow them to steal your joy and rain on your parade. However, if you have made up in your mind, that you will not or cannot be happy until all your problems are eradicated, you will be waiting a very LONG, LONG, LONG time. Been there done that and got the T-shirt in multiple colors.

I challenge you to compare your perspective with that of the famed hymnologist, Fanny Crosby. She was born on March 24, 1820, but her life took a tragic turn when she developed an eye infection at six weeks old. A quack doctor put a hot mustard compress on her eyes to cure her, but instead the compress so scarred her eyes that she was blinded for the rest of her life. That was tragic, but what's more astounding is Fanny's perspective on her pain. She concluded:

> If I had not lost my sight, I could never have written all the hymns God gave me… It seemed intended by the blessed providence of God that I should be blind all my life, and I thank him for the dispensation. If perfect earthly sight were offered me tomorrow, I would not accept it. I might not have sung hymns to the praise of God if I had been distracted by the beautiful and interesting things about me.[4]

Fanny reframed her tragic blindness, at the hands of a fraudulent doctor, as something that God providentially allowed to happen to her, in order that He might use her pain for a greater purpose. Fanny Crosby wrote over 2000 hymns that are sung by the Body of Christ nationally and internationally and will continue to be sung until Christ's triumphant return. Among her most popular hymns are "All the Way My Savior Leads Me," "I Am Thine, O Lord," "Jesus, Keep Me Near the Cross," "Sweet Hour of Prayer," and, "To God Be the Glory." It's often said, when life hands you a lemon, make lemonade, and that is, by the grace of God, exactly what Fanny did. Will you?

Like Fanny Crosby and the Apostle Paul, if you are going to think yourself happy, it is expedient that you stop focusing on your problems and find a purpose for your pain. Granted, your parents may have rejected you by putting you up for adoption, or you may suffer emotional and physical scars from living through a botched abortion. Others of you, by no choice of your own, have undergone a gut-wrenching divorce, or you have had an accident that may have left you paralyzed or with severely limited mobility. I say this with the utmost respect, as have thousands of others. It's time for you to move on with your life. Please, do not spend the remainder of your life being *angry* about all the things you've been through. Please do not spend the remainder of your life harboring bitterness and resentment toward the people who hurt you, all the while blaming God. Find a purpose in your pain and pay Satan back for messing with you and trying to destroy your life. While it took me decades to figure this out, understand that your misery is the soil in which your ministry is cultivated and nourished. This *21-Day Plan*, that you are reading, was born out of my personal pain and struggle, but when I grew tired of justifying my misery and turned to God for help, He helped me just as He promised He would.

God gave me the wisdom to learn how to slow my thoughts down so that I could deal with one thought at a time. Daily, I practiced pushing back on my negative thoughts and faithfully practiced using the (CCCR) thought management paradigm. Practicing what you've learned seals the connections between the new cells and the existing ones.[5] Learning new things stimulates that cell division. All the learning you have experienced in *The 21-Day Plan*, if consistently applied daily, is sealing, bonding and rewiring your brain. Your thoughts are either life-giving or life-threatening. The choice is yours. Being and remaining happy requires that you set your mind and keep it set. Confess your *I Am Significant* mantra and your *My Spiritual Identity* – N-O-W-M-O-V-E-F-O-R-W-A-R-D acrostic 10 to 12 times a day over the next 21 days and neurologically you will begin to experience some "brain change".[6] Scripture affirms, "As a man thinks so he will become" (Proverbs 23:7). Remember, where the focus goes, the energy flows.

> *Practicing what you've learned seals the connections between the new cells and the existing ones.*

Questions for Reflection

Unmet expectations are often the major causes of sadness, disappointment and depression. Think of one or more expectations that you've been holding onto that are causing you much frustration and emotional pain. Is it something God promised you, or is it something you assumed He would do for you? If you are certain He promised you, are you willing to wait on His "perfect timing" to bring it to pass? If it is something you assumed, are you willing to let it go?

Yes/No

> *Unmet expectations are often the major causes of sadness, disappointment and depression.*

Focus on God's Provision Instead of Your Perceived Lack

Happy-minded Paul, having passionately and persuasively argued his case, is now awaiting a final judgment. King Agrippa will decide his fate. But Paul is at peace because he has made it his practice to think about God's promises instead of his problem and God's purposes instead of his pain. Paul, standing strong and speaking boldly before Agrippa, acknowledges to his audience the true sources of his strength. Paul says, "Therefore, having obtained help from God, to this day I stand" (Acts 26:22 NKJV). Paul's peace of mind and his strength comes from the Lord. Finally, we discover that Paul thought himself happy by thinking about God's provision instead of his perceived lack. Paul acknowledges that God had provided him with the emotional, spiritual, physical and mental fortitude to endure all that he'd gone through. Paul made it very clear to all those under the sound of his voice that he stood strong in God's strength and not his own. So, inspired by Paul's defense and testimony, King Agrippa responds to Paul saying,

Paul, "You almost persuade me to become a Christian." And Paul said, "I would to God that not only you, but also all who hear me today, might become both almost and altogether such as I am, except for these chains. When he had said these things, the king stood up, as well as the governor and Bernice and those who sat with them; and when they had gone aside, they talked among themselves, saying, "This man is doing nothing deserving of death or chains." Then Agrippa said to Festus, "This man might have been set free if he had not appealed to Caesar" (Acts 26:28-32).

Through King Agrippa's judgment, God provided Paul a stay of execution. So, Paul was going to live to see another day, live to fight another battle, and, most importantly, live to preach the Gospel and share his testimony one more day. Paul's appeal to Caesar not only meant protection from his Jewish accusers, but it set Paul up to qualify for an all-expenses paid cruise to Rome, an outside cabin with balcony, meals and drinks included. God, just as He promised, was providing all of Paul's needs according to His riches in glory in Christ Jesus (Philippians 4:19). You might be asking, well, with all that God provided him, what was Paul's perceived lack? Paul references it in verse 29 when he responds to King Agrippa by saying, "I desire that you and all men and woman would become a Christian like, I am, except for these chains" (Acts 26:29). Paul's perceived lack was the fact that he was a prisoner bound in chains. He was not a free man as he had been all of his life, and that is what Paul means when he says, "except for these chains." But in order to think himself happy, Paul chose to think about his opportunities rather than his opposition. Paul was spiritually mature enough to know how to balance his blessings and his burdens without allowing the latter to rob him of his joy. Paul didn't allow the little that he lacked—his freedom—to rob him of the joy of all of God's magnanimous provisions.

Today as you are reading this lesson, is your countenance sad because you are thinking about all that you don't have rather than focusing on what you do have? Granted, you may not have the fancy new car you saw advertised on the TV commercial, but can you thank God for your hoop-dee? At least it's paid for. I believe all believers should carry around in their shirt pocket, sport jacket, dress pocket at least three *But God*" cards. So, when the devil comes harassing you with unhealthy comparisons concerning your house *versus* your neighbor's house you can pull out your "But God" card and say, "My new house is a lot bigger and better than the apartment I used to live in. Furthermore, one day, I plan to have a nicer house than my neighbor, but in the meantime, I going to enjoy the house that the Lord has provided for me." You're standing in front of the mirror getting dressed for work and feeling good about the fact that you have lost ten pounds. The enemy attacks again by saying "You look alright, but you're not as thin or as pretty as Suzie Q., your co-worker." That's when you pull out your "But God" card and say, "But God said I am fearfully and wonderfully made in the image of God. I couldn't possibly look any better to God." Run him off, but he'll come again. That's why you need to keep those "But God" cards close by you.

What are you choosing to focus on? God's provision or your perceived lack? Speaking of perspective, allow me to share with you an incident from the life of hymnologist Horatio Spafford. Horatio experienced a tremendous loss, but instead of focusing on his loss, he chose to stand strong in the strength the Lord provided him. Horatio was a retired attorney who lived in Chicago, a devoted Christian and loyal friend of D.L. Moody. Equally important, he was a devoted husband and father of four daughters. Wishing to spend more time with those he loved most, Horatio planned a European vacation with his family. However, some unexpected business delayed him, so he sent his wife and children ahead expecting to join them in a day or two. However, in November of 1873, the ship *S.S. Ville du Harve*, was struck by an English vessel as it was passing through the Atlantic Ocean. Tragically, the ship sank within 12 minutes, killing some 266 passengers. Among the dead were Horatio's four daughters. Mrs. Spafford was one of the few that were miraculously saved.[7] Shocked and heartbroken, he boarded another ship to join his grieving wife in Cardiff, Wales. As he stood on the deck of that ship, to gaze upon the exact place where his daughters had drowned, the inexplicable peace of God engulfed his heart, leading him to write the following words:

When peace, like a river, attendeth my way,
When sorrows like sea billows roll-
Whatever my lot, Thou hast taught me to say,
It is well with my soul,
it is well, it is well with my soul.[8]

To find such comfort from God, when his soul was in anguish, demonstrates that this man of God, obviously, had deposited a lot of God's promises deep in his mind and heart. Hence, when his day of calamity struck, the Holy Spirit could make a withdrawal and bring back to his mind the promises of God. Horatio, empowered by the Holy Spirit was able to think himself happy because he probably practiced meditating upon God's promises, God's purposes and God's provision instead of his personal problems; his pain and his lack. Due to human error, not God, he lost his four daughters, but he didn't lose his praise, his hope, his faith nor his trust in God. By way of provision, God graciously spared his beloved wife. Facing life without his daughters was going to be unimaginably difficult, but the fact that he ran to God for strength and comfort, as opposed to running from God gave him hope to cope with his loss. He knew that he'd not just survive but thrive. He knew that Satan, the wretched thief had targeted and attacked his family. He says as much in the second stanza of the hymn.

Though Satan should buffet
Though trials should come
Let this blest assurance control
That Christ has regarded
My helpless estate

When you can't see God's hand, you can always trust God's heart.

364

And has shed His own blood for my soul
It is well with my soul,
It is well, it is well with my soul.[9]

Mental toughness is a byproduct of a strong and supernatural faith, a strong faith, one that is Word focused rather than feeling focused, a strong faith that suppresses manipulating fears that cause one to not doubt God's love for them when tragedy hits home. Fears are overcome by two things: a strong faith and a deep awareness of God's love for you.

The Bible affirms, "We need have no fear of someone who loves us perfectly; his perfect love for us eliminates all dread of what he might do to us. If we are afraid, it is for fear of what he might do to us and shows that we are not fully convinced that he really loves us" (1 John 4:18 TLB). When you know that God loves you unconditionally, your heart will not be overrun with fear, because your knowledge of God's love is perfect or mature; it's NOT just an intellectual assent, rather it's a heartfelt knowing deep down on the inside. Your soul finds rest in knowing God loves you and is therefore at peace. A perfect/complete understanding of God's love will drive out your worries, anxieties and fears. Knowing that God loves you can get you through the most horrendous trials. This was brought home to me by the testimony of a dear friend, named Barb. She's married to my brother from another mother. Her story encapsulates many of the thought management principles discussed in *The 21-Day Plan*. She is a living example of someone who, by God's amazing grace and strength, learned to perpetually think herself happy while facing the darkest days of her life.

Real Life Testimonies to Help Build Your Faith

Barbara's Cancer Journey: Amazing Grace

At the age of 36, I had just had my second daughter, Lauren. It had been a difficult pregnancy, requiring me to be on bed rest for three months, but in the end, I delivered a beautiful and healthy baby girl. We soon found out that our daughter wasn't as healthy as we had hoped. After months and months of sleepless nights, projectile vomiting, not gaining weight and numerous appointments with specialists, it was determined that Lauren had reflux as well as a hole in her heart and needed immediate surgery. Also, during this time my mother was diagnosed with breast cancer and had to have surgery, which prompted me to check myself. It was during that check that I found a lump. I was sent for a mammogram but was told "nothing was there" and it was "normal breast tissue" and to follow up in six months. During this time, I continued to take care of my mother as well as my sick daughter, not knowing that the cancer was growing inside of me. I have always felt that the Lord doesn't give us more than we can handle, and that everything happens for a reason. Before my daughter's surgery, during one of our sleepless nights while cleaning up vomit and dealing with a screaming baby, I can remember sitting in the rocking chair feeling angry with God and questioning how much more I could take. Shortly after that, I really found out the answer to that question. In September, Lauren had successful heart surgery, and Mom was doing well after her recent breast cancer diagnosis and mastectomy. For a brief moment all seemed to be calm until I remembered that lump in my breast as it seemed to be getting larger as well as becoming painful. It was then that I saw a specialist and was immediately told that I had breast cancer. I remember that day like it was yesterday. Sitting there with my husband by my side as the doctor informed me of the devastating news along with the grueling treatments that I would have to endure over the next year would prove to be the most difficult time of my young life. I was told that my tumor was too large to do surgery right away. I would have to have 4 to 6 rounds of chemotherapy first to shrink the tumor, then surgery followed by more chemotherapy, a stem cell transplant and finally radiation. Just imagine hearing that news after everything that we had been through during the previous 9 months. It was as if my entire life was flashing in front of my eyes.

During the car ride home, between the tears, the disbelief of being misdiagnosed, and the silence, I remember looking out the car window. I was thinking of my girls and asking what will happen to them? How will Rick ever be able to do this on his own? I won't be here to see them grow up, graduate, and get married. It was the worst day of my life. I remember looking into the clouds and seeing the beautiful rays of sunlight shining through them, and I knew that somehow, some way, by the grace of God, I would get through this.

When we returned home, the first thing I did was hold my girls tightly and broke down and cried. I cried that night in my bed as I pulled the covers over my head, and I just wanted to hide, disappear, and never come out again. The next morning, as I woke up hoping it was all a bad dream, knowing that it wasn't, and that this was my reality for the next year of my life, I dug down deep inside and asked God for the strength, the strength to move forward. I knew if I gave into this, I would be missing out on a whole lot of living so I picked myself up, brushed myself off and said, "God, let's do this!"

I have always been a planner and have always wanted things just so. I guess that's the teacher in me. I now realized that I wasn't the one in control, it was in God's hands now. Over the next year I made a promise to myself to live my life as normally as possible (in-between cancer treatments that is). It was literally like a roller coaster ride that I couldn't get off soon enough. There were ups and downs, like the time after the two chemo treatments that made me sick and lose my hair but didn't shrink my tumor. I said, "Well, what do we try next?" Trying not to focus on the negative, like it not working, but focusing on the positive, that there was something else that they could try, I would envision the chemo eating up all of those cancer cells as I was getting my treatments. Even during the times while I was sick or watching my hair fall out, I tried to make it a positive situation. We had a little hair buzzing party, so my mom gave me a buzz cut, and my husband buzzed his hair, too. I would take each step, trying to find the positive and move forward. The positive was that even though the tumor didn't shrink, **at least** it didn't get bigger, and there's something else they could try.

Finally, after 6 months of a new chemo, I was ready for surgery. I was so glad to finally get this cancer out of my body. Unfortunately, after all of the chemo, I was still stage 3B (stage 4 being the worst) with 14 positive lymph nodes! We knew it was going to be bad, but 14 positive lymph nodes!! That's scary, but still I tried to find the positive. Stage 3B stinks, but at least it hasn't spread anywhere else.

Now onto the next step, more chemo, more vomiting, and losing the little hair that started to grow back once again. YUK! I already knew what to expect with that. Six more months of chemo while recuperating from surgery and trying to make life "normal" for my girls and my husband.

Next was the really big decision on whether to have the stem cell transplant or not. What should I do? Do I take the chance of dying by trying to prevent my cancer from returning in the future and possibly saving my life in the long run? One doctor says yes, one says no, and one even told me that it was a "crap shoot." Wow, what do I do? I prayed long and hard and asked God to help me make my decision. I knew in the end I had to do everything possible to save my life, everything to prevent my cancer from returning, everything so that I would be here for my husband and most importantly my girls. While they were growing up, they needed a mother to be there for them. Selfishly, I wanted to be there for them, too. With me being the glass half full kind of girl and my husband being the glass half empty kind of guy, I made up my mind to do it! I would move forward with the transplant.

It seems like yesterday, the day I met my transplant doctor, Dr. S. He walked through the door, and immediately I thought, "This is the man that's going to help save my life." I knew that I had to do it. I couldn't live with looking back and thinking that I didn't do everything possible to prevent my cancer from coming back. If I did have a recurrence, then I could look my girls in the eyes and say that Mommy did everything possible to be there for them.

After a week of collecting my own stem cells and freezing them, the day was finally here. I knew that it would be a difficult three weeks without my girls, but I knew in my heart it was what I had to do. I received three different chemo treatments for 96 hours straight. The object was to kill any cancer cells hiding out in my body. During this process, the chemotherapy not only killed the bad cancer cells, but it also killed all of the good red blood cells, white blood cells and platelets. They bring you down to zero only to then give you back your own stem cells to build you back up again. Over the next 17 days, I was very scared, nauseous, vomiting, and extremely tired. Thankfully, with the help of family and friends and a lot of praying, I made it through with flying colors. I surprised all of my doctors by getting out in 17 days!!

The ride home was absolutely beautiful. It was like I was born all over again and seeing everything for the first time. Feeling the warmth from the sun on my face, seeing the trees, and the sun shining through the white fluffy clouds, it was all just beautiful. Then I noticed the blue sky, and there they were again, those rays coming down through the clouds. It was as if God were telling me that I made the right decision and that everything would be ok.

I remember asking Dr. S. what my chances of recurrence were now. I was shocked when he responded, "50/50." What? After all that, it's still 50/50? I thought for a moment and then looked at him and said, "Well then, that means that there's a 50% chance that it won't come back, right?" Yes, he said. "Well then, that's going to be me. I'm going to be in that 50%!!"

My final step in my cancer treatment was radiation. It consisted of 28 radiation treatments every day with weekends off. That was truly like a walk in the park compared to everything else that I had been through.

With all of my treatments complete, it was now time to start living "normally" once again. I completed my treatments over 18 years ago. I have been cancer free for 18 years! It hasn't always been easy. The chance of recurrence is always in the back of my mind. At first, it was like I was always waiting for the other shoe to fall. It was also difficult when friends that I met during my journey were no longer with us, or every time I felt a new pain thinking, "Oh no, my cancer is back" only to find out that the pain would go away once I received good news from recent scans and checkups. I would even wonder why? Why had God chosen me to do so well? Why was I able to survive such an advanced cancer for so long while others who had much less than me were no longer here? I almost felt guilty for doing so well.

As I look back on my cancer journey, I find myself very thankful. Each and every day I give thanks to God for allowing me to be here, strong, healthy and cancer free. I'm thankful to be able to be here for my family. I know that there were many factors that contributed to my successful journey. First, I could not have done it without the help of family and friends. Also, my team of great doctors, and finally my strong faith in God and a positive attitude all contributed to my successful journey. I truly believe that God chose me to do so well for so long for a reason. Who knows, maybe it's so I could raise my girls and share my story so that I could help others. Who knows? What I do know is that God has a plan for all of us, and I'm sure that this was meant to be just part of His plan all along.

Upon reading the intimate details of her cancer journey, I asked Barb what is your favorite hymn? She replied, "Amazing Grace." I should have figured. She is one amazing woman who serves an Amazing God. Read the lyrics of a few select verses.

Through many dangers,
toils and snares.
I have already come.
Tis Grace that brought me
safe thus far
and Grace will lead me home
The Lord has promised good to me
His word my hope secures
He will my shield and portion be
As long as life endures
Amazing Grace how sweet the sound-That saved a wretch like me![10]

Fight the good fight of faith. Fight against fear! Fight against discouragement! Fight against depression! Fight against sadness! Fight against hopelessness! I've heard it said, there are no hopeless situations, just people who have lost hope. No matter what you may be facing, keep hope alive by daily remembering to meditate on God's promises, God's plan and God's provision. Remembering the words of hymnologist, Annie Johnson Flint's, song, "He Giveth More Grace":

He giveth more Grace
when the burdens grow greater,
He sendeth more strength
when the labors increase;
to added affliction
He addeth His mercy,
To multiplied trials, His
multiplied peace.[11]

God loves you. God's got your back. Therefore, in the midst of adverse circumstances think yourself happy by thinking about...

1. God's promises instead of your problems.
2. God's purposes instead of your pain
3. God's provision instead of your perceived lack.

Think Positive!
Think Victory!
Think Healed!
Think Set free!
Think Delivered!

See it! Say it! Seize it!
You now have the tools, to manage your thoughts for the rest of your life. Apply them daily, and in time you'll discover that your best days are in front of you—not behind you. The best is yet to come, if you only believe! (Mark 9:23).

**A Closing Prayer**

Dear God, I thank You for blessing me to complete The 21-Day Plan. Help me daily to draw upon Your strength moment by moment to employ the thought management strategies to overcome my negative thinking and to renew my mind one thought at a time. I fully recognize that every day is not going to be perfect, but that doesn't mean every day doesn't have a purpose. Help me to discover that purpose so I'll be motivated to overcome any and all obstacles. Lord open my eyes to see what You are doing in and through me. In Jesus' name. Amen.

For an inspirational pick me up, I recommend:

- *Happy Dance* by Mercy Me
- *Power* by Deitrick Haddon
- *If You're Not In It* by Danny Gokey
- *Blessings On Blessings* by Anthony Brown

Until tomorrow, do this:

1. Look over The Toxic Ten (pp. 238-239); reflect upon which thought distortions you may be entertaining. (Where there is relational conflict, somebody is most likely engaging in one or more of The Toxic Ten.)

2. Tomorrow, read the Conclusion: **What's Next?**

**Memory Work**

3. Continue repeating your *I Am Significant* mantra (p.65).

4. Repeat your *My Spiritual Identity* N-O-W-M-O-V-E-F-O-R-W-A-R-D acrostic. In the future (now?), memorize the Scriptures associated with this acrostic. The Scriptures are found on pages 108-109.

5. Continue to write down The Filthy Five Memory Verses on 3x5 cards and practice memorizing them (Figure 14. 2, p. 242).

6. Daily employ your (CCCR) Thought Management 101 strategy (p. 182).

Conclusion

What's Next?

You've been exposed to, and learned a lot of powerful, life changing information. However, information is powerless to change you unless there is the internalization—the application of that information—which leads to life transformation. Without question, you have the information necessary to manage your thoughts for the rest of your life. Whatever benefits you derived from *The 21-Day Plan*, they are temporary at best unless the thought management principles are maintained daily. Practice is the most important key to rewiring/retraining your brain to overcome negative thinking. Should you fail to consistently practice these thought management and thought replacement strategies, I can virtually assure you that you'll find yourself back in bondage to a more sophisticated strain of toxic thoughts and emotions. Why? Because once you unmask Satan's schemes, he comes up with even more deceptive ones!

Even after completing *The 21-Day Plan*, there will be moments, hours and perhaps days that you will struggle to gain mastery over some of the negative thoughts that seek to master your mind. However, ultimate victory is won through prayer, daily meeting with God in a formal QT, reviewing your 3x5 cards, and avoiding those things that are fueling your negative thoughts. Additionally, practice your thought management strategies in *real time life situations* daily. Make this practice a habit whether you feel like it or not, knowing that the principles will work if you'll work them. At times you will have to force yourself because while your spirit is willing, your flesh is weak. It is your choice since no one can rewire your brain except you.

What's next? There are **four** specific action steps that I feel will help you to successfully maintain the benefits of the principles discussed in *The 21-Day Plan*.

First, stay at it until you have fully committed to memory the *I Am Significant* confession and the N-O-W-M-O-V-E-F-O-W-A-R-D acrostic and corresponding scriptures (p. 108-109). It will take you some time but make yourself do it anyway. Why? *Failure to do so will permit your brain to default to negative thinking.* Additionally, in so doing, you will be able to curtail much of your negative self-talk. Until you learn to answer the voice of your inner critic, you will continue to be mentally dogged and harassed by an onslaught of negative accusations. Use your SATS to replace the ANTS. Stomp out those ANTS!

Second, now that you have completed the plan, I encourage you to reread this book to gain deeper insights. This is the type of book you might reread in order to master the thought management principles and memorize all the Scriptures. I also encourage you to begin reading other books on neuroscience and thought management. I have included a recommended reading list in Appendix C. Two books that helped me tremendously are Norman Wright's, *A Better Way to Think* and *Your Thoughts are Killing You* by Marybeth Wuenschel. I recommend you read these two books first. The more you educate yourself on the subject, the more successful you will become at rewiring your brain to overcome negative thinking. There are countless quality YouTube videos online made by practitioners and professional educators, counselors, psychologists, psychiatrists and other noted neuroscientists. Build into your weekly routine a time to listen to many of the gifted speakers and lectures. As you listen and read, jot any motivational quotes on 3x5 cards and recite them to yourself. Additionally, since exercising faith is the number one brain exercise, read the Bible and other books about faith in order to grow your faith and strengthen your brain.

Third, because depression doesn't always look like depression, it would benefit you greatly to discover whether you suffer from it or not. So, to aide you in discovering this, I have included a 12-point depression checklist. See Appendix A. In addition to that, I have also included a 15-point check list to help you assess whether you need to seek help from a caring professional. See Appendix B.

Finally, once you've mastered the *I Am Significant* confessions and the N-O-W-M-O-V-E-F-O-W-A-R-D acrostic, I encourage you to make your very own personal positive faith (acrostic) confessions about your marriage, your children, your relationships, your health, your finances, your ministry, your future, or any area in which the enemy is attacking you. For example, I coupled my *I Am significant* mantra with an I Can …T-A-K-E-A-C-T-I-O-N mantra.
I repeat to myself multiple times daily…

I Can…
Tackle any challenge and handle any obstacle that stands in my way. (Dan. 11:32)
Ask the Father for anything in Jesus name and He will do it. (Matthew 7:7-8, 11)
Keep my promises to my Savior, my spouse, myself and all others. (Ps. 15:4)
Earnestly pray, worship God, memorize His Word and obey it. (Ps. 16:11 GNT)

I Can…
Accept responsibility for my life and pursue God's plan for my life. (Phil 4:13)
Call forth those things that are not as though they are. (Mark 11:22-24)
Triumph over temptation. (1 Corinthians 10:13)
Inspire people to think right so they can live right. (Hebrews 10:24)
Own up to my own faults without blaming others. (Psalm 139:23-24)
Negate all negative thinking by employing my CCCR paradigm. (2 Cor.10:5)

There is an inherent benefit to devoting the time and effort to developing these acrostics and committing them, along with the corresponding Scriptures, to memory. By doing so, you are significantly decreasing your worry time. Neurologically speaking, you are starving to death those worrisome fear filled thoughts by restricting blood flow and oxygen to those negative brain cells (neurons) and redirecting that oxygen and blood flow to cultivating the creation of positive faith-filled brain cells.

Let me be clear. I am not saying that you can eradicate *all* your negative thoughts. As a matter of fact, avoid that all-or-nothing thinking. As a result of "The Fall" (Genesis 3), our brain stem has been compromised, and, therefore, we **all** will be harassed by negative thoughts to varying degrees. However, being bothered by occasional negative thoughts is a far cry from being in bondage to them. When toxic, negative thoughts and emotions seek to overrun your mind, keep pushing back by employing your CCCR thought management strategy.

Once you begin to think better, you will begin to live better. Rewiring your brain to overcome negative thinking is the by-product of deliberate practice. As your mind is renewed, one thought at a time, you'll soon discover that your best days are out in front of you, not behind you. The best is yet to come! I'm not just saying that, I'm speaking what I know. I'm happier now! I'm stronger and I'm wiser now. I still have a ways to go, but I've learned the importance of successive approximations. *I don't focus in on how far I have to go; rather I focus in on how far I've already come.* By learning to control my thoughts, I now have the mental toughness to face any and every challenge with faith and patience. Truth be told, the things that once broke my heart and brought me to my knees in tears, I'd welcome them today with a smile—child's play.

It's my prayer that this book will be to you what it has been to me—a life saver. Begin NOW to consistently apply these thought management strategies. Don't delay another day. It was Dr. Martin Luther King, Jr. who said, "It's always the right time to do the right thing." As has been said, "A mind is a terrible thing to waste." So, with each negative thought, fight to retrain your brain to overcome negative thinking—one thought at a time. "So roll up your sleeves, put your mind in gear... Don't lazily slip back into those old grooves of evil [negative thinking]..." (1 Peter 1:13MSG). Instead, fight the good fight of faith. You'll be glad you did!

> *Once you begin to think better, you will begin to live better. Rewiring your brain to overcome negative thinking is the by-product of deliberate practice.*

Appendix A

Depression Doesn't Always Look Like Depression:
A 12-Point Depression Check List

In ignorance, I, the author, spent many years in a depressive state of mind but never really knew it. Researchers maintain, "Even though depression is a very treatable mental illness, *80% of people don't receive any treatment.*"[1]

Because depression doesn't always look like depression, you may be depressed. Why don't you take the time to evaluate yourself now based on this 12-point checklist? Below are 12 symptoms of depression[2]:

You might be depressed if...

1. **You're often tired.**
   If you find yourself frequently feeling lethargic, feeling under a load, feeling overwhelmed by doing perfunctory daily tasks such as doing household chores, washing dishes, doing the laundry, paying the bills, etc.

2. **People and things frequently annoy you.**
   If you find yourself short tempered and frequently fly off the handle with your wife, children, a slow-moving cashier, your neighbor, etc. you may be depressed. Being "quick to anger, quick to tears" is a classic sign of depression.

3. **You sleep too little or too much.**
   You have trouble motivating yourself to get out of bed. Changes in your sleeping patterns are a sign of depression. If you normally sleep throughout the night, but now find yourself frequently awakening during the night, it may be that you are depressed. If, on the other hand, you don't often sleep, but now find yourself sleepy and tired, that is also a tell-tale of sign of depression.

4. **You have eating issues.**
   You may be depressed if you find yourself eating too much—turning to food for comfort—or, on the other hand, often times severely depressed people have little to no appetite at all.

5. **Your body is often in pain.**
   Those who suffer from depression have three times the average risk of developing chronic pain.

6. **You don't care that you look messy.**
   When you temporarily lose interest in your physical appearance and personal hygiene, it is a symptom of depression. You may have not showered or combed your hair in days or your apartment, house or cars are messy.

7. **You're hiding.**
   Are you isolating yourself from those you used to associate with? Your proclivity to withdraw into isolation is emblematic of depression

8. **You have a decreased interest in things that were once interesting.**
   If you find yourself, unable to motivate yourself to do the things that once brought you excitement and joy such as a hobby, sex, etc., you are probably depressed.

9. **You're beating yourself up.**
   We all engage in negative self-talk at different times of the day. However, when we find ourselves beating up on ourselves for an entire day or longer, our depression may be to blame.

10. **You're forgetful or have trouble concentrating.**
    If you find yourself forgetful, unable to focus, can't remember where you were earlier, such mental confusion may be a sign of depression.

11. **You feel numb.**
    You feel no emotion, either happy or sad. You just may feel empty inside—numb. This is a clear sign of depression.

12. **You think about dying.**
    There are two types of suicidal thoughts:
    Active suicidal thoughts: You have a plan and you are planning to execute your plan. *Passive suicidal* thoughts: You don't plan to kill yourself; you just wish that you would die in your sleep or in a car accident.

Questions for Reflections

1. How many of the 12 symptoms applied to you? Write the numbers below:

   —   —   —   —   —   —   —   —   —   —

2. What do you plan to do about it?

A 15-Point Check List:
You Probably Need Professional Counseling If....

My mind is a neighborhood I try not to go into alone.
--Anne Lamotte

Whether one should pursue counseling in the form of seeing a "trained professional" (i.e. a therapist, psychologist, or psychiatrist) or not is a complicated question for many people. Ironically, most people have no problem going to see a doctor when they severely bump or bruise their head, break an arm or a leg, or their bodies are experiencing acute flu like symptoms. However, when their minds are overridden with melancholy toxic thoughts and emotions or symptoms of recurring mental fatigue, sadness, depression, guilt or intense anger linger, they assume it's normal or okay without first checking with a trained professional. The Substance Abuse and Mental Health Services Administration discovered that while "One in five American adults suffers from some form of mental illness, only about 46-65 percent with moderate-to-severe impairment are in treatment."[1] Did you catch that? One in five Americans suffer from mental illness, but roughly only half are in treatment. Why?

According to psychologists Daniel J. Reidenberg, Mary Alvord, and Dorothea Lack, authors of the article "8 Signs You Should See A Therapist," argue that people shy away from counseling because there are three primary stigmas associated with seeking professional help. First, the assumption is that one must be "crazy" if he needs to see a therapist. Second, admitting you need help is a sign of weakness. Finally, counseling is too expensive, and they simply cannot afford it.[2]

Covert Signs

Below, I've provided you a list of subtle symptoms of unhealthy thinking patterns that if not addressed at their onset could morph into more severe mental and emotional problems. If you are experiencing these types of thoughts and emotions, you could probably benefit from seeking pastoral or professional counseling. The subtle signs are as follows: [3]

1. You often assume the worst.
2. You mentally beat yourself up.
3. You take responsibility for other people's problems.
4. You feel helpless when you are stressed.

5. You tend to avoid difficult situations.
6. You care too much about what other people think.
7. You are of the mindset/attitude that everyone else has a problem except for you. Your motto: I'm okay, but everybody else has a problem.

These are tell-tale signs that something is wrong. "The earlier someone gets help, the easier it is to get through the problem."[4] Don't delay. Become proactive and nip these distorted thinking patterns in the bud before they grow into larger mental, emotional or physical challenges.

Overt Signs

Drs. Daniel J. Reidenberg, Mary Alvord, and Dorothea Lack, make the case that you should seek a therapist if...

1. **You feel intense negative emotions**. You feel intensely sad and negative. You feel intensely helpless and depressed. You feel condemned. You feel angry. You feel afraid, and those intense feelings sometimes lead to panic attacks. Should these feelings disrupt your normal day-to-day functioning, you need to see a professional because these thoughts and feelings are indicative of a deeper problem or some underlining issues.

2. **You've suffered a trauma, and you can't seem to stop thinking about it.** You could be an adult suffering from an adverse childhood experience (ACE) or some form of PTSD. You may have suddenly lost someone through death, divorce or a friendship that ended abruptly. Or, perhaps you lost something important to you like a job, a limb, a ministry, your money, or your self-respect. As a consequence, you might isolate yourself from others or find yourself experiencing intense insomnia.

3. **You have unexplained and recurrent headaches, stomach-aches or a rundown immune system.** "Toxic emotions can cause migraines, hypertension, strokes, cancer, skin problems, diabetes, infections, and allergies just to name a few."[5] These ailments may very well be signs of stress or emotional duress. Seeking professional help could help you to learn to better manage your stress by introducing you to stress relieving strategies.

4. **You're using a substance to cope.** If you find yourself using drugs and/or alcohol to numb your pain, it's a sign that you are undergoing some sort of emotional pain and/or struggling with an addiction. You've tried

stopping because of the negative consequences but have not been able to on your own. You need to seek counseling. Other pain blockers could involve food and or sex.

5. **Changes in work performance.** If your supervisor or coworkers are complaining about your poor work performance, or you find yourself lacking concentration or no longer enjoying a job you once enjoyed, that could be a sign that you may need to make an appointment for counseling. In the event you find yourself avoiding work all together, you are probably dealing with an underlying fear that a counselor could help you work through.

6. **You feel disconnected from previously beloved activities.** If you find yourself withdrawing from actives and hobbies you once enjoyed and find yourself overall feeling unhappy and lacking a sense of direction and purpose in life, you may need to seek counseling.

7. **Your relationships are strained.** If you are no longer happy in the relationship that once brought you joy and satisfaction and are having difficulty consistently identifying your feelings and communicating those feelings, it could be a sign that you need to seek counseling.

8. **Your friends have told you they're concerned.** "If anybody in your life has said something to you along the lines of: "Are you talking to anybody about this?" or "Are you doing okay? I'm concerned about you" — that's a sign that you should probably take their advice."[6]

Questions for Reflections

1. How many of the overt or covert signs applied to you? List them in the space provided below:

_____

_____

2. What do you plan to do about it? Beginning today I plan to….

_____

_____

Appendix C

Communicating Your Needs: His Needs, Her Needs

Having a happy and fulfilling marriage can be one of the toughest relational challenges to navigate. With divorce rates mounting, couples are coming face to face with the stark reality while *love may be blind—marriage is a real eye opener*! To help couples fight for their marriages rather than take flight, Dr. William Harley has written a captivating book, *His Needs, Her Needs: Building An Affair-proof Marriage.* The book is based on a survey of some 10,000 couples who listed their top needs to remain happily married (p.10).

"A husband should satisfy his wife's *needs* and a wife should satisfy her husband's *needs...*"   (1 Corinthians 7:3NIRV).

His Needs	Her Needs
1. Sexual fulfillment	1. Affection
2. Recreational companionship	2. Conversation
3. An attractive spouse	3. Honesty and openness
4. Domestic support	4. Financial support
5. Admiration (Respect)	5. Family commitment

The purpose in meeting your partner's needs is to keep your partner's *love bank* full. Quarrels and conflict result in a withdrawal from your spouse's *love bank*.

Dr. Gary Chapman is his best-selling book, *The Five Love Languages*, avows couples have a particular love language that makes them *feel loved* (p.10).

1. Words of Affirmation	2. Quality Time	3. Gifts
4. Acts of Service	5. Physical touch	

Root Causes of Confusion Over One's Sexual Identity

I, Dr. Chipman, through my research have concluded most individuals who are confused about their sexual identity are so because of five contributing factors:

- Sexual abuse
- Hurts not properly processed
- Influences of peers, pornography, societal trends and ideologies
- Parental influences (generational bondages)
- Satanic Influences (demonic accusations and lies you believe)

Appendix D

Conflict Resolution: Rules of Engagement

Conflict is an inevitable part of most relationships. Here, I offer a coherent plan of action to resolve such conflict.* In seeking to peacefully resolve your differences, be *prayerful, speak respectively, and* remember to **attack the problem—not the person**.

Follow these ten steps:
1. Arrange a time and a place to patiently dialogue—*no cutting each other off. Wait!*
2. Define the *single* point of contention: The problem is _____
3. Acknowledge the ways you yourself may contribute to the problem.
   Partner 1: I contribute by _____
   Partner 2: I contribute by _____
4. Reflect upon past attempts at resolution that were **not** successful.
   1) _____ 2) _____
   3) _____ 4) _____
5. Brainstorm several possible solutions. *Take care not to judge or criticize the other's perspectives.*
   1) _____ 4) _____
   2) _____ 5) _____
   3) _____ 6) _____
   4) _____ 7) _____
6. Humbly evaluate each possible solution.
7. Agree on *one* initial solution to try that *you both feel good about.* _____
8. Agree on how each will contribute toward resolution of the problem.
   Partner 1: I will commit to_____
   Partner 2: I will commit to _____
9. Schedule a time to discuss the progress you're both (hopefully) making.
   Place: _____ Date: _____ Time: _____
10. Express thanks for the other's contributions.

Taking a Time-Out

In our efforts to resolve conflict often it is necessary to take a time-out before tempers flare. Here is how to take a time-out:

1. Acknowledge your need for a time-out.
2. Ask for a time-out.
3. Decompress, relax, and calm down. *(Ex. pray, practice stress relieving breathing exercises; take a walk, a drive or play relaxing music).*
4. Recognize the need to work toward a solution that *both individuals can feel good about.*
5. Resume the conversation at an agreed upon time preferably within 24 hours (Ephesians 4:26-27, 29-31; James 1:19).

These conflict resolutions and time-out strategies are adapted from the PREPARE-ENRICH: Workbook for Couples (p. 13).

380

Appendix E

Recommended Reading

Adams, Junita. *Yes, You Can Begin Again*. Kingdom Publishing Group, Inc., 2012.

Amen, Daniel G. *Change Your Brain, Change Your Life*. New York: Three Rivers Press, 1999.

Chipman, Vonda. *Faith Talk: Word of God Speak A 90-Day Devotional*. Chesterfield, VA: Hope For The Home Inc., 2019.

Eckman, David. *Becoming Who God Intended: A New Picture for Your Past a Healthy Way of Managing Your Emotions a Fresh Perspective on Relationships*. Eugene, OR: Harvest House Publishers, 2005.

Helmstetter, Shad, Ph.D. *Negative Self-Talk and How to Change It*. Gulf Breeze, FL: Park Avenue Press, 2019.

McDowell, Josh. *Building Your Self-Image*. Wheaton, IL: Tyndale House Publishers, 1988

Newberg, Andrew, and Mark Robert Waldman. *How God Changes Your Brain. New York: Ballantine Books Trade Paperbacks*, 2009.

O'Conner, Richard. *Rewire: Change Your Brain to Break Bad Habits, Over Come Addictions, Conquer Self-Destructive Behaviors*. New York: Plume Printing, 2014.

Tchividjian, Tullian, *One Way Love: Inexhaustible Grace For An Exhausted World*. Colorado Springs, CO: David C. Cook Publishers, 2013.

Witt, Lance. *Replenish: Leading From a Healthy Soul*, Grand Rapids, MI: Baker Books, 2011.

Wright, Norman H. *A Better Way to Think: Using Positive Thoughts to Change Your Life*. Michigan: Revell, 2011.

Wuenschel, Marybeth. *Your Thoughts are Killing You: Take Control of Your Mind and Close the Door to Those Negative, Depressing, Fearful Thoughts Forever*. Baltimore, MD: Spirit-Filled Catholic Publishers, 2018.

Appendix F

All Scripture Translations

Unless otherwise indicated, all scripture notations are from the New American Standard Bible, © 1960, 1962, 1963, 1968, 1971, 1972, 1973, 1975, 1977, 1995 by the Lockman Foundation. Used by permission. (www.lockman.org)

Scripture quotations labeled AMPC are from the Amplified Bible, Classic Edition, © 1954, 1958, 1962, 1964, 1965, 1987 by the Lockman Foundation. Used by permission. All rights reserved worldwide.

Scripture quotations labeled AMP are from the Amplified Bible, © 1965 by Zondervan. Used by permission. All rights reserved.

Scripture quotations labeled ASV are from American Standard Version. Public Domain.

Scripture quotations labeled CEB are from the Common English Bible, CEB, © 2010, 2011 by Common English Bible. Used by permission. All rights reserved worldwide.

Scripture quotations labeled CEV are from the Contemporary English Version, Second Edition, © 2006 by American Bible Society. Used by permission. All rights reserved worldwide.

Scripture quotations labeled CJB are from the Complete Jewish Bible, © 1998 by Messianic Jewish Publishers. Used by permission. All rights reserved worldwide.

Scripture quotations labeled CSB are from the Christian Standard Bible, © 2017 by Holman Bible Publishers. Used by permission. All rights reserved worldwide.

Scripture quotations labeled DRA are from Douay-Rheims 1899 American Edition. Public Domain

Scripture quotations labeled EHV are from the Evangelical Heritage Version, New Testament & Psalms, copyright © 2017. Used by permission. All rights reserved worldwide.

Scripture quotations labeled ERV are from the Easy Read Version, © 1987, 2004 by Bible League International. Used by permission. All rights reserved worldwide.

Scripture quotations labeled ESV are from the English Standard Version Text Edition, © 2001 by Crossway Bible. Used by permission. All rights reserved worldwide.

Scripture quotations labeled GNT are from the Good News Translation Second Edition, © 1992 by American Bible Society. Used by permission. All rights reserved worldwide.

Scripture quotations labeled GW are taken from God's Word, © 1995 by God's Word to the Nations. Used by permission of Baker Publishing Group. All rights reserved worldwide.

Scripture quotations labeled JUB are from the Jubilee Bible, © 2000, 2001, 2010 by Life Sentence Publishing, Inc. Used by permission. All rights reserved worldwide.

Scripture quotations labeled KJV are from the King James Version. Public Domain.

Scripture quotations labeled MEV are from the Holy Bible, Modern English Version, © 2014 by Military Bible Association. Used by permission. All rights reserved worldwide.

Index

Index to Diagrams

About the Author

Paul Chipman is a graduate of Dallas Theological Seminary (Th.M.) and Liberty Baptist Theological Seminary (D Min.). He has served as a senior pastor for 17 years. He is a pastoral and marriage and family counselor, author, church consultant, and conference speaker. Dr. Chipman is the founder of *Think Right Live Right Ministries* and conducts TRLR workshops and travels extensively speaking on Biblical mind renewal and thought management strategies to overcome negative thought. He views himself as a thought management specialist. His passion is to help people think more clearly and behave more productively, so they can with greater focus fulfill God's plan for their lives. Paul and his wife, Vonda, have been married for 34 years and are the proud parents of three adult sons.

I would love to hear from you. Please send your comments about this book to the address below. I want to stay in contact with you and send you inspirational emails occasionally, if you would like. I would also like to notify you when/if I will be speaking in your area. If you would like to contact me about the possibility of speaking in person, you can email or call me.

To Contact the Author, Write:

Think Right Live Right Ministries
6933 Commons Plaza Suite 242
North Chesterfield, VA 23832

Internet address:
www.thinkrightliveright.com
(804) 271-2423

Should you have need of our counseling services please email or call me. Your prayers as well as your requests are welcome. If the book has helped you, please share your testimony with us and encourage someone else to read the book.

Notes

The 21 Day Challenge

[1] Keith S. Dobson, *Handbook of Cognitive-Behavioral Therapies* (New York: Guildford Press, 2010), 4.

[2] Harold G. Koening, *"Religious versus Conventional Psychotherapy for Major Depression in Patients with Chronic Medical Illness:* Rationale, Methods, and Preliminary Results." Depression Research and Treatment (2012): 1.

[3] Frank Lawlis, *Retraining the Brain: A 45-Day Plan to Conquer Stress and Anxiety* (New York: Plume.
2008), 6.

[4] Rick Warren, *The Purpose Driven Life: What On Earth Am I Here For?* (Grand Rapids, MI: Zondervan 2002), 9.

[5] Ibid.,25.

[6] Caroline Leaf, *Who Switched Off My Brain?* (Dallas: Improv, Ltd., 2008), 80.

[7] Caroline Leaf, *Think, Learn, Succeed: Understanding and Using Your Mind to Thrive at School, the Workplace, and Life* (Grands Rapids, MI: Baker Books, 2018), 217.

Author's Note

[1] Paul Chipman, *Overcoming The Five Primary Negative Thoughts: A Twenty-One Day Mind Renewal Plan For Men,* Liberty Baptist Theological Seminary, (Lynchburg, VA: Thesis/Dissertation, 2014), 161. https://www.digitalcommons.liberty.edu/doctoral/967

[2] Susan Gaidos, *More Than a Feeling: Emotionally Evocative, Yes, But Music Goes Much Deeper,* Science News. 178.4 (Aug. 14, 2010): p24-26.
https://www.sciencenews.org/sites/default/files/more_than_feeling.pdf (Ibid.,25)

[3] Ibid.,26.

[4] Ibid.

[5] Brain Stuff from TED Talk Dr. Laura Boyd
https://www.youtube.com/watch?v=LNHBMFCzznE&vl=en_Dec 15, 2015 - Uploaded by TEDx Talks

Day 1 Do You Wish to Get Well?

[1] Norman Wright, *A Better Way To Think: Using Positive Thoughts to Change Your Life* (Michigan: Revell, 2011), 57.

[2] Ibid., 33.

[3] Lance Witt, *Replenish: Leading from a Healthy Soul* (Grand Rapids, MI: Baker Books, 2011), 18-19.

[4] Ibid.

[5] "Statistics," National Institute of Mental Health, accessed September 27, 2012,
<http://www.nimh.nih.gov/statistics/1ANYDIS_ADULT.shtml>.

[6] Amy Simpson, *Troubled Minds: Mental Illness and the Church's Mission* (Downers Grove, IL: InterVarsity Press, 2013), 33.

[7] Ibid.

[8] *What Is Mental Illness: Mental Illness Facts, National Alliance on Mental Illness,* accessed September 27, 2012,

<http://www.nami.org/Content/NavigationMenu/Inform_Yourself/About_Mental_Illness/About_ Mental _Illness. htm>.

9 Wright, *A Better Way to Think,* 57.

10 Leaf, *Who Switched Off My Brain?,* 15.

11 Ibid.

12 Ibid., 13.

13 Wright, *A Better Way to Think,* 20-21.

14 Simpson, *Troubled Minds,* 34.

15 Archibald D. Hart, *Habits of the Mind: Ten Exercises To Renew Your Thinking* (Dallas, TX: Word Publishing, 1996), 5.

16 Ibid.

17 Ibid., 33.

18 Leaf, *Who Switched Off My Brain?,* 81.

19 Hart, *Habits of the Mind,* 23.

20 Joyce Meyer, *Battlefield of the Mind: Winning the Battle in Your Mind* (New York: Faith Words, 1995) 49.

21 Leaf, *Think, Learn, Succeed,* 34.

22 Carlo C. DiClemente, *Additions and Change: How Additions Develop and Addicted People Recover* (New York: The Guilford Press, 2003), 27.

23 Anthony Robbins, *Awaken The Giant Within: How to Take Immediate Control of Your Mental, Emotional, Physical & Financial Destiny* (New York: Summit Books, 1991), 133.

24 *Webster's New World College Dictionary, 3rd Ed.* (New York: Simon & Schuster, 1997),1213.

Day 2 You're Not Crazy—You're Human: *The 10 Sources of Your Thoughts*

1 National Science Foundation. National Science Foundation. Accessed December 16, 2013. http://www.nsf.gov/.

2 Wright, *A Better Way To Think,* 12.

3 Ibid., 11-12.

4 Ibid., 12.

5 Hart, *Habits of the Mind,* 5.

6 Leaf, *Who Switched Off My Brain?,* 14.

7 Wright, *A Better Way to Think,* 13.

8 Samuel C. Verghese, *Brain Power: How to Fine-Tune Your Brain Naturally* (Enumclaw, WA: Winepress publishing 2007), 52-53.

9 Daniel G. Amen, *Magnificent Mind at Any Age: Treat Anxiety, Depression, Memory Problems, ADD, and Insomnia* (New York: Three Rivers Press, 2008), 13.

10 Leaf, *Who Switched Off My Brain?,* 13.

11 Ibid.,14.

12 Amen, *Magnificent Mind at Any Age,*13.

13 Leaf, *Think Learn Succeed,* 34.

14 "National Science Foundation. National Science Foundation. Accessed December 16, 2013.http://www.nsf.gov/.

15 Bob Proctor, Subconscious Mind Reprogramming https://www.youtube.com/watch?v=0Mm0Ln1X2sA

16 Amen, *Magnificent Mind at Any Age,* 13.

17 Wright, *A Betty Way to Think,*28.

18 Leaf, *Who Switched Off My Brain?,* 20.

19 Wright, *A Betty Way to Think,* 28.

20 Ibid.,16.

21 Amen, *Magnificent Mind At Any Age,* 29.

[22] Ibid.,14.

[23] Pierce J. Howard, *The Owner's Manual for The Brain: Everyday Applications from Mind-Brain Research* (Texas: Bard Press, 2006) 797.

[24] Wright, *A Betty Way to Think*, 62-63.

[25] David Ziegler, *Traumatic Experience and the Brain*, (Phoenix: Acacia Publishing, 2002), adapted, 42-43.

[26] Wright, *A Betty Way to Think*, 63.

[27] Ibid., 63-64.

[28] Peter McWilliams, *You Can't Afford the Luxury of a Negative Thought* (CA: Prelude Press, 1995), 355.

[29] Kenneth Mcintosh and Phyllis Livingston, *Youth With Alcohol & Drug Addiction: Escape from Bondage* (Philadelphia, PA: Mason Crest Publishers, 2008), 37.

[30] http://sugarcrash.org/sugar-crash-symptoms/

[31] Ibid.

[32] http://www.denverpost.com/2011/04/23/avoiding-the-after-lunch-carb-crash/

[33] *Webster's New World College Dictionary, Third Edition* (New York: Simon & Schuster 1997).

Day 3 A Case of Mistaken Identity: *Discovering the Real You*

[1] Frank Lawlis, *Retraining the Brain: A 45-Day Plan to Conquer Stress and Anxiety* (New York: Plume, 2008), 19.

[2] Tim, Clinton, and Joshua Straub. *God Attachment: Why You Believe, Act and Feel the Way You Do About God* (New York: Howard Books, 2010), 21.

[3] *http://www.bjs.gov/content/pub/pdf/vit14.pdf*

[4] http://www.washingtontimes.com/news/2015/sep/28/identity-theft

[5] Definition adapted from a television interview with Dr. Creflo Dollar aired on December 21, 2013.

[6] Verghese, *Brain Power*, 68.

[7] Clinton, and Straub, *God Attachment*, 21.

[8] Ibid.

[9] *Joseph Prince, The Power of Right Believing: 7 Keys to Freedom From Fear, Guilt and Addiction (New York: Faith Works, 2014), 64.*

[10] Max Lucado, Experiencing the Heart of Jesus: Knowing His Heart, Feeling His Love (Nashville, TN: Thomas Nelson Publishers, 2003), 123-124.

Day 4 The Power of Your Imagination: *What You See is What You Get!*

[1] Wright, *A Better Way to Think,* 49.

[2] A.W. Tozer, "*The Value of a Sanctified Imagination*, in Warren Wiersbe, *Developing a Christian Imagination* (Wheaton, IL: Victor, 1995), 212.

[3] Wright, *A Better Way to Think,* 49.

[4] Bruce L. Doyle III, Think Your Way to the Life You Want: A Guide to Understanding How Your Thoughts and Beliefs Create Your Life (New York: MJF Books, 2011), 5.

[5] Ibid.

[6] James Strong, *Strong's Exhaustive Concordance of the Bible* (Abington, MD: Abingdon Press, 1890), G2507.

[7] David Eckman, *Becoming Who God Intended: A New* Picture for Your Past A Healthy Way of Managing Your Emotions A Fresh Perspective on Relationships (Eugene, OR: Harvest house Publishers, 2005), 116.

[8] Ibid., 116.

[9] Wright, *A Better Way to Think,* 48.

[10] Ibid.,49.

[11] Sharot T. Riccardi AM, Radio CM, Phelps EA. Neural mechanisms mediating optimism bias. Nature. 2007 Nov 1;450(7166):102-5.

[12] Newberg and Waldman, *How God Changes Your Brain,* 164.

[13] http://www.mayoclinic.com/health/positive-thinking/SR00009.

[14] Newberg and Waldman, *How God Changes Your Brain,* 169.

[15] Ibid., 166.

[16] Statement extracted from sermon entitled, You Must Win the Battle of Your Mind First, preached (11-3-19)   by Bishop Daniel Robertson Jr, Pastor of Mt. Gilead Full Gospel International Ministries, Richmond, VA.

Day 5 What You Think About You Bring About.

[1] Richard O'Connor, *Rewire* (New York: Plume Printing, 2014), 28.

[2] Ibid., 4.

[3] Norman Vincent Peale, *Power Your Life with Positive Thinking* (New York: Guidepost Publications, 2013), 15.

[4] O'Connor, *Rewire,* 4.

[5] Laurence R. Tancredi, *Hardwired Behavior: What Neuroscience Reveals About Morality* (New York: Cambridge University Press, 2005), 43.

[6] Michael S. Gazzaniga, *Who's in Charge? Free Will and the Science of the Brain* (New York: Harper Collins Publishers, 2011), 33.

[7] Diana Fosha, Daniel J. Siegel, and Marion F. Solomon, *The Healing Power of Emotion: Affective Neuroscience, Development, and Clinical Practice* (New York: W.W. Norton & Company, 2009), 238.

[8] Tancredi, *Hardwired Behavior,* 43.

[9] Hart, *Habits of the Mind,*15.

[10] Tancredi, *Hardwired Behavior,* 44.

[11] O'Connor, *Rewire,* 28.

[12] Amen, *Change Your Brain, Change Your Life,* 56.

[13] Hart, *Habits of the Mind,* 4.

[14] Charles Duhigg, *The Power of Habit: Why We Do What We Do In Life and Business* (New York: Random House, 2012), 92.

[15] Hart, *Habits of the Mind,* 38.

[16] Ibid.,39.

[17] Duhigg, *The Power of Habit,* 17-18.

[18] O'Conner, *Rewire,* 8.

[19] Leaf, *Who Switched Off My Brain?,* 20.

[20] Ibid.

[21] Charles Swindoll, *Come Before Winter* (Portland, OR: Multnomah, 1985), 29.

[22] O'Conner, *Rewire,*10.

[23] Ibid.

[24] Hart, *Habits of the Mind,* 39.

[25] O'Conner, *Rewire,* 10-11.

[26] Ibid., 28.

[27] Joel Osteen, *Break Out! Journal: A Guide to Go Beyond Your Barriers and Live and Extraordinary Life* (New York: Faith Words, 2013), 114.

Day 6 What You Talk About You Bring About.

[1] Leaf, *Who Switched Off My Brain?*, 20.

[2] O'Connor, *Rewire*, 4.

[3] Wright, *A Better Way To Think*, 16.

[4] http://health.usnews.com/health-news/blogs/eat-run/2015/06/09/how-negative-self-talk-is-killing-your-health-and-weight-loss-goals

[5] http://www.gateways-to-inner-peace.com/self-talk.html

[6] Joseph Stowell, *Fan The Flame* (Chicago, IL: Moody Publications, 1986), 13.

[7] https://www.pgeveryday.com/family-life/family-bonding/article/when-does-your-childs-personality-develop-experts-weigh-in

[8] https://www.td.org/Publications/Blogs/Human-Capital-Blog/2013/07/How-Words-Affect-Our-Brains

[9] Fosha, Siegel, and Solomon, *The Healing Power of Emotion*, 238.

[10] Leaf, *Who Switched Off My Brain?*, 20.

[11] https://www.td.org/Publications/Blogs/Human-Capital-Blog/2013/07/How-Words-Affect-Our-Brains

[12] Verghese, *Brain Power,*68.

[13] Amen, *Magnificent Mind at Any Age,* 29.

[14] Wright, *A Better Way to Think,* 69.

[15] Ibid., 71.

[16] Ibid.

[17] Use Your Subconscious Mind Power & Affirmations to Awaken The Law of Attraction In You. Youtube.com/Growing Forever, November 30, 2016.

[18] Ibid.

[19] Ibid.

[20] Hart, *Habits of the Mind,* 39.

[21] Wright, *A Better Way to Think,* 49.

[22] Verghese, *Brain Power,*68.

Day 7 Why You Do What You Do?

[1] Charles Duhigg, *The Power of Habit: Why We Do What We Do In Life and Business* (New York: Random House, 2012), 15.

[2] Ibid., 17-18.

[3] James Clear, *"The 3 R's of Habit Change: How To Start New Habits That Actually Stick"* accessed October 1, 2016, http://jamesclear.com/three-steps-habit-change.

[4] Ibid.

[5] Hart, *Habits of the Mind,*15.

[6] Duhigg, *The Power of Habit,*17-18.

[7] Ibid.,15.

[8] Ibid.,19.

[9] Clear, *The 3 R's of Habit Change,* http://jamesclear.com/three-steps-habit-change.

[10] Newberg, and Waldman, *How God Changes Your Brain,* 56.

[11] Duhigg, *The Power of Habit,* 92.

[12] Newberg and Waldman, *How God Changes Your Brain,* 158.

[13] Robbins, *Awaken The Giant Within,* 204.

[14] Ibid.,15.

[15] Duhigg, *The Power of Habit,* 92.

[16] Daniel G. Amen, *Change Your Brain Change Your Life: The Breakthrough Program for Conquering Anxiety, Depression, Obsessiveness, Anger, and Impulsiveness (*New York: Three Rivers Press, 1998), *299.*

[17] Tancredi, *Hardwired Behavior,* 43.
[18] Duhigg, *The Power of Habits,* adapted, 47-48,157.
[19] Ibid.,15.
[20] Ibid., 47-48.
[21] Newberg and Waldman, *How God Changes Your Brain,* 167.

Day 8 A Balancing Act: *How Your Brain Manages Your Thoughts and Emotions.*

[1] Newberg and Waldman, *How God Changes Your Brain,* 125.
[2] Joel Osteen, *It's Your Time: Activate Your Faith, Achieve Your Dreams, and Increase in God's Favor (*New York: Free Press, 2009), 72-73.
[3] Leaf, *Who Switched Off My Brain?,*15.
[4] Newberg and Waldman, *How God Changes Your Brain,* 125.
[5] Reader's Digest Association. *No More Brain Drain: Proven Ways to Maintain Your Mind and Memories* (Pleasantville, NY: Reader's Digest Association, 2009), 27.
[6] Newberg and Waldman, *How God Changes Your Brain,* 126.
[7] Ibid.
[8] Kenneth and Gloria Copeland, *Your 10-Day Spiritual Action Plan for Overcoming Stress, Anxiety and Depression* (Fort worth, TX: Kenneth Copeland Publications, 2015), 84.
[9] Newberg and Waldman, *How God Changes Your Brain,* 150.
[10] Ibid., 126
[11] Ibid., 150.
[12] Ibid., 152.
[13] Amen, *Change Your Brain, Change Your Life,* 152.
[14] Frank Lawlis, *Retraining the Brain: A 45-Day Plan to Conquer Stress and Anxiety* (New York: Plume, 2008), 13.
[15] Amen, *Magnificent Mind at Any Age,* 186-187.
[16] Amen, *Change Your Brain,* 172-173.
[17] Ibid., 174.
[18] Ibid.
[19] Ibid., 175.
[20] Ibid.
[21] Ibid., 176.
[22] Kenneth Mcintosh and Phyllis Livingston, *Youth With Alcohol & Drug Addiction: Escape from Bondage* (Philadelphia, PA: Mason Crest Publishers, 2008), 37.

Day 9 The Filthy Five: *5 Negative Thoughts You MUST Take Captive to Remain Positive.*

[1] Leaf, *Who Switched Off My Brain?,* 19.
[2] Neuroskeptic, "The 70,000 Thoughts Per Day Myth?" Discover (May, 2012): accessed December 16, 2013, blogs.discovermagazine.com/neuroskeptic/2012/05/09/the-70000-thoughts-per-day-myth/
[3] Leaf, *Who Switched Off My Brain?,* 20.
[4] O'Conner, *Rewire,* 67.
[5] Newberg and Waldman, *How God Changes Your Brain,* 125.

Day 10 Thought Management 101: *Check. Challenge. Change. Reframe.*

[1] Reader's Digest Association, *No More Brain Drain: Proven Ways to Maintain Your Mind and Memories.* (Pleasantville, NY: Reader's Digest Association, 2009), 27.
[2] Ibid.

[3] Ken Ashwell, *The Brain Book* (New York: Firefly Book, 2012), 341.
[4] Leaf, *Who Switched Off My Brain?*, 52.
[5] Newberg and Waldman, *How God Changes Your Brain*, 126.

Day 11 Mind Games: *A Winning Strategy for Defeating The Filthy Five.*

[1] Connor, *Rewire*, 8.
[2] Duhigg, *The Power of Habits,* 17-18.
[3] Connor, *Rewire*, 8.
[4] How to Force the Subconscious Mind to Manifest What You Want Faster www.The Science of
DeliberateCreation.comhttps://youtu.be/dRUso32LRSg August 13, 2017.
[5] Leaf, *Who Switched Off My Brain?,* 22-23.
[6] Newberg and Waldman, *How God Changes Your Brain,* 126.

Day 12 Mood Swingers: *How to Turn Around a Bad Attitude—Fast.*

[1] Daniel J. Siegel, *Mindsight: The New Science of Personal Transformation* (New York: Bantam
Books Trade Paperback Edition, 2011), 198-199.
[2] Robbins, *Awaken The Giant Within,* 156-157.
[3] Ibid.
[4] "Facts and Statistics," Anxiety and Depression Organization of America,
http://www.adaa.org/about-adaa/press-room/facts-statistics (5/12/2015).
[5] Depression Fact Sheet, No.369, Oct.2012, WorldHealthOrganizationMediaCenter,
http://www.who.int/mediacentre/factsheets/fs369/en(5/12/2015).
[6] Copeland, *Your 10-Day Spiritual Action Plan for Overcoming Stress, Anxiety & Depression,* 15.
[7] "Depression, Anxiety,"beyondblue,http://beyondblue.org.au/the-facts (5/12/2015).
[8] Susan Gaidos, More Than a Feeling: Emotionally evocative, yes, but music goes much deeper,
Science News. 178.4 (Aug. 14, 2010): p24-26.
https://www.sciencenews.org/sites/default/files/more_than_feeling.pdf
[9] Ibid.,24.
[10] Ibid.
[11] Ibid.
[12] Ibid.,25.
[13] Ibid.,26.
[14] Ibid.
[15] Ibid.
[16] Copeland, *Your 10-Day Spiritual Action Plan for Overcoming Stress, Anxiety & Depression,*
49.
[17] Ibid.,74.
[18] Reader's Digest Association. *No More Brain Drain: Proven Ways to Maintain Your Mind and
Memories* (Pleasantville, NY: Reader's Digest Association, 2009), 132.
[19] Ibid.,133-139.
[20] Ibid.,36-37.
[21] Ibid.,37.
[22] Daniel J. Siegel, *Mindsight: The New Science of Personal Transformation* (New York: Bantam
Books Trade Paperback Edition, 2011) 198-199.

Day 13 The Toxic Ten: *10 Distorted Patterns of Thinking, (Part 1)*

[1] Newberg and Waldman, *How God Changes Your Brain,* 126.
[2] Wright, *A Better Way To Think,* 150-151.
[3] Keith Dobson, *Handbook of Cognitive-Behavioral Therapies* (New York: Guildford Press,
2010), 4.

[4] Colbert, *Deadly Emotions*, 78.
[5] Arthur Freeman, *Comprehensive Handbook of Cognitive Therapy* (New York: Plenum Press, 1989), 22.
[6] Dobson, *Handbook of Cognitive-Behavioral Therapies*, 4.
[7] Ibid.
[8] David Burns, *The Feeling Good Handbook* (New York: Penguin Group, 1999), 9.
[9] Ibid., 9.
[10] *The Expositor's Bible Commentary* Frank E. Gaebelein Volume 4 (1Kings-Job) Zondervan Publishing House Grand Rapids, Michigan 1988).
[11] Newberg and Waldman, *How God Changes Your Brain,* 126.
[12] Burns, *The Feeling Good Handbook,* 9.
[13] http://media.psychology.tools/Worksheets/English/Unhelpful_Thinking_Styles.pdf
[14] Amen, *Magnificent Mind At Any Age,* 172.
[15] Ibid.
[16] Burns, *The Feeling Good Handbook,* 8.
[17] Ibid.
[18] Amen, *Magnificent Mind At Any Age,* 172.
[19] http://media.psychology.tools/Worksheets/English/Unhelpful_Thinking_Styles.pdf
[20] Colbert, *Deadly Emotions,* 157.
[21] Burns, *The Feeling Good Handbook*, 8.

Day 14 The Toxic Ten: *10 Distorted Patterns of Thinking, (Part 2)*

[1] Leaf, *Who Switched Off My Brain?,* 13.
[2] Dobson, *Handbook of Cognitive-Behavioral Therapies,* 4.
[3] Ibid.
[4] Burns, *The Feeling Good Handbook,* 8.
[5] Ibid.
[6] Amen, *Magnificent Mind At Any Age*, 172.
[7] Burns, *The Feeling Good Handbook,* 10.
[8] O'Conner, *Rewire,* 49.
[9] Burns, *The Feeling Good Handbook,* 8.
[10] Ibid.
[11] Colbert, *Deadly Emotions,* 156.
[12] Burns, *The Feeling Good Handbook,* 10.
[13] Ibid.
[14] Ibid., 11.
[15] Ibid.

Day 15 Replacing Unforgiveness with Forgiveness.

[1] Fosha, Siegel, and Solomon, *The Healing Power of Emotion,* 238.
[2] Duhigg, *The Power of Habits,* adapted, 47-48,157.
[3] Don Colbert, *Deadly Emotions,*162.
[4] Jerry Mungadze, *Managing Your Brain Managing Your Life* (Bedford, TX: Sound Mind Media and Publications 2016), 43.
[5] Ibid.
[6] Concept taken from a sermon by Elena Robertson in a message entitled, Raise Above Your Circumstances May 19, 2019.
[7] Hart, *Habits of the Mind,* 19.

[8] Leaf, *Who Switched Off My Brain?,* 20.
[9] Don Colbert, *Deadly Emotions,* 162.

Day 16 Replacing Negative Thoughts and Images of God: *God, What Did You Do that For? (Part 1)*

[1] Leaf, *Who Switched Off My Brain?,* 21.
[2] Grace is commonly understood as God's unmerited favor.
[3] 5 Stages of Grief https://grief.com/the-five-stages-of-grief/
[4] Leaf, *Who Switched Off My Brain?,* 20.
[5] Juanita Adams, *Yes, You Can Begin Again! Insights into Picking up Life's Broken Pieces and Starting Over* (Henrico, VA: KPG Publishing and Education, 2012).

Day 17 Replacing Negative Thoughts and Images of God: *How to Feel God's Love? (Part 2)*

[1] Hannah Hurnard, Winged Life (Wheaton, IL. Tyndale, 1978), 49.
[2] Newberg and Waldman, *How God Changes the Brain,* 167.
[3] David Eckman, *Becoming Who God Intended: A New Picture for Your Past A Healthy Way of Managing Your Emotions A Fresh Perspective on Relationships* (Eugene, OR: Harvest house Publishers, 2005), 123.
[4] Ibid.
[5] Ibid.,124.
[6] Ibid., 126.
[7] Mungadze, *Managing Your Brain Managing Your Life,* 27.
[8] Eckman, *Becoming Who God Intended,* 116.
[9] Clinton, and Straub, *God Attachment,* 21.
[10] Duhigg, *The Power of Habits,* adapted, 47-48, 157.
[11] Newberg and Waldman, *How God Changes Your Brain,* 167.

Day 18 Replacing a Negative Self-Image, *Building a Healthy Self-Image.*

[1] Neil T. Anderson, *Victory Over the Darkness: Realizing the Power of Your Identity in Christ* (California: Regal Books, 2000), 56.
[2] McDowell, *Building Your Self-Image,* 39.
[3] Ibid., 53.
[4] Ibid., 53-54.
[5] Mungadze, *Managing Your Brain Managing Your Life,* 60-61.
[6] Joel Osteen, *Think Better Live Better, A Victorious Life Begins in Your Mind, Faith Words* (New York: Hachette Book Group, 2016), 29.
[7] A point taken from a sermon given by Dr. David Early at an SBCV quarterly church planters meeting at Colonial Heights Baptist Church, in Colonial Heights, VA 2012.
[8] Tony Evans, *Theology You Can Count On* (Chicago, IL: Moody Publications, 2008), 580-581.
[9] J.D. Grear, *Gospel: Recovering the Power that Made Christianity Revolutionary (*Nashville, TN: B&H Publishing, 2011), 44.
[10] McDowell, *Building Your Self-Image,* 215-216.
[11] O'Connor, *Rewire,* 28.
[12] Anderson, *Victory Over the Darkness,* 47.
[13] Prepare Enrich Workbook for Couples (IL: Tyndale House Publishers, 2017),5.
[14] Ibid.

Day 19 Replacing Fear with Faith: *The Four Levels of Faith.*

[1] Sharot T. Riccardi AM, Radio CM, Phelps EA. Neural mechanisms mediating optimism bias. Nature.2007 Nov 1;450(7166):102-5.

[2] Newberg and Waldman, *How God Changes Your Brain,*163.

[3] Ken Nichols, *Untie the Fear Knots of Your Heart,* 67.

[4] Leaf, *Who Switched Off My Brain?,*15.

[5] Newberg and Waldman, *How God Changes Your Brain,*125.

[6] Ibid.,126.

[7] Ibid.

[8] Ibid.,151.

[9] Ibid.,153.

[10] Ibid.,155.

[11] Ibid.

[12] Ibid.,159.

[13] Ibid.,160.

[14] Ibid.,62.

[15] Ibid.,163.

[16] Ibid.

[17] Ibid.,164.

[18] Sharot T. Riccardi AM, Radio CM, Phelps EA. Neural mechanisms mediating optimism bias. Nature.2007 Nov 1;450(7166):102-5.

[19] Jack Canfield, Mark Victor Hanson, Patty Aubery and Nancy Mitchell Autio, *Chicken Soup for the Christian Family Soul* (Deerfield Beach, FL: Heath Communications, 2000), 14.

[20] Phrase taken from a sermon by Steven Furtick in a sermon series entitled Functional Faith 2017.

[21] Ibid.

[22] Jentzen Franklin, *Fear Fighters: How to Live With Confidence In a World Driven by Fear* (Mary Lake, FL: Charisma House, 2009), 27.

[23] Ibid.

Day 20 Replacing Weakness: *Building Mental Toughness to Withstand Life's Storms.*

[1] Mark R. McMinn, *Cognitive Therapy Techniques in Christian Counseling* (Eugene, OR: WiPF & Stock Publishing, 2007), 23.

[2] "Hurricane Katrina Statistics Fast Facts." CNN. Cable News Network, 23 Aug. 2016. Web. 25 Apr. 2017.

[3] John F. Walvoord and Roy B. Zuck, *The Bible Knowledge Commentary: New Testament* (Wheaton, IL: Victor Books, 1983), 647.

[4] Amen, *Change Your Brain Change Your Life,* 172-173.

[5] Walvoord and Zuck, *The Bible Knowledge Commentary,* 663.

[6] Warren W. Wiersbe, *The Bible Exposition Commentary: An Exposition of the New Testament Comprising the Entire "Be" Series* (Wheaton, IL: Victor Books, 1989), 94.

[7] *Growing Strong in God's Family: A course in Personal Discipleship to Strengthen Your Walk with God* (Colorado Springs, CO: NavPress, 1978), 62.

[8] Leaf, *Who Switched off My Brain?,* 20.

[9] McMinn, *Cognitive Therapy,* 23.

[10] Dennis McCallum and Gary DeLashmutt, *Developing a Theology of Failure,* 1 http://www.xenos.org/classes/leadership/failure.htm

[11] McCallum and DeLashmutt, *Developing a Theology of Failure,* 3.

[12] Ibid.

[13] Ibid.

[14] Ibid.

[15] Clinton, and Straub, *God Attachment,* 21.

[16] Fosha, Siegel, and Solomon, *The Healing Power of Emotion,* 238.

[17] Tancredi, *Hardwired Behavior,* 43.

[18] Brain Stuff from TED Talk, Dr. Laura Boyd, https://www.youtube.com/watch?v=LNHBMFCzznE&vl=enDec 15, 2015 - Uploaded by TEDx Talks

[19] The Bridge, *10,000 hours: Does Practice Really Make Perfect?* Jeff Vrabel Messiah College Alumni Magazine, Spring 2017 p. 16-21.

[20] Tancredi, *Hardwired Behavior,* 43.

Day 21 I Think Myself Happy!

[1] O'Connor, *Rewire,* 11.

[2] Fosha, Siegel, and Solomon, *The Healing Power of Emotion,* 238.

[3] Ibid.

[4] http://bereanbibleheritage.org/extraordinary/crosby_fanny.php

[5] O'Connor, *Rewire,* 11.

[6] Leaf, *Who Switched Off My Brain,* 80.

[7] http://www.tanbible.com/tol_sng/sng_itiswellwithmysoul.htm

[8] *Hymns for the Family of God,* (Nashville, TN: Paragon Associates, 1976), #495.

[9] Ibid.

[10] Ibid., #107.

[11] Ibid., #112.

Conclusion: What's Next?

Appendix A: Depression Doesn't Always Look Like Depression: *A 12 Point Check List*

[1] *12 Common Symptoms Of Depression That Shouldn't Be Ignored, Healthy Way* by Lisa Douglas May 8, 2017 https://www.healthyway.com/content/common-symptoms-of-depression-that-shouldnt-be-ignored/

[2] Ibid

Appendix B: You Probably Need Counseling If: *A 15 Point Check List*

[1] *Substance Abuse and Mental Health Services Administration. Behavioral Health Barometer:* United States, 2013. HHS Publication No.SMA-13-4796. Rockville, MD: Substance Abuse and Mental Health Services Administration, 2013.

[2] *Meredith Melnick, "8 Signs You Should See A Therapist." The Huffington Post. TheHuffingtonPost.com, 11 Aug. 2015. Web. 26 May 2017.*

[3] https://www.bustle.com/articles/64880-7-surprising-signs-you-need-therapy-not-that-theres-anything-wrong-with-that

[4] Melnick, "8 Signs You Should See A Therapist."

[5] Leaf, Who Switched Off My Brain?, 15.

[6] Melnick, "8 Signs You Should See A Therapist."

Appendix C: Communicating Your Needs: *His Needs, Her Needs*
Appendix D: Conflict Resolution: *Rules of Engagement*
Appendix E: Recommended Reading
Appendix F: All Scripture Translations

Made in the USA
Columbia, SC
20 April 2021

35806026R00220